From Morality to Law and Back Again

From Morality to Law and Back Again

A Liber Amicorum for John Gardner

Edited by

MICHELLE MADDEN DEMPSEY AND
FRANÇOIS TANGUAY-RENAUD

OXFORD
UNIVERSITY PRESS

OXFORD
UNIVERSITY PRESS

Great Clarendon Street, Oxford, OX2 6DP,
United Kingdom

Oxford University Press is a department of the University of Oxford.
It furthers the University's objective of excellence in research, scholarship,
and education by publishing worldwide. Oxford is a registered trade mark of
Oxford University Press in the UK and in certain other countries

First Edition published in 2023

Published in the United States of America by Oxford University Press
198 Madison Avenue, New York, NY 10016, United States of America

British Library Cataloguing in Publication Data

Data available

Library of Congress Control Number: 2023932760

ISBN 978–0–19–886059–4

DOI: 10.1093/oso/9780198860594.001.0001

Printed and bound by
CPI Group (UK) Ltd, Croydon, CR0 4YY

For Jennifer, Henrik, Annika, and Audra.

Contents

List of Contributors

Aditi Bagchi, Professor of Law, Fordham University School of Law

Peter Chau, Associate Professor, Department of Law, University of Hong Kong

Luís Duarte d'Almeida, Professor, NOVA School of Law, Lisbon; and Honorary Professorial Fellow, University of Edinburgh

Michelle Madden Dempsey, Harold Reuschlein Scholar Chair and Professor of Law, Villanova University Charles Widger School of Law

James Edwards, Fellow and Tutor in Law, Worcester College University of Oxford

Kate Greasley, Associate Professor in Law, University of Oxford

Scott Hershovitz, Thomas G. and Mabel Long Professor of Law and Professor of Philosophy, University of Michigan

Leora Dahan Katz, Assistant Professor, Faculty of Law, Hebrew University of Jerusalem

Sophia Moreau, Professor of Law and Philosophy, University of Toronto

Maria Amalia Amaya Navarro (published under Amalia Amaya), British Academy Global Professor, Edinburgh University; and Research Professor, Institute for Philosophical Research at the National Autonomous University of Mexico and School of Law, University of Edinburgh

Dwight Newman, Professor of Law and Canada Research Chair in Indigenous Rights in Constitutional and International Law, University of Saskatchewan, Saskatoon

Irit Samet, Dickson Poon Law School, King's College London

Prince Saprai, Professor of Law, Faculty of Laws, University College London

François Tanguay-Renaud, Associate Professor, Osgoode Hall Law School, York University

Jean Thomas, Associate Professor, Faculty of Law, Queen's University

Grégoire Webber, Canada Research Chair in Public Law and Philosophy of Law, Faculty of Law, Queen's University

Introduction

John Gardner (1965–2019) was elected Chair and Professor of Jurisprudence at the University of Oxford in 2000 and held this post until 2016, when he was elected to a Senior Research Fellowship at All Souls College. Shortly after he stepped down from the Chair, we approached John to suggest organizing a festschrift to celebrate his work during his time as Professor of Jurisprudence.

We worried that proposing a festschrift for someone so young (only 52 years old at the time) might make it seem as if John was 'heading off to pasture' upon relinquishing the Chair. So, in our email suggesting the idea, we noted that we simply wanted to mark the occasion, and 'honour someone whose work, example, and friendship has meant so much to us'. John's response was characteristically humble.

> Dear Michelle and François,
>
> Yikes! Am I at that point in my life already? Seriously, though, I'm touched and flattered. It's very generous of you both. I'm a bit concerned that it's premature, though, not for the reason you give—of course you're not putting me out to grass just yet, and nobody will think you are. Rather, I'm not sure whether my body of work so far is enough to merit the attention ...
>
> I guess you could test the water. I'd have no objection to that.
>
> To maximize your chances of making it work, I humbly suggest aiming at a group of contributors mainly drawn from my former students and others I have supported along the way ... Doing it that way would minimize any implication that I am being canonized/pensioned off, or that you have ideas for me that are above my station. More of a liber amicorum than a festschrift.
>
> But far be it from me to attempt to dictate terms. You guys surely know what you're doing!
>
> Many thanks to you both,
>
> John

In keeping with John's suggestion, this volume was conceived as a *liber amicorum*—a book of friends—with contributions by John's doctoral students during the time he served as Professor of Jurisprudence, along with other junior and mid-career scholars whom he mentored.

From Morality to Law and Back Again. Michelle Madden Dempsey and François Tanguay-Renaud, Oxford University Press.
 DOI: 10.1093/oso/9780198860594.001.0001

The original plan was to identify contributors, collect draft chapters, and organize an in-person conference in Oxford, so that John would be able to provide comments. We envisioned the workshop as something like a group tutorial, with John's brilliance improving the quality of each chapter. The goal was to bring together a true gathering of friends, further developing the community of scholars inspired by John's work, and benefiting from yet another opportunity to learn from him.

Every single person we approached as a possible contributor jumped at the opportunity. Indeed, each one of them made a point of telling us how grateful they were to have been asked. That fact alone impressed upon us how many academics, of all genders and parts of the world, and now high-flying in their own right, had been profoundly touched by John's mentorship at an earlier point in their careers.

Little did any of us know at the time that John would soon be diagnosed with oesophageal cancer. With him having received excellent care from the NHS, and believing the cancer had been trounced, we proceeded with plans to hold the workshop. Tragically, in the spring of 2019, the cancer returned and John died a few months later, but not without making sure to bless our planned conference and the subsequent compilation of its proceedings into this book.

Ordinarily, a volume such as this one would provide details regarding the biography and accomplishments of the scholar being honoured. However, many such tributes have already been published, including an important and comprehensive overview of John's scholarship authored by Antony Duff and Hugh Collins.[1] A vast compilation of letters and tributes from friends, colleagues, students, and other admirers sent to John before his passing has also been archived online, offering rich first-hand accounts of the man and his life.[2] Thus, we do not intend to reprise all the impressive details of John's life here, be it as a scholar or an all-round mensch. Instead, our goal in this introduction is to briefly highlight who John was as a supervisor and a mentor.

John's scholarship focused primarily on issues of general jurisprudence and philosophical issues in criminal law, tort law, and discrimination law. We say 'primarily' because no issue was truly beyond the scope of John's interest, including questions related to more general moral and political theory, practical reasoning, human rights, public and constitutional law, and other aspects of private law. He was influenced by and attracted to legal positivism and made use of broadly Aristotelian insights. Yet, he was never one to be hemmed in by existing

[1] Hugh Collins and Antony Duff, 'John Gardner', posted to Biographical Memoirs of Fellows of the British Academy, 20 (23 March 2021), online: https://www.thebritishacademy.ac.uk/documents/4254/20-Memoirs-01-Gardner.pdf. See also notably Annalise Acorn, 'John Gardner 1965–2019', Faculty of Law, University of Oxford, online: https://www.law.ox.ac.uk/content/john-gardner-1965-2019 and Nicola Lacey, 'John Gardner obituary', *The Guardian* (22 July 2019), online: https://www.theguardian.com/law/2019/jul/22/john-gardner-obituary.

[2] See online: https://johngardnerathome.info/memory.htm.

frameworks, methods, or sets of conceptual assumptions beyond being influenced, as is to be expected, by his immediate forebears and mentors—notably, his doctoral examiners Bernard Williams and Antony Duff, his All Souls College mentor Derek Parfit, and his doctoral supervisor Joseph Raz. His own philosophical commitments, he observed, were 'extremely diverse and often unpredictable'. They were 'not part of a broader philosophical programme'. Rather, his method was to take '[o]ne question at a time, the answer usually being unknown until I run the arguments'.[3] This lesson—namely, to value arguments above conclusions, and resolutely refuse to generate the former simply to fit the latter however self-evident or appealing they may otherwise appear—is one that all younger scholars who encountered John and his work learned to appreciate through his example, and a lesson which, for many of us, induced our first experiences of unsettling yet often fruitful philosophical angst and self-doubt.

Thankfully, John was a patient, generous, and endlessly encouraging scholarly mentor. Such traits were crucial in helping his protégés labour through their early philosophical explorations, and guiding them to the tangible satisfaction that comes from clear, systematically developed, and oft-unexpected insights. John's method of tackling big problems by chipping off small parts, as opposed to seeking to construct or build on pre-existing grand theories, also had the effect of making one's philosophical enterprises seem more manageable from the start, and one's eventual contributions seem more readily graspable and genuine.

Still, John was a demanding supervisor. After giving his students the latitude to come to a topic from their own perspective, he would painstakingly ensure that no stone was left unturned, often zeroing in on details which his students had too rapidly glanced over, pointing out blind spots, or introducing novel angles that shed light on what initially appeared to be dead ends or incontrovertible truths. To be sure, John's humility and deep concern for being accessible to graduate students generally ensured that his critiques were received as constructively and painlessly as can be. While not often wrong, John was always willing to be persuaded. He made certain that the weight of his eminent Chair, and of the history behind his Logic Lane office, never got in the way of a productive exchange. It should be no surprise, then, that John always objected to his students' attempts to enshrine his distinctive positions in less than approachable eponymous epithets. While there were many Hartian, Dworkinian, and Razian views shaping Oxonian legal philosophy, there should be no Gardnerian domain (or so John insisted!). Only arguments, counterarguments, and a healthy dose of inspiration derived from life and its morality—all then applied to law, only to be applied back to life and its morality again.

[3] John Gardner, 'Inconclusive as Ever', Jerus Rev Leg Stud (2019) 19(1) 204, 224.

John's death will continue to evoke a sense of grief and loss for all of us. Indeed, it is difficult to distinguish what we lost through John's passing in terms of scholarly mentorship as opposed to friendship. This is so because John's excellence in pedagogy was imbued throughout, and quite distinctively, with the virtues and values of friendship. Thus, for example, Logic Lane was the place where his students came to thrive intellectually under his tutelage during individual supervision meetings, and where we gathered as a community to socialize and sample John's fine Italian cooking. Or again, while John would spend hours preparing his graduate students for their viva voce examinations, he would characteristically also seek to join them, soon after, in celebratory meals at the Old Parsonage or the Trout Inn, either alone or with their loved ones.

As friends, we hold a deep sorrow that we will never again experience the wit, compassion, and uplifting energy of such a remarkable human being. As students and mentees, we are all very conscious that we have lost access to the guidance of one of the most brilliant philosophical minds of his generation. Through this volume we wish to pay tribute to both of these aspects of John's persona by bringing together friends of his, whom he once guided so deftly, to engage with his multifaceted work.

The workshop we had envisioned, with John commenting on each chapter, never came to be. Yet, out of tragedy and pain in the wake of his loss, we did manage to gather at All Souls College on 18–19 December 2019 to discuss the chapters included in this volume. The contributors were joined by many commentators, who were also invited based on their professional closeness to John, including Annalise Acorn, Andrew Ashworth, Antony Duff, Timothy Endicott, Sandra Marshall, Joshua Pike, Joseph Raz, Guy Sela, Stephen Shute, Sandy Steele, and Ekow Yankah. We are also grateful to Timothy Endicott, Michael Giudice, John Oberdiek, and Denise Réaume, for providing additional written commentary on some of the chapters. The event was an opportunity to further build the community of scholars who have been inspired by John's work, something that was particularly important to him, as he impressed upon us in his final weeks.

We certainly hope this volume lives up to John's confidence that we 'know what we're doing'. At the very least, though, we hope that it provides an opportunity to revisit and engage with a broad range of John's scholarship, and illustrates the many ways in which it has inspired, and continues to inspire, his students and mentees.

The volume aims to reflect the kind of multifaceted intellectual that John was. It engages with many of the concepts, themes, and issues that were central to his philosophical work and outlook. In particular, the volume comprises discussions of duties to try and succeed in relation to Hume's maxim that 'ought implies can' (Bagchi, Duarte D'Almeida); the role of continuity, conservatism, and corrective justice in private law (Chau, Saprai); the interrelations between wrongdoing, blame, punishment, and the justification of criminal law (Dahan Katz, Dempsey, Hershovitz); justifications, excuses, and responsibility (Edwards); and the distinctiveness of the wrongs of rape and discrimination (Greasley, Moreau), as well as general jurisprudence and how it may, or may not, illuminate the questions of normativity and the nature of constitutions (Thomas, Webber). The volume also attempts to show how John's thought was so rich and capacious that it can elucidate many other legal, moral, and political issues that he, unfortunately, did not have time to turn his attention to systematically. The further concepts and questions addressed here, in light of his work, include Indigenous rights and law (Newman); Equity (Samet); corporate responsibility and the possibility of state crimes (Tanguay-Renaud); and the nature, structure, and phenomenology of virtue (Amaya).

Together, the chapters collected in this volume pay homage to the breadth of John Gardner's legal philosophy across fields, from private and criminal law to some aspects of public law and jurisprudence more generally. The chapters also put on display how John's deep engagement with moral philosophy, but also with practical reason, political philosophy, the philosophy of language, and, to some extent, the philosophy of action, yielded a formidable body of work in which each field of philosophical inquiry informs the other while also being integrated with it. Thus, the picture of law that emerges from his scholarship is one that is firmly rooted and shaped by what we may call a broader philosophy of life, but also one that, in turn, helps mould and refine it.

John Gardner may not physically be with us anymore, but as this *liber amicorum* makes clear, his spirit and influence are still very much alive. It is our belief, and hope, that they will continue to be carried by all those whom John touched, and that his insights will also continue to light the way for many others in decades to come.

On behalf of all your students and mentees, John, we thank you.

1

Law and Social Practice: Foundations of the Leap of Faith

*Jean Thomas**

A. Paradox, Faith, and Law

In *Law as a Leap of Faith*,[1] Gardner's analogy of faith in law to faith in God may seem outlandish. But consider the implications of the positions which Gardner's jurisprudential views assemble: law can give us reason to do what we would otherwise not have reason to do—in fact, it can give us reason to do what would otherwise be immoral. This is the implication of a commitment to law's capacity to give exclusionary reasons, on one hand, together with the commitment, on the other, that any given law is valid because of its sources and not its moral merits.

So far this already seems to present a somewhat startling state of affairs. Gardner is also committed to the proposition that law claims to give us the reasons it does authoritatively. And this authority which it claims is not only legal, but moral. That law claims the moral authority to tell us what to do means that it would, at least in law's own eyes, be morally wrong to disobey law's commands, and morally right to obey them. And, if this were not enough, Gardner's intellectual honesty embraces a still more startling idea: while law claims that we would be morally wrong to fail to obey its commands, that claim makes not even a pretence to a correlatively entailed claim to moral correctness. Gardner is careful to point out that law's claim in this regard is just that—a *claim*: it could always be false.

Law has chutzpah, on this way of seeing it, and it does not even leave its subjects with clear assurance about what is required of them. For despite all these ways in which the law could be boldly leading us astray, we are, on law's own view of things, *morally obligated* simply to be directed by it—to do what it tells us to do, because it said so. So it is all the more puzzling that in the background rests a further implication. If law rests on a foundation of social practice, then at least some participants in that practice must be treating law as normative for them—as giving them the kind of reasons it purports to give them. And here lies the puzzle to which

* For comments and discussion I thank the participants in the workshop held at All Souls' College, Oxford.

[1] John Gardner, *Law as a Leap of Faith* (Oxford University Press, 2012)

Jean Thomas, *Law and Social Practice: Foundations of the Leap of Faith* In: *From Morality to Law and Back Again*.
Edited by: Michelle Madden Dempsey and François Tanguay-Renaud, Oxford University Press. © Jean Thomas 2023.
DOI: 10.1093/oso/9780198860594.003.0001

Gardner's assemblage of views points us. If we are autonomous creatures that are rational and self-directing, why would we treat as even *plausible* the surprisingly bald claim that law makes: to be entitled to tell us, with moral authority, what to do, even where its imperatives may lead us astray morally speaking?

With these various commitments and the puzzle they generate in view, it becomes clear why Gardner turns to the Euthyphro dilemma, and then to a more Judeo-Christian version of it, to explore the paradoxical situation that law seems to present. The Euthyphro dilemma as Gardner describes it is analogous to the situation of the legal subject because it presents two distinctly authoritative and yet apparently incompatible normative points of view: God can command us to do something profoundly wrong, and in thus commanding us he can make doing that thing right. If a resolution to that awesome dilemma is achievable it might help us with our slightly more prosaic legal paradox.

Gardner argues that we can have *reasons* to adopt the divine point of view. This means that, once adopted, one point of view can give us moral reasons to do what, from the other point of view, would have a different normative valence. In other words, faith in God that is properly supported by reasons can allow us to have *moral* reason to do what would, absent faith in God, be morally wrong.[2] The trick in this solution lies in the fact that the reasons that get us from the practical or moral point of view to the divine point of view need not themselves be moral ones. This move makes the overlay of the Euthyphro dilemma onto the legal paradox seem to work: we can adopt the legal point of view—in Hart's famous formulation, we can 'accept' it—for any reason, and we can even do so in a detached way, on Gardner's own Razian view. And, according to his Euthyphro logic, once we have reason to have faith—in God, or in the law—the key move taking us from one point of view to the other has already been made, and at that point law's claim to moral authority becomes at least plausible: less outrageous, even if still falsifiable and thus defeasible.

So it is *faith* in law, or its possibility, that makes law's somewhat startling claims about itself plausible. For Gardner, the analogue of the reason for divine faith is a reason to have faith in the law, such as a good experience of it, or instrumental reasons that make it good for us. But faith seems an inapt attribute for an attitude to law, as opposed to God; and so Gardner translates the role of faith, moving from the Euthyphro context to the legal one, into a presupposition, or the cognitive apprehension of a presupposition. The necessary presupposition backing up law's apparently outrageous claim is that law's original source is valid, since that validity is what confers on legal officials moral authority to tell people what to do.

In this way, Gardner reaches the first solution to the Euthyphro dilemma—one that makes law and its normativity seem less mysterious because the two normative

[2] *Law as a Leap of Faith*, pp. 5–6.

points of view can, at least in some way, be rendered less paradoxical. I am myself somewhat dubious about this resolution, however: even given Gardner's explanations of law's instrumental benefits, I continue to find the claims he attributes to law startling, and people's tendency to treat law as normative correspondingly puzzling.

Gardner's solution is made attractive, in light of his wider array of views, because of the assumption that law can have the authority it claims by giving us reasons that allow us to better comply with the reasons we already have. But of course unless we think law must have any particular content—which I do not take Gardner to believe—then a legal system must be capable of getting up and running and producing valid law even if that law patently does *not* have the authority it claims. Law's chutzpah, the boldness of its necessary claim to authority, is precisely that it asks us to treat it as though it is giving us reasons that improve our capacity for responding to reason even if that is *not* what it does. This is the force of the analogy with the Euthyphro paradox that Gardner so insightfully invokes.

Indeed, Gardner himself thought that the dilemma was not ultimately resolved by the instrumental benefit of the law, as he makes evident by persisting in the analogy with faith. Gardner moves from the Euthyphro dilemma to the more forcefully illustrative story of Abraham and Isaac to convey his thought about law's normativity. And it seems odd, although Gardner gestures at this possibility, to say that Abraham would slaughter his own son because, ultimately, he had had a good *experience* of faith or that there is value in *expressing* his faith.[3] In fact, we might argue, the point of this paradoxical way of seeing faith is that even if, like Job, we have nothing but terrible experiences of faith, and even if *we* see no value in expressing our faith, nonetheless faith is required of us.

I find Kierkegaard's inclination—that faith is simply separate and apart from reason and thus that the two positions are in their nature separate and paradoxical—to be more intuitively compelling.[4] But in the case of law, faith of that kind will not help us, because we cannot resort to faith in a supernatural 'personification of goodness in the universe' to explain why people treat law's claim as normative, where this means that we can understand its startling claim as being at least plausible.

So what can be the analogue for faith-in-personified-goodness in the case of law's normativity? What could cause a person to shift from a point of view of self-interest, prudence, real, practical, and 'not-merely-claimed-or-supposed reasons',[5] to one in which they allow *law* to give them those latter kind of reasons? Gardner's analogue for faith in law is something like the *Grundnorm*, or the somewhat

[3] *Law as a Leap of Faith*, pp. 5–7.

[4] Ibid, pp. 2–18. Gardner here cites Kierkegaard's *Fear and Trembling*, trans Hong & Hong (Princeton University Press, 1983).

[5] Ibid, p. 134.

mystical existence of a 'presupposition' that the original source of law is valid, to imbue law's source with merit.[6] Gardner endorses the idea that this presupposition can be held entirely at arm's length—so that one can understand the law without being committed to it. One can be an anarchist, on this view, and still be a competent lawyer. So law's 'merit' here, in the passages I am citing from *Law as a Leap of Faith*, can be taken to be legal merit only—legal validity, in other words. As we shall see, however, Gardner's argument in 'Nearly Natural Law' puts pressure on the idea of the completely hypothetical character of the presupposition in question.[7]

Presupposition merely re-creates the two parallel normative points of view, leaving intact the paradox of legal normativity in the gulf between them. This is because a presupposition is simply too much *like* faith to do anything but re-describe the original dilemma in other terms. To *suppose* something is to put credence in a proposition in a defeasible way. This sounds quite a lot like what we might think is many people's actual attitude to law's moral claim on them—and indeed Gardner later describes the proper attitude to law in something like these terms.[8] But since law's claim is normative, this Kelsenian solution presents the very problem of fact and norm that Kelsen faced.[9] Probably for this reason, the idea of the *pre*supposition seems more attractive, and more in keeping with Gardner's search for an analogue for faith, than a supposition.

Given the facially implausible nature of law's claim—that it has moral authority to tell us what to do, although its claim is not to moral correctness—the question I posed earlier seems to reappear where a supposition or presupposition is necessary: what would make autonomous creatures like ourselves *suppose* this to be true? This is not a psychological inquiry, for reasons that will become evident below in considering the two points of view Gardner embraces in *Law as a Leap of Faith*—the acceptance of a 'central case' of law or of the legal point of view puts conceptual pressure on law's claim: what would make the claim plausible enough to generate the kind of social practice necessary for an abstract legal point of view to

[6] Ibid, pp. 8–11.

[7] In 'Nearly Natural Law', Gardner rejects the possibility of law's normativity being entirely formal, like that of a game or a recipe, on the basis of the fact that law has moral implications. 'Every legal issue', he says, 'is a moral issue, for its resolution inevitably has morally important consequences for someone'. But from that indisputable fact, Gardner draws the inference that 'every legal norm ... is a putative (or purported or supposed) moral norm: it is a proposal, on the part of the law, for tackling and resolving one or more moral problems'. This would, if true, help to bridge the Euthyphro-type dilemma of law's normativity from *Law as a Leap of Faith*. But the inference is not warranted: that something has moral implications does not mean that it is trying to solve a moral problem. That much is self-evident. Gardner gives warrant for the inference by accepting the premise that law has *in its central case* a moral purpose, as I will discuss below. See *Law as a Leap of Faith*, pp. 171–173.

[8] Gardner accepts Finnis's claim that 'the central case of the "legal *viewpoint*" is indeed the "point of view in which legal obligation is treated as at least presumptively a moral obligation"' (emphasis mine). He goes on to deny that this implies that legal obligations *are* presumptively obligatory, but does accept that they are defeasibly so. Ibid.

[9] Gardner considers Kelsen's own dilemma at pp. 10–11, in his discussion of the latter's *General Theory of Law and State*, trans Wedberg (Harvard University Press, 1945) and 'On the Pure Theory of Law', *Israel Law Review* 1 (1966): 1.

emerge? Law *might* have the authority it claims, since it is *possible* for it to have that authority,[10] but if law is made valid by its sources not its merits, then that simply can't be a satisfactory answer. Qualifying the supposition as a *pre*supposition is no help: it avoids the need to answer the question of *why* we would 'suppose' that law's claim on us is true, but only by making the solution more mysterious.[11]

While I think Gardner was right to look to the source of legal validity in searching for an answer to this dilemma, the presupposition does not seem to take us further than the original dilemma. Even if presupposition is a form of faith, that does not explain why we would have that kind of faith in law's validity. A more plausible answer lies in the *social* practice of normativity that grounds legal systems. For in that normative social practice, we find plausible human reasons for making the kind of leap of faith from one normative point of view to another that, as I will argue in the next section, Gardner implies that law asks of us.

B. Two Points of View

I have so far been focusing just on Gardner's presentation of two highly abstract normative points of view in *Law as a Leap of Faith*. If we compare his positions in 'How Law Claims, What Law Claims' and 'Nearly Natural Law', the 'Euthyphro' gap between the two pictures of law's normativity seems insurmountably wide. Indeed, its two sides are normally associated with a version of hard positivism on one side and of natural law on the other: on one hand we have a picture of legal normativity held together by a legal point of view which can detach its exponents from their *own* commitments, let alone from a moral one; on the other hand we have a picture of legal normativity in which the legal point of view is internal and rationally inescapable.

The fact that Gardner even contemplated both these views at the same time invites us to consider ways of bridging their divide. But the importance of Gardner's insight in bringing them together becomes unmistakable when we recognize this to be the implication of holding two jurisprudential positions which are often taken to both be true: (1) law's moral potential, and (2) its humble, socially real foundations. If one accepts both, then our account of legal normativity ought to allow for the possibility of moving *towards* the ideal in which law can fulfil its moral potential *from* a non-ideal case. The upshot of this, as I will argue, is that the nature of social normative practice has a lot of work to do in even making it *possible* for law to fulfil its moral potential.

[10] This is so if one accepts Raz's service conception of authority—in itself a contentious idea. See Joseph Raz, *The Authority of Law* (Oxford University Press, 1979) and *The Morality of Freedom* (Oxford University Press, 1986).

[11] Indeed, Gardner calls the *Grundnorm*, or, we can infer, the presupposition of validity and authority, the 'juristic God': *Law as a Leap of Faith*, p. 10.

In the early chapters of *Law as a Leap of Faith,* and especially in 'How Law Claims, What Law Claims', the legal point of view is presented as having only a rather tenuous relationship with moral or 'not-merely-claimed-or-supposed' normativity.[12] The position that law necessarily claims moral authority,[13] though not moral correctness, allows for two ways in which the law can be both valid and morally wrong, even morally abhorrent. First, there is logical space, Gardner points out, in virtue of the illocutionary form of *claiming*: to claim something is to allow conceptual space for the claim's falsity.[14] The second possible gap between valid law and morally good law lies in the distinction between moral authority and moral *correctness*. Gardner points out that law's claim pertains to the former but not the latter.

The claim of moral authority means, then, that law claims that its subjects are morally obligated to obey it[15] entirely apart from any implication that it is morally correct.[16]This seems to make the truth status of law's claim obviously precarious, even while the claim itself is a necessary feature of law. There is a further precariousness, too, implied by the relation between the legal point of view and the practical or moral one, because of Gardner's position on the legal point of view itself. Hart thought that if we are *using* legal norms, then we take the internal point of view in respect of them, making them, in at least one way, our own. But Gardner, following Raz and others, accepts that one can use norms from a detached point of view. To take the detached point of view is just to be able to cognitively apprehend the legal point of view, while remaining entirely uncommitted to it. This seems to enable the legal subject to keep even the law she uses at a distance from her *own* practical or moral reasons.

In these ways legal normativity sits on one side of what appears to be a chasm between the legal and moral points of view. But Gardner introduces another possibility regarding law's relation to morality, one suggested dimly by his earlier caveat about its instrumental benefit, which would put legal normativity on the other side of that chasm. Whereas in 'How Law Claims, What Law Claims', Gardner articulates a distant relation between the legal and moral points of view, in the following chapter he entertains the possibility of a central case of law whose relation to morality is much tighter.

In 'Nearly Natural Law', the legal point of view appears to be much closer to practical reason and even to morality than it seemed to be in the earlier chapter: here Gardner presents the law as having a distinctive moral potential. He very seriously entertains the possibility that law has a moral aim—that immoral law is failed law,

[12] Ibid, p. 134.
[13] Ibid, p. 125.
[14] Ibid, pp. 143–144, 147.
[15] Ibid.
[16] Ibid, p. 147.

and, as such, is a non-central or peripheral case of law.[17] Moreover, Gardner to some extent adopts Finnis's characterization of the law's central case as being one in which the legal point of view *is* the internal, committed one.[18] While maintaining his fidelity to the 'central' positivist position that any given law is valid in virtue of its sources rather than its moral merit,[19] this second way of thinking appears to present, at least intuitively, a quite different picture of the relation between legal normativity and morality or practical reason.

These two views re-create the paradox of the Euthyphro dilemma. The apparent gap between them invites us to consider the conceptual space between the two positions and whether and how they might be reconciled. Following Gardner's suggestion that the solution lies in a leap of faith made possible by the *source* of law, I will suggest that the two positions can be reconciled, to some extent, by shifting our focus from law's aim and its claim to the social normative practice on which legal normativity rests.

Consider first the idealistic view: law has a distinctive capacity to bring morality to fruition in social life—to allow us to live more morally than we would be able to do without it; to bring into being certain kinds of moral goods that only law makes possible. On this view, law has certain distinctive features that, plausibly, make it specially suited to allow morality to flourish: these include the objects of regulation it shares with morality, and its co-ordination function—which allows for the realization of greater goods for more people—as well as allowing for co-operation among a wider populace than might be possible in a society that has to rely on relations of personal trust in order to co-operate.

Even in its central case, though, law is *somehow* distinct from morality; it must be so because otherwise it could not enable morality's flourishing. Law's normativity is the wind at morality's back, on this view. It cannot fulfil this role if it does not have some kind of distinct normativity of its own. There are several ways to illuminate the idea that the distinctiveness of legal normativity from morality enables law's moral potential. Famously, even if moral precepts were known and if everyone was disposed to follow them, morality's particular requirements in each situation are unclear. In many cases, to bring about the fulfilment of moral precepts—and in particular in the case of co-ordination and co-operation norms—we need a system of social specification that will tell each person to whom it applies what following the moral precept in question requires of them.

[17] Ibid, pp. 149–177, discussing John Finnis's *Natural Law and Natural Rights* (Oxford University Press, 2011). Gardner's difference with Finnis appears to be one of emphasis only: Gardner allows that the morally successful case of law is its central case, but insists that the study of law ought to pay equal attention to its non-central cases and that a theory of law ought to include, as he says, quoting Raz, the 'limits of law'. *Law as a Leap of Faith*, p. 166.

[18] Ibid, pp. 171–173.

[19] See ibid, chapter 2, pp. 19–54.

Law is thus, in its ideal case, a kind of particularized social practice of morality. Yet all the ways in which law can help realize morality in social life require a form of normativity distinct from morality itself: in a large and complex society, especially, legal normativity fits the bill. And in order to serve its moral master, law's normativity must be sufficiently robust—it must be effective, and its reasons must carry distinctive force for those whose compliance they are to attract. The trouble is that, as Gardner presents the startling nature and manner of law's claims, they stop considerably short of what would be required for the central case of law as so far described to *emerge*.

This raises the question: how can this central case of law, with its suitably robust normativity, come about? It surely can't emerge fully formed as Athena from the head of Zeus, complete with her suit of armour. This is because of three other premises consistently at work in Gardner's view. The first is that, among its other characteristics, law is *made*; so even that idealistic picture of law's central case must be brought about by real people. Second, law has no abstract agency—Gardner is clear, in his discussion of how law makes its claims, that it has no voice of its own simply as an abstraction. If it is to claim, or to do anything at all, it must do so through the voices and actions of actual people.[20] Finally, there is the central positivist premise that law rests on a social foundation—a social normative practice which crystallizes the ultimate rule of the legal system. If the central case of law is to be even conceptually possible, then, we must face the question of how it could emerge from that foundation of social practice. The conceptual possibility of the central case of law, and of the legal viewpoint it entails, means that the social normativity that engenders it must also be possible—and possible for what we, as humans, are actually like. This puts the burden of law's moral potential squarely on the social normative practice that grounds legal systems.

With social normative practice, though, we seem to be back on the far side of the Euthyphro gap from the idealistic view of things. Law claims to give people reasons to do things they would not otherwise have reason to do, or to give them a special kind of additional reason to act in light of reasons they may already have had. This makes law seem to be essentially about simply telling us what to do, rather than—since it doesn't claim moral correctness—being about making our conduct morally better or correct. And recall the three of Gardner's propositions brought together above. The fact that law is of necessity made and that lacks abstract agency means that (1) only people can make law's claims. And (2) law's validity rests on social practice. These two propositions together mean that, at least on this non-ideal side of the gap, valid law can emerge without inconsistency simply, even if distantly, as follows. People make claims on each other's conduct—*tell one another what to do*—in a sufficiently consistent and persuasive way that at least some people treat those

[20] *Law as a Leap of Faith*, pp. 130–132.

imperatives of others as authoritative. To treat the imperatives of others such that, eventually, it can make sense to say that law has its own distinctive point of view and can in *some* sense, in its *own* voice, make claims on us.

At first glance, this seems deeply puzzling: why would a practice that revolves around people successfully claiming the moral right simply to tell one another what to do seem at all plausible? What could get such a practice off the ground at all, let alone bring us all the way across the gap to the ideal case of law?

To better appreciate this puzzle, consider the role of the legal point of view in getting law up and running from social normative practice. If the detached point of view was the legal point of view, it would be seriously problematic for engendering the moral potential of law as envisioned in its central case. The detached point of view is consistent with people saying to one another, 'it's against the law to do that, but I wouldn't pay any attention to the law if I were you'. In other words, the detached point of view simply involves the recognition and communication of the legal point of view and its requirements. What is 'detached' about this point of view is the communicant's own distinctive voice and normative perspective from the statements or imperatives she issues. But if the central case of law is one in which law's source lies in a social practice which *engenders* the fruition of moral life, it seems implausible that that social practice undergirding law's normativity involves this kind of detachment of its participants from the normativity it is supposed to support. The view of the social normative practice on which law rests in 'How Law Claims, What Law Claims', in other words, does not seem to involve people making law's claims in their own voices. Given the tight connection that would seem to be required between law's normativity and its moral aim as described in 'Nearly Natural Law', this seems puzzling.

Gardner recognizes this gap between the morally disconnected implications of the way normative social practice is characterized in his discussion of the nature and manner of law's claims, on one hand, and the moral commitment involved in law's central case, on the other. His solution is to agree with Finnis, in 'Nearly Natural Law', that in the central case of law 'the legal point of view is the one in which legal obligation is treated as at least presumptively a moral obligation',[21] and is thus the internal, or internal-committed, one.

How would *this* come to be, though? Even if we assume that everyone in our central case society is disposed to live morally and to use law's normativity to bolster morality, we still need a social foundation—a social normative practice—out of which legal validity, and the *legal* point of view, can be born. At the stage where the social practice is merely that which establishes the rule of recognition, and where the rule of recognition is practised socially on an ongoing basis, there *is* no *legal* point of view on the matter; there is only the point of view of those participating in

[21] Ibid, p. 171.

the social practice. We cannot, I want to suggest, solve the problem of how to bridge the gap between the morally arid, conditional claims of law made through people telling others what to do, on one hand, and the ideal or central case of law, on the other, simply by stipulating that everyone involved in the foundational social practice (and indeed people in the wider society as well) is disposed to act morally.

One reason for this is, as I have suggested, that, for law to do its morality-supporting work, it must have a normativity that is distinct from that of morality itself. Even if we take everyone to be morally disposed, and the central case of the legal point of view to be one which presumes that law is presumptively morally obligatory, a particular legal system must achieve its moral fruits through a social practice that requires doing things in certain particular ways rather than others, where there are a range of morally permissible answers to the question of which way to do things. Furthermore, distinctively legal normativity is necessary to specify the vague requirements of morality in a sufficiently particular and determinately *shared* way so that co-operation and co-ordination in moral practice is possible. Mere moral disposition on the part of all the relevant individuals is not enough to generate sufficient regularity of conduct grounded in a point of view internal to the *social* rule governing that regularity, because any given social rule could be mistaken as a way of achieving a moral purpose. So we are left with the need for law's own normativity. A distinctively legal point of view will have to come into being, and, if it is to give rise to the central case of law, at least some people will have to commit to it.

It follows that if we are to get from the sterile picture of social normative practice that grounds law's distinctive normativity on one side of the gap to the ideal case of law on the other side, we must answer the question of why anyone would come to assent to law's claims—treat the law as normative—such that they come to make those claims of others and adopt the legal point of view as their own. Sustaining the conceptual possibility of both Gardner's ways of conceiving of law's relation to morality, it seems, necessitates an account of how the central case could emerge from social normative practice.

We might object, at this point, that the central case need not emerge from anywhere—that it can simply exist on its own side of the Euthyphro gap—because the presentation of law's central case is merely an idealization. But that would be a mistake. It would have to involve stipulating internal commitment on the part of everyone in our ideal case of law; such stipulation cannot solve the problem of the gap between the moral aridity of the detached point of view characteristic of one view of legal normativity and the morally rich or aspirational view characteristic of what Gardner presents as law's central case. One problem with this solution is that if stipulating internal commitment on the part of everyone in our central case society is our solution to the problem of the gap, we will have an ideal of law built on an illusion, as much as on an abstraction.

A related problem is that we cannot simply stipulate that everyone adopts the legal point of view—especially in the committed sense necessary for the ideal—or our picture of the relation between central case and peripheral case of law would not exist as points on a single spectrum but rather as entirely separate conceptual entities. We would have an account of law made conceivable by what people are like—this would generate every possible case of 'peripheral' or 'failed' law—and we would, separately, have an account of law explained by what *could* be possible given stipulations that are only conceivable in abstraction from reality.

I do not think this can be what Gardner had in mind in invoking central case analysis. One of his most significant insights about the value of the central case method for thinking about law is precisely that it does not force that kind of separate conceptualization, where ideal law is 'real' law and non-ideal law is somehow *not* law. Gardner deftly interprets the central case analysis so that 'peripheral' cases of law are understood to be failed as realizations of law's *moral* aim or potential, but not necessarily to be failed *as law*. In invoking central case analysis, Gardner is careful to insist that non-central cases remain important for study and consideration about what law is like. A shift from peripheral case to central case is thus not a move from a defective *concept* to a successful one, but from an instance of something that has failed to live up to its promise in one, evaluative, respect. On this way of thinking, our conceptualization ought to have a way of making sense of a legal system's progress from morally sub-optimal to morally good or correct; in other words, to *get to*, or to move toward, a central case of law from a non-central one.

The central case of law, then, is not made from whole cloth: it emerges from social life; and we cannot hypothesize the central case into being by imagining humans to be different than we are. Even if we can conceive of a central case of law in which everyone occupies an internal point of view committed to law's moral promise, I take Gardner's point to be that the central case of law is ideal, yes, but an ideal toward which non-central cases can actually move. And for anything like that to be possible, we must begin with a picture of what people are actually like.

Finally, we would be wrong to think we could build a central case of law simply by stipulating that its *content* conform to moral requirements. The particular version or specification of those requirements in any given legal system would have to manifest in the social normative practice of the particular legal system in question—we would have to get its participants to adopt a particular set of norms. And, in doing so, we wouldn't be able to rely only on coercing conformity; the central case of law must, like all law, be built up from a foundation of social practice. That means that although the law is made, it must be made organically, from within, by its own social practices. And just as we can't simply assume that even most people in the society will take an internal, *committed* point of view with respect to the law, we also can't assume that they will be disposed to do what is morally right—to create law with morally good content.

An account of social normative practice, or the social practice of a norm, is therefore crucially important, on anything like the picture of law suggested here. It is social normative practice that will have to get us from people simply criticizing one another's conduct, to acting in accordance with a shared norm, to the point where the original social norm can sort other norms into legal and non-legal—valid and invalid. And if it is true that a valid legal norm claims moral authority, then the social normative practice with which we begin must be capable of sustaining at least the facial plausibility of that ultimate *claim* to moral authority even if the claim is ultimately falsified by the law's content. If this is true, then there is an important connection between the social practice that grounds and sustains a legal system and the plausibility of law's claim to moral authority.

This burden on the nature of social normative practice is heightened when we realize that if law is to fulfil its moral potential, its social practice must extend beyond the foundation of legal systems. We can, in delineating law's ideal case, presumably rule out the 'deplorably sheep-like condition' in which only officials of the system practise legal norms socially while all others are merely goaded into submission;[22] that condition does not look like a system that has a moral aim, and certainly not like one that fulfils it. Rather, at least in the central case, the social normativity of law will have to extend upwards from the base of the rule of recognition to the more general social practice of legal rules. Therefore, in its central case, the practice of legal norms will have to be significantly built on widespread *compliance* rather than mere conformity.

Moreover, the social normative practice that sustains the legal system has a recursive or reflexive relation to the 'original' social practice of the rule of recognition on which the whole edifice is based. This reflexivity is partly what makes an ultimately social rule of recognition possible: it remains 'live', as it were; through adjudication, its practice extends from past to present and presumptively into the future. This means, though, that as new people begin to practice the rule of recognition, and apply the norms it recognizes, law's claim to moral authority must retain the plausibility it inherited from the original crystallization of social practice that manifested in the rule of recognition in the first place. It is thus ongoing social normative practice that can allow for the emergence of anything like the central case of law as Gardner describes it, in which its members take the (committed) internal point of view with respect to the laws of the system. I will merely suggest the beginnings of an account of law's source in social normativity, in the hope that it might offer a complement to the various aspects of Gardner's jurisprudence which invite the analogy with faith he offers.

[22] Jeremy Waldron, 'All We Like Sheep', *Can. J. L. & Jurisprudence* 12 (1999): 169.

C. Social Normative Practice

The social foundation of law has traditionally been taken to be important because it allows law to be built up from empirical facts—acts, attitudes, dispositions—thus fulfilling the central intuitive thrust of legal positivism. As a general matter, when jurisprudents talk about social normative practice, or social normativity, they simply mean norms that are shared, or norms that are not necessarily justified. But these ways of understanding social normative practice cannot meet the burden of allowing law to meet its moral potential, given what people are actually like.

Philosophical accounts of social norms and, especially, social conventions, are—somewhat surprisingly—highly individualistic in their orientation. They focus on the reasons *individuals* have and how those reasons can be interlocking. To differentiate a conventional norm from a regular activity, for instance, Marmor, Gilbert and others point to the fact that while an action may be *regular*, and thus a practice—brushing one's teeth every night, for instance—and it may also be wrong not to do it on any given night, it is not wrong to fail to do it because of a convention one has to brush one's teeth.[23] Marmor cashes this difference out in his definition of a convention: he says that something C can be a convention if, for any C, there is a different rule, C*, which the same reasons for doing C would support.[24] This is the sense in which conventions have been argued to be necessarily arbitrary. If some value V could *only* be achieved by way of *one* practice VP, that practice would not be arbitrary with respect to V. Conventional norms have also been isolated on the basis that they are grounded in the individual preferences of their participants,[25] on the basis of their participants' joint acceptance,[26] or on the basis that they solve co-ordination problems.[27]

These various elucidations of social norms share an emphasis on the structure and nature of the reasons they offer rather than on anything like the significance of interpersonal relations, or to social *connections* between people. To the extent that such explanations are concerned with the social character of the norms, that concern focuses on the reasoning structure of individuals: in general, the normativity of social rules is taken to be explained in terms of individual self-interest. The social character of norms could then be relevant because of a purely arbitrary co-ordination solution: that enough people taking act X rather than act Y thereby creates a reason for each of them to take X rather than Y. The social character of the norm in that case is just that it converts a reason that might not pertain to anyone into a reason that pertains to everyone. The social character of the norm could,

23 Andrei Marmor, 'On Convention', *Synthese* 107 (1996): 352.
24 Marmor, pp. 351–352.
25 I take this to be part of Lewis' explanation: see D. Lewis, *Convention, A Philosophical Study* (Oxford University Press, 1969) pp. 5–24
26 See Margaret Gilbert, 'Social Convention Revisited', *Topoi* 27 (2008): 5–16
27 See, e.g., Lewis, 1969, pp. 5–24.

relatedly, be relevant because enough individuals have a preference for X over Y that that fact makes X the *better* practice for all members, on a kind of game-theoretic analysis. The social character of a norm could, alternately, be relevant because it engenders the *joint commitment* of its members, which is then taken to be normatively significant. It could be relevant, instead, because each member of the social group has reason to live well, and that reason extends to living together with others in a particular way that gives rise to the social norms of the group.

In contrast to these individualized explanations of social normativity, Hart emphasized the *social* character of norm-practice: he focused on the role of the *interpersonal pressure* co-members of the group put on one another to conform to rules.[28] This allowed him to make sense of the use of normative language in the practice of social rules and to draw attention to the attitude of the members of the group practising the rule.

Hart's account did not go far enough, though, in my view, in explaining the nature of social normative practice, or in articulating the conditions that make it possible. It is all too easy to think of social normativity merely as a kind of herd mentality in which people goad one another through expression of disapproval. Notice that inhabiting the internal point of view—the primary object of much analysis of Hart's account of social normative practice—is a feature of the *individuals* who constitute the relevant social group. That approach to understanding social normativity is seriously limited: it fails to attend to the distinctively *social* mechanisms at work in the practice of norms among a group of people.

If we are to allow for the possibility of law having a central case towards which any given actual legal system can move, a fuller account of the social practice of legal norms is essential. But we cannot simply assume that a sufficient number of people in any given legal system simultaneously come to inhabit the internal point of view or anything like it. Social normative practice requires that norms transfer from one individual to another—that norms be *transmitted* socially.

This means that the clear case of social normative practice must be able to explain the transmission of the internal point of view within the group. So the central case of social normative practice cannot only involve one person—call her Speaker—criticizing someone else—call her Hearer—for failing to comply with a norm and thus producing conformity with that norm in Hearer's conduct. Rather, social normative practice must be able to explain the transfer of the *norm itself*, rather than just the shaping of *conduct*, from one person to another. Social normative practice in its clearest case involves the transfer of the internal point of view itself from one person to another.

To fully understand social normative practice, then, we must expand our scope of inquiry from Speaker to include her Hearer. The internal point of view, in other

[28] H.L.A. Hart, *The Concept of Law* (Oxford University Press, 3rd ed, 2012), pp. 56–57 and 255–256.

words, is only *one side* of the social practice of a norm. Social practice must also include *effective transmission of norms* from one person to another.

Effective transmission of norms means that a Speaker says something to a Hearer[29] with normative content N such that somehow, eventually, Hearer will herself accept N.[30] This does not require that the Hearer actually conform her action to the norm's *requirements* on any particular occasion.[31] Nor does it require that either Speaker or Hearer thinks N morally justified. Rather, what must be transmitted, at least often enough to reach a level of sufficiency, is the internal point of view *itself* vis-à-vis the norm in question. Even if the Hearer need not act as the norm requires, she must, at least sometimes, allow that there is a practical reason for *her* to accept it—to use it in the first person to evaluate her conduct *and* make internal statements about it to others. Transmission thus involves two: Speaker and Hearer (the occupier of the normative point of view and the person whose conduct stands to be guided). So much has been said about the significance of the Speaker's point of view that the Hearer, and her role in effective norm-transmission, has received insufficient attention. I will call the passing of the internal point of view from Speaker to Hearer the requirement of normative *uptake* to effective transmission. In brief, then: normative uptake is necessary to the emergence of social normative practice.

Conventional jurisprudential emphasis on the Speaker's role in the process of norm-communication has led us to cease our inquiry into the norm-transfer process at the point where the Speaker makes an internal statement of the right kind. But in the context of any of the kinds of statements used to illustrate the internal point of view, the question arises: why would a Hearer of such a statement *take* it in the mode in which it was expressed? In other words, why would a Hearer of even a statement *made* in the normative mode *take* it that way *for herself*? To make sense of social normative practice, we need a way of explaining normative uptake in the context of communications of norms that do not explicitly appeal to their justifications. For social norms to get off the ground and to sustain themselves, Hearers are going to have to care that Speakers take themselves to have reason to treat N as normative, to use it as a norm with which to evaluate Hearer.

It matters to people what others in their social group think, and what they think *of them*; social normative practice is possible because of the affective and associational ties people have to one another. My proposal is that we characterize truly *social* normativity as generated from social *ties*. Whereas Gardner's paradigm case

[29] By using 'speaker' and 'hearer' I do not mean that the content need be verbalized explicitly: the British are fond of the 'tsk-tsk' sound or the shaking of the head, say, when someone jumps the queue at a bus stop. I mean 'speaking' and 'hearing' under this terminology to mean saliently communicating.

[30] I use quotes around the term here simply to indicate that what is happening is a kind of willing suspension of disbelief—an act of presuming the veracity of something *only* for some specific purpose and in the context pertinent to that purpose.

[31] But not, of course, on no occasions ever. She will have to conform her action to the norm at least enough that the point of sufficiency can be met.

of the human being is the rational being, the paradigm case of the human person upon which legal normativity can rest must *also* be the social person. This is what makes social normativity—and thus also law's normativity—possible. It is also, therefore, what makes *plausible*, even if not necessarily probable, law's audacious claim to moral authority.

The leap of faith involved in social normativity is not faith that the content of norms are correct, or faith that the lawmaker has the authority she claims to make the law and to make it binding. Hearers need not have faith that Speakers actually believe in the truth of the norms they transmit. Rather, they must believe that those Speakers are acting on the basis of practical reason, in that they take themselves to have a reason to treat the relevant norm as true,[32] and to encourage others to treat it that way. The central case of the legal point of view *can* emerge, then, from the faith of legal subjects that those with whom they share social ties of various kinds are, in passing norms along to them in the normative mode, themselves acting—appropriately enough—in good faith.

[32] Adam Perry, 'The Internal Aspect of Social Rules', *Oxford Journal of Legal Studies* 35.2 (2014): 283–300.

2
Can the Constitution of a Fruit Fly Be Written?

Grégoire Webber[*]

A. Pedagogy and Public Debate

Can there be a written constitution? That is the title question of an essay by John Gardner first published in 2011 in the inaugural volume of the *Oxford Studies in the Philosophy of Law* series and republished the following year in his collection of essays, *Law as a Leap of Faith*.[1] The essay began as a lecture delivered at Oxford in July 2008,[2] being one year to the month after Prime Minister Gordon Brown outlined before the House of Commons a series of proposals for constitutional change. Among them was a proposal to 'involve the public in a sustained debate whether there is a case ... for moving towards a written constitution'.[3]

I do not know if John conceived of his lecture and essay as a contribution to that sustained debate, but I doubt it. He repeats, more than once, that he wishes to stay clear of 'political hot potatoes'[4] and he adds twice in the essay's first few pages that there is 'no live proposal' for the UK to have 'a canonical constitutional master-text'.[5] I read the essay as pursuing a different objective, one summarized in the preface to *Law as a Leap of Faith*. John there says that many of the essays included in the collection 'were originally written with pedagogical objectives in mind, responding to perennial misconceptions on the part of [his] students'.[6] The preface does not single out which essays come under this pedagogical umbrella,

[*] For comments and discussion, I thank participants at the *From Morality to Law and Back Again: Liber Amicorum for John Gardner* workshop held at All Souls College on 16–17 December 2019 as well as Nick Barber, Timothy Endicott, Richard Ekins, Jean Thomas, Leah Trueblood, Mark Walters, and Paul Yowell.

[1] John Gardner, 'Can there be a written constitution?' in Leslie Green and Brian Leiter (eds), *Oxford Studies in the Philosophy of Law, volume 1* (OUP 2011); John Gardner, *Law as a Leap of Faith* (OUP 2012) ch 4 (hereafter *LLF*).

[2] In the Acknowledgements pages of *LLF*, Gardner reports that the essay 'grew from a lecture in July 2008 to mark 25 years of Southern Methodist University's Law Program in Oxford' (xi).

[3] 'In full: Brown on constitution' (BBC News, 3 July 2007), online: http://news.bbc.co.uk/2/hi/uk_news/politics/6266526.stm (accessed 2 March 2023).

[4] *LLF* (n 1) 89–90, 111, 119.

[5] *LLF* (n 1) 90, 92.

[6] *LLF* (n 1) vi. The objective is repeated in John Gardner, '*Law as a Leap of Faith* as others see it' (2014) 33 *Law & Philosophy* 813, 813.

Grégoire Webber, *Can the Constitution of a Fruit Fly Be Written?* In: *From Morality to Law and Back Again*. Edited by: Michelle Madden Dempsey and François Tanguay-Renaud, Oxford University Press. © Grégoire Webber 2023. DOI: 10.1093/oso/9780198860594.003.0002

but John's essay on the constitution is a contender for inclusion. Insofar as the perennial misconceptions live among Oxford students are also live within the wider public, John's essay illuminates important aspects of a constitutional debate that long predates the Prime Minister's invitation and that continues to agitate many today.[7]

What is the perennial misconception that the essay addresses? It is hinted at obliquely in the essay's title: 'Can there be a written constitution?' Stripped of context, the title question gestures towards a speculative inquiry, inviting reflection on a conceptual possibility with respect to a constitution, be it the constitution of the United Kingdom or the United States or another constitution, real or imagined. But when situated in the context of a general loss of faith in the United Kingdom's constitutional arrangements,[8] the title question is a clever play on the question that is more often formulated by those who study constitutional affairs: 'Can there be an *unwritten* constitution?' That question is often put in a more pointed fashion in the United Kingdom, where, given the absence of a canonical constitutional master-text, the inquiry sometimes takes the following form: 'Does the United Kingdom have a constitution?'[9] John situates this more pointed question as his essay's opening sentence.

The question, and the misconception that underlies it, owe much to the shadow cast by the US Constitution, which obscures from view constitutions that do not share its features, at least as those features are understood in some of their more romanticized readings.[10] Among some of those romanticized features are that a constitution marks a founding in time that breaks with the past; is an original written compact that serves as a constant reference through time;[11] has the status of supreme law resulting from higher law-making by 'the People';[12] and is protected by judicial guardians from the encroachments of government and legislature.

[7] For a sample of academic contributions to the debate, see JAG Griffith, 'The political constitution' (1979) 42 MLR 1; NW Barber, 'Against a written constitution' [2008] PL 11; Jeff King, 'The democratic case for a written constitution' (2019) 72 CLP 1; Jo Eric Khushal Murkens, 'A written constitution: a case not made' (2021) 41 OJLS 965.

[8] On which, see Martin Loughin, *The British Constitution: A Very Short Introduction* (OUP 2013) and Grégoire Webber, 'Eulogy for the constitution that was' (2014) 12 I-CON 468.

[9] John entertains the possibility that the United Kingdom has not one but three or four constitutions, but, for the purposes of his essay, 'speak[s] brazenly' of 'the UK constitution': *LLF* (n 1) 90. I follow him in simplifying the discussion in this way.

[10] For an illuminating comparison between romantic and historical accounts of the US Constitution, see Ruti Teitel, 'Transitional jurisprudence: the role of law in political transformation' (2009) 107 Yale LJ 2009.

[11] I explore aspects of these two features in my challenge to originalist constitutional interpretation in Grégoire Webber, 'Originalism's constitution' in Grant Huscrot and Bradley W Miller (eds), *The Challenge of Originalism* (CUP 2011).

[12] See e.g. Bruce Ackerman, *We the People: Foundations* (Belknap Press 1993); AR Amar, *America's Constitution: A Biography* (Random House 2006) 8: 'In the beginning, God said, *fiat lux*, and—behold!—there was light. So, too, when the American people ... [said] "Let there be a Constitution"—and there would be one.'

Measured against these features, the UK has no constitution: many of its constitutional arrangements are, in Burke's formulation, 'an entailed inheritance derived to us from our forefathers, and to be transmitted to our posterity';[13] though some aspects of the constitution are written and some of what is written has the status of law, these are but 'some written fragments of the otherwise unwritten ... constitution';[14] many of those aspects of the constitution that are written law are in Acts of Parliament 'passed and promulgated in the ordinary way'[15] and have special legal status only insofar as they make exception to the doctrine of implied repeal;[16] and while British courts exercise authority over some aspects of the constitution, the doctrine of parliamentary sovereignty qualifies their role as constitutional guardians.[17] As for 'the People' and its authority over the constitutional order, the idea of constituent authority in the UK is complicated by the standing of the Westminster Parliament, which, in the words of Alexis de Tocqueville, is 'at once a legislature and constituent assembly'.[18] All this to say, if one's conception of a constitution is captured by the American Constitution, then the question whether the UK has a constitution invites a ready reply.

These different conceptions of a constitution suggest that John's title question—Can there be a written constitution?—invites a prior question about the nature of the constitution one is interrogating. This will be a theme of my review of John's constitutional essay. It is true that John's essay can be understood to be an investigation into that prior question. He offers, as answers, ideas about secondary rules, legal systems, inherent and delegated powers, and more. Yet, as he explains in the preface to *Law as a Leap of Faith*, his constitutional essay is focused on investigating 'the essential place of a customary "ultimate rule of recognition" in every legal system', albeit 'under cover of studying the nature of constitutions'.[19] Perhaps because his primary interest is in secondary rules, a number of John's claims about the nature of a constitution will be surprising and counter-intuitive for constitutional lawyers. Among them are that a constitution constitutes a legal system, that the constitution can be reduced to the ultimate secondary rules of change and of adjudication, that the UK Supreme Court does

[13] Edmund Burke, *Reflections on the Revolution in France* (first published 1790, Penguin 2004) 119 (hereafter Burke, *Reflections*).

[14] *LLF* (n 1) 91.

[15] *LLF* (n 1) 91.

[16] *LLF* (n 1) 93–94.

[17] Though the doctrine has been questioned by some senior members of the judiciary: see *R (Jackson) v Attorney General*, 2005 UKHL 56 (Lord Steyn, [102]; Lord Hope, [104]–[107]; Baroness Hale, [159]), and *R (Privacy International) v Investigatory Powers Tribunal* [2019] UKSC 22 (Lord Carnwath, [131], [144]). See also *AXA General Insurance v The Lord Advocate* [2011] UKSC 46 (Lord Hope, [42]–[52]).

[18] Alexis de Tocqueville, *Democracy in America* (first published in 1835, Henry Reeve trans, Vintage Books 1990). See further Martin Loughlin, 'Constituent power subverted: from English constitutional argument to British constitutional discourse' in Martin Loughlin and Neil Walker (eds), *The Paradox of Constitutionalism: Constituent Power and Constitutional Form* (OUP 2007).

[19] *LLF* (n 1) vii.

not have constitutional status, that inherent powers can be delegated, and that delegated powers can be inherent. On a closer examination, none of this is surprising given that John's essay does not interrogate the nature of constitutions writ large. The scope of his argument is more modest: he interrogates the nature of the constitution of a legal system. Of this constitution, one can ask whether it can be written. But can the question of written-ness be asked of any constitution whatsoever?

That is the question that my chapter title aims to raise. The reference to a fruit fly is inspired by an analogy John made in one of the first meetings of the postgraduate BCL seminars in Constitutional Theory in Michaelmas Term 2004. 'Even a fruit fly has a constitution', he said in a seminar interrogating the nature of constitutions. (In his generous way, John meet with me after the seminar to help me explore what was, for me then, a most arresting thought.) Would it make sense to ask whether the constitution of a fruit fly can be written? I think not, and think that the question reveals that, in asking whether a constitution can be written, one has in view an understanding about the nature of the constitution one is interrogating. As I aim to show, John's focus is on the constitution of a legal system. But if one is instead interrogating the constitution of a state or of a government or of a country's governing arrangements, it is less clear whether John's title question remains apposite. Without a clear view on the nature of the constitution one is interrogating, asking whether a constitution can be written may be akin to asking whether the constitution of a fruit fly can be written.

To explore John's argument, I begin by contrasting his invitation to investigate the nature of a constitution in the frame of Hart's secondary rules with two historically competing accounts of the nature of a constitution (section B). I do so not because John is best read as contributing to the debate between Edmund Burke and Thomas Paine, but rather to show how his focus on the secondary rules of a legal system leaves some important questions about the nature of a constitution to the side. I then set out a series of propositions defended in the course of John's dialectical argument (section C). This helps to show how the meaning of 'constitution' changes across his essay, though his focus remains always on the constitution of a legal system (section D). I then offer some reasons for thinking that secondary rules may be part of, but not the whole of, what interests constitutional lawyers when they inquire into whether a constitution can be written (section E). I conclude by suggesting that John's essay helps us see how the very idea that the UK could move to a written constitution presupposes that there is something that can be written (section F). A different way of putting the thought is this: if not every constitution can be written, then something about the UK constitution is presupposed in claims that the UK could or should move to a written constitution.

B. Burke and Paine (or Hart)

The battle over the nature of a constitution has a long history, exemplified in the clash of ideas between Burke and Paine at the time of the French Revolution. For Burke, the British constitution was distinguished by a 'principle of conservation, and a sure principle of transmission', all without 'excluding a principle of improvement'.[20] The Glorious Revolution of 1688 was conceived by him not as a break with the past and a new beginning, but as a restoration—a way of securing the preservation of 'our *antient* indisputable laws and liberties'.[21] Revolution here denoted a 'recurring, cyclical movement' borrowed from astronomy,[22] with the term's metaphorical use in human affairs signalling a commitment to 'revolve back to old times when things had been as they ought to be'.[23] The Glorious Revolution signified a restoration of the old, a return to a previous state of affairs. Burke offered a similar reading of other moments of constitutional note, including the Magna Carta 1215 ('our oldest reformation'[24]) and the Petition of Right 1628 ('a patrimony derived from their forefathers'[25]), which, taken together with the Bill of Rights 1689, affirmed the 'uniform policy of our constitution to claim and assert our liberties, as an entailed inheritance'.[26]

Paine, by contrast, insisted that a constitution must be 'produced in a visible form', as a document can be; that a constitution is 'antecedent to a government' rather than developed in the evolutionary workings of government; and that a constitution, rather than being sustained by the commitment of government actors to the standards of the done and the not-done things, is beyond the authority of the constituted authorities to alter.[27] To some French counter-revolutionaries, Paine's 'evil book' had the distinction of making it 'difficult to get more errors into fewer lines'.[28] And in Great Britain, the King's Bench would try and convict Paine *in absentia* for seditious libel for things said in *The Rights of Man*.[29] But, with time, the

20 Burke, *Reflections* (n 13) 119–120.
21 Burke, *Reflections* (n 13) 119.
22 Hannah Arendt, *On Revolution* (Penguin 1963) 41.
23 Arendt (n 22) 44.
24 Burke, *Reflections* (n 13) 117.
25 Burke, *Reflections* (n 13) 118.
26 Burke, *Reflections* (n 13) 119. See further Loughlin, *The British Constitution* (n 8) 87 and Graham Gee and Grégoire Webber, 'A conservative disposition and constitutional change' (2019) 39 OJLS 526. The idea of a conservative disposition is not to be confused with political conservatism. See Prince Saprai's contribution to this volume.
27 Thomas Paine, 'Rights of man' (1791) in Mark Philip (ed), *Rights of Man, Common Sense and other Political Writings* (OUP 1995) 122–123. For discussion, see Martin Loughlin, *Foundations of Public Law* (OUP 2010) ch 10.
28 Joseph de Maistre, 'Study on sovereignty' (1794–1795) in Jack Lively (ed), *The Works of Joseph de Maistre* (Allen & Unwin 1965) 107, cited in Loughlin, *Foundations of Public Law* (n 27) 279 n 14.
29 *The Genuine Trial of Thomas Paine, for a Libel, contained in the Second Part of Rights of Man; at Guildhall, London, Dec. 18, 1792, before Lord Kenyon and a special jury: Together with the Speeches at Large of the Attorney-General and Mr. Erskine, and Authentic Copies of Mr. Paine's Letters to the Attorney-General and others, On the Subject of the Prosecution* (London: printed for J.S. Jordan, 1793).

influence of the American and French revolutions on constitutional thought elevated Paine's thinking on the constitution to the rank of received wisdom, and demoted Burke's to the rank of dissent.

John's title question plays on today's received wisdom, turning it on its head or, as he puts it at one point in the essay, turning the tables against the written constitution.[30] Yet, John's method in his constitutional essay is not to appeal to the history of ideas, but to the philosophy of law. His main source of inspiration for affirming that there is 'no room for doubt' that the UK has a constitution is Hart, not Burke.[31] As he explains in the preface to *Law as a Leap of Faith*, his essay on the constitution contributes to his defence or support of two jurisprudential theses: first, although all law is made, 'not all is made intentionally, or even knowingly, and in particular not all is made by legislating'; and second, the content of all law is the content it was given by its makers and changers and this 'includes the law that determines who counts as an ultimate maker or changer of law (what Hart calls "rules of recognition")'.[32] John expounds his understanding of a constitution by reference to Hart's secondary rules and, with the exception whether a constitution can be written, he takes no position on the features of a constitution debated between Burke and Paine.

John's appeal to Hart is not an appeal to intellectual authority: he differs from Hart and highlights ambiguities in *The Concept of Law* at various points in this and other essays. Rather, John appeals to the idea of a rule of recognition to explore the thought that, *if* the ultimate rule of recognition in a legal system is customary, and *if* it is the ultimate rule of recognition that constitutes at least part of the legal system, *then* the constitution of a legal system is, as a matter of conceptual truth, at least partly unwritten. And *if* the written parts of a constitution have constitutional status only 'because of their reception into the unwritten law that is made by the customs and decisions of the courts and other law-applying officials', *then* a constitution—in part *and* in whole—'cannot be, or be contained in, documents'.[33] If the argument is sound, then the response to the title question is straightforward: no, there cannot be a written constitution.

That is the 'heretical view' that John explores, but it is not the view with which he concludes.[34] True to his essay's pedagogical purpose, the argument proceeds in a dialectical manner: laying out the case for doubting that there can be a written constitution, then laying out the case for doubting that there cannot be a written constitution, raising and answering objections all along the way, and then restating the question under consideration before answering it. The result is, for me, a case

[30] *LLF* (n 1) 97.
[31] *LLF* (n 1) 90, citing to HLA Hart, *The Concept of Law* (OUP 1961) 95–96 (hereafter Hart, *Concept of Law*).
[32] *LLF* (n 1) ix.
[33] *LLF* (n 1) 98.
[34] *LLF* (n 1) 98.

for much admiration and for some uncertainty as to where the argument ultimately concludes. That uncertainty comes, in part, from what I perceive to be shifting understandings of the nature of the constitution that answers to his title question. At times, such as in the passages referred to in the previous paragraph, John includes the rule of recognition within his understanding of a constitution. At other times, he 'set[s] aside ... the ultimate rules of recognition of the system'.[35] But always, John's focus is on the constitution of a legal system.

By the end of the essay, we learn that, for John, there can be a written constitution if the following conditions hold: *if* the focus is exclusively on law; *if* the rule of recognition is excluded from the category of law; *if* one of the ultimate rules of recognition is that a written constitution made by an authority is law; *if* that authority is sufficiently unlikely to revoke the constitution; and *if* the case law interpreting the text of the constitution is understood to be part of the written law. If these conditions are all satisfied, then there can be a written constitution—a constitution that is entirely written and that has constitutional status as written rather than as received by courts.

C. A Dialectical Argument

John's essay has four parts. The first explores the possibility of an unwritten constitution in close conversation with the UK constitution; the second examines whether the arguments in the first part allow for the conceptual possibility of a written constitution; the third makes room for that conceptual possibility by way of three meditations on the rule of recognition; and the fourth defends an affirmative answer to the essay's title question, with special reference to the US Constitution.

The first set of arguments includes conceptual claims about (1.1) the necessity of a constitution for a legal system,[36] (1.2) how the rules specifying the major institutions and offices of government make up the constitution of that system,[37] and (1.3) how no constitution is exhausted by its law.[38] The arguments also include claims about the UK constitution according to which (1.4) Acts of Parliament have constitutional status by virtue of their treatment in the customs or the decisions of certain law-applying officials,[39] with such status affirmed by (1.5) the decisive test whether an Act makes exception to the doctrine of implied repeal.[40]

[35] *LLF* (n 1) 118.
[36] *LLF* (n 1) 90.
[37] *LLF* (n 1) 90.
[38] *LLF* (n 1) 96 (and 117).
[39] *LLF* (n 1) 92.
[40] *LLF* (n 1) 93–95. At least as articulated by Laws LJ in *Thoburn v Sunderland City Council* [2002] EWHC 195 (Admin), [2003] QB 151, the decisive test does not conceive of the constitution in John's frame of 'rules that specify the major institutions and officials of government, and determine which of them is to do what, and how they are to interact, and how their membership or succession is to be determined, and so forth' (*LLF* (n 1) 89). Instead, *Thoburn* outlines that 'a constitutional statute is one which

The second set of arguments reaffirms the conceptual claim (1.2) that the rules specifying the major institutions and offices of government make up the constitution of a legal system, and clarifies that (2.1) an institution and office of government is 'major' if the institution's or office's power is inherent or original, rather than delegated.[41] A power's inherent or original status is not a function of its history, but rather (2.2) a function of how it is received and regarded in the practice of law-applying officials, especially the courts.[42] The institutions of inherent power are also (2.3) those identified by the ultimate rules of recognition,[43] which (2.4) cannot be enacted or canonically formulated or exist in legislation, because they exist only in the practices of officials.[44]

The conceptual case for an unwritten constitution developed over the essay's first two parts seems strong. It affirms that *if* the constitution regulates institutions of inherent power, and *if* those institutions are identified by the ultimate rules of recognition of the legal system, and *if* those ultimate rules 'exist only in the practices of officials', *then* 'a constitution, as the part of the law that regulates institutions of original or inherent power, can't be legislated', a constitution 'can't take the form of written law', and '[a]ll constitutions must therefore be unwritten like the UK one'.[45] Yet, in the next two parts of the essay, John sets out the case for a written constitution and ultimately resolves the debate between the conceptual cases for and against the possibility of a written constitution in favour of the conceptual possibility of a written constitution.

John's third set of arguments is more difficult to grasp. He unpacks the conceptual claim (1.2) that the rules 'specifying' the major institutions and offices of government make up the constitution of that system by drawing a distinction between (3.1) the rules 'identifying' institutions of inherent power and the rules 'regulating' those institutions[46] and adds (3.2) that the rules identifying such institutions are the ultimate rules of recognition whereas (3.3) the rules regulating such institutions are the ultimate rules of change and of adjudication.[47] He adds that an institution may be said to have (3.4) inherent power if its power was delegated but the delegation is 'irrevocable enough' to qualify as a constitutional power.[48] Whereas the ultimate rules of recognition (3.5) cannot be written and, being a borderline

(a) conditions the legal relationship between citizen and State in some general, overarching manner, or (b) enlarges or diminishes the scope of what we would now regard as fundamental constitutional rights': [62]. For general discussion, see Farrah Ahmed and Adam Perry, 'Constitutional statutes' (2017) 37 OJLS 461.

[41] *LLF* (n 1) 98–99.
[42] *LLF* (n 1) 101.
[43] *LLF* (n 1) 101.
[44] *LLF* (n 1) 102.
[45] *LLF* (n 1) 102.
[46] *LLF* (n 1) 103.
[47] *LLF* (n 1) 103.
[48] *LLF* (n 1) 114–115.

case of law, (3.6) lie 'beyond', 'outside', or 'above' the constitution,[49] (3.7) the ultimate rules of change and of adjudication can be written. The differences between the ultimate secondary rules include the possibility that (3.8) they may identify different institutions.[50] This for John is a 'route' by which 'a customary rule of recognition can be squared with a written constitution', as we will see.[51]

The fourth set of arguments in the essay includes the claims (4.1) that a constitution may encompass both the written law as well as the case law and customary law that is developed from authoritative adjudication by law-applying officials[52] and (4.2) that such case law and customary law can be said to be part of the text's meaning, be it because such meaning is authoritatively extracted from or because it is authoritatively attached to the text by interpretive retrievers or innovators.[53] It follows that (4.3) the law of the constitution—understood to exclude the ultimate rules of recognition and the constitution's non-legal features—can be 'entirely written'.[54]

The dialectical nature of the essay's argument serves a rich pedagogical purpose, but it also calls for a reconstruction of the many steps in the arguments if one is to engage with John's ultimate answers to his title question. Such reconstruction discloses, I think, that the meaning of 'constitution' shifts over the course of the essay, so that the answer formulated in the essay's final sentence—Yes, there can be an *entirely* written constitution—is an answer to a different question than is answered at the beginning of the essay—Yes, the UK has a constitution that is unwritten. The significance of the shift will be clearer if the argument is reconstructed in propositional form, excluding from such a reconstruction arguments that John entertains only to reject.

As I read John, the set of arguments that supports the claim that the UK has an unwritten constitution is this:

> A constitution is a conceptual necessity for a legal system (1.1)
>
> The constitution of a legal system is made up of the rules identifying and the rules regulating the institutions of inherent or original power (1.2, as modified by 2.1, 2.2, and 3.1)
>
> The rules *identifying* the institutions of inherent power are identified by the ultimate rules of recognition (2.3 and 3.2)

49 *LLF* (n 1) 107, 109, 117.
50 *LLF* (n 1) 116.
51 *LLF* (n 1) 116.
52 *LLF* (n 1) 117.
53 *LLF* (n 1) 123.
54 *LLF* (n 1) 124.

The ultimate rules of recognition only exist in the practices of officials (2.4 and 3.5)

The rules *regulating* the institutions of inherent power are identified by the ultimate rules of change and of adjudication (3.3)

The ultimate rules of change and of adjudication may be written or unwritten (3.7)

In the UK, even those aspects of the ultimate rules of change and of adjudication that are written in Acts of Parliament have constitutional status by virtue of how they are received in the customs and decisions of law-applying officials (1.4 and 1.5)

Therefore, the UK has an unwritten constitution.

According to these propositions, no constitution can be entirely written, for there is at least one part of every constitution that only exists in the practices of officials: the ultimate rules of recognition, which John equates with the rules *identifying* the major institutions of a legal system. In turn, the propositions in this reconstruction suggest that it is only the rules *regulating* the major institutions that are candidates for being written and, as written, they must secure their constitutional status otherwise than by virtue of how they are received by law-applying officials. The path for a written constitution left open by John's first set of arguments is therefore a narrow one.

Does John track this narrow path in arguing for the claim that the US could have an entirely written constitution? He does, but he also modifies some propositions and adds new ones:

A constitution is a conceptual necessity for a legal system (1.1)

The constitution of a legal system is made up of the rules identifying and the rules regulating the institutions of inherent or original power (1.2, as modified by 2.1, 2.2, and 3.1)

The rules *identifying* the institutions of inherent power are identified by the ultimate rules of recognition (2.3 and 3.2)

The ultimate rules of recognition only exist in the practices of officials (2.4 and 3.5)

The ultimate rules of recognition lie beyond, outside, or above the [legal] constitution (3.6)

One of the ultimate rules of recognition in the US is: 'Whatever is laid down in the constitution produced by the 1787 Philadelphia Convention, as amended, is law'[55]

[55] *LLF* (n 1) 116.

The rules *regulating* the institutions of inherent power are identified by the ultimate rules of change and of adjudication (3.3)

The ultimate rules of change and of adjudication may be written or unwritten (3.7)

The rules identifying and the rules regulating the institutions of inherent or original power may identify different institutions (3.8)

In the US, the ultimate rules of change and of adjudication are written in the Constitution produced by the 1787 Philadelphia Convention (3.7, read with 1.4 and 1.5)

The President, the Congress, and the US Supreme Court are mentioned for the first time in the 1787 Constitution[56]

Though delegated by the Philadelphia Convention, the powers of the President, the Congress, and the US Supreme Court are irrevocable enough to qualify as constitutional powers (3.4)

The interpretation of the written constitution is part of the text's meaning (4.1 and 4.2)

The constitution, understood to exclude the ultimate rules of recognition and to exclude the non-law features of the constitution, may be entirely written (4.3)

Therefore, the US Constitution may be entirely written in the canonical master-text called 'The Constitution of the United States'.

(Below, I review why John refrains from the more affirmative conclusion that the US Constitution *is* entirely written.[57])

The argument to sustain the conclusion that the US Constitution may be entirely written is more complex and more controversial than John's argument in respect of the UK constitution. The greater complexity arises from the introduction of new premises distinguishing the legal from the non-legal aspects of a constitution of a legal system, the premise that the ultimate rules of recognition are not law, and the expansion of the scope of inherent powers to include delegated powers if the delegation is 'irrevocable enough'. The greater controversy turns on John's reading of the Philadelphia Convention's more or less spent constituent authority, on the under-articulated revocability threshold ('irrevocable enough') for delegated powers to qualify as constitutional, and on the relationship between interpretation (even 'innovative interpretation') and the text being interpreted such that the text encompasses the meaning it has and the meaning that was added to it by authoritative interpreters.

[56] *LLF* (n 1) 116.

[57] *LLF* (n 1) 124, n 75: 'I am not suggesting that the US constitution falls into this category [of an entirely written constitution].'

D. Answers to Questions

When set out alongside each other, John's two sets of arguments suggest different answers to different questions. If one reads the title question ('Can there be a written constitution?') in the way suggested by the claim that the rules specifying the major institutions and offices of government make up the constitution of that system (1.2), then the answer is a straightforward no: no constitution can be *entirely* written, because every constitution contains at least one rule (the ultimate rule of recognition) that exists only in the practices of officials. If, in turn, one reads the title question by stipulating 'constitution' to exclude the ultimate rules of recognition, then the answer is again a straightforward no: no constitution can be *entirely* written, since 'no constitution is exhausted by its law'.[58] If, in turn, one reads the title question by stipulating 'constitution' to exclude the ultimate rules of recognition and to exclude the non-legal aspects of the constitution, then the answer is a qualified yes: it is conceptually possible that '(the rest of) constitutional law' be written.[59]

The conceptual case that the rest of constitutional law can be entirely written is a narrow one, for it turns on the following: (a) the major institutions must have powers that were delegated in a written instrument enacted by another institution higher in authority; (b) there must be an ultimate rule of recognition that refers to that institution and the written instrument it enacted; and (c) the institution higher in authority must either cease to exist or, if it continues to exist, must be sufficiently unlikely to revoke the powers delegated in the written instrument so that those powers may be said to be 'irrevocable enough'. To these conceptual possibilities must also be added the following conceptual claim with respect to the interpretation of the written instrument: (d) the authoritative interpretation of the instrument's meaning is part of the text's meaning.

As presented by John, claims (a), (b), and (c) may hold or not in a given legal system. John reports that they hold in the United States; others may raise some doubts. Doubts with respect to claim (b) may challenge the reference to the Philadelphia Convention. John's argument turns on one of the ultimate rules of recognition identifying an institution (the Philadelphia Convention) that delegated powers in a written instrument (the 1787 Constitution). If, instead of formulating one of the ultimate rules of recognition in the US as 'Whatever is laid down in the constitution *produced by the 1787 Philadelphia Convention*, as amended, is law', the ultimate rule of recognition is instead formulated as 'Whatever is laid down in *the 1787 Constitution*, as amended, is law', then, on John's argument, the US Constitution is no longer written. Of course, the text remains written, but the text owes its constitutional status to how it is received by law-applying officials

[58] *LLF* (n 1) 96, 117.
[59] *LLF* (n 1) 118.

rather than to the authority of its maker. The Constitution is written, but does not have constitutional status *as written*; its constitutional status is owed to practice and custom.

There may be other grounds to question John's reading of conditions (b)[60] and (c)[61] in the US, as well as (d) more generally, at least to the extent that John extends the claim to encompass 'interpretive innovators'.[62] Let us put these doubts aside and note the narrow path to a written constitution on John's argument. Against the standard of John's philosophical disposition to wear 'every thought down to its rightful little size' and then to keep 'it in its rightful little place',[63] it is no objection to say that John's path to a written constitution is narrow. Rather, I wonder whether John's path is narrow enough. In the spirit of his commitment to 'unbundle' the conceptual possibility of an entirely written constitution, we may add one further premise. It is this unarticulated premise that, on my reading, keeps John from the more affirmative conclusion that the US Constitution is entirely written.[64]

At the very end of his essay, John writes that '[d]oubtless some parts of US constitutional law are judge-made, but not by way of interpretation of the canonical text or of previous interpretations of it'.[65] He makes oblique reference to this reality in saying that the rule of recognition that, on his account, refers to 1787 Philadelphia Convention is but '*one* of the ultimate rules of recognition of the US'.[66] What is the significance of the possibility that there is one or more *other* ultimate rules of recognition? It is this: it would deny that the canonical constitutional master-text entitled 'The Constitution of the United States' is the whole of the US Constitution. Consider the possibility that, in addition to the ultimate

60 On the ultimate rule of recognition, see e.g. Kent Greenawalt, 'The rule of recognition and the Constitution' (1987) 85 Michigan L Rev 621, 622: '[it is an] illusion that the rule of recognition for the United States can be reduced to any simple statement, such as "The federal Constitution is our rule of recognition".' See also Scott Shapiro, 'What is the rule of recognition (and does it exist)?' in Matthew D Adler and Kenneth Einar Himma (eds), *The Rule of Recognition and the US Constitution* (OUP 2009). On the ultimate rule of adjudication, one may note that it is set out in a rudimentary way in the US Constitution, leaving much to Congress to 'ordain and establish' 'from time to time' (Article 3, Section 1). I am grateful to Paul Yowell for this thought.

61 Some may claim that the authority of 'the People', expressed in the Philadelphia Convention, remains live, such that claim (c) is challenged. See e.g. Akil Reed Amar, 'Philadelphia revisited: amending the Constitution outside Article V' (1988) 55 U Chicago L Rev 1043.

62 Some may question whether (d) can include text that, by design, invites meaning to be supplemented, rather than interpreted. For example, some draw a distinction between 'interpretation' and 'construction', the latter being a 'supplementary theory' of meaning once the 'search for meaning already in the text' runs out. The meaning provided by 'construction' is, on this view, 'external to the text'. See Keith Whittington, *Constitutional Interpretation* (University Press of Kansas 1999) 3, 6. For discussion with respect to the open-ended wording of many bills of rights, see Grégoire Webber, *The Negotiable Constitution* (CUP 2009) ch 5.

63 *LLF* (n 1) v.

64 See text corresponding to n 55.

65 *LLF* (n 1) 124 n 75.

66 *LLF* (n 1) 116 (emphasis added).

rule of recognition identifying as law the written constitution produced by the Philadelphia Convention, there is another ultimate rule of recognition. This possibility tracks jurisprudential debates on how to relate different sources of law to Hart's idea of the rule of recognition.[67] Does the same rule of recognition recognize both the common law and statutory law or are there two corresponding rules of recognition, one each for common law and for statutory law? Analogously, could there be an ultimate rule of recognition that recognizes the rulings of the US Supreme Court independently of the ultimate rule of recognition that recognizes the 1787 Constitution and its reference to the Court's authority in Article III?[68]

John noted this possibility in the final footnote on the final page of his essay, reporting that 'some parts of US constitutional law' are 'doubtless ... judge-made' in the sense that they are 'independent judicial or legislative contributions to constitutional law of the kind that are characteristic of UK constitutional law'.[69] If this is the case, then a constitution like that of the US is not entirely written, even on the narrow path outlined by John. It would follow that the conceptual case for a written constitution requires a fifth condition in addition to conditions (a), (b), (c), and (d) outlined above: (e) the ultimate rule of recognition that refers to the historically most major institution and the written instrument that it enacted is the *only* ultimate rule of recognition.

E. Secondary Rules and the Constitution

Perhaps the most telling truth about John's focus on the constitution *of a legal system* is that his answers to his title question can be reported, without loss of meaning, by removing the word 'constitution' altogether and inserting instead 'Hartian secondary rules'.

Consider two related accounts of the constitution that John employs. John's first account is on the essay's first page: 'The rules without which there would be no legal system ... make up the constitution of that system'.[70] As support for the claim, John refers to Hart's secondary rules according to which the constitution of a legal system is made up of the rules identifying and regulating the major institutions and officials of government. John's second, related account of the constitution turns on the difference between inherent or original powers and delegated (and so

[67] For contributions to the debate whether the ultimate rule of recognition is a single rule or can be a set of rules, see John Finnis, 'Revolutions and continuity of law' in *Philosophy of Law: Collected Essays, Volume IV* (OUP 2011) and Joseph Raz, *The Authority of Law* (2nd edn, OUP 2009) 98 n 32.

[68] For discussion, see Thomas C Grey, 'Do we have an unwritten constitution?' (1975) 27 Stanford L Rev 703, 706.

[69] *LLF* (n 1) 124 n 75.

[70] *LLF* (n 1) 89. The ellipses replace the following: '(or some of them, invariably in combination with some other rules)'.

revocable) powers. The constitution, he says, 'is what regulates institutions of inherent power'.[71] Although John nowhere says so explicitly, I read him as equating 'major institutions' with 'institutions of inherent power', such that the two accounts of 'constitution' are different ways of communicating the same idea.

Given that the rules identifying and regulating the major institutions are the ultimate rules of recognition and the ultimate rules of change and adjudication, respectively, and given that the ultimate secondary rules are the rules without which there would be no legal system, John's accounts of a constitution can be re-stated entirely in the frame of secondary rules. In the spirit of unbundling, one could unbundle the references to 'constitution' in John's essay, such that his title question may be re-stated as: 'Can there be written ultimate secondary rules?' Or, reformulating slightly in a manner that corresponds to the question asked and answered at the end of the essay, John's title question may be formulated as: 'Can there be entirely written ultimate rules of change and of adjudication?'

These are questions in search of answers, and John offers answers. But these are likely not quite the questions asked by those who seek answers to whether the UK should move towards a written constitution. The question asked by the Prime Minister in 2007 and by others before and since—should the UK move to a written constitution?—is not best conceived as a question whether the constitution *of the UK legal system* should be written or not. Rather, the ambitions of those who favour such a constitutional reform would appear to encompass more than a reform to the legal foundations of the legal system.

Some evidence for this can be found in the attention awarded to Hartian secondary rules in American constitutional thought and its investigation into constitutional foundations. In the year following John's 2008 lecture on the constitution, the editors of a volume on Hart's rule of recognition and the US Constitution remarked that, '[d]espite the centrality of *The Concept of Law* to jurisprudential debates over many years, the book has been virtually ignored by United States constitutional theorists'.[72] The remark can be softened, and extended: without being ignored,[73] Hart's secondary rules have not been an organizing framework for thinking about the nature of a constitution, in the US or beyond. Why might that be?

One reason is the one already highlighted: Hart's secondary rules can be understood to constitute a legal system. Though understandably the focus of a legal philosopher, the constitution of a legal system does not demarcate the scope of a

[71] *LLF* (n 1) 101.

[72] Matthew D Adler and Kenneth Einar Himma, 'Introduction' in Matthew D Adler and Kenneth Einar Himma (eds), *Rule of Recognition and the US Constitution* (OUP 2009) xiv.

[73] In UK constitutional scholarship, it is not uncommon to frame the doctrine of parliamentary sovereignty with reference to Hart's summary of the UK rule of recognition: 'whatever Parliament enacts is law.' See Hart, *The Concept of Law* (n 31) 106–108. But cf Peter Cane, 'Public law in *The Concept of Law*' (2013) 33 OJLS 649, 655: 'central to Hart's account is an abstraction—the rule of recognition—that finds no place in standard accounts of the public law of modern legal systems' (hereafter Cane, 'Public Law').

constitutional theorist's interest in a constitution, which may extend more generally to the constitution of a state[74] or a 'more perfect Union'[75] or government or political authority and its arrangements. The title of many canonical constitutional master-texts captures this more encompassing constitutional interest: the Constitution of the United States is not only the Constitution of the *legal system of* the United States and the references to the UK constitution are not usually taken to be shorthand for the constitution of the UK legal system.

Of course, one may, with John, demarcate the scope of one's interest to the legal system, but then the nature of the constitution that one is interrogating will be delimited by the constitution of a legal system. The answer to the question whether the constitution of a legal system may be written will be an answer to that question and not to the more encompassing question whether the constitution of a state or union or government or political authority may be written. As John says, even if his focus is on 'the legal aspect of constitutions', '[n]o constitution is exhausted by its law'.[76] Without purporting to be exhaustive, one could encompass within the non-legal aspects of a constitution those aspects that travel under the banner of the 'political constitution', including the day-to-day workings of political life such as ministerial accountability, cabinet decision-making, the relationships between legislative chambers, the privileges of their members, and more.[77] In the UK, the constitution in its more encompassing sense includes the Crown and its prerogatives and the conventions that direct their exercise. To ask whether these aspects of the constitution can be written is to ask a question that differs from the question whether the constitution of a legal system can be written. When some ask whether the UK constitution should be written, I suspect that they have this more encompassing version of the question in mind.

A second, perhaps correlated reason why secondary rules have not generally been an organizing framework for thinking about the nature of a constitution relates to the place of the executive within Hart's account. Hart's ultimate rule of change and ultimate rule of adjudication correspond closely to the institutions of the legislature and the court,[78] respectively, but there is no obvious ultimate secondary rule corresponding to the institution of the executive. Of course, much of the executive function is regulated by what John calls administrative rather than constitutional law, as when the executive branch exercises powers delegated to it by the legislature. These delegated powers may be legislative or adjudicative and may be regulated by non-ultimate rules of change and of adjudication. In exercising

[74] NW Barber's title is a welcome illustration: *The Constitutional State* (OUP 2010).
[75] US Constitution, preamble.
[76] *LLF* (n 1) 97, 96.
[77] See Graham Gee and Grégoire Webber, 'What is a political constitution?' (2010) 30 OJLS 273.
[78] For discussion of the relationship between Hart's secondary rules and institutional design, see Grégoire Webber, 'Past, present, and justice in the exercise of judicial responsibility' in Geoffrey Sigalet,

such delegated powers, the executive is not a 'major' institution because it exercises no inherent power. Yet, as John recognized, the Privy Council is an institution of inherent power under the UK constitution.[79] Yet, it is not obvious which secondary rule identifies or regulates the Privy Council or the Crown more generally when one or the other exercises what the US Constitution refers to, in Article II, as the 'executive Power'.

The absence of an ultimate secondary rule corresponding to the executive may be explained by Hart's method for identifying the secondary rules. Hart developed his account of secondary rules by showing how each offered a remedy for the defects of uncertainty, stasis, and inefficiency faced by members in a pre-legal community. In his outline of the deficient state of affairs in such a community, Hart identified no defect in need of remedy by an executive function. Hart's pre-legal community does not engage with other communities; it does not confront the need to defend itself against aggression from others; it faces no public health emergency or natural disaster. On Hart's account, the members of a pre-legal community confront specific needs in relation to the specific defects that emerge when the 'simple form of social control' achieved by primary rules of obligation fails and an order of complexity in the management of life in common is called for.[80] But, save for unofficial primary rules of obligation—rules that Hart would have called 'custom' but for the term's unwelcome connotations[81]—the circumstances confronting Hart's community members disclose no general need for a coordinating authority or governing body.

There is in Hart's pre-legal community no *defect of impotence* akin to the defects of uncertainty, stasis, and inefficiency, and so no need for a remedy that Hart might have formulated as a rule of authority or of power or of governance that would correspond to the 'executive Power'.[82] In his review of the absence of the executive power in Hart's account, Cane offers a 'possible explanation' for Hart's

Grégoire Webber, and Rosalind Dixon (eds), *Constitutional Dialogue: Rights, Democracy, Institutions* (CUP 2019).

[79] I note that John's references to the Privy Council are all to the power of the Privy Council to make primary legislation via Orders in Council under the Royal Prerogative, which could be said to fall under the secondary rules of change. See *LLF* (n 1) 91–92 n 8 and 98 n 22.

[80] Hart, *Concept of Law* (n 31) 92–93.

[81] Hart, *Concept of Law* (n 31) 91.

[82] The expression 'defect of impotence' is taken from Cane, 'Public Law' (n 73) 656. Cane's proposal for a remedial secondary rule is that of a 'rule of implementation and enforcement', which confers on executive or administrative officials power to implement general rules, enforce compliance, and sanction non-compliance (ibid). This is in line with Cane's special emphasis on the administrative state, together with the exercise of discretion as 'perhaps *the* central issue in administrative law' (ibid, 656, n 35). My focus here is on executive functions that are not delegated by primary legislation. I read Cane as recognizing that administrative functions could, in a way, be accounted for by way of Hart's secondary rules, as John's distinction between inherent and delegated powers aims to show, but as nonetheless insisting that Hart's account of *rules* fails to capture how 'more-or-less specific directives are a pervasive and characteristic form of law' (ibid, 659).

emphasis on rules rather than institutions.[83] On Cane's reading of Hart, 'rules precede institutions and law creates the state', whereas Cane favours 'a different story', one according to which 'officials who wield political power and run the country precede the laws that legitimize those activities'.[84] Cane's story may better reflect historical truth, but his claim's full force is conceptual, not historical: the executive's responsibility to govern may be prior to the responsibility to govern *through law*. What is the nature of that responsibility? Let us say, too simply, that it is to act for 'peace, order, and good government', identifying defeats and finding remedies,[85] including, we might say, identifying the defects of uncertainty, stasis, and inefficiency and finding the remedies in rules of recognition, change, and adjudication. If this is right, there is much left unsaid by a study of the constitution that focuses on the distinctively legislative and distinctively adjudicative functions. Those are the functions that Hart rightly focused on in his interrogations into the concept of law. But those are not the only functions that interest those who interrogate the constitution of a state or union or government or public authority.

A third possible reason why secondary rules have not been an organizing framework for thinking about the nature of a constitution is in relation to rights. With some exceptions, constitutional rights are difficult to situate in the frame of secondary rules. Some rights, such as Hohfeldian liberties and immunities, can be understood as qualifications on the power to change the law, and so can be accommodated within the frame of the rules of change. The First Amendment to the US Constitution is illustrative: the power of Congress to change the law is subject to the declaration that 'Congress shall make no law respecting an establishment of religion, or prohibiting the free exercise thereof; or abridging the freedom of speech, or of the press'.[86] By contrast, other constitutional rights, such as those that require legislative action to create, in law, Hohfeldian claim-rights and powers, are an awkward fit within secondary rules. The Canadian and South African constitutions, for example, each guarantee a right to education and this right requires legislative specification and realization.[87] So, too, does the right to vote, which is rarely set out in the constitutional text with every modality necessary for its realization. These rights, which require positive legislative realization,[88] are more difficult to capture in the frame of secondary rules: the *power* to change the law is here coupled with a *responsibility* to change the law. And yet, in the familiar division of labour between

[83] Cane, 'Public Law' (n 73) 660.

[84] Cane, 'Public Law' (n 73) 660.

[85] Constitution Act, 1867 (Canada), s 91; Commonwealth of Australia Constitution Act, s 51.

[86] The judicial interpretation of the First Amendment is another matter. For discussion, see Grégoire Webber, 'Proportionality and limitations on freedom of speech' in Frederic Schauer and Adrienne Stone (eds), *The Oxford Handbook of Freedom of Speech* (OUP 2021).

[87] Canadian Charter of Rights and Freedoms, s 23; South African Bill of Rights, s 29.

[88] For the claim that this is generally true of rights, see Grégoire Webber, Paul Yowell, Richard Ekins, Maris Köpcke, Bradley Miller, and Francisco Urbina, *Legislated Rights* (CUP 2018).

secondary rules, duty falls under the rule of recognition, not the rule of change, such that a duty to change the law is more difficult to capture.

John's recourse to Hart's secondary rules to explore the nature of a constitution has other implications too, some of which may surprise constitutional lawyers. One of them is that the threshold for counting an institution as 'major' for the purposes of the constitution appears to exclude some unexpected institutions. The UK Supreme Court, for example, fails to meet John's threshold: being a creature of statute, the Supreme Court, like the Court of Appeal, is, for John, not regulated by constitutional law: its powers are neither original nor inherent, but delegated by Parliament.[89] The same will be true of the powers of the Scottish Parliament, the Welsh Assembly, and the Northern Ireland Assembly.[90] Owing their powers to Acts of Parliament, these institutions are governed by administrative law, not constitutional law, on John's account.

This strict division between administrative and constitutional law is explained by what John says he 'was given to understand—or maybe simply came to understand' as 'a student of UK constitutional law'.[91] There are indeed reasons to demarcate constitutional from administrative law for some purposes and, in turn, there are reasons to demarcate inherent and delegated powers for some other purposes, and the purposes for one and the other demarcation may even overlap some or much of the time. But it may be another thing to investigate the nature of a constitution by relying on such demarcations. The recital in the Scotland Act 2016 that 'The Scottish Parliament and the Scottish Government are a permanent part of the United Kingdom's constitutional arrangements' suggests a different compass for interrogating the nature of a constitution.[92] One such compass allows one to affirm that the recital articulates 'a political and constitutional commitment but not a legal limitation'.[93] The distinction between a 'constitutional commitment' and 'a legal limitation' is intelligible if one expands the reach of the UK constitution beyond the constitution of the UK legal system.

Let us return, then, to the beginning with John's title question, 'Can there be a written constitution?'. I have suggested that it is a question that may be best reformulated as 'Can there be written ultimate secondary rules?' or, more precisely, 'Can there be entirely written ultimate rules of change and of adjudication?'. The answers to *these* latter questions will also be answers to John's more generic title question if we read that more encompassing question, with him, as bounded by

[89] *LLF* (n 1) 99. Although John's constitutional essay post-dated the statutory creation of the UK Supreme Court in the Constitutional Reform Act 2005, he does not mention the Court, instead referring to the Appellate Committee of the House of Lords.

[90] In the reference *The UK withdrawal from the European Union (Legal Continuity) (Scotland) Bill* [2018] UKSC 64 [41], the UK Supreme Court ruled that 'the UK Parliament remains sovereign, and its legislative power in relation to Scotland is undiminished'.

[91] *LLF* (n 1) 98.

[92] Scotland Act 2016, s 1.

[93] Richard Ekins, 'Legislative freedom in the United Kingdom' (2017) 133 LQR 582, 583.

Hartian secondary rules. If our interest in his title question extends also to the non-legal aspects of a constitution and to the constitution of a state or union or government or political authority, then John's answer will not be an answer to the question we ask.

F. The Constitution of a Fruit Fly

'Even a fruit fly has a constitution.' As I recall the discussion in which John made the remark, he was inviting us to think of a constitution as that which configures, composes, constitutes. It was an idea of 'constitution' that John had committed to print some years earlier.[94] On this understanding, what a constitution is will fluctuate according to that which is configured, composed, constituted. The constitution of a fruit fly, for example, will differ from the constitution of a legal system, and the things that may be said or interrogated about one constitution need not also be said or interrogated about the other. The nature of a constitution, on this understanding, takes its cue from that which it constitutes.

The constitution of a legal system may, on John's brilliant argument, conceivably be written, but it would make no sense to say that the constitution of a fruit fly can be written. Of course, one may write down information about it, but that writing is not the fruit fly's constitution, not being the thing in the world that does the constituting. One may commit to writing the DNA of a fruit fly, setting out the genetic coding of what a researcher will refer to as the *drosophila melanogaster*. In this sense of 'written', no one doubts that the UK constitution can be written. After all, it is generally accepted that 'much (indeed, nearly all) of the constitution *is* written, somewhere'.[95] John's title question is not asking whether a constitution can be written in this sense. He is asking whether *that which* configures, composes, constitutes can be written.

Early in this chapter, I reported that John's constitutional essay takes no position on the features of a constitution that animated Burke and Paine and others, except for the question whether a constitution may be written. I conclude this chapter by interrogating whether the question of a constitution's written-ness can be separated from these other features. These other features help to identify *that which* is configured, composed, and constituted by the constitution. To recall some aspects of the great debate between Burke and Paine, those other features may be a tradition or a document; they may be a state, a government, or a legal system; or they

[94] See Mads Andenas and John Gardner, 'Introduction: can Europe have a constitution?' (2001) 12 KCLJ 1, 1: 'Can Europe have a constitution? This question is in one way a silly one. Obviously Europe ... can have a constitution, for it has had a constitution ever since it was constituted.'

[95] Adam Tomkins, *Public Law* (OUP 2003) 7.

may be the politically fundamental laws or the legally superior laws, to touch on but some among the contested features of a constitution.

If one does not follow John in thinking about the nature of a constitution in the frame of secondary rules and legal systems, then his answer that there can be a written constitution will not be an answer to the question one asks in repeating his title question. Even if one employs the same words, one will ask a different question if one is with Paine or with Burke and inquires whether there can be a written constitution. John's essay is devoted to interrogating the nature of the constitution *of a legal system*. That is a constitution of which it can be asked whether it can be written. But if one is interrogating the nature of the constitution of a state or a union or a government, one will appeal to more than the secondary rules of recognition and of change and of adjudication. In relation to that interrogation, John does not attempt an answer.

To say all this is in no way to call into question John's answer to his question as he defines it. John explains that his constitutional essay investigates secondary rules 'under cover of studying the nature of constitutions'. It may have been more accurate to say that John's essay investigates secondary rules under cover of studying the constitution of a legal system. One may ask, with John, whether the constitution of a legal system can be written. But, or so I have been attempting to show, one may not ask whether a constitution, *just as such*, can be written. It is not in the nature of a constitution to have the capacity to be written or not. That capacity, rather, inheres in the nature of that which is constituted. John's essay therefore makes an all-important contribution to the debate whether there is a case for the UK to move towards a written constitution. He helps us see how that very idea presupposes that there is something that can be written. To put the thought another way, John's essay helps us see that whatever is to be written in any proposed constitutional reform will only be those aspects of the constitution of the UK that are liable to be written. To assume that everything about the UK constitution can be written is akin to thinking that the constitution of a fruit fly can be written simply because it is a constitution.

3

Gardner's Pluralistic Virtue Jurisprudence

Amalia Amaya[*]

A. Introduction

John Gardner is not usually associated with virtue jurisprudence, but his work, I argue, significantly contributes to this field. Gardner has provided important insights into the concept of virtue and the structure of virtue theory: he has vindicated the relevance to law of a rich set of character traits beyond the prototypical judicial virtues, such as humanity, charity, benevolence, neighbourliness, loyalty, solidarity, and public-spiritedness; he has given a detailed account of controversial virtues, such as justice, and underdiscussed virtues such as charity; and he has applied notions of virtue and character to a variety of legal doctrines and branches of law, most prominently to discussions of excuses and justification in criminal law, the law of charity, anti-discrimination law, torts, and the reasonable man doctrine in common law.[1]

In this chapter, I shall not attempt to provide a thorough account of Gardner's work on virtue and law. Rather, I will focus on one aspect of his virtue jurisprudence that I find particularly intriguing, namely his claim that the virtues are foils to each other, which leads to a version of virtue jurisprudence in which conflict occupies centre stage. Gardner embraces the Aristotelian thesis—denied by the so-called master-virtue views—according to which virtues are distinct goods that cannot be reduced to one single overarching virtue. However, he goes further (and departs from the Aristotelian tradition) in claiming that it is not only that the virtues are heterogeneous and irreducible goods, but that they endow their possessor with incompatible and mutually incomprehensible moral priorities; that is, they are 'foils' to each other. As I will argue in this chapter, Gardner's account of virtues-as-foils is highly problematic, but nonetheless has far-reaching implications for

* I am very grateful to Frederico Bonaldo, Luis D'Almeida, Michelle Dempsey, Francois Tanguay-Renaud, and Ekow Yankah for valuable comments on an earlier draft.

[1] See, especially, his 'The Virtue of Charity and Its Foils', in C. Mitchell and S. Moody (eds), *Foundations of Charity*, Hart Publishing, 2000 and 'The Virtue of Justice and the Character of Law', *Current Legal Problems*, vol. 53, 2000. See also 'Reasons for Teamwork', *Legal Theory*, vol. 8, 2002 and 'Finnis on Justice', J. Keown (ed.), *Reason, Morality and Law*, Oxford University Press, 2013. On Gardner's applied virtue jurisprudence, see 'The Gist of Excuses', *Buffalo Criminal Law Review*, vol. 1 (2), 1998; 'The Mark of Responsibility', *Oxford Journal of Legal Studies*, vol. 23 (2), 2003; and 'The Logic of Excuses and the Rationality of Emotions', *Journal of Value Inquiry*, vol. 43, 2009.

Amalia Amaya, *Gardner's Pluralistic Virtue Jurisprudence* In: *From Morality to Law and Back Again*.
Edited by: Michelle Madden Dempsey and François Tanguay-Renaud, Oxford University Press. © Amalia Amaya 2023.
DOI: 10.1093/oso/9780198860594.003.0003

virtue jurisprudence. Specifically, Gardner's account of virtues as foils paves the way for the development of an attractive, and thus far unexplored, pluralistic approach to virtue jurisprudence.

The argument of the chapter will proceed as follows. Section B explains Gardner's virtues-as-foils view and identifies a number of features that make this thesis a distinctive and important one. Section C provides a number of arguments against this view. In brief, I will argue that the virtues-as-foils view is at odds with central tenets of virtue theory and fails to give a satisfactory account of the phenomenological and developmental aspects of virtue. In addition, when applied at an institutional, rather than personal, level, this view is also objectionable. Section D shows that the virtues-as-foils view ultimately depends on a disputable assumption, namely, the assumption that harmony among the virtues may be brought about only by endorsing the master-virtue view. An appeal to meta-virtues, I will argue, may impose order among the virtues in a way that not only squares better with basic tenets of virtue theory, but also affords a more plausible depiction of the virtuous person's moral experience, virtue acquisition, and the dynamics of virtuous legal institutions. Section E concludes by claiming that, despite its problems, Gardner's virtues-as-foils view has far-reaching implications for virtue-oriented work in law, in that it suggests the possibility of developing a pluralistic version of virtue jurisprudence.

B. The Virtues-as-Foils View

In virtue jurisprudence, as much as in virtue ethics and virtue epistemology, it is very common to provide 'lists' of virtues.[2] Similarly, a 'bag-of-virtues' approach, which focuses on enumerating desirable traits of character, is prominent in both positive psychology and moral education.[3] The virtues, however, are not merely individual traits of character that one can develop and exercise independently from one another. This was already appreciated by the ancients, who posited a thesis about how virtues relate to each other, namely, the well-known (and highly controversial) unity of virtue thesis.[4] Whether or not the virtues are tightly interconnected in the way in which the unity of virtue thesis contends, a virtuous character

[2] Specifically, of judicial virtues. See L. Solum, 'Virtue Jurisprudence: A Virtue-Centred Theory of Judging', M. Brady and D. Pritchard (eds), *Moral and Epistemic Virtues*, Blackwell, 2003.

[3] See B. Kent, 'Moral Growth and the Unity of the Virtues', D. Carr and J. Steutel (eds), *Virtue Ethics and Moral Education*, Routledge, 1999.

[4] For useful discussions of the unity of virtue thesis, see S. Wolf, 'Moral Psychology and the Unity of the Virtues', *Ratio*, vol. 20, 2007; E. Halper, 'The Unity of the Virtues in Aristotle', *Oxford Studies in Ancient Philosophy*, vol. 17, 1999; J. M. Cooper, 'The Unity of Virtue', *Social Philosophy and Policy*, vol. 15, 1998; T. H. Irwin, 'Disunity in the Aristotelian Virtues', *Oxford Studies in Ancient Philosophy*, suppl. vol., 1988; J. Annas, *Intelligent Virtue*, Oxford University Press, 2011, ch. 6; and D. Russell, *Practical Intelligence and the Virtues*, Oxford University Press, 2009, ch. 11.

exhibits some sort of structure and the virtues seem to relate to each other in more dynamic ways than are conveyed by the list-of-virtues approach. Gardner's virtues-as-foils view provides an account of virtue and of how the domain of virtue may be mapped that accounts for the interactions—which are, as we will see, mostly conflictual in Gardner's view—among the different virtues.

A brief explanation of Gardner's concept of virtue is in order before we are in a position to discuss his views about how the virtues relate to each other. On Gardner's view, moral virtues endow those who possess them with a disposition to perform certain actions in a distinctive 'spirit' and for specific reasons.[5] People with different moral virtues vary in the spirit in which they act, 'warmer or colder, more spontaneous or more deliberate, with more levity or gravitas, etc.'[6] Critically, they also have distinctive 'rational horizons', that is, they are animated by different rationally significant features of actions.[7] Since actions may have more than one rationally significant feature, one and the same action may be required by different virtues. In these cases, people who possess diverse virtues may agree on the action to be performed but disagree on the reasons why it has to be performed.[8] For example, writes Gardner, 'what strikes, say, an honest person as sufficient reason to perform some action may strike a loyal person as being an insufficient reason to perform the same action, and *vice versa*.'[9] On other occasions, however, people with different virtues will be led to favour different, even opposed, courses of action. For instance, 'the honest person will be disposed to betray in order to avoid deceiving, whereas the loyal person leans the other way.'[10] Thus, people with different moral virtues 'tend to react to reasons and prioritise them in different ways, sometimes leading them to different, even mutually antagonistic, actions.'[11] The value of the virtues thus conceived, claims Gardner, has two sides: an 'instrumental' and an 'expressive' one.[12] The former has to do with the 'instrumental contributions to the state of the world', that is to say, the values that acting virtuously bring to the world. The latter is a matter of what the exhibition of a virtue expresses, as acting virtuously 'not only improves one's chances … of bringing certain value to the world, but also plays a constitutive role in shaping the value that one thereby brings.'[13] This

[5] See Gardner, 'The Virtue of Charity', pp. 1–2 and 'The Virtue of Justice', pp. 152–153.

[6] See Gardner, 'The Virtue of Charity', p. 1.

[7] Gardner, 'The Virtue of Justice', p. 152.

[8] These are the 'coincidence problems', as different from the 'conflict problems', in which the virtues give different guidance for conduct. See L. Becker, 'Unity, Coincidence, and Conflict in the Virtues', *Philosophia*, vol. 20 (1–2), 1990.

[9] Gardner, 'The Virtue of Justice', p. 152.

[10] *Ibid.*, p. 153.

[11] *Ibid.*, p. 154.

[12] Gardner does not deny that there is intrinsic value in being virtuous, but such value depends on the value of the actions of the virtuous, which may turn out to be wholly instrumental. He writes: 'There is intrinsic value in being a polite person, for example, even if what counts as being polite is entirely determined by the good consequences of politeness.' What 'it is virtuous to do' depends on 'what it is good to do … *quite apart from one's virtue*'. J. Gardner, 'As Inconclusive as Ever', *Jerusalem Review of Legal Studies*, vol. 19, 2019, p. 219 (my italics).

[13] Gardner, 'The Virtue of Charity', p. 37.

expressive value, in Gardner's view, is critical to the status of each moral virtue as a virtue, for a trait of character is a moral virtue 'only if it expresses a morally acceptable attitude towards others'.[14]

Gardner's analysis of virtue concepts interestingly adds complexity to the view, developed by Linda Zagzebski and amply endorsed in virtue theory, according to which the virtues have two components: motivation and success.[15] For motivation, if Gardner is right, cannot be simply expressed in terms of reasons: there is also a spiritual element, as it were, in the distinctive motivational outlook with which virtues endow their possessors. In order to be virtuous, actions need to be done not only for the relevant reasons but also in the relevant spirit. Similarly, the success of virtuous actions does not exclusively depend on their instrumental value, but also on the meaning that the fact that they were virtuously performed lends to them, that is to say, on their expressive value.

Now, how do the virtues—understood as distinctive moral horizons which have both instrumental and expressive value—relate to each other? In Gardner's view, some virtues stand in a special relationship with others and may be grouped together into certain virtue types. Gardner distinguishes between the 'humanitarian' virtues, which include justice and charity; the 'civic' virtues, such as public-spiritedness and neighbourliness; and the 'partisan' virtues, such as loyalty, patriotism, and solidarity.[16] Presumably, Gardner's view on virtues as traits of character that may be grouped together could be extended to all virtues. What emerges is a picture of the domain of virtue that resembles what some psychologists have defended as a 'cluster view'.[17] In this view, traits of character are not isolated from one another, but rather there is an order within the catalogue of virtues, as the virtue set exhibits a sort of modular structure.

Different versions of cluster views will result depending on the criteria chosen for identifying virtue types. Gardner seems to group virtues together in an original and provocative (although ultimately, as I will argue in the next section, implausible) way. Gardner employs a conflict-based criterion for grouping virtues together.[18] Thus, charity, for instance, relates to other humanitarian virtues, such as justice, which are 'foils'. He writes:

> That the two virtues [justice and charity] stand in a special relationship cannot be denied. But it is the stormy relationship of foils. Of course, only two characters closely bound together can be foils. And so it is with the just and the charitable.

[14] *Ibid.*

[15] See Linda Zagzebski, *The Virtues of the Mind*, Princeton University Press, 1996, p. 137.

[16] Gardner, 'The Virtue of Charity', pp. 23–25.

[17] See C. Peterson and M. E. P. Seligman, *Character Strengths and Virtues*, American Psychological Association, 2004. See also L. Gulliford and R. C. Roberts, 'Exploring the "Unity" of the Virtues: The Case of an Allocentric Quintet', *Theory and Psychology*, vol. 28 (2), 2018.

[18] Other criteria also play a role in distinguishing among virtues clusters. See Gardner, 'The Virtue of Charity', pp. 23–35.

> Of any just action or reaction there is an intelligible charitable variation, and *vice versa*. And whoever can be treated justly can also be treated charitably, and *vice versa* ... the just and the charitable are not just occasionally and accidentally at odds over tricky cases ... On the contrary, the just and the charitable are *set up* to collide; to be more charitable *is*, you might say, partly a matter of being at odds with one's more just friends.[19]

There is, moreover, also inter-group conflict, as virtues within a group are also claimed to be foils to the virtues within another group; for example, the partisan virtues are foils to the humanitarian virtues.[20] Furthermore, in addition to conflicts among virtues, within and among clusters, Gardner claims that virtuous agents experience another kind of conflict, namely, conflicts within the virtues. Just as, to take Gardner's illustrative example, justice may conflict with humanity, so can reasons of corrective justice conflict with reasons of distributive justice; furthermore, reasons of corrective justice might pull in different directions, and the same holds for reasons of distributive justice.[21]

Critical to Gardner's version of the cluster view is that virtue conflicts are not merely accidental, but are enshrined within the structure of virtue. It is not that the virtues may impose conflicting demands in hard cases; rather, the virtues relate to each other—within a cluster but also among clusters—as foils. Conflicts between the just and the charitable, the charitable and the public-spirited, as well as conflicts between the loyal, on the one hand, and the just and the charitable, on the other, are unavoidable not because of the garden-variety constellation of facts that may come to be relevant in a particular case and that may give rise to conflicting reasons for action, but because of conceptual reasons. Virtues are differentiated from one another, as indicated above, in that they have different moral horizons, that is, they put in place different moral priorities. Thus, it is not that the virtues may align moral priorities differently in a particular case, but that one cannot be impeccably virtuous (according to one virtue) except at the price of compromising one's other virtues.[22] Virtues recommend 'incompatible and mutually incomprehensible ways to be morally impeachable' and their relation is thus best understood as one of foils.[23]

This incompatibility, argues Gardner, surfaces as ambivalence when people have a modicum of different virtues. The source of this ambivalence, in Gardner's view, is the existence of mutually incompatible yet internally correct prioritizations, put forward by distinct virtuse. While the reasons do have an independent rational force and sometimes there are cases in which 'there is only one rationally acceptable way

[19] *Ibid.*, pp. 22 and 28.
[20] *Ibid.*, p. 31.
[21] See Gardner, 'The Virtue of Justice', p. 156.
[22] Gardner, 'The Virtue of Charity', p. 32. See also Gardner, 'Finnis on Justice', pp. 153–154.
[23] Gardner, 'The Virtue of Charity', p. 28.

to go', which is 'the way that will be chosen by all morally virtuous people', 'more often than not' there are various alternative rationally acceptable ways to prioritize reasons.[24] In these situations, people who have a modicum of two virtues, such as justice and humanity, or charity and public-spiritedness, will be ambivalent as to which ranking of reasons they should endorse.[25] Since different rankings may favour one and the same action, ambivalence may not translate into indecisiveness as to which course of action one should take, but even in those cases ambivalence may arguably be present in the virtuous person in that different virtues will support action for certain reasons and in a certain spirit.

In claiming that the virtues are foils to each other, Gardner joins a number of philosophers who have argued for the incompatibility among the virtues.[26] However, Gardner's thesis is distinct in important and illuminating ways. First, the claim that virtues are foils to each other does not imply the claim that the virtues are disunited, where such disunity signals mutual independence.[27] The foil relationship can only be established between characters, as mentioned above, that are 'closely bound together'. There is a 'special relationship' between the virtues that are foils to each other, although it is not a 'harmonious' relationship but rather a 'stormy' one.[28] Gardner's virtues-as-foils view is thus importantly different from both the disunity of virtue thesis, according to which the virtues are logically independent from each other, and the limited unity thesis, which holds that the virtues are disunited across domains.[29]

Second, the relationship of foil need not be a pairwise relation, but it may connect up a number of different virtues: for example, charity is a foil to—says Gardner—justice, public-spiritedness, and loyalty. On this point Gardner significantly departs from most incompatibility theses, which focus exclusively on conflict relations between pairs of virtues, such as, for example, Michael Slote's notion of partial virtues, that is, virtues that are organized into pairs of opposing character traits.[30] In claiming that the virtues cluster in multi-member contrast sets, he also stands apart from most discussions of virtue conflict, which similarly centre on the analysis of dyadic conflicts.[31] It is worth noticing that Gardner's virtues-as-foils view deviates from contemporary work on virtue conflict in a further aspect. This

[24] Gardner, 'The Virtue of Justice', p. 154.

[25] *Ibid.*, p. 158.

[26] For a discussion of some of these views, see A. D. M. Walker, 'The Incompatibility of the Virtues', *Ratio*, vol. 6, 1993.

[27] Mutual independence (i.e., disunity) is thus to be distinguished from mutual incompatibility. See, N. K. Badhar, 'The Limited Unity of Virtue', *Nous*, vol. 30 (3), 1996, p. 307.

[28] Gardner, 'The Virtue of Charity', p. 22.

[29] On the disunity of virtue, see G. Screenivasan, 'Disunity of Virtue', *The Journal of Ethics*, vol. 13 (2/3), 2009. On the limited unity thesis, see Badhar, 'The Limited Unity of Virtue'. For a discussion of the psychological plausibility of both theses, see S. Barbosa and W. Jiménez-Leal, 'Virtues Disunited and the Folk Psychology of Character', *Philosophical Psychology*, vol. 33 (3), 2020.

[30] See M. Slote, *The Impossibility of Perfection*, Oxford University Press, 2011, p. 39.

[31] See Slote, *The Impossibility of Perfection*, p. 31 and Walker, 'Virtue and Character', p. 352.

work focuses on binary conflicts between a few, selected, virtues, such as tact and frankness or kindness and justice, whereas Gardner defends the virtues-as-foils view by examining incompatibility relations among a number of virtues that have received scant attention in the literature.

Third, as mentioned, Gardner does not explicitly argue for the claim that the foiling relation connects up the whole domain of virtue, but rather limits his analysis to the humanitarian, civic, and partisan virtues. However, given that his virtues-as-foils thesis depends on his views about the nature of virtue as a trait of character that endows its possessor with a distinct moral priority, it seems reasonable to assume that all virtues may be understood as foils to some other virtues—that is, those that establish incompatible moral priorities. In this sense, Gardner's account differs from related views, such as Slote's, according to which only some virtues are 'partial'—that is, they are paired opposites—whereas other traits are virtues in an unqualified way.[32]

Fourth, Gardner's use of 'foil' to describe the opposition among the virtues—which is idiosyncratic, to my knowledge—brings into the discussion (perhaps unintentionally) important insights about the nature of virtue. To begin with, it evokes the idea that some virtues make the distinctive features of the virtues that are its foils more noticeable and better understood. For example, one may come to understand the virtue of charity better by contrast with the virtues that are its foils. Moreover, it may turn out that full understanding of the requirements of a virtue may be only achieved by contrasting it with its foils. Gardner's claim that '[c]harity has to be understood in opposition to justice—as justice's foil' suggests that much.[33] Virtue concepts would only be fully grasped in opposition to each other: a thesis that is, unsurprisingly, diametrically opposed to the unity of virtue thesis, according to which the understanding of each virtue requirement broadens and deepens as one is able to integrate it with the requirements imposed by other virtues.

In addition, the concept of 'foil' also points to the idea that virtue reasons may have important contrastive features. The notion of foil has received a significant amount of attention in discussions over 'contrastive' explanations. Contrastive questions have the form 'Why P rather than Q?' where P and Q stand in a fact/foil relationship. There are different views about how to understand the relationship between the various members of a contrast set, that is, the class of propositions including P and alternatives to P, such as Q.[34] An important one appeals to what Eric Barnes calls 'substitutional transformation'.[35] For instance, 'Lewis went to Monash' and 'Lewis went to Oxford' are both members of a legitimate contrast set as we

[32] Slote, *The Impossibility of Perfection*, p. 39.

[33] Gardner, 'The Virtue of Charity', p. 41.

[34] See E. Barnes, 'Why P Rather than Q? The Curiosities of Fact and Foil', *Philosophical Studies*, vol. 73, 1994.

[35] See Barnes, 'Why P Rather than Q', p. 36.

may aptly ask why any of these propositions is true rather than the other. That is to say, I could ask why Lewis went to Oxford rather than to Monash, but not why Lewis went to Oxford rather than why elephants are able to fly.[36] Thus, the claim that justice and charity are foils—on this understanding of foils—would imply that it makes sense to ask, for instance, why Lewis was treated justly rather than charitably, but not whether he was treated charitably rather than honestly. This understanding of the foil relationships seems congenial to Gardner's idea, mentioned above, that foils, although incompatible, are bound together in that for any virtue there is as intelligible 'foil' variation. Thus, virtues that are foils to each other may be thought to provide contrastive explanations of why someone acted the way they did; that is, virtue reasons are contrastive in that they are reasons for doing one thing rather than another, for doing one thing in a certain spirit, or for doing one thing out of a range of alternatives.[37]

Fifth, Gardner's virtue-as-foils claim brings together two arguments for the incompatibility of virtues that are usually viewed as independent from each other, namely, a conceptual argument and a psychological one.[38] Gardner's argument is conceptual in that virtue incompatibility follows from his concept of virtue and virtue possession. The full possession of one virtue, in Gardner's view, impedes the full possession of its foil, so that the 'impeccably charitable and the impeccably public spirited simply part company'.[39] The incompatibilities also obtain at levels short of perfection, as 'to be more charitable *is*, you might say, partly a matter of being at odds with one's more just friends'.[40] Thus, Gardner endorses the claim—forcefully defended by A. D. M. Walker—that it is in the nature of the virtues that the degree to which one possesses one correlates inversely with the possession of its foil(s).[41] But Gardner's arguments in support of the virtues-as-foils view also have a psychological underpinning. Psychological arguments for incompatibility hold that certain virtues are incompatible because of incompatibilities between the personal qualities necessary for possession of each of these virtues or the way in which they are acquired.[42] Gardner's discussion of the contrast between charity and its foils as a contrast between 'character types',[43] as well as a contrast between the 'just person' and the 'charitable person' and the 'public spirited',[44] suggests that psychological considerations also play a role in that some types of personality are

36 *Ibid.*, p. 37.

37 For a defence of a contrastive view of normative reasons, see J. Snedegar, *Contrastive Reasons*, OUP, 2017.

38 For the distinction between these two kinds of arguments in support of virtue incompatibility, see Walker, 'The Incompatibility of the Virtues', pp. 45–56.

39 Gardner, 'The Virtue of Charity', 28.

40 *Ibid.*, p. 23.

41 See Walker, 'The Incompatibility of the Virtues', p. 47.

42 For a psychological argument against virtue compatibility, see Walker, 'Virtue and Character', *Philosophy*, vol. 64, 1989.

43 See Gardner, 'The Virtue of Charity', p. 15. See also *ibid.*, pp. 19 and 22.

44 See *ibid.*, pp. 16 and 28. See also Gardner, 'The Virtue of Justice', p. 156.

congenial to one virtue and inimical to its foils.[45] Conceptual and psychological considerations are arguably intertwined in the virtue-as-foils view in that it is in the nature of the virtues that they instil in their possessor a selective astuteness to (incompatible) moral reasons, which are then prioritized in a distinct way by each individual character.

Last, in claiming that virtue incompatibility gives rise to ambivalence, Gardner distances himself from a highly influential model of virtue, most prominently defended by John McDowell, according to which the virtuous person immediately knows what to do in situations of moral conflict. In this view, the virtuous person is able to see the situation of choice in a way that misses nothing of relevance and in which some reasons are viewed as requiring a specific course of action, while opposing reasons remain silenced.[46] A virtuous life, however, as McDowell admits, is not free of conflict, as there might well be cases that pose moral dilemmas which not even the virtuous person may be able to resolve. However, in McDowell's view, even if a virtue-based approach does not eliminate the possibility of deep moral conflict, the virtuous person will know what the right answer is, if there is one.[47] Against this effortless view of what virtuous behaviour entails, Julia Annas has argued that the virtuous person's decisions are oftentimes the result of conscientious moral reasoning.[48] Virtuous people are not those for whom all decisions are easy, but rather those who have the devices to engage in the arduous moral work that goes into deciding hard cases.[49] Gardner interestingly builds on this view of the virtuous person's moral experience as one that involves engaged deliberation in the face of conflict, by illuminating the important sense in which moral ambivalence may also characterize the virtuous person's response.[50]

In sum, in contrast to the fairly static view that is characteristic of standard virtue catalogues, Gardner puts forward a dynamic model of virtue in which the virtues relate to each other as foils. Gardner's virtue-as-foils view is a distinctive incompatibility thesis that is not restricted to binary relations between virtues, that is potentially applicable to the whole domain of virtue, that brings to light the contrastive nature of virtue reasons, that is interestingly grounded in both conceptual and psychological considerations, and that signals ambivalence as an important feature of the virtuous person's moral experience. However, despite its attractiveness, the virtues-as-foils view faces serious objections. Indeed, for all virtues, virtue

[45] Nonetheless, this does not preclude that one person develops one virtue and its foils to some degree, for this is what explains that a virtuous person may feel ambivalence.

[46] John McDowell, 'Virtue and Reason', in *Mind, Value and Reality*, Harvard University Press, 1998.

[47] McDowell, 'Virtue and Reason', fn. 5.

[48] J. Annas, 'The Phenomenology of Virtue', *Phenomenology and the Cognitive Sciences*, vol. 7 (1), 2008.

[49] A. Amaya, 'Virtue and Reason in Law', in Maksymilian del Mar (ed.), *New Waves in Philosophy of Law*, Palgrave Macmillan, 2011.

[50] For a discussion of ambivalence and virtue, see K. Kristjánsson, 'The Trouble with Ambivalent Emotions', *Philosophy*, 85, 2010.

requirements may come into conflict with other virtue requirements. But, as I will show in the next section, it is highly problematic to contend, as Gardner does, that virtue requirements should be defined so that they are necessarily in conflict with one another.

C. Objections against the Virtues-as-Foils View

The virtues-as-foils view is objectionable on several grounds. To begin with, Gardner's claim that the conflict among virtues is not merely contingent on context, but rather enshrined in the very concept of virtue, is in stark opposition to the thesis of the unity of virtue. According to one influential version of this thesis, one cannot have one virtue without having all others.[51] If this thesis obtained, the virtues-as-foils view would be a non-starter, for it would require the impossible: that one simultaneously possesses and acts upon incompatible character traits. One cannot be fully just unless one is also fully charitable—says the defender of the unity of virtue thesis—but since it turns out that justice requirements and charity requirements are, by definition, in conflict, then the combination of the unity of virtue thesis and the virtues-as-foils thesis would make it impossible for anyone to possess any virtue. However, rather than arguing against Gardner's view by straightforwardly appealing to the controversial thesis of the unity of virtue, I will deploy two arguments that are based on widely accepted tenets in virtue theory: namely, that virtues are constitutive components of the good life and that the virtuous person embodies a normative ideal. I will also provide two additional arguments to the effect that the virtues-as-foils view is also wanting from a phenomenological and developmental point of view. Finally, I will show that the virtues-as-foils view has troublesome implications when we move from the personal to the institutional level.

1. The Argument from Coherence

The claim that virtues embody incompatible values is opposed to a thesis—central in both classical and contemporary virtue theory—according to which the virtues *jointly* contribute in distinct ways to the good life.[52] From the Aristotelian point about the heterogeneity of value and the irreducibility of such values to a single one (which Gardner fully endorses), it does not necessarily follow that such values

[51] As the (Aristotelian) reciprocity of the virtues holds. This thesis is to be distinguished from the (stronger) thesis according to which all virtues are one. See Irwin, 'Disunity in the Aristotelian Virtues' and Cooper, 'The Unity of Virtue'.

[52] That virtues are constitutive components of the good life is a central tenet of (eudemonistic) virtue ethics, which, in fact, Gardner endorses. See his 'Reasons for Team Work', p. 505.

are in permanent and ineluctable conflict (as Gardner argues). It is a mystery how, if virtue requirements align moral priorities in incompatible ways, the virtues could add up to a coherent conception of the good life. Each virtue endows its possessor with a specialized sensitivity to certain reasons, but the appreciation of such reasons does not proceed in a way that is insulated from the requirements of other reasons. Virtues are not straightforward dispositions that lead their possessors to pursue the specific objectives that are their proper concern so that the more merciful actions one does, the more merciful one is.[53] Quite to the contrary, each virtue bestows its possessor with a 'peripheral' sensitivity to virtue requirements other than those that are specific to the virtue in question.[54] Thus, the evaluative judgments of a virtuous person are 'global' rather than 'pointwise', so that the virtuous person's assessment of what mercy requires in the particular case involves an assessment of the role that mercy plays in the good life as a whole and how it relates to the values that other virtues promote.[55] On the virtues-as-foils view, the virtues are, in Nietzsche's words, 'jealous' of each other, and thus, rather than standing in relations of mutual support which enhance the holistic knowledge of what a good life is, are connected through relations of incompatibility that undermine its coherence.[56]

2. The Virtuous Person as a Normative Ideal

The virtuous person embodies a normative ideal to aspire to.[57] The virtues-as-foils view would make the ideal of the virtuous person not merely unachievable in principle, for it would be impossible to satisfy the requirements of virtue, as these are mutually incompatible but also hardly an ideal at all. The virtuous person, insofar as she is acutely aware of the conflicting requirements that the virtues impose on her behaviour, would be a deeply fragmented and unquiet self that seems worthless as an ideal one should strive to approximate.[58] Virtuous people have a psychic

[53] This is what Watson has dubbed the 'straight' view of virtues, as opposed to the 'due concern view', according to which the virtues are dispositions to feel and act well in certain respects. See G. Watson, 'Virtues in Excess', *Philosophical Studies*, vol. 46, 1984, p. 58. See also Russell's related distinction between the 'trajectory view' and the 'direction view' of the virtues in *Practical Intelligence*, pp. 339–343.

[54] See Cooper's claim that each virtue focuses in its own considerations primarily but is also secondarily sensitive to the considerations belonging to others. See Cooper, pp. 246.

[55] On the distinction between pointwise vs global styles of evaluation, see N. White, 'Conflicting Values and Conflicting Virtues', P. Baumann and M. Betzler (eds), *Practical Conflicts*, Cambridge University Pres, 2004.

[56] J. Annas, 'Nietzsche and the Ethics of Virtue', unpublished manuscript, fn. 19, p. 8.

[57] Annas, *Intelligent Virtue*, p. 109.

[58] Interestingly, Gardner himself might perhaps not have found these implications of the virtues-as-foils views unpalatable, given his distaste for master-view theories and, more generally, of comprehensive visions, as his self-description as an 'intellectual squirrel' tellingly conveys. See J. Gardner, *Law as a Leap of Faith*, Oxford University Press, 2012, p. vi. See also Gardner, 'As Inconclusive as Ever', p. 223–224. I thank Michelle Dempsey for bringing this point to my attention.

unity that is incompatible with a vision of the virtuous person as someone who is constantly under the pressure of antagonistic forces that tear her apart. It is, in part, this integrated quality of the virtuous person's character that we find admirable and that makes it an attractive normative ideal that inspires us to improve. The virtues-as-foils view does not permit to give an account of two important features that, as Julia Annas has persuasively argued, virtue dispositions have; namely, that they involve a need to learn and a drive to aspire.[59] If the virtues, as the virtues-as-foils view holds, provide competing normative perspectives, then it turns out to be inexplicable why one should aim to develop the virtues and place oneself in a situation of constant inner conflict. Why is not then more desirable to pursue, for example, single-minded charity than to develop both charity and justice, with the inevitable disharmony, in Gardner's view, that this would bring about? The virtues-as-foils view, in short, deprive us of any sense in which the virtuous person may be a desirable normative ideal that moves us to thrive.

3. The Argument from the Phenomenology of Virtue

If the virtues-as-foils view were correct, the virtuous person's experience would be systematically one of conflict and ambivalence. Gardner's virtue-as-foils view makes conflict not only present but pervasive in the life of the virtuous. While there are extreme, relatively rare, cases in which the conflict is such that a virtuous person may feel ambivalence (as Gardner brings to light), cases in which not even the efforts of the virtuous person succeed in pointing unproblematically a way forward, it is unlikely that the virtuous person would, 'more often than not', as Gardner says, experience ambivalence and the distress that goes into facing irresolvable conflict. Just as a depiction of virtue as an unerring and effortless insight into the right seems at odds with the phenomenology of virtue, for it minimizes the extent to which the virtuous person experiences moral conflict and strives to deal with it in a satisfactory way, Gardner's view of virtues as devices which endow their possessors with incompatible and mutually incomprehensible moral points of view does not accord with the phenomenology of virtue, in that it portrays the virtuous person as someone who is permanently at the crossroads. The virtues-as-foils view also fails to account for another feature that is central in the virtuous person's experience, namely, that acting virtuously is enjoyable, and ultimately that living happily is, at least in part, living virtuously.[60] If virtues conspire against each other in the way the virtues-as-foils thesis holds, they would not be a source of pleasure and happiness for the virtuous person, whose life would be rather marked off by conflict and fragmentation.

[59] *Ibid.*, ch. 3.
[60] *Ibid.*, chs 3 and 9.

4. The Argument from Virtue Acquisition

Virtues are not traits of character that one may cultivate independently from one another. If one were to select just one or a few traits as 'one's signature strengths' for their development (as positive psychologists Peterson and Seligman recommend), one would end up developing a highly unbalanced and compartmentalized self.[61] Gardner would not have us develop one trait independently of another, for virtues are tied up as foils, but his view of how virtues are related to each other also puts in place a distorted picture of moral development. If virtues are foils to each other, the development of some traits (to which one's personality is more hospitable) comes at the price of not (fully) developing others. The development of justice, for example, precludes one's development (to a certain point) of charity, so that in the end one has to fall into either a 'sharing' or a 'caring' type. This is, however, incompatible with the deeply seated view that moral development aims at yielding an integrated personality. In acquiring the virtue of justice, one is also learning how its requirements play out in different cases, on which reasons from charity may also impinge. As one learns more about what charity requires, one also becomes more just, for one deepens one's understanding of justice by learning how justice applies across situations (including those in which charity reasons are relevant) and its place within a broad conception of the good life (which includes the virtue of charity). Thus, moral development aims at instilling virtues that are consistently expressed in different situations (i.e., they are global character traits) and integrated into one's character as a whole.[62]

5. Virtues-as-Foils and the Fragmented Character of Law

In Gardner's view, it is not only people who ought to exhibit moral virtues: institutions, and the law itself, in view of its capacity for moral agency, should exhibit them as well.[63] The legal system and the institutions of law—such as legislatures, courts and tribunals, police forces, and law firms—should thus be 'honest, humane, considerate, courageous, prudent, temperate, trustworthy, and so on.'[64] The arguments that I have provided against the virtue-as-foils view as a conception of

[61] See M. S. Vacarezza, 'The Unity of Virtues Reconsidered. Competing Accounts in Philosophy and Positive Psychology', *Review of Philosophy and Psychology*, vol. 8, 2017, p. 646; K. Kristjánsson, *Virtues and Vices in Positive Psychology*, Cambridge, Cambridge University Press, 2015, p. 154 and 171, and Kent, *passim*.

[62] See Annas, 'Nietzsche and the Ethics of Virtue', p. 3. See also J. Annas, 'Virtue Ethics and Social Psychology', *A Priori*, vol. 2, 2003.

[63] Gardner, 'The Virtue of Justice', p. 151.

[64] *Ibid.*, p. 183. The issue of whether one may attribute virtuous character traits to collective agents and institutions is an important and controversial one. I will grant for the sake of the argument that there can be institutional virtues and focus on the implications that the virtues-as-foils view would have for the virtue of law and legal institutions.

individual moral virtue equally apply, I suggest, to the virtue of laws, legal institutions, and doctrines. At an institutional level, the virtue-as-foils view depicts the law as a polyphony of voices, a chorus that is far from being harmoniously integrated. To be sure, the law would not speak with one voice (*à la* Dworkin), but rather would speak simultaneously in several voices that pitch against each other. It is difficult to see, in this view, how the law could advance a coherent conception of a social life that is responsive to the diverse values that legal systems are meant to serve. Gardner's virtues-as-foils view would also make it hard to explain how the law could ever be exemplary or embody an ideal worth working towards realizing.[65] In addition, people occupying different institutional legal roles would be constantly subjected to the incompatible demands that the different virtues that the law should manifest impose on them, and thus legal decision-making will be pregnant with conflict, struggle, and frustration, which is at odds with its phenomenology.[66] Finally, the law would evolve in unbalanced ways, as the development of some legal values could only be promoted at the cost of undermining others, so that the possibility of firmly advancing in the direction of promoting the whole set of values that a legal system takes to be central is precluded.

In sum, Gardner's claim that the virtues are foils to each other is vulnerable to a number of serious objections. Now, it is important not to exaggerate the extent to which, on a virtues-as-foils view, the virtuous person's moral experience and the life of the law would be marked by conflict. As indicated above, Gardner accepts that, in many cases, there is only one virtuous way to go, so that even if the virtues are responsive to incompatible reasons, they will all point towards one and the same action. Nonetheless, insofar as virtue conflict is not merely accidental and far from occasional, the virtues-as-foils view creates within the virtuous person and virtuous institutions a constant source of instability and disharmony that is, as argued, objectionable on several grounds.

D. The Motivation for the Virtue-as-Foils View

The virtues-as-foils view is, as claimed, highly problematic. What motivates Gardner to propose a view that is so much out of line with key tenets of (Aristotelian) virtue theory and that makes conflict, implausibly, pervasive in a virtuous life? Gardner seems to be pushed to defend the virtues-as-foils thesis because of his denial of a thesis very prominent in moral philosophical thought, namely, the master-virtue

[65] On law's exemplary character, see K. Brownlee, 'What's Virtuous about the Law?' *Legal Theory*, vol 21 (1), 2015. On the relevance of ideals in law, see S. Taekema and W. Van Der Burg, *The Importance of Ideals: Debating Their Relevance in Law, Morality and Politics*, Peter Lang, 2004.

[66] Of course, this is not to deny that legal decision-making may at times be a very hard and frustrating business.

thesis.[67] Master moral views—claims Gardner—simplify moral life by positing 'one master-virtue' that would allow us to identify 'one true path'[68] in situations of value conflict. These views identify a single trait of character that is expected to consistently align correct moral priorities for any moral agent and arbitrate between the moral priorities of specific virtues. Utilitarianism and Kantianism, says Gardner, endorse a version of the 'master-virtue' view, with 'impartial benevolence' and 'diligence' or 'conscientiousness', respectively, occupying the space of the prime virtue. In these views, traits of character such as honesty, loyalty, or generosity are not distinct virtues but subsidiary aspects of the central master-virtue.[69] It is not only modern philosophers who succumb to the temptation to ground all the structure of virtue on one single character trait, from which the value of all moral virtues derives; the search for a foundational virtue is also characteristic of contemporary philosophy. In Gardner's view, Rawls' defence of 'justice' as the prime virtue of social institutions—specifically, of the law—as well as Michael Sandel's prioritization of 'solidarity'[70] partake in the project of identifying one master-virtue, to which current views about the foundational status of 'humility' or the search for a foundational argumentative virtue could be added.[71]

Master-virtue theories, claims Gardner, wrongly assume that there is always a 'real moral priority' in each case.[72] On Gardner's view, to the contrary, 'there are many distinct non-derivative moral values, and these are not comprehensively ranked in respect of their relative importance', so there is no 'unified master-prioritisation' by which to rank the diverse moral priorities that are characteristic of the different individual virtues.[73] Indeed, the plausible (Aristotelian) thesis according to which values are plural and irreducible precludes the possibility of reducing them all to one single overarching value. However, from the plurality and irreducibility of value, which the master-virtue thesis denies, it does not follow that all virtues are in permanent conflict with one another, as the virtues-as-foils view asserts. This would be the case if the only way to secure harmony among the virtues were to posit a master-virtue, as Gardner seems to assume. However, this assumption is not granted, for one could address value conflict without resorting to a master-virtue. One prominent method in virtue theory appeals to meta-virtues, most importantly, to *phronesis*. Practical wisdom may arbitrate between

[67] Cf. Slote, whose main motivation for the claim that (some) virtues are partial, i.e. pairs of opposing character traits, is to argue for the impossibility of perfection. See Slote, *The Impossibility of Perfection*, ch. 2.

[68] See Gardner, 'The Virtue of Justice', p. 184, fn. 38.

[69] See Gardner, 'The Virtue of Charity', p.1.

[70] See Gardner, 'The Virtue of Justice', p. 184, fn. 32.

[71] See T. Nadelhoffer and J. C. Wright, 'The Twin Dimensions of the Virtue of Humility: Low Self-Focus and High Other-Focus', in W. Sinnott-Armstrong and C. Miller (eds.), *Moral Psychology, vol. 5: Virtue and Character*, MIT Press, 2017.

[72] Against master-virtue views, Gardner also argues that they wrongly assume that direct moral success is automatically superior to indirect moral success. See Gardner, 'The Virtue of Charity', p. 3.

[73] See Gardner, 'The Virtue of Charity', p. 5.

the different demands imposed by the virtues as well as identify, in a given context, what virtue requires. This is not to fall back on a master-virtue view, as Gardner may perhaps claim, given that he describes it at some point as a 'master virtue'.[74] *Phronesis* unifies the virtues in a way that does not imply monism—that is, the reduction of all virtues to one—nor their ordering in a single comprehensive scale, but does it instead by integrating their expressions as well as their diverse requirements in light of a conception of the good life, to which they contribute in distinct ways.[75]

Critically, even though *phronesis* may successfully deal with value conflict, this is not to say that a virtue theory that assigns a prominent place to *phronesis* would explain conflict away. There are cases in which there might be more than one correct way to go—or rather, in which not even virtuous people may succeed at identifying one correct way to go but may only, as it were, make the best of a bad job. But in these exceptional cases the conflict arises because of the extreme circumstances of choice, rather than the incompatible nature of the values involved. Thus, in between the oppressive peace imposed by one single virtue and the state of constant war that the virtues-as-foils brings about there are intermediate positions, relative peace with moments of crisis, in which we need to negotiate and redefine the self and its priorities. In normal times, so to speak, *phronesis* helps us deal with the challenges posed by ordinary moral life, and in times of crisis, we may not have a safe way to go. We (the virtuous included) may feel ambivalence and there may be more than one correct way forward—or none. But happily, we do not live in permanent crisis, and moral life, as life in general—while always challenging to varying degrees—is not permanently putting us up against the ropes.

E. Conclusions

Gardner's virtues-as-foils view is an important contribution to contemporary discussions on virtue and normative conflict. Gardner articulates a dynamic approach to virtue according to which virtue's domain is closely interconnected through multi-member relations of dependency and incompatibility, which are psychologically and conceptually motivated, and that highlights the contrastive dimensions of virtue reasons and the place of ambivalence in a virtuous character. Despite its merits, Gardner's claim that virtues are foils to each other faces, as argued, serious objections. Gardner defends this view as an alternative to the master-view thesis, which he finds wanting. The rejection of the master view, however, does not compel us to accept the virtues-as-foils view, as there are ways in which the

[74] See Gardner, 'Finnis on Justice', p. 154.

[75] On *phronesis*'s integrative role, see Annas, *Intelligent Virtue*, pp. 83ff. See also Kristjánsson, *Virtues and Vices*, pp. 156–160 and Russell, *Practical Intelligence*, ch. 11.

virtues may be harmoniously integrated (as opposed to what the virtues-as-foils thesis holds) that do not amount to either reducing all virtues to one or imposing a priority among virtue requirements by comparing them on a single scale (as the master thesis contends). *Phronesis*, as argued, is a meta-virtue that may impose order among the virtues in a way that preserves their plurality.

Even if the rejection of the master-view thesis does not provide adequate support for the virtues-as-foils view, Gardner's driving motivation (that is, the claim that rather than 'one true path' of moral virtue[76] there could be incompatible correct ways, which people and institutions with different virtues may endorse) is an important one to preserve. That there may be more than one course of action that is correct, because values are plural, heterogeneous and irreducible, is the key insight of value pluralism.[77] Value pluralism was more explicitly developed in the twentieth century, most prominently by Isaiah Berlin, but its origins can be traced back to Aristotle.[78] Indeed, a commitment to value pluralism is central to contemporary (neo-Aristotelian versions of) virtue ethics.[79] However, the implications of this commitment for virtue jurisprudence remain unexplored.[80] Gardner's virtues-as-foils thesis interestingly suggests the possibility of developing virtue jurisprudence along pluralistic lines.

From Gardner's work on virtue and conflict, there emerge two different ways in which the pluralistic project in virtue jurisprudence could proceed. In Gardner's view, the irreducibility of virtue to one master virtue results in the impossibility of identifying one uniquely correct moral response. Instead there are 'various rationally acceptable alternatives', which follow from the different moral prioritizations favoured by people and institutions with different moral virtues, as well as 'different ways of being morally impeachable',[81] which, for instance, a 'sharing type' and a 'caring type' would exemplify.[82] Two kinds of pluralism may be distinguished here: pluralism about moral value, that is, that there are irreducible moral values; and pluralism about moral excellence, that is, that there are irreducible types of moral excellence.[83] Virtue jurisprudence could consequently aim at exploring

[76] See Gardner, 'The Virtue of Justice', p. 184, fn. 38.

[77] See A. Vicente and A. Arrieta, 'Moral Ambivalence, Relativism and Pluralism', *Acta Analytica*, 2016, pp. 209–210.

[78] See I. Berlin, 'The Pursuit of the Ideal', *The Crooked Timber of Humanity*, Pimlico, 2013. On the Aristotelian origins of pluralism, see J. D. G. Evans, 'Cultural Realism: The Ancient Philosophical Background', D. Archard (ed), *Philosophy and Pluralism*, Cambridge University Press, 2009, p. 48 and M. Nussbaum, *The Fragility of Goodness*, Cambridge University Press, 1986, pp. 290–317.

[79] See M. Nussbaum, *Love's Knowledge*, Oxford University Press, 1990, pp. 56–66.

[80] For a discussion of the implications for law of another pluralist version of virtue ethics, defended by Swanton, which is importantly different from the (neo-Aristotelian) one, see G. Bassam and O. Ostrowski, 'A Pluralistic Virtue-Centered Theory of Constitutional Adjudication', unpublished manuscript. See C. Swanton, *Virtue Ethics: A Pluralistic Approach*, Oxford University Press, 2003.

[81] Gardner, 'The Virtue of Charity', p. 28.

[82] *Ibid.*, p. 23.

[83] On the distinction between these two kinds of pluralism, see Wolf, 'Moral Psychology and the Unity of the Virtues', pp. 156–159.

the implications of both kinds of moral pluralism for a number of relevant issues, specifically, questions concerning disagreement in law, legal indeterminacy, and differing conceptions of legal exemplarity.

Indeed, the proposal of pluralistic version(s) of virtue jurisprudence would be a significant development. Such a theory may be better placed to meet two challenges that are commonly raised against virtue theories in law, to wit, that they have troublesome relativistic implications and that they are incompatible with the conditions of diversity that are distinctive of contemporary liberal societies. Value pluralism asserts that there may be plural, justified outcomes in a way that is importantly different from relativism—in that this plurality is a corollary of the nature of values, not the result of asserting that justifications are always indexed to specific moral practices or traditions.[84] It is also opposed to objectivist views that are tied to a single conception of the good and thereby do not sit well with a liberal legal order. In opening the space for an alternative, middle way between relativist and absolutist approaches, Gardner's work on virtue and law makes an innovative and lasting contribution to the field of virtue jurisprudence.

[84] On the differences between pluralism and relativism, see Evans, 'Cultural Realism', pp. 47–48, D. E. Thorsen, 'Value Pluralism and Normative Reasoning', unpublished manuscript, 2004, pp. 20–25; and C. Yumatle, 'Pluralism', M. Gibbons (ed.), *The Encyclopedia of Political Thought*, John Wiley and Sons, 2015.

4
The Importance of Being Effective

Aditi Bagchi[*]

One element of John Gardner's distinctive normative outlook was the idea that consequences matter. Of course, utilitarians have long emphasized consequences. But Gardner helped bring this core insight into deontological thinking. It was central to his argument that complicity properly understood should require actual contribution to a primary wrong, not mere endorsement of, or association with, it.[1] It was also at the core of Gardner's influential argument that our moral duties are more likely to take the form of a duty to succeed than a duty to try, such that strict liability rather than negligence is the normal or default form of moral responsibility.[2] It also motivates Gardner's potentially even more controversial view that, if one cannot succeed, there is no duty to try.[3]

Although Gardner's views are closely interlinked, at first blush the absence of a duty to try in the face of futility might seem at odds with a duty to succeed, rather than an extension of it. If both views are true, it sounds as if one can commit a wrong (by failing) without ever doing anything wrong (failing to try). One might think to the contrary that, even if the duty to succeed is primary, it implies a duty to try wherever the duty to succeed applies. This chapter will explore how Gardner's view that there is sometimes no duty to try because one cannot succeed fits with the view that, even then, the duty to succeed persists. Gardner can hold these views because he rejects a certain version of the idea that ought implies can. He holds that a duty to succeed at, for example, saving a child implies a reason to save the child. But if one lacks the capacity to save the child then one has no reason to try, even if the reason to save the child applies. Gardener rejects, however, the idea that one has a duty to save the child only if one can save her. After elaborating on Gardner's views on duty under circumstances of futility, this chapter will consider the jarring

* Many thanks to Guy Sela for commenting on a previous iteration of this chapter. I am grateful to Michelle Dempsey and Francois Tanguay-Renaud for inviting me to participate in this volume celebrating John Gardner. I first met John when I audited his seminar on Jurisprudence as a history student, out of curiosity. It was an addictive first encounter with legal philosophy. No one else made thinking hard and clearly look like so much fun.

[1] John Gardner, 'Complicity and Causality' (2007) 1 Criminal Law and Philosophy 127.

[2] John Gardner, 'The Wrongdoing that Gets Results' (2004) 18 Ethics 53 (hereafter Gardner, 'Wrongdoing').

[3] Ibid.

Aditi Bagchi, *The Importance of Being Effective* In: *From Morality to Law and Back Again*.
Edited by: Michelle Madden Dempsey and François Tanguay-Renaud, Oxford University Press.
DOI: 10.1093/oso/9780198860594.003.0004

but inevitable implication of Gardner's views; namely, that pervasive wrongdoing is inevitable—not just in the world but by our own hand.

A. The Edifice at which Gardner Aimed

If the idea that consequences matter—that is, what actually happens matters—sounds alien to most deontological thinking, we might point the blame at Kant. Kant argued that only a good will is of moral value, and it is valuable irrespective of whether it is effectual.[4] That is not to say that consequences do not figure into moral deliberation at all. The moral duties that constrain our practical judgement with respect to any action are identified by way of the categorical imperative. The categorical imperative is offered in three variations but in its first formulation it requires that one 'act only in accordance with that maxim through which you can at the same time will that it become a universal law'.[5] Whether one may act on the maxim under consideration depends on whether a world governed by that maxim-turned-law is desirable, and this will turn on what that world would look like, that is, on the consequences of the proposed maxim. But the rightness of action does not depend on what *actually* happens, or even what could be expected to happen, in the real world in which the agent in fact acts. The moral quality of her action—in the Kantian framework, not only its permissibility but probably also its moral worth tout court—turns on an assessment of the maxim on which the agent acts, and the maxim is assessed by reference to an imaginary world in which that maxim is universal law.

The literature on moral luck departs from the Kantian picture initially in the vantage point it adopts, or the perspective of practical judgement. The categorical imperative is forward-looking: it defines moral duties ex ante. Its ex ante orientation makes more palatable its disinterest in consequences because it trades on the endemic uncertainty about what the consequences of our actions will be. By contrast, the discussion of moral luck and even the idea of a duty to succeed tends to focus on the ex post perspective. That is, once something has gone wrong, it speaks to the evaluative stance we should adopt towards the ill-fated act. Indeed, it is difficult to imagine phenomenologically what it would mean for an agent to act on a duty to succeed separate from a duty to try. The duty does conceptual work mostly in the breach.

From that difference in orientation, the contemporary literature takes a sharp turn away from Kant. The literature on moral luck challenged the basic idea that intention wholly controls the moral quality of an act. Moral luck allows that we

[4] Immanuel Kant, *Groundwork for the Metaphysics of Morals* 4:394 (ed. Mary Gregor, Cambridge University Press 1998).

[5] Ibid, 4:421.

are responsible for the causal upshot of our actions even if those actions were not wrongful, perhaps even when the harms we cause were unlikely.[6] We appropriately experience agent-regret when our actions produce harm to others, even if we would not wish to revise our course of conduct—perhaps even with the benefit of hindsight.

The idea of moral luck does not directly challenge the categorical imperative. On its own, the concept of moral luck has its place in a view that would attach culpability only to those actions with some faulty intention. The idea of moral luck posits only that moral *responsibility* is broad: foreseeability and control are sufficient to render us responsible for the ill we bring about, even when we did not intend it and even when we did nothing wrong, that is, where we complied with all relevant duties (excepting a duty to succeed).[7]

Still, even if we can reconcile moral luck with ordinary Kantian thinking, we are left with two related changes in our disposition that run counter to the Kantian project. First, we are more vulnerable in our normative status than Kant would have allowed; it is not under our control. The aim of control is actually fundamental to the Kantian project, which links moral reasoning closely with freedom. The reason why it is imperative that we abide by moral obligations deducible by reason is that subjecting ourselves to such a rule of reason renders us self-governing. To the extent that we are moved by inclinations or desires that are rooted in our phenomenal selves, we are merely part of the causal chain in the natural world.[8] Because we cannot practically conceive of action except on the assumption that we are free, we must act as if we are free—again, governed by law derived from our capacity for reason and not by externally driven forces. The basic moral intuition here is powerful and resonates with many people who are not directly influenced by Kant. Many people likely believe that we are only morally responsible for our *choices* because the moral quality of our actions and our moral character more broadly are conceptually assumed to be under our control.

The picture of a moral agent that emerges from contemporary moral philosophy differs from the Kantian ideal and related moral intuition in another related respect: We are connected to the material world—and no amount of theoretical gymnastics can save us from it. If we allow for moral luck, our status as material beings who interact with the world is integrated into our moral identity; it is not an alternative or rival to it. This too is antithetical to the Kantian project, the highest aim of which was arguably to disentangle and thereby free us from the tyranny of natural

[6] Thomas Nagel, *Mortal Questions* (Cambridge University Press 1991) 24–38 (defining concept of moral luck and exploring the challenge it poses for Kantian moral theory); Bernard Williams, *Moral Luck* (Cambridge University Press 1981) 20–39.

[7] Stephen R. Perry, 'Responsibility for Outcomes, Risk, and the Law of Torts' in Gerald J. Postema (ed) *Philosophy and the Law of Torts* (Cambridge University Press 2001) 72, 83.

[8] Henry Allison, *Kant's Transcendental Idealism: An Interpretation and Defense* (Yale University Press 1983) 287–293 (discussing two aspects of self in Kantian theory).

forces; to assert the priority of the noumenal over the phenomenal dimensions of the self. Today we tend to regard the material dimension of persons as essential to our self-understanding and not a feature we can or would aim to escape.

If the concept of moral luck shifted our thinking about the morality of our conduct in these ways, Gardner takes us further along each dimension. As discussed in the next section, he describes us as lacking control not merely over our normative position but over the moral character of individual actions. On Gardner's view, having committed an action that went wrong might mean that we breached a duty to succeed; it is not just that we brought about something bad—we did something *wrong*.[9] And still Gardner takes the view that we have no duty to try to avoid committing that wrong if we cannot succeed. The idea of moral luck rejects only the idea that avoiding wrongdoing absolves one completely. Gardner goes further to reject the idea that one can avoid wrongdoing at all.

The implication of his view is that we are, even as moral beings, not only dependent on and connected with the material world but knocked about by it. We are scarred by it, morally. Our life narrative is not just subject to a vague cloud of opprobrium for the various consequences to which our innocent acts gave rise. Because our actions themselves are properly regarded as wrongs, the scars inflicted on us run deeper. Section 3 of this chapter explores Gardner's view that our own wrongdoing is inevitable.

B. Can We Have Reason to Succeed but No Reason to Try?

We would normally think a duty to succeed gives rise to a duty to try. This seems consistent with Gardner's view that the duty to succeed is conceptually prior to the duty to try. The latter derives from the former; it is because we have a duty to succeed that we have a duty to try.

While the two kinds of duty normally operate together, Gardner argues that this is not always true. Why might a duty to succeed apply without generating a duty to try? Because trying does not imply success. He explains: 'Someone who recognizes that his trying will not contribute to his succeeding cannot conceivably try. This is because of the nature of trying. Trying is acting for the reason that one's action will (supposedly) contribute to one's succeeding.'[10] While successfully completing an action satisfies a duty to perform it, merely trying—if there is no reason to believe one will succeed—accomplishes nothing. It is precisely because consequences matter that trying only counts as trying if it is calculated to bring about morally significant results.

[9] Gardner, 'Wrongdoing'.
[10] Ibid, 57.

Limitations of capacity and circumstance sever not only the link between intentions and actions but also the link between the duty to try and the duty to succeed. This is jarring because the influential Kantian claim that 'ought implies can' is normally taken to mean that we cannot have a duty to do what we cannot do. Gardner is sceptical of this understanding, though he does not clearly reject the Kantian claim itself. The key is to understand how Gardner understands duty:

> To have a duty to do something is to have a reason to do it that, (i) does not depend for its existence on one's goals at the time, and (ii) is also a reason not to act for certain conflicting reasons.[11]

That is, a duty is supported by a reason that is both categorical and protected.[12] For example, a person has a reason to save a child, irrespective of her particular attitude towards the child or children in general. Moreover, one cannot decline to save the child because one is having a bad morning or wearing expensive shoes, or even because one has a phobia that will make saving the child particularly burdensome, even traumatic.

Although the definition of duty above helpfully deconstructs the concept into meaningful elements, it is actually a very demanding view of what a duty entails. As discussed further below, we are regularly subject to many conflicting reasons, more than one of which is both categorical and protected.[13] In Gardner's conceptualization of duty, conflicting reasons are not necessarily defeated. Moreover, there is no 'reality' constraint built into the identifying criteria, so a reason for an action might apply to an agent even though she is unable to perform the action.

Even if duty were not conceived so as to render conflict impossible, or to ensure the possibility of compliance, a tighter boundary around duty could limit the simple frequency of duty. One alternative would be to recognize that many moral reasons (categorical and protected) fail to generate duty per se, though acting on those reasons is commendable and morally valuable. At least part of the grounds for conceiving of duty more narrowly would be that it would render the phenomenon of duty less overwhelming.

The idea that we must be capable of meeting moral requirements manifests in other contexts as well. For example, those who deny that we can be subject to competing moral requirements are likely concerned that it would then be impossible to fulfil both and regard that dilemma as an unacceptable result.[14] And one of the most powerful arguments against consequentialism has been that its demands are

[11] John Gardner and Timothy Macklem, 'Reasons' in Jules Coleman and Scott Shapiro (eds), *The Oxford Handbook of Jurisprudence and Philosophy of Law* (Oxford University Press 2002).
[12] Ibid.
[13] See Part III.
[14] See, e.g., Earl Conee, 'Against Moral Dilemmas' (1982) 9 Phil. Rev. 87.

excessive and are so incompatible with human motivation as to be implausible, or, at least, non-guiding in the way that moral principles should be.[15]

It is, then, at least tempting to think that we are not duty-bound to perform an impossible action.[16] But Gardner's view is deontological rather than utilitarian; while consequences matter, they do not control the moral terrain. Subjective intentions cannot redeem an agent's action when she fails to comply with a duty in fact. But whether she is subject to a duty turns on the reasons that apply to her, not just on the consequences of her action. The duty to save the child diverges from the duty to try to save the child if the agent has a compelling reason to save the child but no reason to try only to fail. While on the consequentialist view it is hard to fathom even the distinction between a duty to succeed and a duty to try, on Gardner's view the reasons to persist may be impervious to impossibility while the duty to try is not.

Gardner discusses Kant's 'ought implies can' proposition in an unpublished essay.[17] He does not comprehensively consider the topic—which he suggests might require a book of its own—but rejects some contemporary interpretations of the maxim and offers his own interpretation. One interpretation that he describes as pervasive but implausible is as follows (he labels it 'OC2'):

> A has a reason to Φ only if A has the ability to Φ.[18]

Gardner concludes that this proposition is false. He begins by exploring an ambiguity in the statement. 'Ability' can be read to refer to capacity, opportunity, or both.[19] That is, in assessing whether an agent has the ability to perform an action, we can put aside limitations in herself or outside herself, or neither. One might be tempted to include all barriers to performing an action. However, Gardner observes that, if we take this too literally, the statement is meaningless: A can Φ only if she does. If she does not, apparently she is subject to *some* limitation, if only her own disinclination or lack of motivation. In light of that, Gardner argues that at the least we have to put aside limitations that arise from moral failings of the agent, such as cowardice. After all, an agent does lack a reason to perform an act merely

[15] The demandingness of utilitarianism is the basis for powerful arguments against it. See, e.g., Samuel Scheffler, *The Rejection of Consequentialism: A Philosophical Investigation of the Considerations Underlying Rival Moral Conceptions* (Oxford University Press 1994) 62. See also Shelly Kagan, 'Does Consequentialism Demand Too Much? Recent Work on the Limits of Obligation' (1984) 13 Phil. & Pub. Affairs 239.

[16] For a more general defence of the idea that duties are limited by the constraints of reality, see James Griffin, 'The Human Good and the Ambitions of Consequentialism' (1992) 9 Soc. Phil. & Pol. 118, 123 (there is no point to a moral rule that is utopian, in that it requires something we cannot do—in fact, it ought not to be regarded as a moral rule at all).

[17] John Gardner, *Reasons and Abilities: Some Preliminaries* (11 June 2012) (Oxford Legal Studies Research Paper No. 30/2012), available at <https://ssrn.com/abstract=2081960>.

[18] Ibid, 3.

[19] Ibid, 7.

because she is too cowardly to perform it; we could not even recognize her failure to perform that act as cowardly if she lacked reason to perform it.[20]

But now Gardner has (knowingly) set us along a slippery slope. If the popular interpretation of ought-implies-can does not imply that a person lacks reason to perform an act that she is not courageous enough to perform, then she similarly does not lack reason to perform acts that she cannot because of limitations in her capacity that are not moral faults at all, such as clinical neuroses.[21] Personal limitations, as a category, do not make reasons to act disappear. Whatever an agent's personal capacity, she is subject to 'the same reasons to act that she would have were she an ideally rational being'.[22]

This manner of cashing out the ambiguity in baseline 'ability' does not generate light with respect to physical capacities, that is, barriers to performing an action that are based outside of the agent. Gardner argues that 'the problem' of defining which physical barriers to include in assessing whether an agent has the ability to perform an act 'comes of the Kantian maneuver of abstracting the rational being from the human being. Really, the human being is the embodied rational being that interests us for the purpose of interpreting and assessing' the proposition that ought-implies-can.[23] Kant unhelpfully ignores physical limitations because he deliberately conceives of moral duty as independent of the noumenal world. Since he is not similarly prepared to set aside the reality in which practical judgements are relevant, Gardner concludes that the best workable meaning of OC2 is that:

> A has a reason to Φ only if at least one conceivable human being has the capacity to Φ and A is a human being.[24]

Gardner's solution has its own ambiguities. First, it is not clear whether he means one human being that is conceivably alive right now or any human being that we can conceive of ever having existed, or even any human being that we can conceive will exist given all the unknowns about how humans will evolve over time. Each of these has a plausible rationale behind it. More important, the threshold seems arbitrary. Why does the reason not attach only if the average human being has the relevant capacity, or perhaps most human beings? A moral requirement that we do what at least one person could conceivably do is perhaps less demanding than a requirement that we do what is physically impossible, but it is still startlingly demanding and leaves us with a wide range of reasons upon which we cannot act, and therefore (given Gardner's conception of duty) duties we cannot fulfil. Interestingly, Gardner does not distinguish among physical limitations, which include all

[20] Ibid, 12.
[21] Ibid, 13.
[22] Ibid, 14.
[23] Ibid, 15.
[24] Ibid.

constraints on performance that are outside our control. He does not differentiate among obsessive compulsive disorder, limitations that derive from physical laws, physical constraints that the agent could have altered, or physical barriers that are the work-product of other agents.[25] It does not matter, for Gardner's purposes, why we cannot succeed. Reasons having to do with our mental functioning stand on a par with reasons that have to do with the weather.

Gardner objects to another aspect of how ought-implies-can is commonly interpreted as well. Many people intuit that an agent has reason to try to perform an act only if she has the ability to succeed. He captures this notion in 'OTCS2':

> A has reason to try to Φ only if A has the ability to Φ.[26]

Gardner disputes the proposition because 'having the ability to Φ is not ... a condition of having a reason to try to Φ'.[27] He argues that what people really mean—or should mean—is that she only has a reason to try to perform an act that is derivative from her reason to perform it if she has the ability to succeed at it. Thus, she might have reasons independent of her ability to succeed.

Certainly, Gardner is right that we sometimes have reasons to try independent of our ability to succeed.[28] But this point distracts a bit from the more controversial, affirmative claim that Gardner makes, which is the version of ought-implies-can that he endorses:

> A has a reason to try to Φ derived from A's reason to Φ only if A has the ability to Φ.[29]

We have reason to try to perform an act *in order to* perform that act only if we have the ability to perform it. The implication of *that* statement is that, if we do not have the ability to succeed, then we do not have a reason to try derivative from a reason to succeed. Thus, Gardner arrives at the conclusion that reasons to perform an act might apply even absent any duty to perform the act.

[25] Some arguments against recognizing a moral duty to perform the impossible are more limited to specific kinds of impossibility. See, e.g., Bart Streumer, 'Reasons and Impossibility' (2006) 136 Phil. Stud. 351, 362 (arguing that a person without the ability to perform an action is in the same position as an object, and, like an object, can have no reason to perform the action).

[26] Ibid, 17–18.

[27] Ibid, 18.

[28] See Ulrike Heuer, 'Reasons and Impossibility' (2010) 147 Phil. Stud. 235, 237 (a person may have reason to try to do something because it will make it possible for her to do it on another occasion).

[29] Ibid, 18.

C. Pervasive Wrongdoing

Consistent with the argument in his unpublished essay discussed above, in 'The Wrongdoing that Gets Results' Gardner argued that 'within morality in the broad sense, there can be duties to succeed even where trying does not entail success, so that there can be strict liability for wrongdoing'.[30] R.A. Duff has described Gardner's position as 'extravagant' in how widely it spreads wrongdoing.[31] Duff himself distinguishes between 'when we are involved in a situation as agents who have reason to act, and when we are there only as spectators whose plight might consist partly in the fact that they can only be spectators, rather than agents who can recognize and respond to reason to act'.[32] By contrast, Gardner's position seems to imply that ceasing to regard ourselves as accountable agents with respect to particular problems amounts to denying some permanent and paramount feature of ourselves. In this respect, he sounds like Kant. Kant, as Gardner himself cited, held that:

> We must not determine moral duties according to our estimate of a man's power to fulfill the moral law; on the contrary we must estimate man's moral power by the standard of the moral law, which commands categorically. Hence we must appraise this power on the basis of our rational knowledge of what men should be ... not on the basis of our empirical knowledge of men as they are.[33]

Gardner's stringency on the scope of one's duties is all the more striking in light of his position that there is no reason to attempt to fulfil such a duty where trying is futile.[34]

As discussed above, the sweeping scope of duty in Gardner's view is driven by the fact that he sees duty as present wherever categorical and protected reasons apply. Protected reasons might preempt some kinds of reasons-balancing without excluding all other reasons. Some of the untouched reasons might themselves be categorical and protected and dictate inconsistent actions. More often, there is no direct conflict but there is a lot of co-existence. That is, an agent in a given situation might be subject to a wide variety of reasons that have the requisite moral quality. The dilemma is not one of choosing among good reasons but one of avoiding wrongdoing. 'One does the wrong thing in the mandatory sense', Gardner writes, that is, the sense 'for which we normally reserve more emphatic terms like

[30] Gardner, 'Wrongdoing' 86.

[31] R.A. Duff, 'Cliff-Top Predicaments and Morally Blemished Lives' (2019) 19 Jerusalem Rev. Leg. Stud. 125, 129.

[32] Ibid, 133.

[33] Immanuel Kant, *The Metaphysics of Morals* Ak VI. 404-05 (ed. Mary Gregor, 2nd ed, Cambridge University Press 1996) (hereafter Kant, *Metaphysics*).

[34] Gardner, 'Wrongdoing' 56.

"wrongdoing", "wrongdoer", and "wrongful"—if one does not do what one has . . . a protected reason to do'.[35]

Categorical and protected reasons are everywhere, and so, on this account, is duty. While protected reasons on their face appear to be exceptional and 'higher order', because they rule out other kinds of reasons, there is reason to think that many of the reasons for action that are rooted in others' interests will be protected in some sense; that is, they will preempt some but not all other reasons. If moral agents have the capacity to confer value on ends, reasons to advance those ends are as commonplace and varied as human desires and interests. One might dispute that moral agents have the capacity to anoint ends valuable in this way, or in any event that the reasons to which they give rise are properly characterized as protected; Kant certainly does not endorse that view. But it seems to flow from the capacity for reason that marks moral agents.

Our rational capacity to develop a conception of the good, that is, to adopt ends that are not independently compelled, *binds* us to respect each other's pursuit of those ends without independently assessing their worth. The ends we respectively endorse do not thereby take on objective worth but they must be regarded as valuable in our practical judgements, or in our dealings with one another, in order to respect the agents who have adopted those ends. We are bound to respect them without subjecting them to the balancing of reasons by which we ordinarily might assess whether a reason we are contemplating acting on is undefeated. Thus, for example, I can decide how to balance the reasons I have to drive fast against the reasons to drive slower only inasmuch as my own safety is at issue. It is not similarly appropriate for me to weigh my reasons to drive fast against your interest in my slowing down to avoid hitting *you*. Gardner also implies that my reason to defer to your interest in my driving slowly is not defeated by a moral reason to drive quickly, such as your interest in my aid. But the reason that arises from your interest might also be a protected reason, in that it too ought not to be balanced against certain kinds of other self-directed reasons I might have for driving slowly.

It is not only the lives of others that give rise to protected interests. People's lives are valuable in large part because they value them. They value other things as well; indeed, it is one of our distinctive human capacities that we adopt conceptions of the good that are fragile. Unlike a philosophy or ideology that might exist independent of the world, it is in the nature of a "conception of the good" that it aims to be realized. It entails a way of being in the world or life projects that depend on the material world—and the other people that share space in it.

If the ends of others have moral significance, they give rise to a crush of protected reasons on each of us. We are bound to give them weight and at least avoid

[35] John Gardner, *Offences and Defences: Selected Essays in the Philosophy of Criminal Law* (Oxford University Press 2007) (citing Joseph Raz, *The Authority of Law* (Oxford University Press 1979) 17–19 (hereafter Gardner, *Offences*).

interference with them—perhaps in some cases aid them—irrespective of our own endorsement and by simple virtue of their significance for others. If all those reasons can give rise to duties, the resulting web of duty is overwhelming. We stagger under the weight of it.

Morally significant reasons are ubiquitous in the realm of choice because most of our choices involve other people. We cannot understand the constraints that others create for us in terms of duty in the first instance, since we are looking to understand the scope of our duties. Instead, we have to appeal initially to their interests. The categorical imperative implicitly incorporates their interests when it directs us to treat other people as ends and ask whether we would generalize our conduct. The interests of others are not properly understood to be limited to their objective interests, let alone their material needs (such as not being hit by an automobile). Just as we are agents capable of imbuing our selected projects with significance for ourselves, other agents can do the same for theirs. Respecting others as our equals, and agents in their own right, requires respecting the projects that they have undertaken. It does not usually require that we promote their projects directly (unless we are situated in some role or context in which that further obligation applies) but we should understand how we interfere with their projects and avoid that interference just as we would wish them to refrain from interfering with ours. Given the myriad ways in which our choices affect other people and the things they value, we are at every turn confronted by an unwieldy spectrum of reasons.

Gardner is considerably more demanding in this regard than Kant, who not only allowed for imperfect duties that do not give rise to wrongdoing by individual acts, but also regarded competing grounds of obligation as incapable of grounding conflicting duties—and therefore, implicitly, rejected the idea that a morally significant reason was sufficient to create a duty.[36] Gardner, on the other hand, accepts that it may be impossible to meet conflicting duties, that it may be physically impossible for a given agent to fulfil a duty, and that agents may be incapable of fulfilling duties that apply to them. Indeed, he accepts that there is sometimes no duty to even try to fulfil these duties, because it would be impossible to do so. Gardner accepts that agents will fail, again and again.

We might attempt to soften the view by suggesting that an agent who commits a wrong is not necessarily blameworthy.[37] Characterizing an act as contrary to duty merely identifies the act as wrongful. It does not necessarily follow that the agent who commits the wrong is blameworthy. The idea of moral luck seems to run the opposite way; that is, it suggests that an agent may have appropriate agent-regret even if she did not commit a wrong. While Gardner might not agree with

[36] Kant, Metaphysics Ak 6:224 ('[A] collision of duties and obligations is inconceivable. However, a subject may have, in a rule he prescribes to himself, two grounds of obligation, one or the other of which is not sufficient to put him under obligation, so that one of them is not a duty').

[37] Cf. Robert Stern, 'Does "Ought" Imply "Can"? And Did Kant Think It Does?' (2004)16 Utilitas 42, 47.

the expansive account of protected reasons on which I rely here, he did associate wrongdoing with blameworthiness.[38] He might not have held further that that agents who commit wrongs—not once or twice but perpetually—are blameworthy in character. But while Gardner himself was both forgiving and generous, he at least saw many wrongs in need of forgiveness.

The pervasive wrongdoing around us, on Gardner's picture, is borne of both human frailty and the circumstances in which we find ourselves. The idea that we are each—and not just a few—beset with duties we cannot fulfil, and therefore wrongs we cannot avoid, has the air of tragedy. At worst, such a way of thinking could lead to a kind of defeatism. It is hard to motivate oneself to act morally when one knows that one cannot but fail on so many fronts.

But perhaps there is another way to think about the picture that Gardner presents. If duty is ever-present even where compliance is unattainable, then maybe the significance of failure is not so dire as we might otherwise presume. For Kant, our very freedom and humanity are at stake; when we violate the categorical imperative, we objectify ourself. More commonly, we worry that when we fail to meet a duty we are not only making ourselves culpable vis-á-vis a particular action, or even the context or role within which the duty arose; we are making ourselves bad people.

One does not have the impression that Gardner thought this way. Instead, compliance with duties is the noble aspiration of a life lived well. Reasons give rise to duty, and when we fail to fulfil them, they give rise to new duties. Reasons guide us through duties. Their task is such guidance. They do not serve a primarily evaluative function. While Kant similarly understood his moral theory as a theory of practical judgement, we too often associate the deontological perspective with a backward-looking blame game.

Instead of extracting duties from reasons and finding ourselves ensnared in a web of irreconcilable and impossible duty, perhaps the lesson from Gardner's conceptual landscape is that we should focus on the realm of reasons. In that case, we see the agent presented with a range of compelling reasons, and it is her task not so much to find the answer lest she be blamed for choosing the wrong door but to mark out her own path. While I previously suggested that the reasons that present to an agent are overwhelming, maybe the same human capacity to anoint ends with value that generates such an onslaught of morally significant reasons for each agent also enables—indeed entitles—her to pick and choose among the reasons she has. While there is more than one valuable way to spend her Sunday afternoon, the choice is not determined. It is not only that she experiences herself as free to make the choice, but also that there is more than one way she can spend it without inviting blame. The reasons on which she fails are not defeated by the ones on which

[38] Gardner, *Offences* 17–19.

she acts; they persist and may motivate her another day. They may properly motivate another agent across the road on that very Sunday afternoon. Far from being oppressive, the abundance of normative reasons and the impossibility of acting on all of them can be seen to liberate the agent from just the necessity that Kant sought to impose.

This is one way of thinking about duties and reasons and wrongs, as Gardner presents them in relation to one another. I worry, though, about the soot that remains from the label of wrongdoing even after the agent is cleared of any unique wrong. I am not worried that the soot will stain; I am worried that it might lighten.

Wrongdoing is lighter when it is impossible to avoid; it might be less shameful when it is characteristic of human agency rather than particular agents at particular times. At present, most of us approach the prospect of wrongdoing with dread and the concept might be more useful if our dread is preserved. After all, outside the law, we rely on the concept of wrongdoing primarily to help differentiate between good and bad choices before we make them. While it might be liberating to think of ourselves as acting on a menu of compelling reasons, it is the particular task of moral theory to rank those reasons. Nothing in Gardner's account forecloses such a function. But the attitude that makes pervasive wrongdoing bearable also risks rendering wrongdoing almost palatable, if not at the individual level then as a matter of culture. Perhaps we will grow too forgiving, if only of our friends. Depending on how one defines duty, it need not follow as a matter of logic—but rejecting the proposition that 'ought implies can' risks coming to accept that if wrongdoing is impossible to avoid, it is okay.

5

Hume's Law (in Gardner and Otherwise)

Luís Duarte d'Almeida[*]

A. 'To See a World in a Grain of Sand'

More than once at philosophy workshops I was reminded of William Blake's line as John Gardner would ask the speaker a question. Often John would say nothing about the main points made by speakers—or the points speakers *thought* were their main ones. He would concentrate instead on small or even seemingly trivial remarks made in the paper being discussed; remarks sometimes so small or seemingly trivial, in fact, that you could be forgiven—but only if you did not know John—for thinking he had not read the whole piece. And then, little by little, he would tease out interesting implications of such remarks, and bring them together into bold and important claims, and show how those claims might form the basis of some surprising but plausible new thesis or theory. He might then, with typical generosity, say to the speaker: '*That* is what your paper is about!' It was a wonderful thing to witness.

John did similar things in his own writing, too—including in one of his last papers, in which he swiftly weaves a comprehensive discussion of normativity around a short quote from Kelsen on the relation between 'is' and 'ought'. This relation, and the views John expresses on it in that paper, will be my focus in this contribution. I lack his skill for spotting unsuspected theses behind an author's words. In this instance, though, that doesn't matter: John's skills also meant he was a reliable judge of what his own main points were.

I start, in Section 2, by reconstructing and criticizing John's own views on Hume's Law. He takes a formal approach to the distinction between 'is-' and 'ought-' sentences; but his approach, I argue, fails. In Section 3, I take a different approach to Hume's Law (as John seems to want to understand it); I then show, in Section 4, that John's reasons for resisting it are unpersuasive. In Section 5, moving away from John's views, I suggest that under the common 'Hume's Law' banner we can identify two different, independent theses, rather than just one: an 'implication' thesis and a 'relevance' thesis (as I call them). To conclude, I look briefly, in Section 6, at some issues raised by legal statements in connection with such theses.

* I am grateful to Euan MacDonald, Jean Thomas, Patrícia André, Timothy Endicott, and audiences at Oxford and Lisbon for helpful comments on an early draft.

Luís Duarte d'Almeida, *Hume's Law (in Gardner and Otherwise)* In: *From Morality to Law and Back Again.* Edited by: Michelle Madden Dempsey and François Tanguay-Renaud, Oxford University Press. © Luís Duarte d'Almeida 2023.
DOI: 10.1093/oso/9780198860594.003.0005

B. Gardner on Hume's Law

Can an 'ought' be inferred from an 'is'? It is a cloudy question. Before it can be tackled, it needs clarification and even rewriting. In 'Normativity (in Kelsen and Otherwise)' Gardner does try to clarify it somewhat, although, as I will suggest, what he says is not always convincing. But he opens his paper with this quote from Kelsen, who appears to have found the question clear enough to answer:

> An Ought cannot be reduced to an Is, or an Is to an Ought; and so an Is cannot be inferred from an Ought, or an Ought from an Is.[1]

'By these words', Gardner says,

> Kelsen endorses Hume's Law. In fact he fortifies it: Hume worried only about the inference of an ought from an is; Kelsen worries no less about the inference of an is from an ought. This makes his claim stronger than Hume's.[2]

'Hume's Law' is the commonly used label,[3] in contemporary philosophy, for a thesis that can be traced back to this famous passage from David Hume's *Treatise of Human Nature*:

> In every system of morality, which I have hitherto met with, I have always remark'd, that the author proceeds for some time in the ordinary way of reasoning, and establishes the being of a God, or makes observations concerning human affairs; when of a sudden I am supriz'd to find, that instead of the usual copulations of propositions, *is*, and *is not*, I meet with no proposition that is not connected with an *ought*, or an *ought not*. This change is imperceptible; but is, however, of the last consequence. For as this *ought*, or *ought not*, expresses some new relation or affirmation, 'tis necessary that it shou'd be observ'd and explain'd; and at the same time that a reason should be given, for what seems altogether inconceivable, how this new relation can be a deduction from others, which are entirely different from it.[4]

[1] Hans Kelsen, *General Theory of Norms*, translated by Michael Hartney (Oxford: Clarendon Press 1991; originally published in 1979) 58.

[2] John Gardner, 'Normativity (in Kelsen and Otherwise)', in *Die Reine Rechtslehre auf dem Prüfstand*, edited by Matthias Jestaedt, Ralf Poscher and Jörg Kammerhofer (Berlin: Franz Steiner Verlag 2020) 18, footnote omitted.

[3] The label was coined by—or at least is normally attributed to—Richard Hare; see Richard Hare, 'Universalisability', 55 *Proceedings of the Aristotelian Society* (1955) 295–312 at 303.

[4] David Hume, *A Treatise of Human Nature*, edited by L. A. Selby-Bigge and P. H. Nidditch (second edition, Oxford: Clarendon Press 1978; originally published in 1739) 469.

The thesis goes by other names too—'Hume's Guillotine' is one[5]—and is sometimes referred to simply as the 'No "ought" from an "is"' rule. And Kelsen did endorse it in several of his works, even if he did not call it 'Hume's Law' (and whether or not he adopted it from Hume's work itself).

It is far from obvious, though, that Kelsen is 'fortifying' Hume's Law. The question is not whether Hume himself endorsed *both* a 'No "ought" from an "is"' claim and a 'No "is" from an "ought"' claim (although Bentham seems to have thought that he did).[6] The question is also not whether what came, in philosophy, to be *called* 'Hume's Law' includes claims in the two directions (although some think that it does).[7] The question is whether, once we are clearer about what it is to infer an 'ought' from an 'is', the claim that the former cannot be inferred from the latter does not already itself *imply* that the latter can also not be inferred from the former. For now, then, let us set this 'fortification' point to one side—I will take it up again at the end of Section 3—and think first, and more generally, about Hume's Law.

Why do I say we need to be clearer? One reason is that inferences are relations between sentences—and 'ought' and 'is' are not sentences. So any more careful formulation of Hume's Law will have to display it as a thesis about the inference of 'ought'-from 'is'-*sentences*.

To be fair, Kelsen did sometimes make his point this way. At the beginning of the second edition (1960) of *Pure Theory of Law*, for example, he says this:

> Nobody can deny that the statement 'something is'—that is, the statement by which an existent fact is described—is fundamentally different from the statement 'something ought to be'—which is the statement by which a norm is described. Nobody can assert that from the statement that something is, follows a statement that something ought to be, or vice versa.[8]

And elsewhere in *General Theory of Norms* this same point is also presented—with an explicit reference to Hume—as a point about '*Sollen*-sentences' (that is, 'ought-sentences') and 'is-sentences'.[9] Yet this is still far from sufficiently clear, since it now gives rise to a different question: What should we understand by an 'ought'-, or an 'is'-, statement or sentence?

[5] Max Black, 'The Gap Between "Is" and "Should"', 73 *The Philosophical Review* (1974) 165–181 at 166.

[6] Jeremy Bentham, *Chrestomathia*, edited by M. J. Smith and W. H. Burston (Oxford: Clarendon Press 1983; originally published in 1817) 275; and see, on the reception of Hume's thesis, Charles R. Pigden, 'Introduction', in *Hume on Is and Ought*, edited by Charles R. Pidgen (London: Palgrave Macmillan 2010) 11–15.

[7] See, for example, Ota Weinberger, '"Is" and "Ought" Reconsidered', 70 (4) *Archiv für Rechts- und Sozialphilosophie* (1984) 454–474 at 456, or Catherina Z. Elgin, 'Fact–Value Distinction', in *The International Encyclopedia of Ethics*, edited by Hugh LaFollette (London: Blackwell 2013) 1881.

[8] Hans Kelsen, *Pure Theory of Law*, translated by Max Knight (Berkeley: University of California Press 1967; originally published in 1960) 6.

[9] Hans Kelsen, *General Theory of Norms* (n 1) 273.

One possible answer comes from Gardner's discussion of what he calls Kelsen's 'core argument' for Hume's Law. Kelsen's argument (which Gardner quotes as well) runs as follows:

> Since something can be without being *decreed to be obligatory* in a norm, and something can be decreed to be obligatory in a norm without *being* in reality, therefore when something *is* it does not follow that something really *ought* to be, or when something *ought* to be, that something *is*. The relation between Is and Ought is one of irreducible duality.[10]

Gardner says this argument is 'sound as far as it goes', but thinks it does not go as far as it purports to. I agree that Kelsen's argument does not fully establish its conclusion. But I disagree with how Gardner defends the point:

> [H]ow far does it [i.e. Kelsen's argument] go? Suppose we replace the word 'something' with the letter 'P', and see how it looks now:
>
> Since P can be without being decreed to be obligatory in a norm, and P can be decreed to be obligatory in a norm without being in reality, therefore when P is it does not follow that P ought to be, or when P ought to be, that P is.
>
> Can we really conclude from this that '[t]he relation between Is and Ought is one of irreducible duality'? Surely we can conclude only that the relationship between 'P is' and 'P ought to be' is one of irreducible duality. 'You are buying me lunch' neither entails nor is entailed by 'you ought to be buying be lunch'. True enough. But we do not know whether the same goes for the relationship between 'P is' and 'Q ought to be'.
>
> For example, we do not know whether the same goes for the relationship between 'you *promised* to buy me lunch' and 'you ought to be buying me lunch', to borrow John Searle's famous attempt at a counterexample to Hume's law.[11]

There is indeed an important distinction to draw here, but Gardner does not draw it well enough. And it will be worth our while to discuss what Gardner is saying (and how he says it), not only because it bears on his criticism of Kelsen, but also, and more importantly, because it will help us to think about Hume's Law more generally.

That something is not quite right becomes clear as soon as we ask what it is that Gardner's 'P' and 'Q' stand for. Are 'P is' and 'Q is' sentence schemes? That is certainly what they look like. If so, 'P' and 'Q' must stand for nouns or noun-phrases. But that cannot be what Gardner means—and his own examples show it. His example of a 'P is' sentence is 'You are buying me lunch': but this is not an instance of

[10] Hans Kelsen, *General Theory of Norms* (n 1) 63.
[11] John Gardner, 'Normativity (in Kelsen and Otherwise)' (n 2) 18.

'P is' taken as a sentence scheme; nor is 'You ought to be buying me lunch' quite an instance of the scheme 'Q ought to be'.

Why then formalize these example sentences in the way that Gardner does? It obscures what seems to me to be his underlying substantive point: that the fact that you *are* indeed buying me lunch does not mean that you *ought* to be buying me lunch, and vice versa. And given that Gardner takes this to be an example of a more general distinction about *types* of sentences—that is, after all, the point of his misguided formalizations, since his use of the *letters* 'P' and 'Q' makes sense only if he is indeed assuming that his substantive point will hold regardless of what we substitute for each letter—we need a better way of characterizing what those two types would be.

How should we reinterpret his formal point? One way that immediately suggests itself is to say that no declarative sentence *p* either entails or is entailed by any sentence of the form 'It ought to be the case that *p*'. (The point needs to be about *declarative* sentences: they need to be able to feature in syntactically well-formed that-clauses.) Let us mark this out as the following thesis—one *kind* of 'No "ought" from an "is"' claim:

(H1) No declarative sentence *p* entails a sentence of the form 'It ought to be the case that *p*'.

Is this what Gardner means to accept as true? But (H1) cannot yet be an adequate rendition of the kind of 'No "ought" from an "is"' claim that he takes Kelsen to have satisfactorily defended. For one, what about attempts to derive a sentence of the form 'It ought to be the case that *p*' from the *negation* of *p*? Surely that would equally count, by Gardner's own lights, and for precisely the same reason, as an illegitimate attempt to derive an 'ought' from an 'is'; that you are *not* buying me lunch does not entail that you ought to be buying me lunch. And the same holds for the attempt to derive either *negative* 'ought'-sentences of this type (that is, sentences of the form 'It ought *not* to be the case that *p*') or the *negation* of any given ought-sentence (either positive or negative) from either any given sentence *p* or its negation. So we would need to interpret Gardner as both accepting, and taking Kelsen to have established, the claim that:

(H2) No declarative sentence *p* or its negation entail a sentence of the form 'It ought (or ought not) to be the case that *p*' or its negation.

So Gardner, thus reinterpreted, takes Kelsen to have established (H2); and himself thinks that (H2) is true. The problem, then, according to him, is that (H2) does not capture all that we should take Hume's Law to encompass. (H2) proscribes one *kind* of inference of an 'ought' from an 'is'. But Gardner's point—the point he seeks to bring out with his 'P is' and 'Q ought to be' formalizations—is that Hume's

Law, properly interpreted, is meant to also rule out inferences running from *p* to 'It ought to be the case that *q*'; and Kelsen's argument does not show that such inferences are indeed invalid.

But Gardner misses his mark. For his claim, reinterpreted along the same lines, would be that Hume's Law, properly understood, includes not merely (H2) but (H3) as well:

(H3) For any two declarative sentences *p* and *q*: neither *p* nor its negation entails either a sentence of the form 'It ought (or ought not) to be the case that *q*' or its negation.

Now, Gardner is right to resist (H3). Consider an inference of the following form:

(1) It ought to be the case that you φ and it ought to be the case that I φ.
Therefore,
(2) It ought to be the case that you φ.

This is obviously a valid inference. Yet to point out that (H3) is false is not a valid criticism of either Kelsen or any other endorser of Hume's Law. Kelsen says nothing to suggest that we would deny the validity of an inference like the one above; and in any event (H3) does not succeed in capturing any aspect of what is commonly understood as Hume's Law.

Under (H3), indeed—as well as under (H1) and (H2), for that matter—'*p*' can stand for any declarative sentence whatsoever. But the fact that a sentence is grammatically declarative does not suffice to make it an instance of what we ought plausibly to count as an 'Is'-sentence for the purposes of working out the scope of Hume's Law. After all, any sentence of the form 'It ought to be the case that *q*' is itself a declarative sentence; but surely any such sentence would count as an instance of an 'ought'-rather than an 'is'-sentence. So none of (H1), (H2), and (H3) is an adequate rendition of Hume's Law; and—at least under the assumption that 'it ought to be the case that it ought to be the case that *p*' directly entails 'it ought to be the case that *p*', as it arguably does—(H1) and (H2) too are false.

The conclusion to draw, I think, is that we are unlikely to go very far in understanding the precise import of Hume's Law by pursuing Gardner's attempt to characterize 'is'-and 'ought'-sentences formally in terms of *P*s and *Q*s. We need a different way of distinguishing between the two types.

C. 'Is'-and 'Ought'-Sentences

What then? It might be tempting to capture the difference by saying that while a sentence like 'You are buying me lunch' is a sentence about what *is* the case—a 'descriptive' sentence, as such sentences are sometimes called[12]—a sentence like 'You ought to be buying me lunch' is a 'normative' sentence, a sentence about what *ought to be* the case. We might then think of characterizing Hume's Law as the thesis that you cannot derive a normative conclusion from any number of purely descriptive premises.

To say this, however, would be to merely push the problem forward. For again there is a sense in which even a sentence like 'You ought to be buying me lunch' can be characterized as a sentence about what *is* the case. What such a sentence says, one could plausibly argue, is that it *is* the case that you ought to be buying me lunch. The point is not only that every grammatically declarative sentence can be characterized as a sentence that says that something (whatever it is that the sentence declares) is the case. The point is also that it is far from obvious that we should restrict the domain of what we take, metaphysically speaking, to *be* the case—the domain of *facts*, as we might put it—to empirical facts such as the fact that someone is buying someone else lunch. The view that there are *normative* facts, including facts about what one ought to do, is a plausible and indeed popular one in philosophy. Under that view, however, why should we deny that a sentence such as 'You ought to be buying me lunch' is descriptive in precisely the same sense of 'descriptive' that applies to 'You are buying me lunch'?

As it happens, Kelsen made a similar point. Gardner himself quotes Kelsen's remark, in *General Theory of Norms*, that 'by the very nature of things, even a statement about a norm is an *is*-statement, a statement about the *specific* existence (an Is) of a norm (an Ought)'.[13] And Gardner, too, speaks freely in his paper of 'the *world* of norms'.[14] So if the goal is to produce a workable formulation of Hume's Law, it seems a bad idea to contrast normative sentences with 'descriptive' ones.

What then should we contrast normative sentences with? 'Factual' will not do, for similar reasons. Nor would 'empirical', for while 'You are buying me lunch' does indeed state an empirical fact, Hume's Law, properly formulated, should also—or so one would think—rule out the derivation of 'ought' sentences from, say, mathematical propositions, or logical truths, which, though clearly not normative, are also not empirical.

Perhaps the way forward is simply to contrast normative sentences with *non-normative* ones, and to treat the contrast as equivalent to that between 'ought'- and 'is'- sentences for the purposes of Hume's Law. That would give us the following version of Hume's Law:

[12] See e.g. Gillian Russell, 'In Defence of Hume's Law', in *Hume on* Is *and* Ought, edited by Charles R. Pidgen (London: Palgrave Macmillan 2010) 151l; Aaron Wolf, 'Giving Up Hume's Guillotine', 93 (1) *Australasian Journal of Philosophy* (2015) 109–125 at 109.

[13] Hans Kelsen, *General Theory of Norms* (n 1) 164.

[14] John Gardner, 'Normativity (in Kelsen and Otherwise)' (n 2) 19, 20, 22, 25; emphasis added.

(H4) No normative sentence follows from any number of purely non-normative sentences.

If we are to equate the domain of 'ought' sentences with that of normative sentences, though, we need to take care not to be unduly restrictive about what it includes. A sentence like 'You ought to be buying me lunch' is plausibly thought of as normative. But what matters is neither (of course) that the *word* 'ought' is used in it, nor that the sentence is explicitly *about* what someone *ought* to do: for there is a range of other types of sentences that are not explicitly or directly about what anyone ought to do (or think, or feel), nor about what ought to be the case, which must nonetheless also be counted as 'normative' in the relevant sense. One type is that of sentences about the moral duties or obligations we have, alongside sentences about our moral rights and liberties. Another is that of sentences about what we have reason to do or believe. Another, perhaps, is that of sentences about what is morally good and bad, together with other kinds of morally evaluative sentences.

Maybe all these notions—maybe all normative notions—are tied in a philosophically significant way to the notion of what one *ought* to do or think or feel in any given context. Maybe they can all be *explained* by reference to how they relate to judgments about what ought to be the case.[15] But whether or not that is right, calling all such normative sentences 'ought'-sentences need signify nothing more than that they are all 'normative' sentences—where a 'normative' sentence can be defined simply as any sentence that makes a substantive normative claim.

As Gardner points out, Kelsen took a somewhat similar approach. Kelsen used the word 'ought' in a broad, stipulated sense to include a range of normative notions—including permissions and even powers—that are, he says, 'essentially related' to the (stricter) notion of what one ought to do.[16] But Gardner thinks Kelsen ought to have used 'ought' in a broader sense still.[17] Kelsen made no room for *reasons*, for example, because he saw the 'world of Oughts' as co-extensive with the 'world of norms'.[18] He was also confused on the relation between norms and values.[19] Indeed, Gardner says, Kelsen ran together three different and non-equivalent distinctions: 'between the world of norms and what lies outside it', 'between the world of reasons and what lies outside it', and 'between the world of value and what lies outside it'.[20] And Gardner thinks this shows that Hume's Law, as Kelsen endorsed it, can be given no clear import:

[15] For an account of reasons in terms of (what we call) a 'support' relation to ought-judgments, see Luís Duarte d'Almeida and Euan MacDonald, '*Contra Tantum* Reasons' (typescript on file with the author).

[16] See John Gardner, 'Normativity (in Kelsen and Otherwise)' (n 2) 20; and Hans Kelsen, *General Theory of Norms* (n 1) 97.

[17] John Gardner, 'Normativity (in Kelsen and Otherwise)' (n 2) 20.

[18] John Gardner, 'Normativity (in Kelsen and Otherwise)' (n 2) 19.

[19] John Gardner, 'Normativity (in Kelsen and Otherwise)' (n 2) 23–25.

[20] John Gardner, 'Normativity (in Kelsen and Otherwise)' (n 2) 25.

> There are three quite different distinctions here. Kelsen conflates them. But now we know they are different: Which, we may wonder, constitutes the 'irreducible duality' of Ought and Is?[21]

But however pertinent Gardner's criticisms of Kelsen's views (or lack thereof) on norms, reasons, and values, this last question is misplaced. Even if Kelsen conflated Gardner's three distinctions, it does not follow that the claim that 'the relation between Is and Ought is one of irreducible duality' cannot be given a clear, straightforward meaning. For it remains open to Kelsen to insist that the 'irreducible duality' of 'ought' and 'is' concerns the whole domain—however varied—of normative notions, and simply concede that this domain should be expanded further still than he had allowed, to encompass not only norms, but reasons and values as well.

In other words: (H4) seems minimally serviceable both as a clearer (clearer than Gardner's) restatement of Hume's Law as it is normally understood, and as a charitable restatement (which Gardner could have adopted) of what Kelsen must have meant by a claim such as 'the relation between Is and Ought is one of irreducible duality'. Yet had Kelsen not explicitly maintained not only that we cannot derive an 'ought' from an 'is', but that we can also not derive an 'is' from an 'ought'? Indeed, isn't that what he meant by 'irreducible duality'? And doesn't that mean we need to take him as having indeed 'fortified' Hume's Law, as Gardner (as we saw at the start of this chapter) puts it?

Gardner's 'fortification' point would be that alongside (H4)—Hume's Law—Kelsen endorsed its converse as well:

(H5) No non-normative sentence follows from any number of purely normative sentences.

But the point, I think, is wrong. For any inference of an 'ought' from an 'is' that (H4) proscribes directly, the corresponding inference of an 'is' from an ought' is *already* proscribed by (H4), by implication. Take any non-normative sentence *p*, and any normative sentence *q*. To deny that *p* entails *q* is the same (by contraposition) as denying that *not q* entails *not p*. Now this latter inference, from *not q* to *not p*, is (or would be) an inference of an 'is' from an 'ought': the negation of a non-normative sentence ('You are buying me lunch') is itself, it seems, a non-normative sentence ('It is not the case that you are buying me lunch'), and likewise the negation of a normative sentence ('You ought to be buying me lunch') is, it seems, a normative sentence as well ('It is not the case that you ought to be buying me lunch').[22] But if the sets of each type of sentence are, as they arguably are,

[21] John Gardner, 'Normativity (in Kelsen and Otherwise)' (n 2) 25.

[22] Indeed, Hume's original text explicitly speaks of the relation not only between 'is' and 'ought', but between '*is*, and *is not*' and 'an *ought*, or an *ought not*'. See the passage quoted above to note 4.

closed under negation, then (H4) also proscribes (directly) any inference of *not q* from *not p*, and therefore (by contraposition) any inference of *p* from *q*.[23] So for any pair of a non-normative sentence *p* and a normative sentence *q*, (H4) already conveys the 'irreducible duality' thesis: that neither can be inferred from the other. So Gardner's claim that Kelsen somehow 'fortified' Hume's Law doesn't seem to hold.

D. Resisting Hume's Law?

In any event, Gardner is not himself a defender of Hume's Law. He does not say much about it, but he does tell us—if 'mainly by way of a declaration of interest'—that he shares John Searle's 'broadly Aristotelian resistance to Hume's Law'.[24] He has in mind Searle's much-discussed claim that we can derive the normative conclusion 'Jones ought to pay Smith five dollars' from the (supposedly) non-normative premise 'Jones promised to pay Smith five dollars', with the help only of other non-normative premises.[25] Gardner does not defend Searle's point directly, but he seeks to dismiss one possible objection to it—the one he thinks Kelsen might raise:

> We know roughly how Kelsen would reanalyse that [i.e. Searle's] claimed counterexample [to Hume's Law] to explain it away. He would say that there is a hidden 'Ought' in the background. He would say there is a norm in play *sub silentio* according to which you ought to do whatever you promised. You promised to buy me lunch so, according to the *sub silentio* norm, you ought to buy me lunch. That is certainly a possible reanalysis of Searle's claimed counterexample ... But offering the reanalysis is not making an argument for it. If you think that it is the correct reanalysis, that is probably because you already endorse Kelsen's conclusion that '[t]he relation between Is and Ought is one of irreducible duality.' You have done nothing to show that this conclusion is correct.[26]

But this quick-handed reply is not persuasive. The point is not whether we need a premise like 'You ought to do whatever you promised' in order for the inference to run. We do, as Searle himself agrees. Searle's inference includes the crucial premise 'All promises are acts of placing oneself under (undertaking) an obligation to do the thing promised' (which he then relies on to derive 'Jones ought to pay Smith five dollars'—under the assumption that 'other things being equal, one ought to do what one is under an obligation to do', and together with

[23] See also, for similar points, David R. Kurtzman, '"Is", "Ought", and the Autonomy of Ethics', 79 (4) *The Philosophical Review* (1970) 493–509 at 499; and Bruno Celano, *Dialettica della giustificazione pratica: Saggio sulla legge di Hume* (Torino: Giappichelli 1994) 443.

[24] John Gardner, 'Normativity (in Kelsen and Otherwise)' (n 2) 19.

[25] John R. Searle, 'How to Derive "Ought" from "Is"', 73(1) *The Philosophical Review* (1964) 43–58.

[26] John Gardner, 'Normativity (in Kelsen and Otherwise)' (n 2) 19.

a further premise stating that in Jones's case other things are indeed equal).[27] The point is whether the sentence 'All promises are acts of placing oneself under (undertaking) an obligation to do the thing promised' is itself a substantively normative sentence, or rather, as Searle claims, a 'tautological' sentence;[28] and there are good (and to my mind persuasive, although I will not enter that debate here) reasons to think that Searle is wrong on the tautological nature of such a sentence.[29]

This is not to say that Hume's Law is true; Searle was not the only one to offer purported counterexamples to it. Here is another well-known one—one of several devised by A. N. Prior:

(1) Tea-drinking is common in England.
Therefore:
(2) Either tea-drinking is common in England or all New Zealanders ought to be shot.

This is only a counterexample to Hume's Law, of course, if we accept that the conclusion is properly classified as a normative sentence. But if it isn't, then the following *will*, it seems, be a counterexample to Hume's Law:

(1) Either tea-drinking is common in England or all New Zealanders ought to be shot.
(2) Tea-drinking is not common in England.
Therefore:
(3) All New Zealanders ought to be shot.[30]

There have been attempts to revise Hume's Law in such a way that it overcomes this dilemma—including revisions that seek to distinguish between 'vacuous' and 'non-vacuous' normative sentences (where vacuity is an argument-relative notion), in order to then suggest that what Hume's Law, more perspicuously stated, proscribes is the inference of substantive, determinate normative conclusions from wholly non-normative premises.[31] In the face of repeated challenges and successive revisions—none obviously water-tight so far—to Hume's

[27] See John R. Searle, 'How to Derive "Ought" from "Is"' (n 25) 46.
[28] John R. Searle, 'How to Derive "Ought" from "Is"' (n 25) 46.
[29] See, for example, Richard Hare, 'The Promising Game' 70 (4) *Revue Internationale de Philosophie* (1964) 398–412; and, for a short summary, Charles R. Pigden, 'Is–Ought Gap' in *The International Encyclopedia of Ethics*, edited by Hugh LaFollette (London: Blackwell 2013) 4–5.
[30] See A. N. Prior, 'The Autonomy of Ethics', 38 (3) *The Australasian Journal of Philosophy* (1960) 199–206 at 201–202.
[31] See, for instance, Alan Gewirth, 'On Deriving a Morally Significant "Ought"', 54 *Philosophy* (1979) 231–232; Charles R. Pigden, 'Logic and the Autonomy of Ethics' 67 (2) *Australasian Journal*

Law, however, one might wonder whether we have now reason to think that the task is doomed to fail. Gillian Russell has a persuasive 'good company' argument for the conclusion that we ought to believe that Hume's Law can be more precisely formulated, rather than that we ought to abandon it.[32] But Gardner's short discussion of Searle's counterexample does raise a logically prior point: Why should the default position be that some version of Hume's Law is true? And the literature on the topic is by and large silent on *why* we should find Hume's Law appealing to begin with, and worth defending and revising in the light of counterexamples.

But there are at least general instances of Hume's Law that seem intuitively correct. One is the claim that we cannot argue that something ought to be (or to have been) the case, or ought to be (or to have been) done, or permitted or promoted or condoned, purely on the basis that it *is* actually the case, or has been the case for any amount of time, or will or is likely to be the case. More generally, it seems intuitively correct that the *objects* of our normative judgments may well fall short of whatever normative standards we take to be correct; that things as they are may well, and often do, fail to live up to how they ought to be. This is the thought that underlies the claim marked above as (H1), although (H1) was not, as we saw, a satisfactory formulation. But we can now refine and expand it as follows:

(H1*) No non-normative declarative sentence *p* entails a sentence that normatively (and non-vacuously) assesses the object of *p*.

This is still an instance of (H4); but while (H1*) concerns solely the relation between normative sentences and their *objects*, (H4) also encompasses the relation between normative sentences and their own possible inferential *grounds*. (H1*) proscribes the derivation of 'Jones ought to be paying Smith five dollars' from 'Jones is paying Smith five dollars' without one or more further premises along the lines of, for example, 'Jones promised to pay Smith five dollars' and 'One ought to do what one promised to do'—the latter of which is a normative sentence. But (H1*) tells us nothing about whether this

of Philosophy (1989) 127–151; and see also Bruno Celano, *Dialettica della Giustificazione Pratica* (n 23) 438–481 for a thorough discussion of what he too calls 'prescriptively vacuous' attempts at counterexamples to Hume's Law. Prior himself admits that 'there is *something* peculiar' about his counterexamples, and that normative expressions in conclusions that are 'deduced by ordinary modes of inference [like the classical logical rule of disjunction-introduction] from a pure "is"' seem to be 'contingently vacuous': the inference would remain valid if the relevant normative expressions 'were replaced by any expression whatever of the same grammatical type': see A. N. Prior, 'The Autonomy of Ethics' (n 30) 203–204.

[32] Gillian Russell, 'In Defence of Hume's Law' (n 12).

normative sentence can itself be justified, inferentially, on the basis of wholly non-normative premises. In this respect, though, (H4) too has intuitive appeal. We cannot derive, it seems, any normative sentence *q* from premises stating solely, say, that most or even all of us believe or agree (or have believed or agreed for any amount of time) that *q*, or that someone proclaimed or prescribed that *p*, for no such non-normative claim can rule out the possibility that *q* is actually false. (More generally, it seems that there will always be room for normative disagreements between parties who agree on all non-normative matters.) And that is what we would need for (H4) to be false: that there be some pair of a non-vacuous normative sentence *q* and a set of non-normative sentences such that the truth of the latter simply leaves no logical room for the possibility that *q* is false.

E. One Law or Two?

Still, how important is it to be mindful of Hume's Law? How likely is it that anyone in good faith would actually argue for some normative conclusion purely on the basis of non-normative premises? Suppose that someone argues: 'Jones promised to pay Smith five dollars; therefore, Jones ought to pay Smith five dollars.' It would be uncharitable to complain that this is a non-sequitur on the grounds that it breaches Hume's Law, for charity requires that we take the argument, as expressed, to be enthymematic, and that we reconstruct it as relying on the relevant conditional premise (which the arguer must obviously endorse), marked below as (1), that shows the argument to be valid:

(1) If Jones promised to pay Smith five dollars, then Jones ought to pay Smith five dollars.
(2) Jones promised to pay Smith five dollars.
Therefore (from (1) and (2)):
(3) Jones ought to pay Smith five dollars.

And the argument as reconstructed above seems unobjectionable: not only formally valid, but indeed (on the assumption that Jones did make the promise) sound—for the first premise does seem to be true. To be sure, a fuller reconstruction would also interject a *ceteris paribus* clause of some sort (e.g. 'and there are no countervailing considerations') in the antecedent of premise (1) and then include it as a separate premise as well. Whoever argues 'Jones promised to pay Smith five dollars; therefore, Jones ought to pay Smith five dollars' is likely not suggesting that there can be no circumstances under which someone promised to do something and yet—because, say, of exceptional circumstances—it is not the case that they ought, all things considered, to do it. A more fully charitable reconstruction, then, might run as follows:

(1') If Jones promised to pay Smith five dollars, and there are no countervailing considerations, then Jones ought to pay Smith five dollars.
(2) Jones promised to pay Smith five dollars.
(3) There are no countervailing considerations.
Therefore (from (1') to (3)):
(4) Jones ought to pay Smith five dollars.

And this argument seems to be in good standing. So—to put the point differently—if all that is needed to comply with Hume's Law is for the arguer to supply the missing conditional premise that makes the argument run, then Hume's Law would rarely, if ever, be breached by any actual argument.

And yet we do commonly think that there are some kinds of arguments that are actually deployed with at least some frequency and which can be criticized on the grounds that they do breach Hume's Law. As Wolf points out, Hume's Law 'is employed primarily to explain why certain arguments are invalid, like *everyone does x, therefore x is permissible*';[33] and even though this remark conflates (as we will see) two importantly different points, Wolf is right that we do normally think that certain arguments that people sometimes offer can be faulted for failing to heed Hume's Law. Moreover, an argument like 'Jones promised to pay Smith five dollars; therefore, Jones ought to pay Smith five dollars' is *not* the kind of argument that Hume's Law is commonly taken to target to begin with. (What Searle did was not to come up with a new and surprising kind of argument no one had thought of before and present it as a counterexample to Hume's Law. Searle's strategy, rather, was to look into a very familiar kind of argument that no one would ordinarily take to contravene Hume's Law and claim that, properly analysed, the argument did indeed breach it.)

Consider, then, a different example of an argument that *would* normally be open to criticism on the grounds that it breaches Hume's Law: 'Marriage around here has always been between a man and a woman; therefore, we ought not to allow same-sex marriage.' Why is this the kind of inference that we would normally take to contravene Hume's Law? Again, the point is not that the argument as stated is formally fallacious—that it is formally a non-sequitur—for, again, the arguer could simply make it explicit that they *are* indeed committed to the relevant conditional premise that makes the argument valid:

[33] Aaron Wolf, 'Giving Up Hume's Guillotine' (n 12) 123.

(1) If marriage around here has always been between a man and a woman, then we ought not to allow same-sex marriage.
(2) Marriage around here has always been between a man and a woman.
Therefore (from (1) and (2)):
(3) We ought not to allow same-sex marriage.

Now, if we still want to object—as I think we would—that this argument fails to establish its conclusion because it breaches Hume's Law, the point can no longer be expressed as one concerning the argument's formal validity, for the argument above is formally valid. Rather, the substance of the objection—that we cannot argue about what ought to be done on the basis of what has in fact been done—will now manifest itself as a refusal to accept premise (1), and thus as a point about the argument's *soundness*. What then is that point?

It cannot be that the conditional sentence has a non-normative antecedent and a normative conclusion: for that is true too of premise (1') in the above argument about Jones's promise, and we can agree that that premise is true. (More generally, indeed, it is hard to see how good normative arguments on all kinds of matters would be possible without premises of that sort.) Nor is the worry that the argument presents the fact that marriage around here has been between a man and a woman as *sufficient* to establish that we ought not to allow same-sex marriage, ignoring possible countervailing reasons; for once again, as in the example of the argument about Jones's promise, charity would likely require that a fuller reconstruction of the argument would take that into account:

(1') If marriage around here has always been between a man and a woman, and there are no countervailing considerations, then we ought not to allow same-sex marriage.
(2) Marriage around here has always been between a man and a woman.
(3) There are no countervailing considerations.
Therefore (from (1') to (3)):
(4) We ought not to allow same-sex marriage.

But premise (1') would remain objectionable; we would still take it to be false. The point is, I think, that the antecedent fails to specify a fact that supports to any extent the normative claim specified in the consequent. Whether marriage around here has indeed always been between a man and a woman has in and of itself *no bearing* on whether we ought to allow same-sex marriage. The flaw in the argument, then, is not logical. It is, rather, the mistake of wrongly treating a certain non-normative fact as relevant to the normative conclusion the arguer seeks to establish.

Does this mean Hume's Law is not really about inferential entailment—that it concerns argument soundness rather than validity—and that an argument that breaches Hume's Law is guilty, not of a formal fallacy, but of an informal one—indeed, of a fallacy of relevance?

Yes and no. There are, it seems, two aspects to Hume's Law as it is commonly understood and spoken of—or rather, two different points often made under the banner of Hume's Law. One is that in any argument in which some non-normative facts are relied upon to establish some normative conclusion (as in *both* arguments above: the argument about Jones's promise, and the one about same-sex marriage), a conditional (or logically equivalent) premise linking the two is required to make the argument valid—*and that such a premise is itself a normative premise.* The other is that, in any such valid argument, there are certain kinds of non-normative facts that are *never* adequately relied upon to establish the relevant normative conclusion—which means that the relevant conditional premise is false—because they are irrelevant to the truth of that conclusion.

The two points are sometimes conflated, as in Wolf's remark, quoted above, that Hume's Law 'is employed primarily to explain why certain arguments are invalid, like *everyone does x, therefore x is permissible*'.[34] The point of Wolf's example is not that it is an example of an argument from a non-normative premise to a normative conclusion. The point is that it is an argument from a non-normative premise about *what everyone does*—which indeed is one type of argument we would normally criticize for violating Hume's Law. The problem with such an argument when charitably reconstructed, however, is not that it is invalid but that the relevant normative premise is false, because the non-normative fact described in its antecedent is irrelevant to—is *not a reason* that supports—the conclusion.

The lesson to draw, then, seems to be that there are two different, independent theses that are commonly deployed under the *name* of 'Hume's Law'. One is the thesis captured in (H4):

(H4) No normative sentence follows from any number of purely non-normative sentences.

We could call this *Hume's law of implication*. This—or at least a general thesis of this sort—is what in philosophical discussions most people take Hume's Law to state. As we have seen, we will rarely have occasion to deploy this thesis to criticize any actual argument for normative conclusions. But (H4) remains important as a philosophical thesis; and, if sound, it can be used to criticize theories—meta-normative theories—that fail to heed it.

[34] Aaron Wolf, 'Giving Up Hume's Guillotine' (n 12) 123.

What I called the second point, by contrast, is not entailed by (and does not entail) (H4); and is perhaps best understood as a first-order claim (or set of claims) about the substantive relevance—or lack thereof—of certain types of non-normative facts (such as the fact that everybody has always behaved in a certain way) to certain normative conclusions. Unlike (H4), it is neither a logical point, nor a general point about the relation between normative and non-normative sentences. And there is probably no unitary thesis—no 'law'—that fully captures it: we can probably give only a catalogue of types of non-normative facts that cannot be relied upon to defend normative conclusions. A shorthand version, though, might run as follows—and we could call it *Hume's law of relevance*:

(H6) That something *is* (or was, or has been, or will be) the case lends, in and of itself, no support to the claim that it—that very 'something'—*ought to be* (or to have been) the case, or that it ought to be either preserved or upheld.

As Pigden notes, Hume 'has been widely interpreted' as making the general claim that we cannot deduce normative or at any rate 'moral conclusions *of any kind*' from 'entirely non-moral premises';[35] and that is the thought that underlies (H4). It is interesting to note, however, how a reader like Bentham seems to have taken Hume to be making a point closer to the more modest (H6):

> Some fourscore years ago, by David Hume, in his *Treatise on Human Nature*, the observation was, for the first time, (it is believed,) brought to light—how apt men have been, on questions belonging to any part of the field of *Ethics*, to shift backwards and forwards, and apparently without their perceiving it, from the question, what *has been done*, to the question, what *ought to be done*, and *vice versa*: more especially from the former of these points to the other.[36]

F. Hume's Law in Law

Gardner does not in his paper go on to look into *legal* statements—including statements about what we *ought* legally to do. But do such statements raise any particular puzzles with regard to Hume's Law—in either of the two versions identified in the previous section?

There are several points to consider. That there is not only a difference, but no necessary connection, between law as it *is* and law as it *ought to be* is a familiar

[35] Charles R. Pigden, 'Introduction' (n 6) 7.
[36] Jeremy Bentham, *Chrestomatia* (n 6) 275.

idea in legal philosophy.[37] It was once held to be one of the defining theses of legal positivism—and it can even be traced, historically as well as exegetically, to the influence of Hume's *Treatise* itself.[38] But is it a breach of Hume's Law to argue from 'Legally, you ought to φ' to 'It ought to be the case that legally, you ought to φ'?

The question turns on whether sentences like 'Legally, you ought to φ' or 'according to law, you ought to φ' are appropriately characterized as non-normative. On the one hand, sentences of that kind—and legal statements more generally—are normally taken to be *descriptive*. They convey the content of the law—the law as it *is* in some legal system—on some given matter. That means it makes sense to distinguish them from normative statements about how the law *ought* to be. On the other hand, the law itself is taken to be normative, and statements of law are often said to be descriptive of legal *norms*. So are legal statements normative statements too?

I cannot address this point here in any significant detail.[39] But here is one way of thinking about it, inspired by how Gardner himself thinks of such statements. Gardner would likely say that sentences of the form

(1) Legally, you ought to φ

are second-order claims about what the law claims you ought morally to do.[40] As such, they are non-normative. They report that *the law's normative stance* on φ is that you ought morally to φ, but themselves take no normative stance on whether or not you ought to φ. If that is right, then it would be fallacious, and a breach of what I proposed to call Hume's *law of relevance*, to argue on the basis of (1) that

(2) It ought to be the case that legally, you ought to φ

since it is perfectly possible that the law makes claims that it ought not to make. Why is this best construed as a breach of Hume's law of relevance rather than as a breach of Hume's law of implication? Because, again, charity would require that we take anyone attempting to derive (2) from (1) to be implicitly relying on the following conditional:

'If legally you ought to φ, then it ought to be the case that legally you ought to φ.'

[37] See H. L. A. Hart, 'Positivism and the Separation of Law and Morals', 71 (4) *Harvard Law Review* (1958) 593–629.

[38] See José de Sousa e Brito, 'Hume's Law and Legal Positivism', in *Filosofía del Derecho y Filosofía de la Cultura: Memoria del X Congreso mundial ordinario de Filosofía del Derecho y Filosofía Social*, edited by J. L. Curiel (Mexico City: Universidad Nacional Autónoma de Mexico 1982) 245–246.

[39] I have discussed some aspects of legal statements in Luís Duarte d'Almeida, 'Legal Statements and Normative Language', 30 *Law and Philosophy* (2011) 167–199; and in Luís Duarte d'Almeida, 'The Grounds of Law', in *The Legacy of Ronald Dworkin*, edited by Wil Waluchow and Stefan Sciaraffa (Oxford: Oxford University Press 2016).

[40] John Gardner, 'How Law Claims, What Law Claims', in *Institutionalized Reason: The Jurisprudence of Robert Alexy*, edited by Matthias Klatt (Oxford: Oxford University Press 2012), especially at 34–35. James Edwards and I engaged critically with Gardner's views in that piece in Luís Duarte d'Almeida and James Edwards, 'Some Claims about Law's Claims', 33 *Law and Philosophy* (2014) 725–746.

This means the argument is valid; and our quarrel with such a hypothetical arguer would not concern the status—normative or otherwise—of this conditional, for the arguer could well agree that it is indeed a normative sentence. The quarrel would rather concern the fact that this particular antecedent is irrelevant to this particular conclusion, which means the conditional should be rejected as false.

Still, it is not likely that we would ever encounter an actual argument along such lines. A different matter would be an inference seeking to derive from (1) the following conclusion:

(3) You ought to φ.

This inference—from (1) to (3)—is not the same as the inference from (1) to (2), because (2) and (3) do not entail each other. It is possible that the law be exactly as it ought to be—that the claims it makes about what you ought to do are exactly the claims it ought to make—and yet that you ought not to act as law claims. Of course, the inference from (1) to (3) is suspicious too. But is it a breach of Hume's Law?

It is not. The conditional premise on which such an arguer should be taken to be relying would be 'If legally you ought to φ, then you ought to φ'. Now you may want to say that this conditional is false; that it is not the case that we ought to do whatever we ought legally to do. Unless you are an anarchist, however, your claim is not likely to be that the antecedent of this conditional is of no relevance whatsoever to the conclusion. And even if you are an anarchist, you should agree that anarchism is a substantive view that requires defence, and that the putative irrelevance of whatever it is that the law claims we ought to do is by no means a self-evident point. Of course, the conditional above seems to attribute *too much* relevance to what the law claims we ought to do: it presents it as sufficing to determine that we ought to do it, when a more sensible position would be that, even if we may normally have a strong *reason* or even a duty to act as the law claims we ought to, that reason or duty can sometimes be defeated. But this does not mean the argument breaches Hume's law of relevance; and in any event it is likely that—as in the examples discussed above in Section 5—the fully charitable reconstruction of the arguer's commitments would yield the following, more sensible conditional: 'If legally you ought to φ, and there are no countervailing considerations, then you ought to φ.'

But there is—to conclude—another, more important (and also more familiar) type of inference to consider in connection with both the law and Hume's Law. If Gardner is right that we should take a sentence like

(1) Legally, you ought to φ

as a non-normative, second-level report that the law claims that you ought to φ, that suggests that statements made *from* the point of view of the law will be first-order normative statements of the form 'You ought to φ'.[41] What then about inferences that feature such statements as conclusions? According to Hume's Law—to Hume's *law of implication*—no such inference can do without some further normative premise. As is well known, this is precisely the thought that underlies Kelsen's doctrine of the *Grundnorm*—the basic norm of any system of positive norms (legal or otherwise):

> From the circumstance that something *is* cannot follow that something *ought* to be; and that something *ought* to be cannot be the reason that something *is*. The reason for the validity of a norm can only be the validity of another norm ... It looks as if one could give as a reason for the validity of a norm the [non-normative] circumstance that it was established by a [purported] authority, human or divine; for example, the statement 'The reason for the validity of the Ten Commandments is that God Jehovah issued them on Mount Sinai' ... [But] the reason for the validity is not that God or his son issued a certain norm at a certain time in a certain place, but the tacitly presupposed norm that one ought to obey the commands of God ...[42]

And Kelsen goes on to say that in the 'syllogism' whose conclusion is the '*ought*-statement' that 'one ought to obey God's Ten Commandments', the '*is*-statement' that God has issued the Ten Commandments must necessarily be coupled with another *ought*-statement that 'One ought to obey God's commands'.

There is a lot to be said about this, of course. Fortunately or unfortunately, most of it has already been said many times. But one thing has not yet been said often enough. If statements of the law made from the law's point of view are indeed 'ought'-statements, then if Hume's Law (Hume's *law of implication*) is true, no such statement can ultimately be argued for purely on the basis of wholly non-normative premises. But this includes statements of what we are used to calling the 'rule of recognition' of any legal system. What follows, it seems, is that the so-called 'social fact thesis'—the view, often taken these days to be *the* distinctive claim of legal positivism, that 'the existence *and content* of the law are ultimately determined by certain facts about social groups'[43]—is not tenable, at least if we interpret it as (or as implying) a claim about the inferential justification of such legal statements.

41 Does it mean they not only imply, but are indeed equivalent to, straightforward moral statements about what one ought to do? That cannot be right; but the question of how to distinguish a moral ought-statement made from the legal point of view and a moral ought-statement made from the moral point of view is not one I can address here. In any event, attempting to derive one from the other would not itself be a breach of Hume's Law; but we can also not, it would seem, infer an ought-statement relative to a certain normative system from an ought-statement relative to another normative system.

42 Hans Kelsen, *Pure Theory of Law* (n 8) 193–194.

43 Scott Shapiro, 'The "Hart–Dworkin" Debate: A Short Guide for the Perplexed', in *Ronald Dworkin*, edited by Arthur Ripstein (Cambridge, MA: Cambridge University Press 2007) 3, emphasis added; see also Leslie Green, 'Legal Positivism' in *The Stanford Encyclopedia of Philosophy* (Spring 2018 Edition), edited by Edward N. Zalta (ed.), URL <https://plato.stanford.edu/archives/spr2018/entries/legal-positivism/>.

6
Explaining Ourselves in Court

*James Edwards**

A. Introduction

What is a justification? What is an excuse? Orthodoxy tells us that the answers are as follows. To offer a justification is to deny wrongdoing. To offer an excuse is to concede the wrong but deny responsibility.[1] John Gardner taught us that we should give orthodoxies a hard time. All too often, they get an easy ride. In his work on justifications and excuses, Gardner puts the lesson into practice. Isn't it obvious that, if I am justified in φing, it is not wrong for me to φ? Not at all. Wrongs are breaches of duty, and duties can be overridden. Where they are, we have undefeated reason to do what we are duty-bound not to do. If we act for an undefeated reason, our actions are justified.[2] They are justified even though they are also wrong. In cases such as this, those who offer justifications *concede* rather than deny wrongdoing. The wrong is the very thing for which they provide justification.[3]

The orthodoxy holds that, if I have an excuse for φing, I am not responsible for having φed. This, too, may seem obvious. Gardner argues that it is anything but. Responsibility, in its most basic sense, is the ability to respond to reasons.[4] To claim a justification or excuse for having φed is to claim that one exercised this ability in φing.[5] To claim a justification for φing, we just saw, is to claim that there was undefeated reason to φ. And it is to claim that one φed for such a reason. To claim an excuse for φing is to claim that, though one lacked undefeated reason to φ, one had undefeated reason to feel or believe that one had such a reason. And it is to claim that one φed on the strength of this feeling or belief.[6] If D is accused of wrongdoing, and makes these claims, she *asserts* rather than denies responsibility for φing. Responsibility of this kind, Gardner argues, makes both justifications and excuses possible.

* Thanks to Tom Adams, Michelle Dempsey, Andrea Dolcetti, Kate Greasley, Adam Perry, Sandy Steel, and Leah Trueblood for their feedback on earlier drafts.

1 For a useful summary of the canon, see Mitchell Berman, 'Justification and Excuse, Law and Morality' (2003) 53 Duke Law Journal 1, 7–10.

2 John Gardner, *Offences and Defences* (OUP 2007) 91–108.

3 Ibid, 79.

4 Ibid, 177–185.

5 As we will see, Gardner argues that the claim is *itself* an exercise of the ability. More on this later.

6 Gardner (n 2) 86.

James Edwards, *Explaining Ourselves in Court* In: *From Morality to Law and Back Again.* Edited by: Michelle Madden Dempsey and François Tanguay-Renaud, Oxford University Press.
DOI: 10.1093/oso/9780198860594.003.0006

Justifications often concede wrongdoing. Excuses always assert responsibility. The justified have (and act for) undefeated reasons to act as they do. The excused have (and act on the strength of) undefeated reasons to take themselves to have such reasons. So, in a nutshell, says Gardner's contrarian view of the subject. One question is whether the orthodox or contrarian view is the correct one.[7] Resolving the debate about justifications and excuses will not be our aim here. A second question is why, if we are interested in the criminal law, we should take any interest in the correct resolution. Philosophers of criminal law almost universally assume that we should. They assume that to grasp the truth about justification and excuse is to grasp something important about the body of law that is their subject. This assumption is another orthodoxy that gets an easy ride. So it too should be given a hard time. Our question is what we should make of this second orthodoxy.

Two quick answers ultimately prove unsatisfying. According to the first:

> Understanding criminal law requires clarifying the concepts used by criminal courts. As criminal courts use the concepts of justification and excuse to categorise criminal defences, we need to clarify those concepts to understand criminal law.

A first problem with this answer lies in the doctrinal premise on which it rests. In English law, at least, the categories of justification and excuse are largely conspicuous by their absence. As nothing turns for D's liability on how a defence is categorized, courts rarely trouble themselves with the categorization.[8] A more important problem is that the concepts of justification and excuse used by the courts are not the concepts Gardner is concerned to clarify. When it comes to justifications, Gardner makes clear that his interest 'is not in the legal meaning of the word' but in 'the ordinary phenomenon' that figures 'in evaluative thinking at large'.[9] What goes for justification also goes for excuse. Our question is why those who take an interest in criminal law have reason to take an interest in these ordinary phenomena.[10]

A second quick answer moves from the descriptive to the normative:

> That criminal courts take little interest in justification and excuse does not make these phenomena irrelevant to their decision-making. If we want to know

[7] Another is just how contrarian the contrarian view is. Replace wrongdoing with impermissibility, and responsibility with culpability, and you have a view with which Gardner need have no quarrel.

[8] True, these categories are more prominent in other legal systems. We still need to know whether they should be.

[9] Gardner (n 2) 95.

[10] One suggestion is that, because the courts are understood to be referring to the ordinary phenomena, their use of the language of justification and excuse should map onto those phenomena. Perhaps so. But we still need to know why this mapping is desirable. And we need to know whether anything would be amiss if courts were understood to use both terms in a technical sense.

whether criminal law's liability rules are defensible, we need to know whether liability is precluded by justification and excuse under those rules.

Without more, this second answer begs the question. *Why* should the defensibility of the aforementioned rules depend on how the justified and excused fare under them?[11] One suggestion appeals to the character of criminal verdicts:

> Criminal conviction is stigmatic. Not only does it publicly condemn the convicted, it opens the way to various forms of deprivation and hardship. We should not be stigmatised for doing that which it is not blameworthy for us to do. And we are not blameworthy for doing that which is justified or excused. This is why working out whether criminal law's liability rules are defensible requires working out whether liability is precluded by justification and excuse under those rules.

Duly supplemented, the second answer has force. It nonetheless remains unsatisfying. One problem is that, in Gardner's words, it leaves us 'hanging in mid-air'.[12] We know that *if* criminal verdicts are stigmatic, both justification and excuse should preclude liability. We do not know whether (any or all) criminal verdicts *should* stigmatize. So we do not know whether the criminal law we should be trying to create is a criminal law that would have (much if any) reason to concern itself with justifications and excuses. Two other problems also arise. The first is that the second answer is insufficiently general. It fails to explain why justifications and excuses are (and should be) defences to non-stigmatic crimes. The second—and more important—problem is that the answer fails to account for our concern with *authenticity*. Reasons not to stigmatize the blameless are reasons to acquit the justified and excused. They tell us nothing about *how* the justified and excused ought to be acquitted. As far as those reasons go, nothing is amiss if the justified are never acquitted on the basis of their justifications, or if the excused are never acquitted on the basis of their excuses. If the justified get off the hook by portraying themselves as excused, and the excused get off the hook by denying responsibility for their actions, no stigma is misallocated by the criminal law. It seems clear, however, that inauthenticity of this kind is not what we should want from criminal proceedings. A complete account of criminal law's concern with justifications and excuses should explain why this is the case.

A third answer to our question is offered by Gardner. Consider the following passage:

[11] Here and in what follows, references to justification and excuse are references to the ordinary phenomena.

[12] John Gardner, 'Wrongs and Faults' in A.P. Simester (ed) *Appraising Strict Liability* (OUP 2005) 77.

> The criminal law is only secondarily a vehicle for condemnation, deterrence, and punishment. It is primarily a vehicle for the public identification of wrongdoing (by certain standards of evidence and procedure) and for responsible agents, whose wrongs have been thus identified, to *answer for* their wrongs by offering justifications and excuses for having committed them. By calling this latter function 'primary' I do not mean to suggest that it is socially more important. I mean that the proper execution of the other functions depends upon it. Criminal law can be a proper vehicle for condemnation, deterrence, and punishment only because it is a vehicle for responsible agents to answer for their wrongs.[13]

These are striking claims. Before we can evaluate them, we need to do some unpacking. We can already see, however, that if what Gardner says is correct, those interested in the criminal law cannot but take an interest in justifications and excuses. They cannot but do so because the primary function of that area of law is only fulfilled if criminal proceedings elicit justifications and excuses from responsible agents. If this is right, a system of criminal law which fails to make provision for defendants to offer such explanations in the courtroom can at most fulfil secondary functions of that system.

B. Functions

Should we accept Gardner's claims? Let us begin with some preliminaries. Gardner distinguishes between different *functions* of criminal law. In the case of social practices such as the criminal law, he argues:

> The functions of each practice supply the reasons for that practice to be nurtured and maintained, as well as the reasons for particular people to join in with it by performing actions recognizably forming part of its complex.[14]

It is worth distinguishing between two roles a function might play in the justification of a practice. The first is that of supplying reasons to establish the practice and perpetuate its existence. Call a function that supplies such reasons a *genetic function*. A genetic function need not supply *sufficient* reason to establish and perpetuate the practice of which it is a function. It need only supply a reason that both (i) supports establishment and perpetuation, and (ii) is at least sometimes undefeated by reasons that countervail. Not every reason that satisfies (i) also satisfies (ii). The fact that there will be jobs in prisons may count in favour of establishing and perpetuating a system of criminal law. This reason may nonetheless be an

[13] Gardner (n 2) 80, 239.
[14] Ibid, 202.

excluded reason for establishing and perpetuating such a system. Reasons that satisfy (i) and (ii) need not be sufficient reasons. Undefeated reasons are those that are on the winning side. They may be on that side only when and because they have reinforcements. The reason supplied by a genetic function may thus be undefeated only when and because it is fortified by reasons supplied by other genetic functions. In the case of a practice as destructive of the criminal law this may be true of *all* genetic functions. There may be no function which supplies reasons that are themselves sufficient to justify establishing and perpetuating the existence of criminal law.[15]

We can contrast genetic functions with *parasitic* functions. The justificatory role of the parasitic functions of a practice is to enable the practice to fulfil its genetic functions defensibly. These functions supply reasons to arrange the practice in ways that are necessary if the reasons supplied by its genetic functions are to survive defeat. To see what I have in mind, consider universities. One function of universities is to look after the welfare of students. Another is to educate them. The first function, however, is parasitic on the second. Universities have welfare functions *because* of the way in which they fulfil their educative functions: because defensibly educating students, in the way universities do, requires that universities also look after student welfare. The same is not true in reverse. It is not true that universities have educative functions *because* of the way in which they fulfil their welfare functions.

Gardner claims that criminal law has an *explanatory* function. That function is fulfilled when criminal proceedings elicit justifications and excuses from responsible agents. One question is whether the explanatory function is a function of criminal law. A second question is whether that function is genetic or parasitic. A third question is whether, as Gardner also claims, the explanatory function is the primary function of criminal law. The following sections address these questions in turn.

C. The Argument from Self-Respect

If criminal law has an explanatory function, that function is fulfilled by bringing criminal proceedings against responsible agents for offending acts. To defend an affirmative answer to our first question, we need to know what reason there is to encourage such agents to answer for themselves in this forum. For those who think of criminal proceedings in purely instrumental terms, the idea that there is *any* such reason is apt to appear mysterious. If the point of criminal proceedings is to work out who ought to bear the burden of criminal conviction, what matters is

[15] Gardner expresses no little sympathy for this idea. Ibid, 214–215.

working out which defendants *have* justifications or excuses. *Ceteris paribus*, it does not matter how we come to work this out.[16] So it does not matter whether the criminal proceedings that are conducted are proceedings in which justifications and excuses are actually offered.[17]

Predictably enough, Gardner finds the purely instrumental view to be inadequate. Those who take it

> [miss] the most fundamental point of all this legal rigmarole, all these pleas and committals and verdicts and even the physical layout of the courtroom with the dock and the stand and the bench. The fundamental point is to have structured explanatory dialogues in public, in which the object of explanation is ourselves. This point is not a point relative to which the procedure is instrumental; rather the point is *in* the procedure.[18]

Put differently, Gardner's view is that the value of criminal proceedings is 'first and foremost intrinsic rather than instrumental'.[19] That value resides in the explanatory dialogues that take place in criminal court. Those dialogues consist both of accusations of wrongdoing put by prosecutors, and of justifications and excuses offered by defendants for their commission.

It might be said that all this has not taken us very far. We still do not know *what* intrinsic value is realized by the courtroom dialogue just described. So we still do not know why we should accept the claim that criminal law has an explanatory function. To locate the value we are looking for, Gardner appeals to two ideas. One is the idea of basic responsibility that we encountered earlier. Our basic responsibility, to repeat, is our ability to respond to reasons. One way to be responsive to reasons is to comply with them. A second way to be responsive to reasons is to explain oneself in terms of the reasons with which one complied. To be basically responsible, in Gardner's sense, is to have the ability to respond to reasons in both these ways. We exercise that ability both by performing actions that are justified and excused, and by offering the justifications and excuses we have for those actions.[20]

The fact that we have an ability is not (and does not entail the existence of) any reason for its exercise. Gardner nonetheless argues that, when it comes to basic responsibility, such a reason does exist. To make the argument he appeals to a second

[16] True, encouraging defendants to offer justifications and excuses might be a reliable way to work out which defendants actually acted in ways that were justified or excused. But this is a contingent matter.

[17] As Luis Duarte d'Almeida observes, to claim otherwise would be to suggest that whether D offers a justification for φing at trial *itself* bears on whether D φed for an undefeated reason. This, of course, cannot be right. See L. Duarte d'Almeida, *Allowing for Exceptions* (OUP 2015) 252ff.

[18] Gardner (n 2) 189.

[19] Ibid, 188.

[20] Ibid, 183–184.

idea—to the value of self-respect. According to Joseph Raz, we respect ourselves when we believe that the manner in which we conduct ourselves adds value to our lives. Our self-respect is deserved when this belief is well-founded.[21] One condition of the belief being well-founded is that we endeavour to use our basic responsibility as well as we can. We must aspire to live a life that makes sense rationally. And we must aspire to make what rational sense can be made of that life to others, at least where those others take a legitimate interest in how we live. Gardner puts the thought this way:

> As a rational being [D] cannot but aspire to conform maximally to reason, and his self-respect is bound up, not with the conformity itself, but with the aspiration. His self-respect is threatened by his lowering his sights as a rational agent—by his being no less content to make an excuse than to claim a justification, or no less content to deny his responsibility for his actions than to do either of those things. It does not follow that he compromises his self-respect by the mere fact that he actually *is* excused rather than justified, or actually *does* lack responsibility rather than being excused or justified—so long as he is not indifferent to that being the case, so long as he does not approach with equanimity the question of which argument he is going to offer in his defence.[22]

Gardner's claim, to be clear, is not that there is value in rationalization. His idea is not that we have reason to claim that we were more rationally successful than we really were. His idea is rather that we have reasons of self-respect to claim the degree of rational success we achieved for ourselves. Now anyone who has a justification or excuse for φing is someone who has failed to conform to reasons. Absent reasons not to φ, those who φ have nothing to justify or excuse. Crucially, however, the justified and excused also respond to reasons successfully. All else being equal, the former are more successful than the latter. While the justified act for reasons that are in fact undefeated, the excused act for reasons that are in fact defeated. This is why excuses are 'second best' to justifications—why they include an extra 'admission of rational defeat'.[23] We have already seen that the defeat is not total. Though the excused lack undefeated reasons for their actions, they have undefeated reason for the beliefs and feelings on the strength of which they act. This is what distinguishes excuses from denials of responsibility: while defences of the former kind are only available to those who respond to reasons successfully, defences of the latter kind are only available to those who lack the ability to succeed in this way. So while the justified are more rationally successful than the excused, the excused are

[21] Joseph Raz, 'Liberating Duties' (1989) 8 Law and Philosophy 3, 15–17. Gardner attributes his own understanding of self-respect to Raz and Stephen Darwall: Gardner (n 2) 133 n 16.

[22] Gardner (n 2) 273–274.

[23] Ibid, 179.

more rationally successful than those who lack responsibility. If Gardner is correct, it follows that the justified have reason to want to plead their justifications, and the excused have reasons to want to plead their excuses. They have reason to want these things whether or not other pleas would get them off the hook more easily or just as well.

It is one thing to have reason to want to φ. It is quite another to want to φ. One way to get people to want to do what they have pre-existing reason to do is to give them additional reasons to do it. Imagine D kills V in self-defence and is accused of V's murder. D has reasons of self-respect, Gardner argues, to want to claim her justification. For various reasons, D may be inclined to say nothing, or make other claims. In a system of criminal law with justificatory defences, criminal proceedings give D additional reasons to claim that she acted in self-defence. D stands to be convicted if the elements of murder are proved and no evidence of a defence is provided. True, D might be able to secure an acquittal by pleading some other defence. But as long as D increases her chances of being acquitted by pleading the justification she actually has, D has a powerful incentive to plead self-defence. The same goes, *mutatis mutandis*, for all other defendants who have justifications or excuses to offer. As Gardner puts the point, criminal proceedings put responsible agents 'under extra instrumental pressure to give decent public accounts of themselves', by claiming the justifications and excuses they have for offending acts.[24]

If Gardner is correct, whether we are deserving of self-respect depends on whether we aspire to make rational sense of our lives to others, at least where those others take a legitimate interest in how we live. True, some offending acts may be acts in which no one takes a legitimate interest, either because those acts are no one's business but the actor's or because the moral failings of those who take an interest render that interest illegitimate. For present purposes, however, we can set these cases aside. We can assume that we are dealing with cases in which other people legitimately take an interest in why D acted as D did. In cases such as these, Gardner argues, responsible agents who do not aspire to claim their justifications and excuses, when accused of acting wrongly, thereby compromise their self-respect. Criminal proceedings that elicit these explanations from defendants—by giving them extra reason to explain themselves rationally—are criminal proceedings that forestall this compromise. It is bad for any of us to compromise our self-respect, irrespective of the consequences of our compromising it. This is why courtroom dialogue, in which defendants justify or excuse their actions, is dialogue that is intrinsically valuable.

Call the foregoing *the argument from self-respect*. One virtue of the argument, if sound, is that it accounts for our concern with authenticity. It explains why something is amiss in criminal court if the justified get off the hook by portraying

[24] Ibid, 191.

themselves as excused, and the excused get off the hook by denying responsibility for their actions. One worry about the argument stems from the instrumental pressure on which it relies. On the view of self-respect Gardner borrows from Raz, we deserve self-respect only if we conduct ourselves in a manner that adds value to our lives. It is plausible to think that whether this condition is met depends on our motivations. If D wants to kill V out of spite, and refrains only because she is threatened with life imprisonment, it is hard to believe that the way D conducts herself is to her credit.[25] So it is hard to believe that, on the Razian view, D's inaction helps make it the case that her self-respect is deserved. If this is correct, the same goes for those who justify or excuse their actions only because they face conviction and punishment if they say nothing. That these defendants aspire to claim rational success for themselves *also* does not seem to be to their credit. They have the wrong kind of reason, we might say, for their aspiration. It seems to follow that criminal proceedings which elicit justifications and excuses from defendants, by putting them under instrumental pressure to offer answers in court, do not thereby prevent defendants compromising their self-respect. On the Razian view, the fact that such pressure is required only goes to show that the self-respect of those who require it has already been compromised.[26]

D. The Genetic and the Parasitic

Let us set this worry aside and turn to the second of our three questions. Assuming the argument from self-respect goes through, does it show that the explanatory function is a genetic or a parasitic function of criminal law? Gardner sometimes suggests that his view is the former:

> Even if for some reason we abolished the whole apparatus of criminal sentences and civil remedies, we should still think twice about abolishing the trials themselves. In fact, one important (although not sufficient) reason for *having* the apparatus of criminal sentences and civil remedies is to *motivate* the trials themselves. It is to put people under extra instrumental pressure to give decent public accounts of themselves, in the knowledge that doing this will normally help them to eliminate or reduce the burden of consequential responsibility that they might otherwise bear.[27]

[25] Which is not to deny that D avoids the discredit that would attach to the killing. Avoiding discredit is one thing. Deserving credit is another.

[26] Whether the Razian view is correct is a further question on which I take no position here.

[27] Gardner (n 2) 190–191.

These remarks suggest that the reasons supplied by the explanatory function are reasons to establish and perpetuate systems of criminal law. They are reasons to think that, even if we should not sentence those found guilty, we should still have trials that determine guilt. Such reasons do not suffice to show that the explanatory function is genetic. We also need to show that the reasons that function supplies are at least sometimes undefeated. We need to show that there are at least sometimes undefeated reasons to use criminal proceedings to elicit justifications and excuses from defendants who have them.

Are there such reasons? There is cause for doubt. We can see why by considering a case in which we know that the explanatory function will be fulfilled. Imagine we know that D killed V in self-defence, and that D will not offer her justification unless criminal proceedings are brought against her. Because we know this, we also know that any proceedings against D should result in an acquittal. It would be unjust to convict and punish D when D acted in self-defence. Knowing all this, should we bring criminal proceedings against D? It seems clear that we should not. Given the costs of bringing criminal proceedings, and the risk that D may be convicted in error, our reasons to prosecute are defeated by those that countervail.[28] This is the conclusion reached by many legal systems. Take, to give but one example, the Code for Crown Prosecutors in England and Wales. Under the Code, proceedings must not be brought against D unless there is 'a realistic prospect of conviction'. Whether such a prospect exists depends, among other things, on 'the impact of any defence' that D may run.[29] It follows that, if there is sufficient evidence that D acted in self-defence, there is no realistic prospect of conviction. Any prosecution must be discontinued. This matters here because we already saw that the explanatory function is not fulfilled by rationalization. It is fulfilled in cases where D has a justification or excuse to offer for her offending act. If English law is correct—as the above example suggests—these are cases in which no criminal proceedings should be conducted. If this is so, the only cases in which it is possible to fulfil the explanatory function are cases in which our reasons to use the criminal law to fulfil it are defeated.

It might be objected that the last paragraph moved too quickly. It began with cases in which we *know* that D has a justification or excuse to offer. It concluded that there is *no case* in which we have undefeated reason to obtain that justification or excuse by prosecuting D. This might be said to be too quick because it overlooks the existence of uncertainty—of cases in which we have reason to believe both that (i) D's offending act was justified or excused, and that (ii) D committed

[28] So argues Duarte d'Almeida, to whom this paragraph is owed. Duarte d'Almeida attributes the contrary view to Gardner and Antony Duff: 'My issue . . . is with Gardner's and Duff's suggestion that I must still be called to answer for an action, the performance of which has already been shown to have been permissible or even obligatory; and that, accordingly, I should be charged with having committed the criminal offence, and called to defend myself from that charge *on pain of conviction if I fail to do so*, even if the state has sufficient evidence that one of the admissible (and fully exculpatory) defeating circumstances is verified.' See Duarte d'Almeida (n 17) 252ff (emphasis in the original).

[29] Code for Crown Prosecutors 2018, paras 4.6–4.7.

that act culpably. Reasons of type (ii) are reasons to believe that criminal law's other functions—most notably its condemnatory and punitive functions—would be fulfilled by prosecuting D.[30] It is in cases like these, it might be said—where they have reinforcements—that the reasons supplied by the explanatory function are on the winning side.

The problem with this reply is that reasons for belief are not reasons for action. As Gardner himself tells us, while the former open the way to an excuse, the latter open the way to a justification. To show that there is undefeated reason to bring criminal proceedings we need a reason *to bring the proceedings*, not a reason to believe that we should bring them. My imagined objector attempts to reinforce the reasons supplied by the explanatory function with reasons supplied by the condemnatory and punitive functions of the criminal law. This strategy cannot work. It cannot work because the only cases in which it is possible to fulfil the explanatory function—cases in which D has a justification and excuse—are cases in which D should *not* be condemned or punished. They are cases in which there is no occasion to fulfil either the condemnatory or the punitive function.[31] In such cases, we may have undefeated reason to *believe* that we have undefeated reason to condemn and punish. *Ex hypothesi*, however, we have no undefeated reason to do either. Reasons for belief can at most furnish us with an excuse for bringing criminal proceedings. They cannot provide us with a justification.

It might be said in further reply that the explanatory function is more capacious than I have allowed. Perhaps that function is fulfilled both when answers elicited by criminal proceedings *successfully* justify or excuse D's actions and when those answers are merely *taken* to do so.[32] Answers of the latter kind are not mere rationalizations. They are rational explanations that point to reasons (for action, feeling, or belief) which D mistakenly believes to be undefeated reasons. Since explanations of this kind disclose rather than defray culpability, proceedings that elicit them are cases in which reinforcements are available: in which criminal law's condemnatory and punitive functions can also support prosecution, placing the reasons supplied by the explanatory function on the winning side.

Does this show that the explanatory function figures among criminal law's genetic functions after all? Not so fast. On any view, the explanatory function is fulfilled by eliciting rational explanations from criminal defendants. On any view, those explanations fail in their own terms when the reasons to which they point are defeated reasons. If I am right, the only cases in which criminal proceedings are justifiably brought against D are cases in which the rational explanations D has to offer point to defeated reasons. It is hard to believe that eliciting rational explanations is a genetic function of criminal law if the only cases in which we are justified

30 Because there would be undefeated reason to condemn and punish.
31 Because any reasons to condemn or punish are defeated.
32 I thank Michelle Dempsey for this suggestion.

in using criminal proceedings to elicit them are cases in which those explanations fail in their own terms. Consider, by way of comparison, the case of punishment. One thing that distinguishes punishment and reparation is their respective success conditions: while the latter may succeed *qua* reparation even if D is left no worse off, the former necessarily fails *qua* punishment if D suffers no harm or deprivation. Given this, it could not plausibly be claimed that punishing offenders was a genetic function of criminal law if the only cases in which criminal courts were justified in imposing criminal punishment were cases in which no harm or deprivation was visited on defendants. More generally: if *y* is not justified in bringing about successful instances of *x*, then *x* is not a genetic function of *y*. If this is so, we retain reason to doubt that the explanatory function is a genetic function of criminal law.

E. The Symbolic Argument

Might it nonetheless be a parasitic function? Some of Gardner's remarks suggest that he would answer in the affirmative. Recall the last line of the passage quoted earlier: 'Criminal law can be a proper vehicle for condemnation, deterrence and punishment only because it is a vehicle for responsible agents to answer for their wrongs.'[33] This remark suggests that the role played by the explanatory function in the justification of criminal law is that of enabling it to fulfil other functions defensibly. Let us call this thesis (A):

(A) Criminal law can defensibly do what is necessary to fulfil other functions only if it continues to fulfil its explanatory function.

To evaluate this thesis, we need to expose an ambiguity in the explanatory function that I have so far suppressed. That function is fulfilled, I said, when criminal proceedings *elicit* justifications and excuses from responsible agents. On one reading, answers are elicited when responsible agents answer for wrongs in criminal court. On another reading, answers are elicited whenever criminal proceedings give those agents both the opportunity and the incentive to offer their answers. On the second reading, criminal law fulfils its explanatory function by trying to obtain justifications and excuses. It need not succeed in obtaining them. On the first reading, it must both try and succeed. Call the first reading *the complete reading*. Call the second *the inchoate reading*.

We already know that, if we opt for the complete reading, (A) must be false. It cannot be true that criminal law defensibly punishes wrongdoers—thereby doing

[33] See text to n 13 above.

what is necessary to fulfil its punitive function—only if those wrongdoers offer justifications and excuses for their wrongs. Defendants who can successfully justify or excuse their actions are not culpable. So they should not be punished. Criminal proceedings that elicit justifications and excuses from these defendants do not thereby render punishment defensible. They are proceedings which make clear that punishment is indefensible in the case at hand. Things are different, of course, in the case of culpable defendants. But the complete reading implies that, if all such defendants remained silent given the opportunity to defend themselves, punishing any of them would be unjustified. This, obviously, cannot be right.

That leaves us with the inchoate reading. Should we accept (A) when the explanatory function is so interpreted? To answer affirmatively is to say that a system of criminal law can defensibly convict and punish wrongdoers only if it makes provision for them to answer for their wrongs in criminal court. We can distinguish between two possible arguments for this conclusion. According to what we might call *the direct argument*: a system that did not make such provision might fulfil its condemnatory and punitive functions; it would nonetheless wrong defendants by depriving them of the opportunity to answer for their wrongs. According to what we might call *the indirect argument*: a system which did not make provision for defendants to answer would not only fail to fulfil the explanatory function; it would also fail to fulfil its condemnatory and punitive functions as a result. The direct argument holds that criminal law can conform to the reasons supplied by its other functions, whether or not it fulfils the explanatory function, but that those reasons are defeated if the explanatory function is not fulfilled. The indirect argument says that, if the explanatory function is not fulfilled, the criminal law also fails to conform to the reasons supplied by its other functions.

Gardner does not explicitly say which argument convinces him of (A). But there is at least some evidence that the indirect argument is what does so. Responsible agents, recall, are those with the capacity to respond to reasons. Gardner argues:

> It is not hard to see how the possession of this distinctively human capacity—or should I say conjunction of capacities—might come to bear on one's exposure to certain adverse normative consequences. For the consequences we have in mind here, are all of them of a distinctive kind that *symbolize* one's participation in the basic human goods of reason and speech. It is not as if, because one did wrong, the way is open to just any form of retaliation, preventive detention, quarantine, etc. Rather, the way is open to punishing one, extracting compensation or apology from one, and similar (partly) symbolic transactions, which all address one as a being who grasps and listens to reason rather than a mere object to be manipulated for some other being's good.[34]

[34] Gardner (n 2) 85.

Gardner accepts that this line of thought needs further development. The basic idea, however, is straightforward enough. When responsible agents act wrongly, this gives us reason to alter how we interact with them. In some cases, it gives us reason to interact with such agents in ways that burden them. It is nonetheless true that, if we are to conduct these interactions defensibly, our conduct must be conditioned by the fact that it is a responsible agent with whom we are dealing. What goes for each of us also goes for the law. If the law is to avoid treating us as mere objects to be manipulated, it must ensure that the manner in which it adds to our burdens affirms our status as responsible agents—that each of us is addressed, in Gardner's words, 'as a being who grasps and listens to reason'. If this is right, whether criminal conviction and punishment are justified, in any given system, depends on whether they retain this kind of symbolic significance. There are various conditions on which retention depends, but one is that the procedures used to determine who is convicted and punished *themselves* affirm the responsible agency of those caught up in them. Criminal proceedings are affirmative—in the relevant sense—only if they make provision for defendants to exercise their responsible agency, by offering justifications and excuses they have for their wrongs. A system of criminal law that did not make such provision might well continue to convict and punish defendants. It would nonetheless fail to conform to the reasons supplied by its condemnatory and punitive functions. Those reasons, recall, are not reasons for courts to convict and punish *per se*. They are reasons for courts to convict and punish those they are justified in convicting and punishing. If the above remarks are correct, a system that fails to fulfil the explanatory function is a system of criminal law in which this justification no longer obtains.

F. Primacy

Call the foregoing *the symbolic argument*. Space does not permit proper evaluation of its merits here. Suffice it to say that, if sound, the argument rescues the explanatory function from the objections pressed above. It shows that, though that function may not be genetic, it is nonetheless a parasitic function of criminal law.

We saw above that Gardner also makes a stronger claim. He claims that the explanatory function is criminal law's *primary* function. It is worth comparing this claim with some claims of HLA Hart's. Hart says:

> The characteristic technique of the criminal law is to designate by rules certain standards of behaviour as standards for the guidance either of the members of society as a whole or of special classes within it: they are expected without the aid or intervention of officials to understand the rules and to see that the rules apply to them and to conform to them. Only when the law is broken, *and this primary*

> *function of the law fails*, are officials concerned to identify the fact of breach and impose the threatened sanctions.[35]

If Hart is correct, criminal law's primary function is not explanatory but *preventive*. It is important to see that, in making this claim, Hart is not denying that criminal law's primary function is fulfilled by means of our responsible agency. He is only claiming that it is fulfilled by harnessing that capacity in a different way. Criminal law's explanatory function is fulfilled when responsible agents use their ability to respond to reasons by justifying or excusing wrongs they have already committed. Criminal law's preventive function, as Hart understands it, is fulfilled when responsible agents use their ability to respond to reasons by refraining from the unjustified commission of wrongs.[36] We have already seen that criminal law fulfils the explanatory function by putting responsible agents on trial, and by putting those agents under extra instrumental pressure to offer answers at those trials. Criminal law fulfils the preventive function by publicly articulating standards of conduct for responsible agents, and by putting those agents under instrumental pressure to conform to its standards.

It is worth noting that Hart's claims here are claims about criminal *law*, not claims about criminal *punishment*. It is true, of course, that if responsible agents refuse to be guided by standards articulated by the criminal law, prevention may not be possible without the imposition of punishment. It does not follow that prevention is either a necessary or a sufficient condition of justified punishment. Nor should it be assumed that it is by punishing wrongdoers that criminal law ideally, or even standardly, succeeds in preventing wrongs. In truth, a system of criminal law which resorts to punitive means of prevention is a system that has already failed in preventive terms. *Ex hypothesi*, it has failed to prevent the very wrongs for which punishment is imposed. Where fulfilment of the preventive function is an unqualified success, there *are* no wrongs for which criminal law may justifiably impose punishment. There are no such wrongs because those who would otherwise have committed them instead conform to the norms of the criminal law.

If Hart is right, is Gardner wrong? Not necessarily. The concept of primacy is ambiguous. Two senses are worth distinguishing here. One is *normative*:

[35] H.L.A. Hart, *The Concept of Law* (OUP 1961) 38–39 (my emphasis).

[36] Why unjustified wrongs, rather than either (i) wrongs *per se*, or (ii) wrongs culpably committed? If criminal law's preventive function took in wrongs *per se* it would take in both unjustified and *justified* wrongdoing. But wrongs that are committed for undefeated reasons are not wrongs that criminal law should be in the business of preventing. If criminal law's preventive function only took in *culpable* wrongs it would not take in *excused* wrongdoing. But wrongs that are committed for defeated reasons *are* wrongs which criminal law should be in the business of preventing. Criminal law's standards of conduct do not say to us 'you may offend when excused'. What they say is 'you must not offend when unjustified'.

> *X* has primacy in the normative sense if and only if we should prefer *y*'s fulfilment of *x* to *y*'s fulfilment of its other functions.

A second is *lexical*:

> *X* has primacy in the lexical sense if and only if *y*'s justified fulfilment of its other functions depends on *y*'s continued fulfilment of *x*, whereas *y*'s justified fulfilment of *x* does not depend on *y*'s continued fulfilment of other functions.

That a function has primacy in the normative sense does not entail that it has primacy in the lexical sense. That we should most want *y* to fulfil one of its functions does not entail that, where this fails to occur, *y* is not justified in continuing to fulfil any other function.

It is clear that, when Gardner claims primacy for the explanatory function, it is lexical primacy that he has in mind.[37] When Hart claims that the primary function of the criminal law is preventive, it is plausible to think that he is referring to normative primacy.[38] So interpreted, we should accept Hart's claim: we should prefer a criminal law that fulfils its preventive function to one that fulfils its explanatory, condemnatory, or punitive functions. We already saw that, if criminal law successfully fulfils its preventive function, there is no occasion for it to fulfil its condemnatory or punitive functions. A criminal law that succeeds in preventing unjustified wrongdoing leaves nothing that criminal courts are justified in condemning and punishing. A world free of such wrongs is better, all else being equal, than a world that contains them alongside the condemnation and punishment of wrongdoers. We should most want criminal law to harness our responsible agency in ways that bring about this better world.

Criminal law's preventive and explanatory functions are not mutually exclusive. That there are no unjustified wrongs does not entail that there are no wrongs for which genuine justification might be offered. These functions may nonetheless come into conflict: we may have to choose to fulfil one or the other. To see this, imagine we are faced with two individuals—D1 and D2. We have strong reason to believe that D1 has committed a justified wrong—that she killed V1 in defence of others—and that D1 will answer for this wrong only if we demand answers. We have strong reason to believe that D2 is about to commit an unjustified wrong—she is about to kill V2 to secure a promotion—and that D2 will commit the wrong unless we demand that she refrain. Though we would like to make both demands, we

[37] Gardner (n 2) 80: 'By calling this latter function "primary" I do not mean to suggest that it is socially more important. I mean that the proper execution of the other functions depends upon it.'

[38] By providing for wrongdoers to be tried and punished, Hart claims, a system of criminal law 'makes provision for the breakdown or failure' of the system. Hart (n 35) 39. Though this claim implies that we should prefer prevention to trial and punishment, it does not imply that if criminal law fails to prevent it cannot defensibly try or punish.

can only make one. The costs of making the two demands are identical. Our choice will have no other morally significant implications.

It seems clear that we should demand that D2 refrain. This is not only because of the importance of V2's life. It is also because of the importance of D2's. We should all want to avoid committing unjustified wrongs, not (or not only) because of the adverse consequences this may have, but (also) because our lives go worse for containing them.[39] It is true that, if Gardner is correct, our lives *also* go worse when we fail to answer for wrongs. But if we must choose between worsening our lives in one of these ways, it is hard to believe that we should prefer the second. If this is not obvious, first imagine killing an innocent person by mistake. Then imagine failing to explain why you did it. I take for granted that, if you could avoid only one of these failures, you would prefer to avoid the first.

So much for normative primacy. What about lexical primacy? To claim that the explanatory function has lexical primacy is to combine (A) with (B):

(A) Criminal law can defensibly do what is necessary to fulfil other functions only if it continues to fulfil its explanatory function.

(B) It is not the case that criminal law can defensibly do what is necessary to fulfil the explanatory function only if it continues to fulfil other functions.

We have already considered the case for (A). For the explanatory function to have primacy, however, (A) is not enough. That function must not be on a par with any other function. If there is some other function, *f*, fulfilment of which is necessary for criminal law to defensibly fulfil its explanatory function, then *f* and the explanatory function are on a par. The explanatory function then lacks primacy in the lexical sense.

Is (B) true? To defend an affirmative answer, one must fend off two opponents. Both opponents claim that *f* exists, and that (B) is therefore false. They disagree about which function makes (B) false. The first opponent appeals to criminal law's condemnatory and punitive functions. Imagine a system of criminal law that fulfils the explanatory function—by making provision for defendants to answer for wrongs in criminal proceedings—but which does not fulfil either the condemnatory or punitive functions. (B) implies that this system could defensibly put defendants on trial. To evaluate this claim, we need to know what the system does to those found guilty. One possibility is that it continues to punish them. *Ex hypothesi*, these punishments are unjustified.[40] It seems clear that wrongdoers could not defensibly be tried for their wrongs if this was the result of trying them.

A second possibility is that the system punishes no one. It abolishes 'the whole apparatus of criminal sentences' without 'abolishing the trials themselves'.[41] It is

[39] Gardner himself makes this claim. See Gardner (n 12) 54–61.
[40] If they were justified, they would fulfil the condemnatory and punitive functions.
[41] Gardner (n 2) 190–191.

less obvious that trying defendants in this system would be indefensible. But the symbolic argument I suggested Gardner might use to defend (A) might be used in reverse by our first opponent to attack (B). To see how, recall that argument's major premise: the law's interactions with responsible agents remain defensible only if those interactions continue to affirm that this is what they are. The symbolic argument for (A) holds that criminal conviction and punishment retain their symbolic significance only if criminal proceedings provide for defendants to answer for their wrongs. But it might equally be argued that criminal trials retain *their* symbolic significance only so long as they culminate in the condemnation or punishment of those who have no adequate answer. Why so? Because a system of criminal law which refuses to do these things to culpable wrongdoers is a system of criminal law that ceases to blame those found guilty of such wrongs—of murder, rape, theft, insider trading, dangerous driving, and so on. T.M. Scanlon claims that such a rejection of blame is *itself* objectionable: that it 'involves an attitude of superiority toward the person in question (something like the attitude of a parent toward a very young child) and thus represents a failure to take that person seriously'.[42] To treat someone as a very young child, of course, is not to treat them as a responsible agent. If Scanlon is right, a system of criminal law that turned its back on condemnation and punishment would be a system that failed to affirm the responsible agency of those it put on trial.[43] If we accept the major premise of the symbolic argument, such a system could not defensibly bring criminal proceedings against responsible agents. It could not defensibly do what is necessary to fulfil the explanatory function. If this is the case, (B) is false: the criminal law cannot defensibly put responsible agents on trial for their wrongs unless it continues to fulfil its condemnatory and/or punitive functions. This is not to say that the latter two functions have lexical primacy. But it is to say that the explanatory function does not.

What one makes of this argument will depend on one's degree of enthusiasm for blaming the blameworthy. Those for whom it is blame itself, rather than its rejection, that is morally problematic will of course have little sympathy for the first opponent I have conjured up. A second opponent of (B) may nonetheless remain troublesome. That opponent finds *f* not in criminal law's condemnatory or punitive functions, but rather in what I have called its preventive function. Recall that, in order to make (A) plausible, we had to give the explanatory function an inchoate reading. So understood, that function is fulfilled by criminal law when it *tries* to get responsible agents to respond to reasons by offering answers for their wrongs.

[42] T. M. Scanlon, *Moral Dimensions: Permissibility, Meaning, Blame* (Harvard University Press 2008) 168.

[43] True, Gardner might reject Scanlon's claim. But he does not deny that responsible agents have an interest in being punished: 'Since all rational beings want to assert their basic responsibility, all else being equal they cannot but welcome whatever contributes to that assertion. Punishment contributes to that assertion if it expresses their basic responsibility—if that is the public meaning of a punitive action. So all else being equal rational beings do have an interest in being punished whenever they are basically responsible for their actions.' Gardner (n 2) 192.

The explanatory function is not the only function that can be understood in the inchoate mode. We can also offer an inchoate reading of the preventive function. So understood, that function is fulfilled whenever criminal law tries to get responsible agents to respond to reasons by refraining from the unjustified commission of wrongs. According to the symbolic argument, we should accept (A) because it is a condition of criminal law defensibly fulfilling any function that it interacts with us as beings who 'grasp and listen to reason'. The argument from self-respect tells us that responsible agents have reasons of self-respect to offer justifications and excuses for their wrongs. The problem with a system of criminal law that did not even attempt to elicit answers from defendants is that it would imply that defendants were (assumed to be) incorrigible—that they would fail to conform to the aforementioned reasons even with the law's encouragement. The symbolic significance of criminal proceedings—and of their normative consequences—would be undermined accordingly.

The second opponent argues that this line of thought can be redeployed as follows. For the criminal law to stop trying to prevent unjustified wrongdoing would *also* be for it to stop addressing us as beings who grasp and listen to reason. Why so? Because responsible agency is not just the ability to use reasons by explaining why one failed to conform to them. It is also the ability to use reasons to avoid failing to conform to them in the first place. When the criminal law publicly articulates standards of conduct, and puts us under instrumental pressure to conform, it presupposes that we have the ability to use reasons in this latter way. The message sent is that we are agents who—with a bit of encouragement from the law—might come to exercise that ability successfully. A system of criminal law that abandoned all this—that kept its standards secret, say, or punished without articulating any standards at all—would be a system that sent a very different message. It would convey that we were agents who were (assumed to be) incorrigible—who lacked responsible agency that the law might harness to prevent unjustified wrongs. We know that, according to the symbolic argument, it is a condition of criminal law fulfilling any function that it interacts with us as beings who grasp and listen to reason. If the foregoing is correct, the criminal law can only interact with us in this way if it fulfils the inchoate version of the preventive function. It can defensibly fulfil other functions, including the (inchoate version of the) explanatory function, only if it continues to fulfil this preventive function. It follows, according to the second opponent, that (B) is false. Though the preventive function has normative primacy over the explanatory function, the explanatory function does not have lexical primacy over the preventive function.

Let us conclude this section by returning to where we began. The first section of this chapter raised the following question: why would those who take an interest in the criminal law have reason to take an interest in the ordinary phenomena of justification and excuse? Gardner offered us an arresting answer: eliciting ordinary justifications and excuses from responsible agents is the primary function of criminal law. The past few sections offered some reasons to doubt that the arresting answer is the right one. Though I did not deny that the explanatory function is a function of criminal law, I offered some reasons to think that it is a function that is parasitic on others. And I offered some reasons to doubt that the explanatory function has primacy in either the lexical or the normative sense.

G. Coda

I have no doubt that, had John read this chapter, he would have had a great deal to say about why my reservations are misplaced. I wish we had been able to talk it through. Talking philosophy with John was always a joy. It could also be unnerving. To broach a puzzle with him was often to become aware of how much one had failed to grasp, and of how much more work remained ahead of one. It was also to be offered new and dazzling ideas for how that work might be done. It is a mark of John's generosity of spirit that he often presented his ideas as though they were already to be found in the contributions of his interlocutors. I am a serial beneficiary of his generosity. It was my good fortune to know John for a little more than a decade, first as his student and then as his colleague. Our meetings in John's office at University College to discuss my doctoral thesis were formative experiences for me intellectually. The seminars we gave on the BCL, after I returned to Oxford in 2014, will remain highlights of my academic life. I owe so much of my thinking—about how to do philosophy, how to be an academic, how to live a good life—to the time I spent with John.

7

Private, Public, and Punitive Blame

Leora Dahan Katz[*]

A. Introduction

Recent years have seen an explosion of interest in the phenomenon of blame in both philosophical and legal discourse. While the literature has not yet settled the question of whether we should be for or against blame, what does seem to be settled is that if blame is to be endorsed it must be safely divorced from punishment, its brutal brother-in-arms. This has been the presumption of scholars on both sides of the blame debate. Opposition to blame is often driven by a deep association between blaming and punitive responses, while support for blame has been garnered precisely by driving a wedge between the two phenomena. Some supporters of blame have endorsed a 'sanitized'[1] conception of blame, stripping blame of its negative, hostile characteristics.[2] These views generally come under criticism for failing to capture the phenomenon of blame. Others, who endorse conceptions of blame that seek to capture rather than eradicate the 'force' or 'sting' of blame, abide by the general methodology of seeking to justify such sting while maintaining its distance from the practice of punishment.[3]

John Gardner's late-developed defence of blame follows this same pattern, which takes endorsing blame to be associated with maintaining its distance from punishment. Once a long-time, self-pronounced blame-sceptic, Gardner's later work defends blame and blaming, while redirecting his animus towards the outward expression of blame—towards reproach and punishment.[4] This move is not coincidental to his newfound support of blame, but arguably a necessary ingredient of his revised view, and that which allows him to rescue blame from long-held objections

* My sincerest thanks to Michelle Dempsey, David Enoch, Daniel Telech, and Shlomit Wygoda Cohen for their helpful comments on previous drafts.

[1] Victoria McGeer, 'Civilizing Blame' in Coates and Tognazzini (eds), *Blame* (OUP 2013) 165 (hereafter, McGeer, 'Civilizing Blame').

[2] See e.g. T.M. Scanlon, *Moral Dimensions* (HUP 2008) (hereafter Scanlon, *Moral Dimensions*). *See* also Michael Smith, 'Gary Waston: Strawsonian' in Coates and Tognazzini (eds), *Oxford Studies in Agency and Responsibility* Vol. 5 (OUP 2019) 119–122.

[3] See e.g. Angela M. Smith, 'Moral Blame and Moral Protest' in Wallace, Kumar, and Freeman (eds) *Reasons and Recognition* (OUP 2012); R. Jay Wallace, 'Dispassionate Opprobrium' in Wallace, Kumar, and Freeman (eds) *Reasons and Recognition* (OUP 2012).

[4] John Gardner, 'Why Blame' (2019) https://johngardnerathome.info/pdfs/blame.pdf, accessed 1 January 2021 (hereafter Gardner, 'Why Blame').

Leora Dahan Katz, *Private, Public, and Punitive Blame* In: *From Morality to Law and Back Again.* Edited by: Michelle Madden Dempsey and François Tanguay-Renaud, Oxford University Press. © Leora Dahan Katz 2023. DOI: 10.1093/oso/9780198860594.003.0007

to the hostilities he had taken to be bound up with blame *per se*—objections now redirected by Gardner exclusively at public forms of blaming.

Gardner's emergent position on the question of blame will be the topic of this chapter, though I will have some things to say about this general pattern of argument along the way. In section B, I elaborate on this general strategy and on Gardner's proposed defence of blame in particular.[5] In section C, I suggest that the position Gardner motions towards—in defence of private blame and opposition to public blame—is an unstable one. I then propose in section D that we can make sense of Gardner's attraction to the suggested view if we recognize the essentially punitive nature of public blame, despite efforts in the literature to deny this. Nonetheless, accepting the punitivity of blame does not mean we should come out against public blame, as intimated by Gardner. Rather, attending to the excesses and pathologies of public blame, we can proceed with the necessary caution with respect to blaming practices, while defending not only the significance of private blame but that of public blame as well. In section E, I suggest that Gardner would thus have done well to push his reconsidered position even further, in defence not only of private blame but public blame as well, while insisting that we not mistake the *pro tanto* justification of public blame for its all-things-considered justification.

B. Between Blame and Punishment

1. Rescuing Blame—Generally

Addressing blame is complicated by the wide variety of phenomena to which the term has been attached. We might avoid the 'what is blame' debate here by conceding at the outset that there is a wide set of phenomena which the term might capture, and which can be broadly referred to as 'blame-related phenomena'. On one end of the spectrum of such phenomena lie cognitive judgements of blameworthiness. On most accounts, these do not count as blame but are rather a pre-condition for (sincere) blaming, given that one might judge another to be blameworthy while refraining from blaming her. Judgements of blameworthiness are epistemic, liable to standard epistemic fittingness conditions, and are not subject to substantial scrutiny insofar as they are true, that is, insofar as they correctly represent the fact of an agent's blameworthiness.[6] On the other end of the blame-related spectrum lie

[5] Gardner does not offer a comprehensive view of blame, so my exposition of his view involves something like 'anticipatory' reconstruction.

[6] See e.g. Pamela Hieronymi, 'The Force and Fairness of Blame' (2004) 18 *Philosophical Perspectives* 115, 127 (hereafter, Hieronymi, 'Force and Fairness'). Some have suggested that evaluative judgements of blameworthiness might nonetheless be governed by moral norms, insofar as we have control over what we attend to. See e.g. Gary Watson, 'Standing in Judgment', in Coates & Tognazzini (eds), *Blame: Its Nature and Norms* (OUP 2013).

harsh punishments, which insofar as they are condemnatory are blame-related, but which are generally understood to be subject to heavy burdens of justification. On most accounts, that punishment is in response to a blameworthy act may be a necessary condition for justified punishment, but it is far from sufficient for its justification. Between these two poles lie a series of phenomena that may be carved up in different ways which inhabit the primary territory of blame, including private and attitudinal forms of blame, reactive attitudes (emotions such as resentment and indignation), non-private expressions of blame, censure, condemnation, distancing, shunning, and up to and including harsh punishment.

Punishment's position at the high end of this spectrum has played a central role in the unfolding of the contemporary blame narrative. Accounting for blame has become deeply intertwined with the project of rescuing blame from punishment, where contemporary accounts of blame often attempt to paint blame as an integral part of moral life, while punishment is painted as the further, highly suspect, avoidable, voluntary imposition of suffering.[7] A stark contrast is drawn between blame and punishment, generally by thinning the phenomenon of blame to render it immune to the criticisms and justificatory requirements understood to apply to punitive actions and, on some accounts, to render it rationally uncriticizable. A case in point, for example, is views that understand blame to be a cognitive or evaluative phenomenon. If one takes the view that to blame is to make a cognitive or evaluative judgement of a particular kind, then the conclusion that it maintains a safe distance from punishment becomes fairly uncontroversial. Hieronymi's insistence, for example, that blame can primarily involve an evaluative judgement of a distinct and important kind appears to rest on the desire to defend a responsive phenomenon that need not be subject to the justificatory burdens that apply to punishment.[8]

This surgical approach is rejected by many, however, and far more central are approaches that attempt to retain the centrality of attitudes, activities, and behaviour to the phenomenon of blaming, though these too remain manifestly at pains to mark blame off from punishment in some other way. The influential Scanlonian approach, for example, offers an account whereby blaming consists in making relational adjustments that reflect impairments in the relations between the blamee and blamer, stripped of all the hostilities associated with condemnation and

[7] But see J.J.C. Smart, 'Free Will, Praise and Blame' (1961) 70 *Mind* 291; Gary Watson, 'Responsibility and the Limits of Evil' in F. Schoeman (ed.) *Responsibility, Character, and the Emotions* (CUP 1987). Strawson was not at pains to distinguish between the two, and in fact thought them tightly connected, though many of those who later took up his view part ways with Strawson on this point. P.F. Strawson, 'Freedom and Resentment' in Gary Watson (ed.) *Free Will* (2nd ed. OUP 2003), 90–91. See also Christopher Bennett, *The Apology Ritual* (CUP 2008).

[8] She aims to draw a conception of the force of blame that would render *some* forms of blaming immune from the 'target charge of unfairness'. See Hieronymi, 'Force and Fairness'. She does not, however, restrict the phenomenon of blame to the cognitive, and understands blame to be instantiated in reactive attitudes such as resentment, allowing throughout that blame might find its force in other features (beyond judgements of ill will) as well.

retribution.[9] Like Hieronymi, Scanlon takes his proposed conception of blame to isolate blame from the punitive, and thus to immunize blame from the justificatory burdens taken to apply to punishment.[10]

Throughout the literature, punishment's suspect status remains a central theme, driving much of the project of articulating both descriptive and normative accounts of the phenomenon of blame. Illustrative is Wallace's articulation of the project of carving out a space for blame. He writes that an essentially punitive account of blame 'deprives [it] of its legitimacy as a form of interpersonal behavior'.[11] To concede the punitivity of blame is apparently to concede its illegitimacy. Or so goes the common refrain pervasive throughout the contemporary literature, a version of which is taken up by Gardner, as we will soon see.

2. Rescuing Blame: Gardner

Though his motivations are distinct, Gardner follows this same pattern of argument, rescuing blame as it were from the phenomenon of punishment by restricting (defensible) blame to a private, internal phenomenon, though not one restricted to the cognitive.[12] Gardner rather understands blame to be a matter of holding or modifying certain attitudes. He writes: 'Blaming someone is taking the attitude towards her that befits her blameworthiness. It is losing faith in her, or losing admiration for her, or taking a dim view of her.'[13] While Gardner once thought these attitudes dispensable and unjustifiable, he is now poised to defend them as having an important role in 'the rational architecture of human life'.[14] Gardner's intention, however, is to remain a reproach-and-punishment sceptic—sceptical of the justifiability of outwards expressions of blame directed at the blamee, with all the hostility and harshness bound up with such expressions, while changing his view only with respect to his previously held 'private blame' scepticism. Instead, he is now open to becoming a 'blame enthusiast' so long as a safe distance can be maintained between private blame and the troublesome downstream outward responses and interactions that might follow.[15]

On Gardner's account, the private phenomenon he seeks to endorse consists in befitting attitudinal modifications given the blamee's blameworthiness, and he proposes a defence of such responses to blameworthy action: attitudes, he explains, should be judged by whether they befit their object, not by their aims or what they

[9] Scanlon, *Moral Dimensions*.

[10] These include constraints related to fairness, avoidability, and desert.

[11] Wallace, 'Dispassionate Opprobrium' (n 3) 348.

[12] For Gardner's reflection on the tight relationship between his blame scepticism and punishment abolitionism, see Gardner, 'Why Blame' (n 2) 28.

[13] Ibid 26.

[14] Ibid.

[15] Ibid 8.

achieve as in the case of actions, since attitudes do not have aims on his view. While solid judgements of blameworthiness thus for him lead naturally to a defence of such attitudinal modifications, which 'simply' befit their object,[16] they do not, on Gardner's view, lead naturally to a defence of the behavioural modifications that might equally follow. Private, that is, unexpressed, attitudinal blame is defensible. The public or, as Gardner puts it, 'expressed' side of directing blame at others—'expressions[s] of blame conveyed to the person who is blamed', namely, reproach and punishment, which might collectively be termed 'public blame'—escapes this defence.[17] While I do not deny the integrity of a distinction between attitudes and the standards by which they are to be judged, and actions and the relevant standards by which they should be judged,[18] there are a number of concerns to be raised in relation to where Gardner 'lands' on the question of blame. In the next section I argue that the position he promotes, in defence of private blame and opposition to public blame, belies a deep inconsistency.

C. Between Private and Public Blame

Blame, whatever its definition and contours, is an agent-directed and generally interpersonal phenomenon. In its non-self-directed form, it consists in a response of one agent to the perceived blameworthiness of another.[19] On Gardner's view, it consists in having a particular attitude, sentiment, or view of another that is markedly negative or entails a downgrading or dimming of one's attitude or view of the blameworthy agent. Private blame of this sort, on Gardner's view, is an important part of the rational architecture of human life and to be defended, whereas the activities that might be motivated by holding such an attitude, those that consist in the public side of blaming, remain subject to his prior scepticism. This view, however, is not limited to the methodological scepticism of proceeding with caution. Rather, like the other forms of blame scepticism discussed by Gardner (e.g. 'moral responsibility scepticism', 'judgement scepticism'), the scepticism he propounds invites *opposition* to blaming. The position however, which draws a line in the sand between the public and the private, raises worries that Gardner fails to reckon

[16] On Gardner's account, one may yet have reason to avoid blaming; but strictly speaking this would not be a reason against blaming, but a reason to take steps to rid one's self of the attitude. Gardner, ibid, 6–7.

[17] While one might privately express blame, e.g. in one's diary, Gardner is concerned with publicly expressed blame; this chapter follows suit, focusing on public blame, as opposed to private forms of blame (whether attitudinal, emotive, or expressed), that is directed at and *expressed to the blamee* (rather than to others).

[18] See Barry Maguire, 'There Are No Reasons for Affective Attitudes' 127 (2018) *Mind* 779–805.

[19] I set aside here the case of self-blame, which, though intra-personal rather than interpersonal, retains the feature of being directed *at* an agent *for* their blameworthiness. The chapter, however, does not address the unique case of self-blame, since the problem of the bifurcation of private and public blame is broadly irrelevant in this context.

with—for the interpersonal nature of blame, I suggest, renders its restriction to the private untenable.

If blame is a responsive attitude to the actions of others that entails a modification of our view of them, what would it mean to endorse a view that defends private forms of blaming while globally rejecting outwards expressions thereof? Presumably it would mean regularly endorsing negatively charged attitudes and views of others, without making this fact transparent to the other party to the relations through any outwards manifestations or expressions of these attitudinal changes. Notice that the view is not that one ought to forgive the blameworthy. Forgiveness may be a possibility where there is blame, but Gardner's suggestion is not that we should forswear the negative attitudinal responses we have where there is a sound judgement of blameworthiness. Rather, we are invited to hold onto these appropriate, negative attitudinal responses, which are befitting of their objects, though without giving voice or space to them within our interactions with the blamee. Yet such a *modus operandi*, which involves internally harbouring attitudes of blame while never bringing their existence or meaning to bear on the relations with those with whom we interact, seems not only psychologically straining, but also morally suspect.[20]

A first set of troubles that arises, primarily in the context of ongoing personal relations, might be articulated in terms of the lack of transparency, inauthenticity, or dishonesty involved in such a disconnect between one's inner and outer interpersonal life. To keep up a façade of mutual recognition that has in no way been impaired by the blameworthy action despite its actual impact on the blamer's own attitudes and conception of the blamee is to represent one's self as holding attitudes that one does not hold, while acting inconsistently with such attitudes for reasons that are not revealed to the blamee.[21] Though this may mean treating another better than might otherwise be warranted, it appears disrespectful to, as a matter of course, put on a charade of business as usual while harbouring justified negative views and attitudes one has no reason (and sees no reason) to reject. It precludes honest moral engagement with others and inhibits the ability to fully participate in valuable interpersonal relations,[22] which require mutually honest exchange.[23]

Consider the 'friend' who always greets you with a smile, has only good things to say, and is outwardly supportive of your actions and endeavours, yet in fact takes a rather dim view of you given his assessment of your blameworthiness on various

[20] At least in the case of moral blame. While many restrict blame to the case of relevant moral failures, Gardner's conception does not include such a restriction. The worries raised herein may be taken to be restricted to the moral context.

[21] This will be the case if there are interactions with the blamee, and not, e.g., in cases of absent-stranger blame or blaming someone from the past (who is in any event not a candidate for public blame as addressed herein).

[22] See Strawson, 'Freedom and Resentment'.

[23] While these concerns arise primarily in the context of ongoing personal relations, they generate grounds for objecting to Gardner's position.

occasions. This seems to be an inappropriate way of engaging with fellow rational moral agents. Yet if one is to retain the valuable negative attitudes while universally refraining from allowing them to find public expression in the interpersonal interactions with the blamee, it is unclear how this is to be avoided.

Moreover, to blame others attitudinally while universally stifling the public manifestations of blame is to restrict the blamee's role within the practice of blaming to that of being an *object* of blame. While the blamee's agency is not denied, as her agency is presupposed by the very judgements and attitudes involved in private blaming, such restriction to the private fails to more robustly *treat* the blamee as an agent: it fails to engage her agency and incorporate her into the practice of blaming, failing to accord significance to her responsiveness to the blaming attitudes which are directed towards her. It robs the blamee of opportunities to explain, apologize, or otherwise take up the demands of being *held* blameworthy. It focuses solely on the blamer's being in the right and accurately assessing the world—a self-oriented exercise—rather than on blame as an interpersonally significant exercise relevant to two, rather than a single, agent.[24] True enough, if one's blaming response is responsive to true facts about another's blameworthiness, this makes blaming unobjectionable in one respect: it is not 'unfitting' or 'misplaced'. Yet it remains vulnerable to the charge that there are substantive and procedural norms that are violated by failing to take the blamee to be even a potentially significant participant in the practice of blaming.

In some cases, it might further undermine the relations themselves, which given the bifurcated way in which they proceed—with standing opposition between the internal and external—cannot but be damaged by the lack of transparency involved. While relationships are not central to Gardner's preferred account of blame, for those views within which the justification, meaning, and significance of blame (and often blameworthiness) have everything to do with the value of interpersonal relations, if the endorsement of private blame and rejection of public blame will be destructive of the very relations within which blame is a part, this too matters to the sustainability of the view.[25]

Of course, Gardner does not reject addressing the actions of others, nor engaging in practices of accountability vis-à-vis wrongdoers that address agents' (basic) responsibility for their actions.[26] Quite the opposite. But blameworthiness

[24] This does not preclude involvement in being held responsible, as Gardner does not endorse a stance of scepticism towards holding others *responsible*, only towards holding them *blameworthy*. See below.

[25] In fact, where private blame is universally precluded from playing a role in the interpersonal space and interactions between the parties, which are to be sterilized against forms of expressed blame, reproach, or punishment (owing to the hostility or negativity they involve, yet without rejecting the private attitudes themselves), this may itself preclude a level of involvement with others that is an integral part of what makes such relations valuable. Cf. Strawson, 'Freedom and Resentment'.

[26] Thus responses such as those called for in tort—demanding compensation—and even demanding apology or agent regret might be available to the respondent, though not responses such as punishment, which are responsive to the fact of blameworthiness. For Gardner's conception of 'basic' responsibility, see e.g. 'The Mark of Responsibility' in *Offences and Defences* (OUP 2007); 'Relations of Responsibility'

picks out, as Gardner develops, a different property worthy of our attention than responsibility. Thus, if blameworthiness is an important property—and he says it is—that should change our evaluations and attitudes towards others in ways that are not called for by basic responsibility—as he thinks it should—the problem remains.

Gardner is aware of the concealment involved in the pattern of behaviour his view would endorse, and he in fact seems attracted to the idea of actively hiding one's blaming attitudes and emotions. He writes:

> One can be a blamer ... and yet not do anything to reveal or convey how one feels, or even that one blames, to the person blamed (or to anyone) ... Myself, I often make the effort (e.g. when dealing with a cold caller) and sometimes but not always I succeed.[27]

While his description is attractive when considered in the context of managing the excesses of blame (probably the correct diagnosis of the cold caller case), a point to which we will return, it is not at all attractive as a general portrait of interpersonal response and engagement, or lack thereof, if the attitudes themselves are in no way called into question. One could of course reject outward expressions of blame on the ground of the indefensibility of the underlying blaming judgement or attitudes, as might be proposed by moral responsibility sceptics and judgement sceptics who come out against public blame.[28] This, however, is not the view Gardner takes up. He is moved by the significance of blameworthiness, judgements of blameworthiness, and attitudes of blame. He defends these as fitting, even where we may have reason to manage them. But he resists extending this charitable defence (even at the level of *pro tanto* justifiability) to public blame. Yet in the context of blame, there seems to be a 'dynamic trajectory of unfolding events'[29] that runs from the evaluative to the attitudinal to the behavioural. And while reasons not to adopt certain attitudes or to express blame may interfere with this trajectory as often as not at the *local* level, *globally* severing this trajectory at the point at which private attitudes translate into public blame requires disregarding the blamee as an agential participant in the practice of blaming while recommending proceeding on a fragmented path,[30] one which is self-effacing in that it recommends a continuous

in *Crime, Punishment, and Responsibility* (OUP 2011); 'The Negligence Standard: Political not Metaphysical' (2017) 80 *Modern Law Review* 1; Gardner, 'Why Blame' (n 2).

[27] Here he is referring primarily to the way in which affective and public blame can come apart, but the same is true of attitudinal and public blame.

[28] See e.g. Derk Pereboom, *Living Without Free Will* (CUP 2011).

[29] To borrow a phrase from McGeer, 'Civilizing Blame' (n 1) 175.

[30] Cf. Michael Stocker, 'The Schizophrenia of Modern Ethical Theories' (1976) 73 *Journal of Philosophy*, 453–456.

struggle against acting on judgements and attitudes which one is on the other hand invited to endorse.

This is not to say that that public blame should not be kept in check, or that overriding reasons will not have an important role to play in determining how we should ultimately act.[31] There are surely many cases in which public blame is unwarranted or excessive or in which one ought not, all things considered, express blame, whether because public blame would be illegitimate, infelicitous, imprudent, self-righteous, cruel, or otherwise.[32] But it is to expose a fallacy in the point of view that takes itself to be able to endorse private blame while neatly escaping the punitive behaviours that follow.

In fact, it is not even clear that one *can* have the relevant blaming attitudes if the blame trajectory is severed. That is, there might be a tighter relationship between attitudes and dispositions to act than the suggested view allows. There are many who take attitudes to involve dispositions to act,[33] where non-contingently stifling the action tendency might place under question whether one has the relevant attitude at all.[34] Even if action tendencies are not constitutive elements of the relevant attitudes, having the relevant attitudes might at least commit one to be disposed to act in certain ways.

Consider the analogy drawn by Gardner between love and blame, both of which are to be judged (*qua* attitudes and emotions) by whether they befit their objects rather than by whether they achieve aims. Even if one ought, as Gardner intimates, to 'love the lovable' (and 'blame the blameworthy'), an emotion of love globally severed from any disposition to act (in ways that, e.g. per the literature on love, enhance proximity to the subject of love or benefit the subject, etc.) would seem to call into question the nature of the internal phenomenon itself. The principled management of downstream activities seems in such instances to be intimately connected to the attitude itself, in a way that is not acknowledged by a view that would endorse the internal while non-contingently rejecting all its external manifestations. Similarly, if private blame is treated as an attitude that ought never find outlet in the sphere of inter-agential interaction, it is not clear that the underlying attitude would remain intact.

[31] Nor does it mean that we should not recognize the value of dispositions—humility, epistemic stringency, generosity of interpretation, etc.—that would moderate blaming, though this is not the place to offer substantive arguments in their defence.

[32] There are further cases in which expressing blame is impossible because the blamee is unavailable or has ceased to exist. But this is different from endorsing a *standing* opposition to expressing justified attitudes.

[33] With respect to evaluative attitudes that are non-doxastic. See e.g. Nico Frijda, *The Emotions* (CUP 1986); Julien A. Deonna and Teroni Fabrice, *The Emotions: A Philosophical Introduction* (Routledge 2012); Andrea Scarantino, 'The Motivational Theory of Emotions' in D'Arms and Jacobson (eds), *Moral Psychology and Human Agency* (OUP 2014), who take this position with respect to emotions (as attitudes).

[34] The manifestation of a disposition is not generally required for the disposition to 'survive'. Yet the case of agent-directed attitudes of a certain kind may be distinctive here.

On communicative accounts, blame is itself understood to be an incipient form of moral address, one that implicitly makes a demand and calls for uptake, further complicating the recommended severing of the internal and external aspects of blame.[35] Yet even if one does not take this to be a constitutive feature of blame, and Gardner does not, it seems reasonable to wonder about the value and in fact 'role in the rational architecture of human life' of blaming attitudes that ought never find expression or seek uptake in interactions with the blamee.

In other words, regardless of where our descriptive commitments lie with respect to the phenomenon of blame, the normative commitments involved in endorsing the private attitudinal aspects thereof while globally rejecting its public manifestations seem to corrupt the very integrity of the private reactions themselves.

D. Public Blame's Punitivity

One might thus move to either reject the judgements and attitudes that underlie public blame,[36] or affirm the significance of such judgements, attitudes, and corresponding behaviour. But to insist on the indispensability of the former while refusing to let go of a substantively sceptical approach to the latter proves unstable. Why then does Gardner resist extending his newfound appreciation for blame to its public counterparts? Here we return to the relation between blame, in this case public blame, and punishment. Gardner appears sceptical about the project of rescuing expressed blame given its association with punishment. And I submit that Gardner is right to worry that if he passes positive judgement on public blame he is on the path to sanctioning punishment, despite efforts in the literature to deny this. That is, we can make sense of Gardner's resistance by recognizing the essentially punitive nature of public blame. To help motivate this point, I sketch an account of the punitivity of blame.[37] Nonetheless, I will suggest that appreciating this connection is insufficient to motivate the sceptical view on offer and that we can accommodate much of Gardner's normative worries about public blame by directing our opposition towards excessive and pathological blame, a phenomenon he is clearly very concerned with, rather than towards public blame itself.

[35] On McKenna's conversational theory, public blame is in fact explanatorily prior to its private counterpart. Michael McKenna, *Conversation and Responsibility* (OUP 2012). For other communicative views see e.g. Gary Watson, 'Responsibility and the Limits of Evil' (n 6); Stephen Darwall, *The Second-Person Standpoint* (HUP 2006); David Shoemaker, 'Moral Address, Moral Responsibility, and the Boundaries of the Moral Community' 118 (2007) *Ethics* 70.

[36] This is the path offered by Lacey and Pickard in the context of criminal punishment, which Gardner seeks to reject. N. Lacey and H. Pickard, 'From the Consulting Room to the Court Room? Taking the Clinical Model of Responsibility Without Blame into the Legal Realm' 33 (2013) OJLS 1 (hereafter Lacey and Pickard, 'Clinical Model'). See also Erin Kelly, *The Limits of Blame* (HUP 2018).

[37] This account is consistent with earlier proposed conceptions of blame e.g. those proposed by Strawson and Waston (see n 7), and inconsistent with much of the current literature on blame. But see C.E. Franklin, 'Valuing Blame' in *Blame* (OUP 2013).

Whatever blame is, insofar as blame is enacted or manifest in our interactions with the blamee, it is negatively charged, expressive of disapproval, and essentially burdensome.[38] Public blame is a negative response directed at and expressed to an agent for her blameworthy action. It involves the imposition of moral and non-moral burdens on blameworthy agents in response to their failures, and involves liability to suffering on the part of the blamee that is not merely a side-effect of the interaction. In terms of the moral burdens of blame, one is subject to a negative evaluative appraisal of the exercise of one's agency, of one's ill will or lack of respect towards others (or one's failure of sensitivity to reasons) as reflected in one's actions, that is captured by some accounts of the force or sting of blame. As many have argued, this is not merely unpleasant or unwelcome, but carries special moral significance for the blamee. One is also subject to non-moral burdens, which can include forms of deprivation, pain, suffering, and loss. This is an inherent feature of the imposition of the moral burdens of blame when rendered public irrespective of the particular blamee's subjective experience of such burdensome treatment.[39] A blamee might relish in the fact of being blamed, just as a homeless offender may welcome the bed and meal offered when imprisoned and fail to value the liberty she has been deprived of. In both cases, the burdensomeness of the response is not undermined by the idiosyncratic reception of such response on the part of the blamee. Rather, insofar as the response is intelligible as intentionally burdensome and unwelcome, and partly appropriate in virtue of such burdensomeness, this is sufficient for the response to count as burdensome in the relevant sense. Further, this burdensome aspect of public blame is not a contingent feature of the blaming response. It is no coincidence that blaming responses are burdensome in this way. Nor is it incidental to the relevant response. Rather, it is partly in virtue of its burdensomeness that the blaming response is rendered appropriate as a response to blameworthy action.

Blame and punishment are thus far closer than many might hope. Punishment consists in the deliberate imposition of burdens upon wrongdoers in response to their culpable wrongs. Its deliberateness and burdensomeness are the central features in virtue of which punishment is thought to be in need of justification.[40] Yet these are features that public blame shares with punishment.

This is not to deny the distinction between blame and punishment. Each of these phenomena can be descriptively captured by different accounts, and private blame is evidence that there is non-punitive blame.[41] But insofar as outward expressions

[38] The following should be taken to be restricted to moral blame. See n 20.

[39] Cf. Mckenna (n 35), 138–139; Christopher Bennett, 'The Varieties of Retributive Experience' (2002) 52 *Philosophical Quarterly*, 145–163.

[40] See e.g. Joel Feinberg, 'The Expressive Theory of Punishment' in *Doing and Deserving* (Princeton University Press 1970), 95–96; Mitchell Berman, 'Two Kinds of Retributivism' in Duff and Green (eds) *Philosophical Foundations of Criminal Law* (OUP 2011), 433.

[41] Some have expressed sympathy with the view that private blame itself can be harmful: see Dana Nelkin, 'Desert, Fairness, and Resentment' (2011) 16 *Philosophical Explorations*, 124; R. Jay Wallace, 'Moral Address' in Coates and Tognazzini (eds) *Oxford Studies in Agency and Responsibility* (vol. 5)

are a part of the valuable set of practices associated with blame, the question becomes whether public blame and punishment are different in relevant ways such that the justificatory burdens that apply to the two are fundamentally different and the latter a greater moral challenge than the former. There are of course some modes of punishment (e.g. those that violate basic human rights) which require further justification, given, for example, the harms they entail and the question of one's authority to impose a particular burden or deprivation. But the practice of punishment includes a broad range of burdens that might be imposed, and we should be careful not to import worries about particular means into worries about the practice of punishment itself.

This is to reject attempts in the literature to carve out a non-punitive space for public blame in order to allow blame to escape the suspicions and justificatory burdens generally directed at punishment. The most influential account that has attempted to achieve this is that offered by Tim Scanlon. Scanlon purports to offer an account of blame that does not restrict blame to a cognitive or private phenomenon, while allegedly leaving punitivity and sanction out of the picture. On Scanlon's account, to blame an agent is to judge the agent to have acted in a way that shows that person to hold attitudes that impair his or her relations with others and to modify one's attitudes, dispositions, and actions in ways that reflect the impairment. Such modifications might include downgrading one's trust and goodwill, ceasing to confide in another or seek their company, being less concerned for another, and so on. While these are unpleasant ways of treating others, Scanlon proposes that his conception of blame escapes the charge of punitivity because it entails mere appropriate modifications, reflective of the impairments already existent in the relations, whereby the blamee is 'merely' deprived of something that was extended conditional on non-impairment, without appeal to the goodness or intrinsic value of making the blamee worse off.[42]

Yet this conclusion is too quick. Blaming responses, even Scanlon-style, are negative, burdensome responses, within which the burdensome or deprivational nature of the relevant response is not merely a contingent feature of the response, but partly constitutive of what makes the relevant response appropriate. That is, one intends a response to culpable action that is burdensome, which, were it not, would fail to be an appropriate (blaming) response. Irrespective of whether one takes the involved burdens, deprivations, or suffering to be intrinsically valuable, it remains a constitutive element of the response intended, as a response to the culpable wrongdoing.[43] In other words, when we actively blame, we react in an

(OUP 2019), 92. Relatedly, though outside the context of blame, Keller has argued that what others believe of you may constitutively contribute to your wellbeing. Simon Keller, 'Belief for Someone Else's Sake' (2018) 46 *Philosophical Topics*, 19–36.

[42] See Scanlon, *Moral Dimensions* (n 6), 187–188.

[43] Scanlon makes much of the fact that the phenomenon of blame generally refers to the deprivation of goods that are not unconditionally owed—to which one is not *entitled*. Yet, even if this were true, it

intentional way, which is non-incidentally burdensome, in response to wrongdoing, *for* such wrongdoing, and which thus is punitive.[44]

The recharacterization of blame thus fails to rescue the public side of blaming from punitivity. And this will be true on any account that defends public rather than merely cognitive or private blame. This means both that we should question the claim that public blame should be subject to lesser justificatory burdens than many forms of punishment, despite protestations to the contrary, but also that to the extent that one has successfully defended public blaming, one has already cleared a path towards the justification of punishment.

E. Rescuing Public Blame

The relationship between public blame and punishment is thus one Gardner *should* be concerned with. To the extent that one defends public blame, one is defending a fundamentally punitive response. So Gardner is right to be on guard against jumping too quickly from a defence of the private to a defence of the public side of blaming. Public blame involves exposing others to burdens and harms, and not just incidentally, but deliberately so. There will be heavy justificatory burdens that apply: those that apply to punishment, generally construed.

Yet while this seems right as far as it goes, it is not enough to get us to the antagonistic position to public blame to which Gardner is sympathetic. That something bears a heavy burden of justification is insufficient to show it is unjustifiable. Yet Gardner repeatedly suggests that public blame might be excusable, though not justifiable. What he means by this, relying on his own conception of justification and excuse, is that when one publicly blames, one may be justified in believing that

does not distinguish blame from punishment. Punishment is not restricted to stripping another of unconditional entitlements. Further, and more importantly, it can be wrong to deprive another of something that is not unconditionally owed: even if not unconditionally owed, relational obligations, such as promissory obligations, can nonetheless be owed such that it would be wrongful to deprive others of relevant goods in the absence of reason or justification, while 'desert' or something like it might precisely offer the relevant justification for depriving another of such goods. Thus, the conditionality Scanlon appeals to is beside the point.

A further feature that has been appealed to in order to ground the non-punitive character of blame has been the 'harshness' of punishment. But if harshness is to do the relevant work it is undertheorized and too often invoked without further explanation. There are milder and harsher modes of blame and milder and harsher modes of punishment. This is not to deny the relevance of harshness to the normative analysis; it is only to question whether it is the distinctive mark of punishment as opposed to blame. After all, expressed blame can itself be harsh, and insofar as either a particular blaming or punishing response is harsh this may raise the bar for the justification of the response, but this will be true of both.

[44] One might think that punishment must be intended to impose suffering, at least if it is to be retributive. This too is false. See e.g. Bill Wringe, 'Must Punishment be Intended to Cause Suffering?' (2013) 16 *Ethical Theory and Moral Practice*, 863–877; Leora Dahan Katz, 'Response Retributivism: Defending the Duty to Punish' (2021) 40 *Law and Philosophy*, 585–615; Andrei Poama, 'Punishment Without Pain' (2015) 5 *Philosophy and Public Issues*, 97.

which drove one to act ('[one has] reasons for thinking she had reasons to do as she did'), but there are no undefeated reasons in favour of the action in the offing to prevail over the reasons against acting ('reasons for doing whatever she did').[45] If there were, the action would be justifiable.

Why resist the prospect of justification? Gardner would certainly not deny that there can be a wide variety of reasons in favour of public blame. Expressing blame might be 'cathartic or fun', help the blamer move on, allay the aggressive reactions of third parties, facilitate the repair of the relations between the parties, or be conducive to some other (valuable) aim. In exploring an action's justifiability, Gardner makes clear that any reason that might count in its favour, however weighty or trivial, is to be taken into account.[46]

But perhaps part of the story is Gardner's resistance to the non-instrumental value of public blame. Reference to the fittingness of public blame is nowhere to be found in Gardner's discussion of reproach and punishment, despite repeated references to the fittingness of judgements of blameworthiness as well as private blame.[47] And while fittingness may be insufficient for justification, it should clearly play a role if the response is indeed fitting.

It is in fact hard to see how one can assert the fittingness of judgements, attitudes, and emotions of blame without countenancing the fittingness of the responses that render such interpersonal responses robustly interpersonal (even if ultimately one is drawn to the view that these will not turn out to be, all things considered, justified). Yet Gardner remains silent about this possibility. This is consistent with his earlier work on punishment. In the final chapter of *Offences and Defences*, in discussing his idiosyncratic view on the justification of punishment needing all the help it can muster, non-instrumental reasons in favour of punishment are absent from the list of reasons he offers which might lend a hand to the justificatory project.[48] While his sceptical view is further nourished by worries about public blame's

[45] It will be further justified if one acts on those undefeated reasons. John Gardner, 'Justifications and Reasons' in Simester and Smith (eds) *Harm and Culpability* (Clarendon 1996), 103; John Gardner, *Offences and Defences* (OUP 2007), 227 (hereafter Gardner, 'Offences and Defences').

[46] See e.g. Gardner, 'Offences and Defences' (n 45), 214–215. Perhaps on Gardner's view all such reasons are excluded. This seems like an exaggerated position, and in any event one that would have to be explicitly defended as it puts the cart before the horses.

[47] Gardner entertains the possibility that blaming emotions may be fitting, but does not go so far as to entertain that the expression of blame may be as well. Gardner, 'Why Blame' (n 4), 26.

[48] Gardner, 'Offences and Defences' (n 45), 213–238. Per Gardner's view, a prime reason in favour of punishment that might be appealed to in order to vindicate the institution, when added to all other reasons in favour, is rooted in its displacement function. So there is in his earlier work clear openness to justification of reprobative punishment. (Though even then he says, focusing on the harsher forms of criminal punishment, that '[o]ne needs to pray in aid all of the valuable functions of criminalizing and punishing people in order to get even close to an adequate justification': ibid, 203.) But notice that the substance of this justification is that punishment is lent potential justificatory force where it successfully displaces practices of public blame and retaliation, revealing an antagonism to such practices rather than support therefore, and a reliance on their unjustifiability to justify criminal law. As will be discussed below, however, it stands to reason that the instrumental value of punishment as displacing relies primarily on the excesses of pathological blame rather than the defects of public blame itself.

counterproductivity (in line with Lacey and Pickard's attack on condemnatory punishment), his concern throughout seems to be one that countenances a deeper moral or rational vacancy to the whole enterprise of public blame.

An indication that Gardner might once have thought otherwise is found in a comment on Hart, where Gardner speculates that the expressive strand of retributivism may offer an account of some intrinsic value to be found in punishing.[49] Yet he quickly shuts down the potential any such intrinsic value might have when he suggests that even if the expressive retributivist route pans out, the intrinsic disvalue of suffering, à la Hart and Bentham, would quickly dwarf any such value. *This* then seems to be his position on reproach and punishment: that whatever value they may have, or whatever reasons in favour might apply, these are defeated by the reasons against, whether due to absence of sufficient reason in favour, or the weight of standing reasons against. Yet Gardner does not provide an argument in favour of this position. Rather, it seems his abolitionist tendencies—which, he tells us in a wonderfully characteristic moment of honesty, had previously unhealthily nourished his private blame scepticism—in fact continued to nourish his public blame scepticism as well, determining in advance that the balance of reasons should come out against reproach and punishment.[50]

While his suggestion is that we should embrace private blame and lay the 'blame' on public blame, it seems that much of his actual concern is not with public blame itself, but with the excesses of public blame. As Gardner writes, 'The problem, in short, is not so much that we live in a "blame culture" but that we live in a "call-out culture" where accusation, reproach, censure, and punishment run wildly out of control and can no longer be managed back into proportion by mediating institutions such as the criminal courts'.[51] He worries about the mob's excesses and populist reproach and punishment. And he is no doubt right to worry about these. They display wild disproportionality in reproach and punishment, inadherence to even the most modest epistemic standards, inattention to standing, a tendency towards cruelty and unwarranted harshness, and many other vices. But the answer is not the eradication of blame and blaming punishment.[52] It is reining blaming in to its proper proportions.[53] We thus should not take these pathologies to rule out public blame's justifiability, despite Gardner's invitation to scepticism.

[49] John Gardner, 'Introduction' in H.L.A. Hart, *Punishment and Responsibility* (OUP 2018), xxix. In the introduction, Gardner further notes that retributive reasons might suffice to justify some minor punishments.

[50] Gardner, 'Why Blame' (n 4), 27–28.

[51] Ibid.

[52] As Lacey and Pickard's thesis, to which John's paper is a response, recommends. Lacey and Pickard, 'Clinical Model' (n 36). See similarly, Kelly, *Limits of Blame* (n 27); Martha Nussbaum, *Anger and Forgiveness* (OUP 2016).

[53] Cf. Scanlon: 'Blame can be carried to excess, but the complete rejection of blame would rule out important relations with others. Moreover, this rejection itself is likely to involve objectionable attitudes of superiority or inferiority.' Scanlon, *Moral Dimensions* (n 9), 168.

Gardner's scepticism is no doubt motivated by a noble suspicion of harshness and hostility. But in his attempt to hold back the floodgates of excess harshness and hostility he aims at the wrong point on the map as the relevant stopping point for a defence of blame's indispensability. 'Blame itself', in Gardner's own words, 'is not the main problem.' Yet this is not because we have come up with a sufficiently contrived philosophical conception of blame that allows us to avoid the negative and burdensome aspects of blame, or because we have restricted our defence to private blame sans punitivity. It is rather because the negative and burdensome aspects of blame can play as indispensable a role in our social and relational lives as the negative appraisals and attitudes involved in private blame. Or, in Gardner's preferred idiom, insofar as human life is not purely internal—and a good life surely is not—public blame is as much a part of the rational architecture of human life as private blame. And while this is not the place to offer a defence of public blame, it is the place to point out that while we should be vigilant with respect to the pathologies of blame and not blind ourselves to the ways in which even justified blame tends towards excess,[54] offering a defence of public blame is consistent with worrying about proceeding hesitantly in its deployment, whether because of doubt that blame is in fact warranted or because of careful attendance to potential overriding reasons not to blame.

Gardner's evolved approach recognizes this indispensability of responsive blame, while cautiously offering a defence of the private that does not extend to the public. But while the motivations for reining in his defence are laudable, they overextend, and further lead to a position that involves deep tensions in its divergent relation to the private and the public. As above, one cannot get away with a wholehearted endorsement of private blaming, while rejecting *tout court* the expression it finds in interpersonal behaviours and activities. Gardner must either give up the indiscriminate rejection of the punitive or alternatively give up the ability to fully endorse an ethic of blame. And while he may opt for the latter, I suggest that he would have done well to push his defence further and count public blaming practices among those that are defensible and valuable, dissolving the concerns raised above that militate against drawing a line in the sand between the private and the public, while insisting that we not mistake the defensibility of public blame for its all-things-considered justification. On many occasions it will not be right to blame, but on many others it will be appropriate to respond in this fitting, if burdensome, way.

[54] As Victoria McGeer has eloquently put it: 'No normative theory worth its salt can afford to ignore the real empirical nature of the sorts of beings to which it is meant to apply.' McGeer, 'Civilizing Blame' (n 1), ch. 4, 187–188.

8

Blame and Punishment: The Difference Duty Makes

Michelle Madden Dempsey[*]

When it comes to blaming and punishing, what difference does it make if the blame and punishment are in response to a breach of duty rather than simply a failure to conform to an ordinary reason? Put in John Gardner's terms, what difference does it make if the action was 'a wrong', 'wrongful', 'wrongdoing'—or if it was simply 'doing the wrong thing' (aka 'a mistake')?[1] According to Gardner, one's action can be blameworthy even if one commits only a mistake, not a wrong.[2] However, when it comes to punishment, things are different. Or so says Gardner: 'The only actions that deserve to be punished', he claims, 'are *both* wrongful [breaches of duty] *and* blameworthy'.[3] In this chapter, I start by agreeing with Gardner that breach of duty is not necessary when it comes to blameworthiness. I then argue, *contra* Gardner, that breach of duty is *also* not necessary when it comes to punishment-deservedness. Finally, I argue that breach of duty *does* make a difference when it comes to *standing* to blame and punish.

A. The Difference Duty Makes: Some Preliminaries

Before jumping into the argument, it is worth briefly outlining the difference between a duty and an ordinary reason. Duties are reasons with special scope and force.[4] Their scope is categorical, which means they apply to you irrespective of

* My thanks to Sandra Marshall for serving as a respondent to an early draft during the December 2019 workshop on this volume, and to Leora Dahan Katz, Antony Duff, James Edwards, and Kate Greasley for detailed comments on later drafts.

1 To be clear, Gardner reserves the terms 'a wrong', 'wrongful', and 'wrongdoing' to refer to breach of duty and uses the terms 'doing the wrong thing' and 'making a mistake' to refer to an unjustified failure to conform to an ordinary reason. John Gardner, 'Wrongs and Faults' in Andrew Simester (ed) *Appraising Strict Liability* (OUP 2005) 55 (hereafter Gardner, 'Wrongs and Faults'); John Gardner, 'Why Blame?' in Iyiola Solanke (ed), *On Crime, Society, and Responsibility in the Work of Nicola Lacey* (OUP 2021) 85 (hereafter Gardner, 'Why Blame?'). I will follow those conventions here.

2 Gardner, 'Why Blame?' (n 1) 85.

3 Gardner, 'Wrongs and Faults' (n 1) 80.

4 John Gardner and Timothy Macklem, 'Reasons' in Scott Shapiro and Jules Coleman (eds), *The Oxford Handbook of Jurisprudence and Philosophy of Law* (OUP 2004) (hereinafter Gardner and Macklem, 'Reasons').

Michelle Madden Dempsey, *Blame and Punishment: The Difference Duty Makes* In: *From Morality to Law and Back Again*. Edited by: Michelle Madden Dempsey and François Tanguay-Renaud, Oxford University Press.
 DOI: 10.1093/oso/9780198860594.003.0008

your personal goals. Their force is mandatory, which means they exclude (at least some) of the reasons you may have not to conform to the reason the duty gives you.[5] For example, if I'm invited to a conference in a beautiful location, that is a weighty (but ordinary) reason to accept the invitation, but I have no duty to accept the invitation. Once I accept, however, I'm duty-bound to attend. So, if the conference is on criminal law and I've changed my personal goals to focus my scholarly energies on private law, the categorical nature of duty means that my new goals cannot get me off the hook—I still have a duty to attend the conference in virtue of my promise to attend. Moreover, consider a case where, after accepting the first invitation, I'm invited to another conference in an even more beautiful location. That is a weighty reason to skip the first conference and attend the second one. Yet, in virtue of the mandatory force of my duty to attend the first conference, such a reason is excluded from my rational horizons. I cannot justify my breach of duty by acting for such reasons. This is so even if the ordinary reasons in favour of attending the second conference are much weightier than the reasons in favour of attending the first conference (say, in addition to being in a more beautiful location, attending the second conference will also provide the opportunity to visit with family who live in the area). When duties are in play, ordinary reasons do not simply compete in terms of weight—at least some countervailing reasons are excluded by the mandatory force of one's duty.[6]

We will revisit the difference between duties and ordinary reasons below, in explaining how breach of duty impacts standing to blame and punish (section D). But, first, let us review Gardner's explanation of why breach of duty is not necessary for blameworthiness (section B) and explain why it is *also* not necessary for deserved punishment (section C).

B. The Road to Blameworthiness

For Gardner, being blameworthy is a matter of being rationally underresponsive. Blameworthiness consists of non-conformity to a reason, without justification or excuse. That is, at every turn along the road to blameworthiness, the actor either failed to recognize or underestimated the force of the reasons that applied to him.[7]

[5] In Joseph Raz's terminology regarding their force, duties are 'protected reasons'. Joseph Raz, *Practical Reason and Norms* (2nd edn, OUP [1975] 1990) 90–97 (hereinafter Raz, *Practical Reason and Norms*). See further discussion below in section D.

[6] Throughout, I will continue to use the phrase 'ordinary reason' to refer to a non-categorical, non-mandatory reason.

[7] Gardner, 'Wrongs and Faults' (n 1) 75–76. This abbreviated account leaves out the requirement of basic responsibility, which in my somewhat tortured metaphor of driving along the road to blameworthiness is probably best understood as the car that one drives. On basic responsibility, see John Gardner, *Offences and Defences* (OUP 2007) 177–200 (hereinafter Gardner, *Offences and Defences*). The 'turns in the road' metaphor is not meant to imply a time gap, as if one *first* fails to conform to a reason

At the first turn, the actor failed to conform to a reason (not to φ) without justification, which is to say he φ'ed and either lacked an undefeated reason to φ, or had one or more undefeated reasons to φ, but did not act *for* any of them.[8] At the next turn, the actor lacked an excuse for his unjustified φ-ing, which is to say he unreasonably misjudged the existence or force of reasons to φ (incorrectly treating such reasons as if they existed when they did not, or as if they were undefeated when they were not), or ignored or was insufficiently responsive to the force of reasons not to φ (incorrectly treating such reasons as if they were defeated, when they were not).[9]

Importantly, on Gardner's view, the road to blameworthiness can begin with *either* a breach of duty (obligation) or a simple failure to conform to a first-order reason.[10] In his later work, Gardner made the point explicitly: 'Some people associate blameworthiness with breach of an obligation. But that is too narrow.' Drawing on the example of missing the last train home (a hypothetical we will call *Train*), Gardner explains how one can be blameworthy without breaching a duty:

> [Y]ou have only yourself to blame for missing the last train home. You had no obligation [duty] to catch the last train home or to get home at all. Nobody is waiting for you. But staying that extra few minutes at the pub was a stupid mistake. The only reason to stay (one last drink) was easily outweighed, hence defeated, by the main reason for leaving (one last train). That puts you, so to speak, in blame's way.[11]

To better understand the category of blameworthy but not wrongful action, let us consider Gardner's example of a parent taking her children mountaineering.[12] As Gardner observes (and as I am willing to stipulate), 'one has a weighty reason not to take one's children mountaineering' but there is no *duty* not to do so. That is, if one

and *then* (later) lacks an excuse. It is simply meant to clarify the distinct steps in Gardner's analysis of blameworthiness. My thanks to Antony Duff for pressing this point.

[8] On Gardner's account, it may be better to think of justification as involving two turns: whether the action is justifiable (which turns on whether the actor *had* an undefeated reason) and whether the actor is justified all-things-considered (which turns on whether the actor acted *for* an undefeated reason): Gardner, 'Wrongs and Faults' (n 1) 63. '[I]t is a basic principle of practical rationality that one should always act for some undefeated reason': Gardner, *Offences and Defences* (n 7) 100.

[9] Gardner, 'Wrongs and Faults' (n 1) 75. See also Gardner, *Offences and Defences* (n 7) 121–139. The 'gist of [the lack of] excuses' for Gardner is not merely a matter of misjudging the existence or force of defeated reasons or being insufficiently responsive to the force of undefeated reasons. It is a matter of failing to live up to normative expectations which apply to one's roles in life. But that wrinkle need not delay us here. No matter the particular standard of excuse that applies, the gist of blameworthiness is being rationally underresponsive.

[10] Gardner uses the terms duty and obligation interchangeably. Gardner, 'Wrongs and Faults' (n 1) 7.

[11] Gardner, 'Why Blame?' (n 1) 85.

[12] The example appears in Gardner's discussion of 'fault anticipating wrongs' in Gardner, 'Wrongs and Faults' (n 1) 67–70, and Gardner, *Offences and Defences* (n 7) 152. Here, there is no need to attend to the fault-anticipating wrong Gardner identifies in those discussions (taking one's children mountaineering recklessly or negligently).

has an undefeated reason to take one's children mountaineering, one may permissibly do so without breaching any duty. Still, in doing so, one does act against the weighty reason one has *not* to take one's children mountaineering. If one's failure to conform to that reason is to be justified, one must act for an undefeated reason. Consider parents who have reasons on both sides. On the 'don't do it' side, there are reasons such as 'risk of injury' and 'expense'; on the 'do it' side, there are reasons such as 'enhancing the parent–child relationship' or 'cultivating a love of nature in one's children'. Assume these reasons are all undefeated, such that the parents could either take their children mountaineering or not. Either way, they're failing to conform to an ordinary reason, since there are ordinary reasons on both sides. So, either way, their action calls for justification. If they act for one of the undefeated reasons we've already surveyed, they are justified all-things-considered, and thus not blameworthy. If they decline the trip for undefeated reasons of safety, they would be justified and thus not blameworthy. Indeed, since they would be justified all-things-considered, we never even reach the question of excuse. However, if they decline the trip for a defeated reason (say, because they incorrectly believed their children would be better off spending the weekend studying for an upcoming exam rather than out in nature) their action is not justified, but it is probably excused, and thus not blameworthy.[13] The same structure of analysis applies if the parents decide to go ahead with the trip. If they do so for an undefeated reason (enhancing the parent–child relationship) they are justified and thus not blameworthy, whereas if they take the trip for a non-existent or defeated reason which they reasonably believed was undefeated (say, the belief that exposing children to dangerous circumstances builds courage), then they are excused.

Now consider Karen, who takes her children mountaineering to get photos that (she hopes) will impress followers of her Instagram account.[14] Let us call this hypothetical *Instagram*. While Karen's reason might genuinely weigh in favour of the trip, it is easily defeated by the safety-reasons not to take the trip. Thus, if Karen takes her children mountaineering to get the photos, she acts for a defeated reason and is thus not justified. Is she blameworthy? Per Gardner, that depends on whether her failure to be sufficiently responsive to the reasons in play (overestimating the weight of Instagram-reasons, while underestimating the weight of safety-reasons) was itself justified.[15] If so, she has an excuse. If not, she is blameworthy. Specifically, on Gardner's account of excuses, the answer depends on whether Karen lived up to the proper normative expectations which apply to Karen's role (parent). Let us

[13] The question of excuse would turn on whether, in misjudging the relative weight of reasons of studying vs nature, they failed to live up to normative expectations which apply to their role (parent). Presumably, this misjudgement is not such a failure and thus they are not blameworthy.

[14] To translate into Gardner's terminology, if the reason has genuine weight it is a 'guiding reason' and when Karen acts *for* that reason it becomes her 'explanatory reason'. On guiding and explanatory reasons, see Gardner, *Offences and Defences* (n 1) 91.

[15] Gardner, *Offences and Defences* (n 1) 121–139.

stipulate that Karen fails to live up to these expectations in taking her children mountaineering to get Instagram photos. As such, her action is blameworthy. All of this is true, despite the fact that she breaches no duty in taking her children mountaineering.

Finally, consider Beth, who declines to take her children mountaineering (thus failing to conform to the ordinary reasons she has to do so), because she wanted to stay home to binge-watch her favourite television show. Let us call this hypothetical *Binge-Watching*, and stipulate that Beth's reason for staying home was defeated. Thus, her failure to conform to the reasons in favour of going is unjustified all-things-considered. Was it blameworthy? Again, on Gardner's account, that depends on whether, by acting for 'binge-watching' reasons over 'relationship-enhancement' and 'nature-appreciation' reasons, she failed to live up to the relevant normative expectations that attach to her role (parent). Assuming she has failed in this way, not taking her children mountaineering is thus blameworthy. All of this is true, again, despite the fact that Beth breaches no duty in staying home.

The *Train*, *Instagram*, and *Binge-Watching* cases each illustrate a blameworthy failure to conform to an ordinary reason (a blameworthy mistake) without any breach of duty. On this, Gardner and I agree. But things are different, so Gardner claims, when it comes to punishment. For punishment to be deserved, he claims, it must be inflicted in response to a breach of duty.[16] To understand where Gardner and I part ways, let us examine his account of deserved punishment.

C. Deserved Punishment and Regret

Regret is key to understanding Gardner's account of deserved punishment.[17] When one fails to conform to a reason, 'the reason does not evaporate ... [i]t still makes its force felt as a reason for [one] to regret' one's non-conformity.[18] However, not everyone experiences the rational regret that follows from a failure to conform to a reason. Some people are 'rationally underresponsive' to this regret. As noted above, blameworthiness is precisely a matter of being rationally underresponsive.

According to Gardner, '[o]ur lives should feel as good, but only as good, as they are'.[19] Let us call this *Gardner's Maxim*. Insofar as one fails to conform to the reasons one has, one's life goes less well. It is a less good life. '[O]ne's success in seeing reasons, and in using them, and in negotiating conflicts among them is [not

[16] Strictly, Gardner claims it must be imposed in response to *supposed* wrongdoing, but that point need not distract us here. Gardner, 'Wrongs and Faults' (n 1) 73.

[17] For criticism of the role of regret in Gardner's account of deserved blame and punishment, see John Stanton-Ife, 'Strict Liability: Stigma and Regret' (2007) OJLS 151.

[18] 'Regret is the rational response to any measure of non-conformity with any reason.' Gardner, 'Wrongs and Faults' (n 1) 58.

[19] Gardner, 'Wrongs and Faults' (n 1) 75.

only] an instrument of better living, but also a constituent of it.'[20] One's life may still *feel* good (that is, it may be a good life in terms of its hedonic quality)—but insofar as one fails to conform to reasons, it is a less good life in terms of its rational quality. When the hedonic quality of one's life (how good it feels) exceeds its rational quality (how good it is), then *Gardner's Maxim* is violated.

One way in which the scales between the hedonic and rational quality of our lives remain balanced is by feeling regret for our blameworthy actions. In virtue of their rational underresponsiveness, Gardner explains, blameworthy actors are 'prone to suffer less regret than is apt', and thus the blameworthy person 'is prone to live a life that feels better than it is'.[21]

Punishment, 'the deliberate infliction of suffering or deprivation', is another way to balance the scales between the hedonic and rational quality of our lives.[22] It gives blameworthy actors 'something extra to regret' beyond their blameworthy actions. To the extent that they do not regret their blameworthy action *qua* blameworthy, 'they regret it *qua* bearer of unwelcome consequences for them'.[23] Thus, punishment, when deserved, goes some way toward satisfying *Gardner's Maxim*, by making it the case that 'people's lives feel as good, but only as good, as they are'.[24]

Consider deserved punishment in the cases set out in the previous section. In *Train*, recall, the rider (let's call him Tom) misses the last train home because he stayed too late at the pub. While he had no duty to catch that train, he lacked an undefeated reason *not* to catch the train. As Gardner explains, 'The only reason to stay (one last drink) was easily outweighed, hence defeated, by the main reason for leaving (one last train)'.[25] Tom was underresponsive to the rational force of the reasons he had. His missing the train was not merely the wrong thing to do (a mistake), it was also *blameworthy*, despite the fact that it was not a wrong (it breached no duty). If Tom beats himself up for having made such a stupid mistake, his doing so can serve as a form of deserved, self-administered punishment.[26] Beating oneself up (giving oneself a 'hard time') for one's blameworthy mistakes is a form of 'self-critical regret known as *remorse*'.[27] As Gardner correctly explains, 'remorse lies at the borderline between regret, suffered spontaneously, and punishment, inflicted deliberately'.[28] When remorse takes the form of self-inflicted punishment in response to one's blameworthy action, it can serve as a form of deserved

[20] The phrases 'less well' and 'better living' here are meant to refer to rational success—a life that goes less well or better in terms of rationality. They do not refer to a life going less well or better in terms of material wealth, comfort, or hedonic pleasures. Gardner, 'Wrongs and Faults' (n 1) 75.
[21] Gardner, 'Wrongs and Faults' (n 1) 76.
[22] Gardner, 'Wrongs and Faults' (n 1) 75.
[23] Gardner, 'Wrongs and Faults' (n 1) 75.
[24] Gardner, 'Wrongs and Faults' (n 1) 75.
[25] Gardner, 'Why Blame' (n 1) 85.
[26] Gardner, 'Wrongs and Faults' (n 1) 77.
[27] Gardner, 'Wrongs and Faults' (n 1) 76.
[28] Gardner, 'Wrongs and Faults' (n 1) 76.

punishment.[29] This explanation is enough to establish that punishment (at least in the form of remorse) can be deserved in a case such as Tom's, without the extra requirement that Tom breached a duty by missing the train.[30]

Self-administered punishment is especially apt if one does not happen to experience any suffering or deprivation that would otherwise balance the scales between the hedonic and rational quality of one's life. In the ordinary course, we would expect that Tom's missing the last train would cause him suffering or deprivation without anyone (including Tom) needing to deliberately inflict that suffering or deprivation. For example, in the normal course of things, Tom is likely to have to pay for a taxi to get home (deprivation of money) and get a poor night's sleep (suffering) due to getting home later than planned. These negative consequences, while not strictly punishment since they are not deliberately inflicted, are a close cousin of punishment, often referred to as karma.[31] When Tom must pay for the taxi and awakes groggy in the morning, the correct understanding of what happened is 'he got what he deserved'. Indeed, if Tom avoided these consequences (say, the train comes back to the station and he's allowed to board, or a neighbour happens to drive by while he's hailing a taxi and offers him a free lift home), we would correctly be inclined to say that Tom got lucky—luckier than he deserved.

So, too, in *Instagram* and *Binge-Watch*—neither Karen nor Beth breached a duty—but Karen was blameworthy for going mountaineering with her children, and Beth was blameworthy for not going mountaineering with her children. They should both experience regret for their blameworthy actions, but in virtue of their rational underresponsiveness, they are not prone to do so. In the absence of spontaneously regret or bad karma, both Karen and Beth deserve to be remorseful—to beat themselves up (at least a bit) for their selfishness.

In 'Wrongs and Faults', Gardner explains deserved punishment in the terms set out above, but he also includes a requirement that deserved punishment must be in response to a blameworthy *wrong* (breach of duty), rather than merely a blameworthy *mistake*. In discussing the matter he poses a question, which he calls the 'second mystery of deserved punishment': 'Why isn't fault [blameworthiness] alone sufficient [for deserved punishment], let alone wrongdoing?'[32] After posing the question, however, he never presents a clear argument to explain why he thinks breach of duty is required for deserved punishment. Given *Gardner's Maxim*,

[29] Gardner, 'Wrongs and Faults' (n 1) 76–77. On Gardner's view, which I share, if self-critical regret is suffered spontaneously, it does not count as punishment. Rather, if Tom spontaneously experiences remorse, he is (finally) showing himself to be cured of his rational underresponsiveness (at least temporarily, with respect to this particular blameworthy action). Where remorse is deliberately inflicted, by giving oneself a 'hard time' or 'beating oneself up', it constitutes self-administered punishment.

[30] There are, of course, cases of undeserved, pathological remorse. As Gardner observes, '"I regret that I spent so much time regretting what I did" would be an intelligible, if sad, deathbed utterance'. Gardner, 'Wrongs and Faults' (n 1) 75, fn 48.

[31] See Raff Donelson, 'Natural Punishment' (2022) 100 *North Carolina Law Review* 557, 567–568.

[32] Gardner, 'Wrongs and Faults' (n 1) 75.

however, the correct answer to Gardner's question seems clear: fault (blameworthiness) alone *can* be sufficient for deserved punishment—there's no need for wrongdoing (breach of duty). More precisely, blameworthy mistakes *can* be deserving of punishment, insofar as the punishment satisfies *Gardner's Maxim*, by making it the case that the blameworthy person's life *feels* only as good as it *is*.[33]

Another way to put the thought is to revisit the metaphor of the road to blameworthiness from section B. Recall, Gardner claimed that 'the only actions that deserved to be punished are both *wrongful* and *blameworthy*'.[34] That is to say, he claimed deserved punishment turned on two considerations: (1) how one got started down the road to blameworthiness (breaching a duty); and (2) that one eventually reached the point of blameworthiness (their breach of duty was neither justified nor excused). Yet, his account of deserved punishment tells a different story. For Gardner, the deservedness of punishment turns on whether one's rational underresponsiveness makes it the case that one's life feels better than it is. If punishment can make it the case that *Gardner's Maxim* will be satisfied, then the punishment is deserved. From this we can see that the deservedness of punishment does not depend on how one got *started* down the road to blameworthiness. One can start down that road either way: by committing a wrong or making a mistake. Rather, the deservedness of punishment depends on the turns one's life takes as one *continues* along the road, after the point of blameworthiness. At the point of blameworthiness, one's life is blemished by one's faulty action. To that extent, it is a less good life. The deservedness of punishment depends on what happens next. As one carries on down the road, does one's life come to *feel* only as good as it *is*? Does one experience an apt degree of spontaneous regret or suffer bad karma which makes it the case that *Gardner's Maxim* is satisfied?[35] If so, then no (or less) punishment is deserved. If not, then (at least some) punishment *is* deserved. If Tom spontaneously feels regret and must pay for a taxi home, further remorse (self-inflicted punishment by giving himself a hard time) would not be deserved. If Karen's children are killed on the mountain as she distractedly posts to Instagram, or Beth's house fills with carbon monoxide while she binge-watches her show and her children are killed, these are both forms of bad karma which far outweigh the selfish mistakes each made.[36] As such, no further punishment would be deserved. Yet, if blameworthy actors' rational underresponsiveness persists, such that they do not feel apt regret for their mistakes, and they suffer no bad karma to balance the

[33] This is not yet to say that any other person has standing to inflict such punishment. As we will see in section D, they do not.

[34] Gardner, 'Wrongs and Faults' (n 1) 80.

[35] *Gardner's Maxim* can be partially satisfied, thus making the case that less punishment is deserved. Gardner, 'Wrongs and Faults' (n 1) 76–77.

[36] Such cases illustrate tragedy, in which each mother's 'moral failure [is] out of proportion to [her] moral failing'. 'Wrongs and Faults' (n 1) 52–53.

scales between how good their lives *are* and how good they *feel*, then, according to *Gardner's Maxim*, punishment is deserved.

D. The Difference Duty Makes: Standing to Blame and Punishment

If the arguments in the previous sections hold up, both blame and punishment can be deserved irrespective of whether the road to blameworthiness and punishment-worthiness began with a breach of duty or merely a failure to conform to an ordinary reason.[37] From this, it is tempting to conclude that breach of duty makes little difference when it comes to blame and punishment. For, no matter how things got started (with a wrong or just a mistake) blame and punishment can be deserved. Yet, this way of thinking about things is too quick—for there is an important difference between whether blame and punishment are *deserved* and whether anyone else has *standing* to blame and punish the deserving.

In order for one to have *standing* to blame and inflict punishment, the blameworthy action must be one's business. As Gardner counsels, however, it is important not to overstate or misinterpret this point. The phrase 'mind your own business', he explains, is an 'intelligible stricture, but only when shorn of the dramatic implication that one has no reason to attend to another's business'.[38] As Gardner and Timothy Macklem correctly observe, '[e]verybody's personal engagement with [reasons] is in principle everyone's business'.[39]

How are we to understand this claim regarding the scope of 'everyone's business' when it comes to blaming and punishing others? As Gardner and Macklem note, '[t]his way of putting the point raises the spectre of a world of nosy parkers, intruding into each other's lives at every turn'.[40] It seems to suggest that everyone has standing to blame and punish others, so long as the blame and punishment are deserved. But again, this way of thinking about the problem ignores the question of whether the blamer/punisher has standing.

When does another person have standing to blame and/or punish another? A full answer to that question would take much further argument than is possible here. Still, we can make a start by asking a simpler question: When is it the case

[37] For Gardner, blame is an attitude, not an expression. For an illuminating improvement on Gardner's account, see Leora Dahan Katz, 'Private, Public, and Punitive Blame' (this volume).

[38] John Gardner, 'Relations of Responsibility' in Rowan Cruft, Matthew H. Kramer, and Mark R. Reiff (eds) *Crime, Punishment, and Responsibility: The Jurisprudence of Antony Duff* (OUP 2011) 89 (hereinafter Gardner, 'Relations of Responsibility'). Reasons are, as he puts it, 'impersonal in respect of attention'. Gardner, *Offences and Defences* (n 7) 62.

[39] Gardner and Macklem, 'Reasons' (n 4) 458. The bracketed phrase in the original is 'valuable activities'. Given Gardner's understanding of reasons as value-ladened facts, the use of reasons here simplifies the point without changing the meaning. See also Gardner, *Offences and Defences* (n 7) 62; Gardner, 'Relations of Responsibility' (n 38) 89, fn1.

[40] Gardner and Macklem, 'Reasons' (n 4) 458.

that *no one else has standing* to blame and/or punish a blameworthy actor who is deserving of punishment? The answer, I suggest, is when the road to blame began with the actor's non-conformity to an ordinary reason, rather than a breach of duty. While either way of starting down the road can pave the way to blameworthiness and punishment-deservedness, only a breach of duty typically gives someone else *standing* to blame and/or punish another.[41]

To see why this is so, we must revisit the difference between a duty and an ordinary reason, and now add an additional wrinkle regarding the kind of *regret* each reason leaves behind when one fails to conform. On Gardner's account, failure to conform to *any* reason (duty or not) leaves a rational residue of regret. But the regret that remains after a breach of duty has a different scope and force. Let us turn to Gardner for the full explanation:

> Among the many reasons that we do not conform to, there are many that are *non-categorical*. We have them by virtue of our personal goals and we no longer have them when our goals change. Furthermore, many are *non-mandatory*. They simply weigh in the balance of reasons and do not exclude any countervailing reasons from consideration. When we do not fully conform to a non-categorical and/or non-mandatory reason, the reason that remains to haunt us is still non-categorical and/or non-mandatory. Such a reason is therefore permanently vulnerable to the abandonment of old goals and/or to defeat by the new reasons that militate powerfully in favor of getting on with our lives. When things are not so easy is when we are left with old unconformed to reasons that are both categorical and mandatory, i.e., when we had duties that we failed to perform, and hence acted wrongfully. In such cases the reason leftover and still awaiting conformity *does not surrender to a change in our personal goals*. And it continues to exert mandatory force such that *at least some conflicting reasons (some of the otherwise powerful reasons we have to get on with our lives) are excluded from consideration and cannot suffice to defeat it*. Wrongful action, in short, leaves us with regrets that are hard to expunge and the repression of which is hard to justify.[42]

The implications that follow from this account help explain why we typically lack standing to blame and punish others for failing to conform to ordinary reasons,

[41] Two caveats. First, none of this helps to specify which particular 'other people' might have such standing: the victim, one's friends/family, one's employer, the state? It is simply to say that, where there is no breach of duty, it is typically the case that *no one* else has standing to blame and/or punish another, even if blame and punishment are deserved. Second, there are unusual cases where one comes to have standing to blame and/or punish another because the actor asked to be held accountable in this way. 'Next time I miss the last train because I stayed late at the pub', Tom says to his roommate, 'I need you to read me the riot act and make me pay you $10'. Here, Tom's friend has standing to blame and punish Tom in response to Tom's blameworthy mistake, but his friend's standing is grounded in Tom's request, not simply in the fact that Tom's mistake was blameworthy and Tom deserving of punishment.

[42] Gardner, 'Wrongs and Faults' (n 1) 59 (emphasis added).

even when those failures are blameworthy and the actors are deserving of punishment.[43] When one has merely failed to conform to an ordinary reason, the residue of regret that sticks around is non-categorical and non-mandatory. So, one can get rid of those reasons to regret by committing oneself to getting on with life and acting for the reasons that weigh in favour of doing so.

Another way to put the basic idea is this: those who merely fail to conform to an ordinary reason, but do not breach a duty, are in a normative position to defeat another person's standing to blame and/or punish them. By choosing to get on with their lives, they can make it the case that their mistake is simply *no one else's business*.[44]

Consider Beth (*Binge-Watching*), who made a blameworthy mistake by not taking her children mountaineering because she overestimated the rational force of reasons to stay home and binge-watch television. Since she was under no duty to take her children mountaineering, her failure was merely a mistake, not a breach of duty.[45] If anyone were to blame or punish her for this mistake, she would have at least two options. First, she could accept the blame and/or punishment as deserved and apologize, make amends, do better in the future, and so on. It would not be irrational for her to have such a response.[46] But if she had decided to move on rather than experience regret for this mistake, she is free to do so. As such, an appropriate response to blame or punishment meted out by another person might go something like this: 'Look, you don't get to blame or punish me for every *mistake* I made as a parent. Sure, I had my faults, but there's a limit to the things for which I can be blamed and punished. Now, that time I broke my promise to pick up the kids from school and they had to walk home in the rain, sure ... that was *wrong* of me. But, not taking them mountaineering wasn't a breach of duty on my part, so I'm free to move on from that mistake ... I'm not going to beat myself up about it, and neither can anyone else.'[47]

In responding this way, Beth is explaining the sense in which no one else has standing to blame or punish another person for their mistakes—only for their wrongs.[48] There are different ways of putting this thought: one can (correctly)

[43] I include 'typically' to account for unusual cases in n 41.

[44] Ori Herstein explains the normative force of the standing norms I have in mind as an exclusionary permission to disregard or discount another's expression of blame or infliction of punishment in virtue of their lack of standing. Ori Herstein, 'Justifying Standing to Give Reasons: Hypocrisy, Minding Your Own Business, and Knowing One's Place' (2020) 20 Philosopher's Imprint 7. On exclusionary permissions, see Raz, *Practical Reason and Norms* (n 5) 90–97.

[45] I am assuming here that the tragic deaths of their children discussed at n 36 did not occur, such that Karen's children returned safely from mountaineering and Beth's children were not killed by carbon monoxide.

[46] Indeed, if she accepts this blame and/or punishment, her doing so is best understood as supererogatory. Raz, *Practical Reason and Norms* (n 5) 91–95.

[47] Of course, when one's mistakes are committed while acting in a parenting role, they may leave us with regrets similar to those duty leaves behind: ones that are 'hard to expunge and the repression of which is hard to justify', especially insofar as one continues to embrace goals relating to good parenting. Thanks to James Edwards for raising this point.

[48] Again, note the caveats in n 41.

declare that a mistake, as opposed to a wrong, is 'just between me and my conscience' or 'just between me and my God'—or, to riff on the lyrics by Porter Granger and Everett Rodgers, 'T'aint Nobody's Business if I Do [or Don't]'.[49]

E. Conclusion

On Gardner's account, punishment is a deserved response to the 'rational unresponsiveness' of a blameworthy actor whose life feels better than it is. *Pace* Gardner, punishment of the blameworthy can be deserved, irrespective of whether the road to blameworthiness began with a breach of duty (wrong) or merely a failure to conform to an ordinary reason (mistake). Still, the fact that blame and punishment are *deserved* does not mean that anyone else has *standing* to blame or punish. It is here where breach of duty makes a difference.

While this chapter has challenged Gardner's claim that deserved punishment must be in response to a *wrong* rather than merely a *mistake*, it is some comfort that Gardner anticipates the central thesis of this chapter in his discussion of *Train*. After establishing blameworthiness for missing the train, Gardner observes:

> True, there might well be doubts about my standing to blame you, when you tell me the story at work the next day. Yet you clearly do have standing to blame yourself: not for breaching any obligation to yourself, I hasten to add, but just for making such a stupid mistake. So although it's not for me to blame you, I might say, you only have yourself to blame.[50]

On this, Gardner and I are in agreement. If the arguments in this chapter hold, the point above regarding blame extends equally to punishment. That is, both blame and punishment can be deserved responses to blameworthy action, irrespective of whether the action is a wrong or simply a mistake. Further, in virtue of the non-categorical, non-mandatory character of reasons that follow from mistakes, it is typically the case that no one else has *standing* to blame and/or punish another for mistakes. For that, at least typically, we need a breach of duty.

[49] To be clear, the claim here is that we typically lack standing to blame and punish others' mistakes, since the residue of regret that remains after a mistake grounds reasons for them that are neither categorical nor mandatory. As such, one who makes a mistake can escape the force of those residual reasons by switching their goals, and by doing so they typically come to have new reasons that override any lingering reasons to regret their past mistakes. Thanks to James Edwards for pressing me on this point.

[50] Gardner, 'Why Blame?' (n 1) 85.

9
Vindicating Criminal Law

Scott Hershovitz[*]

Start reading John Gardner and you'll immediately be struck by his good sense; it's present on every page. And I don't mean to say that Gardner was clever, though he was clearly that. I mean to say that he was wise. Take, for instance, the last chapter in *Offences and Defences*, an essay called 'Crime: In Proportion and In Perspective'.[1] Gardner starts with a simple question: what is the criminal law for? There are, of course, many familiar answers: deterrence, retribution, rehabilitation, incapacitation, and the like. And partisans push their preferred purposes endlessly. But Gardner cautions against joining a side. He writes:

> As students of the criminal law, we have all been brought up on the idea that the various arguments for having such an institution are rivals, each of which takes the winds out of the others' sails. We must therefore decide whether we are retributivists, or rehabilitationists, or preventionists, or reintegrationists, or whatever else may be the penological flavor of the month … To my way of thinking, this supposed rivalry among justifications for criminal law and its punitive responses is illusory. The criminal law (even when its responses are non-punitive) habitually wreaks such havoc in people's lives, and its punitive side is such an extraordinary abomination, that it patently needs all the justificatory help it can get.[2]

And Gardner means what he says. 'If and to the extent that the criminal law deters wrongdoing', he explains, 'that is one thing to be said in its favor'.[3] Likewise if it 'leads wrongdoers to confront and repent their wrongs'.[4] So far, not so surprising. But Gardner also sees justificatory potential in 'the power of the criminal law … to bring people with mental health problems into contact with those who can treat their conditions';[5] in its capacity 'to settle and maintain the internal standards of

* Thanks to Michelle Dempsey and François Tanguay-Renaud for assembling such a wonderful volume and inviting me to be a part of it. Thanks also to the participants in the Liber Amicorum Workshop for their helpful comments and criticism.

1 John Gardner, *Offences and Defences* 213–238 (OUP 2007) (hereafter Gardner, *Offences*).
2 Ibid, 214.
3 Ibid, 215.
4 Ibid, 215.
5 Ibid, 215.

Scott Hershovitz, *Vindicating Criminal Law* In: *From Morality to Law and Back Again*. Edited by: Michelle Madden Dempsey and François Tanguay-Renaud, Oxford University Press. © Scott Hershovitz 2023.
DOI: 10.1093/oso/9780198860594.003.0009

success for social practices such as marriage and share-dealing';[6] and even in the role it plays in 'validating and invalidating people's household insurance claims'.[7] If it seems like Gardner is scraping the bottom of the justificatory barrel, he is. And that is precisely his point. The criminal law needs every bit of justification it can get. There's an awful lot that's awful about it—an awful lot that needs to be justified. So we should say all that we can in its favour, and see if we can say enough.

Now, you might be thinking, that's all fine and good: say as much for criminal law as you can. But sometimes, the purposes of punishment come into conflict. And when they do, we need to decide which one to prioritize. True enough, Gardner says. But not so true that we need to take sides in the endless debates about the purposes of punishment. The question which purpose to prioritize is highly local—not just across but within jurisdictions—so there is no reason to think there's a general answer in the offing. And cases of conflict, Gardner adds, reinforce the need to say all that we can, since 'by their nature, these cases pit additional arguments against whatever course the law adopts for itself'.[8] If, in some aspect of the practice, we aim for rehabilitation at the cost of deterrence, we cannot call on deterrence to justify that bit of the practice—at least not to the extent that we otherwise could, and perhaps not at all.

So Gardner is, deep down, a pluralist about the purposes of punishment. And bully for that. Pluralism is not the sexiest philosophical position, but it is often the best. And given that, it is no surprise to see Gardner plump for it. But even as he proclaims his pluralism, there is one justification for punishment that Gardner cannot countenance. After noting the historical link between the criminal law and the many modes of retaliation ('the blood feud, the vendetta, the duel, the revenge, the lynching'),[9] Gardner observes that many contemporary thinkers assume that the justifiability of punishment 'is closely connected with the justifiability of our retaliating (tit-for-tat, or otherwise) against those who wrong us'.[10] On this picture, '[t]he spirit of the criminal law', he says, 'is fundamentally in continuity with the spirt of the vendetta'.[11] But to Gardner's mind, 'the opposite relation holds with much greater force. The justifiability of criminal punishment, and the criminal law in general, is closely connected to the *un*justifiability of retaliating against those who wrong us'.[12]

Indeed, Gardner argues that part of the point of criminal law is to displace revenge. He explains: 'That people are inclined to retaliate against those who wrong them, often with good excuse, but rarely with adequate justification, creates a

[6] Ibid, 215.
[7] Ibid, 215.
[8] Ibid, 215.
[9] Ibid, 213.
[10] Ibid, 213.
[11] Ibid, 213.
[12] Ibid, 213.

rational pressure for social practices to take the heat out of the situation and remove some of the temptation to retaliate.'[13] This 'displacement function' of criminal law is, according to Gardner, one of the 'central pillars' of its justification.[14] That is, criminal law is worth having, in no small part, because it dampens retaliatory impulses. The idea is not that those impulses are, in themselves, worth satisfying, such that the criminal law draws some measure of justification from the fact that it is itself retaliatory, or (at least) responsive to the same sorts of reasons that retaliation would be. Quite the opposite. Retaliation, Gardner tells us, is rarely justified, so it has no justificatory power to pass on to the criminal law.

That last bit is the part I want to quibble with. In a community that has well-constituted criminal law, Gardner is right. Retaliation is sometimes excused, but nearly never justified. In a community that lacked criminal law, however, there would be reasons to retaliate in response to serious wrongs—weighty reasons, which would almost surely amount to justification, at least in some cases, and I suspect in many. The criminal law's ability to respond to those reasons *is* something to be said for it—something quite important, since the criminal law can (at least when well constituted) respond to those reasons more fairly, more humanely, and more justly than many victims would manage. And since criminal law provides a better way of responding to those reasons, it dissipates the justification for retaliation that victims would have in its absence.

The upshot is that Gardner misses something that we can say for the criminal law. He says that criminal law displaces the temptation towards retaliation, and he is right about that. But it does that, in part, by dissipating the justification for retaliation— by providing a better way of responding to the reasons which otherwise would warrant it. And it is important that we see that and say it, lest we fail to follow Gardner's suggestion that we say all that we can for criminal law.

A. Reasons to Retaliate

Before we turn to the reasons to retaliate, a quick story. I nearly never tell strangers that I'm a philosopher, in part because I don't want to answer the question that inevitably follows: 'So, what's your philosophy?' Anthony Appiah has a clever answer. He tells people, 'My philosophy is that everything is more complicated than you thought'.[15] But Gardner once told me that he had an even better answer. 'What's your philosophy?' a stranger would ask. And Gardner would say, 'Have you heard of *two wrongs don't make a right*? That was me. I came up with that!' Amazingly, no

[13] Ibid, 213–214.
[14] Ibid, 214.
[15] See Paul Bloom, 'Morality Studies' *New York Times* (3 February 2008), available at https://www.nytimes.com/2008/02/03/books/review/Bloom-t.html.

one ever called Gardner out. They accepted that he was the author of this almost-surely-ancient bit of wisdom.

But is it wisdom? It might be wise counsel. Revenge is, after all, risky business. But there are reasons to retaliate; indeed, there are reasons to think that retaliation can set things right in response to wrongdoing. I've told this story before,[16] so I'll tell it quickly here. Take a simple case: Alfred punches Bert. Does that give Bert a reason to punch Alfred back? Maybe, and it's worth thinking why it would. First, and most obvious, Bert might not want Alfred to punch him again. And if Alfred thinks that there are no costs to punching Bert, then he might well. Similarly, Bert might not want Carol to punch him. And if Carol sees Alfred get away with punching Bert, then she might think she can get away with it too. And of course, it's not just Carol that Bert might worry about—it's David, Ernie, and the rest of the gang too.

So retaliation is in part responsive to the reasons we have to deter mistreatment. But that is not the only reason we might have to retaliate. In addition to worrying whether he might get punched again, Bert might worry that he will be seen in his community as the kind of person who can be punched, and permissibly so. Indeed, it is possible that Bert will worry that he *is* the kind of person who can be punched, permissibly so, and not just that people might think so. That is, he might worry that Albert's treatment of him was not *mis*treatment; it's just the sort of thing that he, being Bert, has to endure.

Lots of people have made a similar point. I think Pamela Hieronymi put it best:

> [A] past wrong against you, standing in your history without apology, atonement, retribution, punishment, restitution, condemnation, or anything else that might recognize it as a *wrong*, makes a claim. It says, in effect, that you can be treated this way, and that such treatment is acceptable.[17]

When Hieronymi wrote that, she was concerned primarily with the rationality of resentment. Resentment, she argued, was a way of rebutting the claim that wrongdoing makes. When you resent, you protest, if only to yourself, that you were *mis*treated—that you had a right not to be treated the way you were.[18]

But though resentment is clearly rational for that reason, there is no reason to think that resentment is the only, or even the best, way to rebut the message implicit in wrongdoing. There are many ways to rebut that message—and many people who can do it, not just the victim. Indeed, the best option may be for the wrongdoer to do the expressive work himself—by apologizing, atoning, or otherwise

[16] See Scott Hershovitz, 'Treating Wrongs as Wrongs: An Expressive Argument for Tort Law' (2017) 10 J. Tort Law 1 (hereafter Hershovitz, 'Treating Wrongs as Wrongs').

[17] Pamela Hieronymi, 'Articulating an Uncompromising Forgiveness,' (2001) 62 Phil. & Phenomenological Res. 529, 546.

[18] Ibid, 546.

acknowledging that the wrongdoing was, in fact, a wrong. As we will see in a moment, the surrounding community can do the work too. But suppose that no one does—not the wrongdoer nor the community. In that case, the victim is left to do the work himself, and he has reasons not to keep his protest private. That is, he has reasons to communicate that he's been wronged, so that others know where he stands on the question how he may be treated.

Now we can see another reason that Bert might punch Alfred back. In doing so, he sends a message—that he believes he's been mistreated, and more than that, that he doesn't plan to tolerate that sort of mistreatment. The second bit takes us back to deterrence. But the first bit matters even if Bert has no reason to think that Alfred—or anyone else for that matter—will ever attempt to punch him again. Alfred's punching Bert put Bert's social standing in question—it became, in a sense, an open question whether it was permissible to punch Bert. In punching back, Bert says no, and rather emphatically. And it matters that the punch is a rather emphatic way of responding. Bert could say, loudly and even emphatically, that Alfred has mistreated him. But actions speak louder than words, at least on some occasions. And Bert's punch communicates his views about Alfred's punch much more emphatically than his words would.

So Bert does have reasons to retaliate. Do his reasons amount to a justification? That depends on whether those reasons are defeated by other considerations. And there are, of course, reasons running in the opposite direction. If Bert punches Alfred back, he might harm him, and there are always reasons to avoid harming others. If Bert punches Alfred back, Alfred might punch him again, or gather up his friends and hurt Bert more severely. Revenge, as we learn from the Hatfields and McCoys, has a habit of cycling into ever greater eruptions of violence. Gardner allows that Bert might have an excuse for retaliating against Alfred, but he seems confident that he will rarely have a justification—that his reasons to retaliate will be almost always defeated. I am not so sure. In fact, I am nearly sure that the opposite is true, as is everyone who has ever counselled a child to stand up for himself—to pop the bully back, as a way of getting him off his back. When no one else will stand up for you, sometimes you have to do it yourself, even in the face of the many reasons to refrain. And that is true no matter what playground you play on.

B. Criminal Law and Community

But it is better if you don't have to stand up for yourself, or at least, it often is. There's strength in numbers, so having others come to your defence can reduce the risks of responding on your own. But just as important: when others stand up for you, they recognize you as the victim of a wrong and reassert your social standing as someone who has a right to live free from the particular mistreatment you've endured. That can shore up your sense of yourself and your standing in the community. It's not just you who thinks you have a right to be free from this sort of treatment; it's everyone who signs on to the protest.

The fact that we can assist a person who has been wronged in that way is, in itself, reason to do so. But there are many other reasons to help victims rebut the messages implicit in wrongdoing. We are all vulnerable in various ways. If Alfred can punch Bert with impunity, he might punch others too. So it is not just Bert's social standing that is at stake. It is everyone who is vulnerable in the way that Bert is. If you are among that number, you have a special interest in helping Bert. But we all have reasons to respond to Alfred, whether or not we share Bert's vulnerability. As I said, we are all vulnerable in one way or another. By responding to wrongdoing collectively, we reassure one another that we are part of a community that stands ready to vindicate the social standing of those that are victimized.

To be sure, there are also pragmatic reasons for a community to respond to wrongdoing. Some of them sound in deterrence. Others relate to the cycles of violence that retaliation risks setting off. Still others stem from the tendency of victims to take things too far—to overestimate the significance of the wrong they suffered, to place too little weight on the well-being of the wrongdoer, and so on. These are the sorts of considerations Gardner had in mind when he spoke of criminal law's displacement function. And they are genuine concerns. But the reasons to displace do not exhaust the reasons to respond to wrongdoing by rebutting the message implicit in it.

So how can a community stand up for a victim like Bert? In lots of ways. People might commiserate with Bert, letting him know that they think he was wronged. Even more effective, they might express that view publicly, perhaps even directing their message to Alfred, as well as to others who might be tempted to act as he did. But though this could all be done informally, there are reasons to institutionalize the practice—too many reasons, perhaps, to list them exhaustively. But here are a few. By institutionalizing the practice, we can regularize the response. We can make sure that it happens reliably. We can make sure the response is consistent across cases. And by developing rules to regulate the response, we can constrain it—with a view towards making sure that we treat both victim and wrongdoer fairly and humanely.

The criminal law, at its best, can accomplish all of these goals. Of course, the criminal law we know is far from the best. And it is a good deal more difficult to justify the criminal law we have than the ideal we might imagine. Indeed, it might not be possible. But it is nevertheless important to ponder what criminal law might accomplish if it was well constituted. And good criminal law has the capacity to achieve all the aims just adduced—responding to wrongdoing reliably, consistently, fairly, and humanely.

C. Why Not Tort?

But wait a minute. Can't tort law do the work I just described? In a tort suit, a plaintiff files a complaint, alleging that she was wronged. In doing so, she calls upon her community to validate that viewpoint, and if it finds in her favour, it rebuts the message implicit in the wrongdoing. It makes clear that she was, in fact, mistreated. So even if you find the argument so far persuasive, you might think it misplaced. Vindicating victims is what tort law does. Criminal law condemns wrongdoing. We should keep each institution in its proper place.

To be sure, that line of thought has a long history. Tort law, we are told, is concerned with corrective justice. Criminal law aims at retributive justice. And this division of labour is supposed to account for many of the most salient differences in the institutions. A tort suit starts with a complaint from the person wronged, and it ends (if it ends in her favour) with compensation. A criminal proceeding starts with charges from the state, and it ends (if it ends in the state's favour) with a sentence to some sort of punishment. But as I have argued elsewhere, the boundary between these institutions is not nearly so neat. Though they are structured in different ways and do different things, they send some of the same messages. If you condemn a defendant for a wrong that had a victim, you inevitably communicate something about the victim's social standing. You communicate that she was a victim—that she was wronged. And moreover, you communicate that she matters—that what happened to her matters enough for her community to respond, and to respond with the force of the criminal law.

Our criminal law is too harsh, too rigid, and too involved in the lives of too many people. But at the same time, it is too lame, too ineffectual, and too indifferent to the serious harms that some people suffer. Think here of sexual assault, cyberbullying, revenge porn, and the like. The judge who sentenced Brock Turner to just six months in prison said something about the significance of Chanel Miller, the woman Turner sexually assaulted, whether he intended to or not. He said that she did not matter much, or at least that what Turner did to her did not. That was the source of the outrage at the sentence. The court had an opportunity to send a message about Miller—to signal to her and everyone else that she mattered, that she'd been wronged, and seriously so, and to reaffirm her social standing in the face of that mistreatment. Turner's conviction did indeed signal that she'd been wronged. But the slight sentence undermined the message. This just wasn't that big a deal, the court seemed to say.

And that was outrageous. But there was another reason to be outraged. Because the slight sentence did not just say something about Chanel Miller. It said something about sexual assault, its significance as a wrong, and the significance of those who are vulnerable to it—especially women. (Which is not to say that the criminal law does well by men who are sexually assaulted. It may do even worse.) It told women that they could not rely on their community to vindicate their social standing. Or rather, it made clear just what their social standing was: it told them that their community viewed sexual assault as a minor offence. A better sentence would have signalled to women that they matter—that wrongs of this sort matter—and that they will be treated as the serious wrongs that they are.

But I don't want to get bogged down in a discussion of Turner's sentence. There is a broader point here: many people are threatened by the messages implicit in wrongdoing, not just the victim. That is a reason to maintain a forum for rebutting those messages that is subject to community control, not to the idiosyncratic decisions of individual victims. In other words, it is a reason to have an institution like the criminal law, notwithstanding the fact that tort law can and does do some of the same expressive work.

And that is far from the only reason. Here are a few more. Tort law puts the onus on victims to initiate a suit. That can be burdensome emotionally and (depending on how attorneys are paid in the jurisdiction) financially. Victims are often pressured not to become plaintiffs—by wrongdoers and others. And while money damages can signal a lot, there are limits to their expressive significance. Putting Turner in prison for a substantial time would say more about what he did than any monetary judgment could. It would communicate that the community's condemnation was so strong that it did not think Turner fit to live with them for an extended period of time. Add all this up and it is easy to make an expressive case for criminal law, notwithstanding the fact that tort can and does do overlapping expressive work.

D. The Dissipation Function

As we saw back at the start, Gardner allows that the criminal law draws some measure of justification from the fact that it displaces retaliation as a response to wrongdoing. He sees this as a sociological fact, or perhaps simply a psychological one. Victims' vindictive impulses, he says, provide 'rational pressure for social practices to take the heat out of the situation and remove some of the temptation to retaliate'.[19] He adds that courts should 'insist on thinking in terms of justice irrespective of whether doing so serves the further purpose of pacifying retaliators'.[20] But as we have seen, it is not just a brute fact that victims are sometimes vindictive; nor is criminal law's capacity to pacify them unconnected to claims that sound in justice. Victims have reasons to be vindictive, some of which relate to their interest in rebutting the messages implicit in wrongdoing. The criminal law 'removes some of the temptation to retaliate' because it is responsive to (some of) the very same reasons that retaliation is. And the question whether we respond to those reasons is (quite often) a question of justice, since it is a question about the basic structure of our social relations. It is no accident (nor is it confused) that we say that the

[19] Gardner, *Offences* 213–214.
[20] Ibid, 221.

criminal law can deliver justice for the victims of crimes. It can deliver the same sort of justice they could deliver themselves.

'Revenge', Francis Bacon famously said, 'is a kind of wild justice, which the more man's nature runs to, the more ought law to weed it out'.[21] But if I am right in what I've said, the law ought to weed it out because it is wild, not because it is not justice. It follows that it is not enough for the law to displace private violence in response to wrongdoing. It must also deliver justice for victims, and in so doing dissipate their justification for retaliation. Doing so might have good consequences, and that is indeed part of the point. If people think the criminal law can do an adequate job in responding to wrongdoing, then they will see less reason to respond on their own. But there is a more important reason to remove the rational warrant for revenge. If we plan to prohibit private violence and punish it, we should be sure that it is not justified; otherwise, we won't be justified in punishing it. So the criminal law licenses the scope of its own prohibitions in part by responding to the reasons that victims have to retaliate—by delivering the same sort of justice that they could, just better.

That does not mean that the criminal law is retaliatory. In rebutting the messages implicit in wrongdoing, the criminal law vindicates victims, not itself. And that is an important fact about the institution, which partly explains its potential (often unrealized) to respond to reasons to retaliate better than victims themselves could. Avengers are often too vengeful. They overweight the wrong done; they underweight the well-being, or simply the humanity, of the wrongdoer. I said all that already, but it bears saying again, because I know (from experience) that any defence of retaliatory impulses yields the charge that one is an apologist for indefensible and inhumane practices—the practices of putting eyes out or putting a wrongdoer's family members to death. I don't want to defend any of that, nor do I feel the least temptation to romanticize revenge. But I do think that we owe it to those who seek revenge to understand why and to offer them something better, if not by their lights, at least by ours. When it is well constituted, criminal law can be that substitute.

E. Finishing a Friend's Thoughts

When I first agreed to write this chapter, I expected it would be part of a conversation that Gardner and I had been engaged in, off and on, for more than twenty years. Alas, I have gotten the last word, but in service, I hope, of his project. As I said at the start, Gardner's good sense pervades his work. And nowhere was he more sensible than in the passage I quoted earlier. The criminal law is an awful

[21] Francis Bacon, 'Of Revenge' (1625).

institution—disruptive and costly beyond measure. And it would be so even at its best (and around here it is far from its best). So if we are to be reformists, rather than abolitionists, it is vital to say all that we can for the institution. The displacement function is, as Gardner says, a central pillar of its justification. But the dissipation function is too. The criminal law is capable of responding to victims' reasons to retaliate, and it is capable of doing so more fairly and humanely than they can do themselves. That is an argument for the institution, which deserves some prominence among all the others that Gardner gathered up.

10
State Crimes

François Tanguay-Renaud[*]

Be it as a scholar or as a doctoral supervisor, John Gardner often liked to provoke. This chapter is meant as a response to one such provocation.

Gardner believed that, through a combination of what he called natural and artificial agency, institutions can be agents whose actions cannot simply be reduced to that of their individual human members.[1] He thought that, through the intercession of their members acting together in accord with a suitably designed normative framework, institutions can act in the world in distinct ways, and even engage in wrongdoing of their own. For example, Gardner moots the possibility that a police force—understood not so much as a collection of officers acting individually, but as 'a whole system'—may sometimes go astray and turn into a distinct institutional 'assassin'.[2] He even maintains that the state as a whole can sometimes engage in wrongdoing. Thus, Gardner cautions, 'the state', like any other moral agent, 'must not murder or be complicit in murder. It must not rape or be complicit in rape. It must not rob or be complicit in robbery.'[3]

When, as a graduate student, I first read this last passage, many questions arose. Among them was the question whether, if one adopts Gardner's theoretical commitments as deployed in the article in question, states should also sometimes be thought of as criminals, when they engage in crimes that in some way recognize in the law moral wrongs such as murder, rape, and robbery. Gardner's response to my query was characteristic of his empowering supervisory style. 'Interesting and underexplored question', he proclaimed, 'since there is no doubt that states also regularly engage in legal wrongdoing'. That was before he added: 'What do *you* think?'

* I thank the participants in workshops held at the University of Toronto Centre for Ethics, University of Saint Andrews, Brooklyn Law School, Queen's University, Osgoode Hall Law School's Nathanson Centre, and Stockholm University, where versions of this chapter were presented.

1 See John Gardner, *Law as a Leap of Faith: Essays on Law in General* (Oxford: Oxford University Press, 2012), at pp. 61–66.

2 John Gardner, 'Criminals in Uniforms' in RA Duff, Lindsay Farmer, SE Marshall, Massimo Renzo, and Victor Tadros (eds), *The Constitution of Criminal Law* (Oxford: Oxford University Press), pp. 97–118, at p. 115.

3 John Gardner, 'Prohibiting Immoralities', *Cardozo Law Review* 28(6) (2007): pp. 2613–2628, at p. 2628.

François Tanguay-Renaud, *State Crimes* In: *From Morality to Law and Back Again*. Edited by: Michelle Madden Dempsey and François Tanguay-Renaud, Oxford University Press. © François Tanguay-Renaud 2023.
DOI: 10.1093/oso/9780198860594.003.0010

Many years later, here is (part of) my attempt at providing an answer,[4] grounded in Gardner's own theoretical commitments about the possibility of distinct state agency, the applicability to the state of the general principles of morality that bind us all, and some version of legal moralism as the best way of understanding criminal wrongdoing.[5] To be sure, since Gardner never attempted to answer this question himself, I must depart from his work in a number of ways to do so, and this chapter may be somewhat less exegetical than others as a result. Still, given that Gardner long encouraged me to pursue this project, which his work inspired and now frames, I believe it is a fitting tribute.

A. Why State Crimes?

Taking seriously Gardner's assumption that states can commit both moral and legal wrongs that cannot simply be equated with those of their individual members, do they also perpetrate crimes?

For years, criminologists have been studying so-called state crimes.[6] However, analytic criminal law and political theorists, more scrupulous about the concepts they employ, are generally much more reluctant to speak of the normative category of crime as applicable to states. Their hesitation is understandable: while states are certainly paradigmatic criminalizers and worthy of theorization as such, what practice of singling them out as agents of crimes is there for us to theorize? In name, at least, there isn't much, either at the international or domestic level.

Admittedly, the wording of Article 9 of the Nuremberg Charter may have allowed the Military Tribunals to declare organizations—possibly, the Nazi state—guilty of crimes.[7] Instead, though, criminal organizations were judicially defined as aggregates of guilty individuals, thus rendering the notion of organizational criminality—including state criminality—obsolete.[8] Early drafts of the International Law Commission's *Articles on State Responsibility* later also made room for the category, defining a state crime as '[a]n internationally wrongful act

[4] See also François Tanguay-Renaud, 'Criminalizing the State', *Criminal Law and Philosophy* 7(2) (2013): pp. 255–284.

[5] On this last commitment, see John Gardner and James Edwards, 'Criminal Law', in Hugh LaFolette (ed.), *The International Encyclopedia of Ethics* (Chichester: Wiley-Blackwell, 2013).

[6] See as far back as Horace King, *State Crimes* (Worthing: Little Hampton Book Services, 1967), and Charles Tilly, 'War Making and State Making as Organized Crime', in Peter B. Evans, Dietrich Rueschemeyer, and Theda Skocpol (eds), *Bringing the State Back In* (Cambridge: Cambridge University Press, 1985), pp. 169–191.

[7] 'At the trial of any individual member of any group or organization the Tribunal may declare (in connection with any act of which the individual may be convicted) that the group or organization of which the individual was a member was a criminal organization.' *Agreement for the Prosecution and Punishment of the Major War Criminals of the European Axis, Charter of the International Military Tribunal*, 8 August 1945, Art. 9, 59 Stat. 1544, 82 UNTS 279.

[8] Judgment of the International Military Tribunal: The Accused Organizations. Online: <http://avalon.law.yale.edu/imt/judorg.asp#general>.

which results from the breach by a State of an international obligation so essential for the protection of fundamental interests of the international community that its breach is recognized as a crime by that community as a whole'.[9] Aggression, genocide, the establishment and maintenance by force of colonial domination, slavery, apartheid, and massive pollution of the atmosphere or of the seas were then listed as paradigmatic examples. Still, the category was ultimately dropped from the final version of the *Articles*.[10] Indeed, international organizations such as the United Nations Security Council are generally very careful not to frame their treatment of states that violate international law as criminal-law-like, opting instead to limit themselves to preventive, regulatory, and reparative language and means.[11] To be sure, many of the crimes initially listed in the International Law Commission's drafts ended up being recognized in the *Rome Statute of the International Criminal Court*. However, despite requirements of actions pursuant to or in furtherance of a state or organizational policy,[12] or of involvement with the use of armed force by a state,[13] these crimes are now explicitly and exclusively understood as crimes of *individuals*—against humanity, of aggression, or of war—not as crimes of states.

Domestic legal systems are no exception. In most of them, 'the state' is explicitly excluded from the ambit of the criminal law.[14] Admittedly, in some rare cases, statutory provisions or court rulings do contemplate the possibility of criminal prosecutions not so much of the state *per se* but of various organs, such as 'municipalities', 'governmental entities', 'public bodies', or 'the Crown'.[15] Yet, insofar as they were ever invoked—which is sometimes not even the case—these provisions and decisions have by now generally fallen in desuetude.[16]

Be that as it may, a lack of practice surely does not prevent one from speculating about the normative prospects of a category of state crimes. To what end? I argue that there are good reasons for both criminal law and political theorists to turn their minds to the possibility of state crimes, including the fact that the issue lies at the intersection of their fields of study, which remains significantly underexplored.

[9] James Crawford (ed.), *The International Law Commission's Articles on State Responsibility: Introduction, Text and Commentary* (Cambridge: Cambridge University Press, 2001), at pp. 352–353.

[10] *Ibid.*, at pp. 16–20.

[11] See further Gabriella Blum, 'The Crime and Punishment of States', *Yale Journal of International Law* (2013) 81(2): pp. 57–122, for a helpful survey of relevant international practice.

[12] Rome Statute of the International Criminal Court, 17 July 1998, Art. 7(2)(a), UN Doc. A/CONF.183/9* (www.un.org/icc), reprinted in 37 ILM 999 (1998).

[13] Resolution RC/Res.6, Review Conference of the Rome Statute, Annex I on the Crime of Aggression (http://www.icc-cpi.int./iccdocs/asp_docs/Resolutions/RC-Res.6-ENG.pdf).

[14] For an example of statutory exclusion, see, e.g., *Code pénal* (France), at s. 121-2 ('Les personnes morales, à l'exclusion de l'État, sont responsables pénalement').

[15] See, e.g., *Criminal Code of Canada*, RSC 1985, c. C-46, at ss. 2, 22.1, 22.2; *Indiana Code Ann.*, at s. 35-41-1-22; *New York Penal Law*, at s. 10.00(7); *Cain v Doyle* (1946), 72 Commonwealth Law Reports 409 (High Court of Australia).

[16] See Stuart P. Green, 'The Criminal Prosecution of Local Governments', *North Carolina Law Review* 72 (1993): pp. 1197–1246.

My main contention is that these theorists' reluctance to consider state crimes is symptomatic of a broader inattentiveness to the difficult question of what remedies for state wrongdoing may be justified. More specifically, I argue that if we take seriously the possibility that the state may be punished for its perpetration of certain wrongs, then, without the idea of state crimes, we lack a concept that would helpfully allow us to single out such wrongs. We lack an important concept, just as we would lack one were we to abandon, without replacing it, the idea that some punishable individual wrongs are crimes. I intend to get to this point by addressing a series of key objections to the idea of state crimes, namely: (1) that different norms that already apply to states satisfactorily regulate the kinds of conduct which legal systems generally treat as crimes, when they are engaged in by individuals or non-state organizations; (2) that institutions and safeguards required for legitimate criminalization are currently unavailable for states; and (3) that states are not kinds of entities that can be valuably punished.

B. State Crimes in Other Guises

If, as John Gardner holds, states can engage in wrongdoing and crimes are wrongs, then it seems at least worth asking why analytic philosophers are so reluctant to even consider the possibility of state crimes. Some, it must be said, are not so averse to the idea. Thomas Nagel, for example, writes quite unhesitatingly of 'certain types of criminal conduct [such as war crimes or crimes against humanity], usually by states, against other states or against individuals or ethnic groups'.[17] Consider also Avia Pasternak, who discusses in passing the legitimacy of 'assigning individual liability for state crimes',[18] or Paul Gilbert, who argues that 'State terrorism is a crime'.[19]

A standard rejoinder to such assertions is that they are merely metaphorical. That is, they refer to kinds of wrongdoing which, although not criminalized when engaged in by states, commonly are—either internationally, domestically, or both—when engaged in by ordinary individuals or officials in their personal capacity. The point is sometimes couched in even more trenchant terms: doesn't the intrinsically metaphorical nature of these assertions account, at least in part, for the ease with which they often veer into hyperbole—as in Emma Goldman's infamous characterization of the state as 'the greatest criminal, breaking every

[17] Thomas Nagel, 'The Problem of Global Justice', *Philosophy and Public Affairs* 33(2) (2005): pp. 113–147, at p. 114.

[18] Avia Pasternak, 'Limiting States' Corporate Responsibility', *Journal of Political Philosophy* 21(4) (2013): pp. 361–381, at p. 20.

[19] Paul Gilbert, *Terrorism, Security & Nationality* (London: Routledge, 1994), at pp. 133, 157.

written and natural law, stealing in the form of taxes, killing in the form of war and capital punishment'?[20]

This kind of rejoinder does not constitute much of an objection to state crimes. Indeed, the authors cited might well genuinely think that the kinds of state wrongdoing to which they refer *should* be recognized as crimes, even if existing legal systems fail to do so. In other words, their mentions of state crimes may be more aspirational than metaphorical. Even if we do not yet have legally recognized state crimes, these authors might argue, the cause is not the unintelligibility or illegitimacy of the category so much as political myopia, hypocrisy, or sheer obstruction. There is no denying that a sustained inquiry would be needed to flesh out the justified parameters of any plausible category of state crime. Yet, is this not precisely, as John Gardner once suggested to me, the sort of task that serious theorists should be willing to consider undertaking?

Ironically, a more significant objection to recognizing state crimes arises from the writings of those very theorists whose work otherwise shows openness towards the category. Such theorists often seem to think that state crimes double up as violations of other more familiar norms, whose applicability to states is already commonly accepted. For example, Nagel understands state crimes as state violations of duties of justice, while Pasternak and Gilbert often seem to associate them with violations of human rights.[21] If, indeed, these norms are equivalent, isn't a category of state crimes at best redundant?

1. State Crimes as Injustices?

Let us first turn to Nagel's suggestion. Are all crimes, and especially all conceivable state crimes, best understood as injustices? This question must be answered in the negative, at least if one adheres to John Gardner's understanding of the domain of justice—in my view, the most perspicuous—as concerned with allocative moral questions, such as who is to get what and how much of it.[22] Many international crimes such as those that Nagel understands as paradigmatic state crimes are cases in point. There are normally no questions, either of a comparative or non-comparative nature, to be asked about who should be enslaved, about the proper grounds of genocide, or about how much one should be tortured. There are

[20] Emma Goldman, 'Anarchism: What It Really Stands For' in *Anarchism and Other Essays* (New York: Mother Earth Publishing Association, 1911): pp. 3–11, at p. 8.

[21] Nagel, 'The Problem of Global Justice', note 17, at p. 114, refers to state war crimes and crimes against humanity as an "aspect of global justice". Pasternak, 'Limiting States' Corporate Responsibility', note 18, at p. 379, writes of 'state crimes in regimes that violate their citizens' basic human rights', whereas Gilbert, *Terrorism, Security & Nationality*, note 19, at p. 133, speaks of the state crime of terrorism as 'a grave infringement of human rights'.

[22] See John Gardner, 'What Is Tort Law For? Part 1. The Place of Corrective Justice', *Law and Philosophy* 30(3) (2011): pp. 1–50, at p. 6.

normally no such allocative questions because these forms of conduct are, quite simply, inhumane. It is their inhumanity—that is, their sheer disrespect for their objects' intrinsic value as autonomous beings—and not their unjust character that makes them wrongful. Except perhaps in some rare tragic scenarios where, for example, the only way to prevent some people from being enslaved would be to enslave others, or where the only means of saving some from being tortured a lot would be to torture others to a lesser extent, the mere asking of allocative questions about such actions reveals moral confusion or, worse, grave insensitivity. Thus, if wrongs that are most likely candidates for state crimes are not best understood as injustices, it seems unwise to seek to reduce the category to violations of duties of justice.

This is not to say that state injustices may not amount to wrongs that could be properly criminalized. Thus, the suggestion is sometimes encountered that a state that distributes wealth unjustly and, thus, generates criminogenic conditions among those it fails to support may be complicit in the crimes they perpetrate as a result. In such a scenario, the claim often goes, the state really 'ought to be a co-defendant'.[23] Surely, though, not all state injustices should be categorized as crimes. Otherwise, all imperfectly just states would be criminals. That is, all existing states would be guilty of crimes every time they cannot account for an injustice of theirs as justified—say, as necessary to avoid larger evils—or as excused—say, as grounded in reasonable epistemic mistakes. While such a radical suggestion would certainly please someone like Emma Goldman, who believes that all attempts by states to redistribute wealth are likely to wrongfully miss the mark, it would fly in the face of how most people—including all liberals—conceive of the normative position of the modern state. Other things being equal, states ought to strive for greater justice, and may be criticized for their failures, but below a certain threshold of injustice the label of crime seems wholly inappropriate. Indeed, general popular discourse tends to echo this assessment, reserving this label for state actions that amount to gross injustices (when injustices are the wrongs at issue), such as widespread expropriations without compensation, endemic misappropriation of public funds, indiscriminate internment or killing of those belonging to a given racial group, or abject neglect of needy communities.

I would like to suggest that an important reason for this intuitively plausible popular demarcation is that characterizing some wrongdoing as a crime is commonly understood as calling for a distinctive set of harsh responses—namely, for the perpetrator's condemnation and punishment. Thus, it is unsurprising that a political anarchist such as Emma Goldman would choose to depict states as criminals, since she otherwise argues that their wrongdoings are so grave and pervasive as to warrant condemning them to death *qua* purportedly authoritative corporate

[23] Victor Tadros, 'Poverty and Criminal Responsibility', *Journal of Value Inquiry* 43 (2009): pp. 391–413, at pp. 391, 410.

organizations, through popular overthrow and dismantlement. Of course, if punishment is understood like John Gardner understands it, as the intentional infliction of an inconvenient or burdensome deprivation, or suffering, in response to wrongdoing (or claimed wrongdoing),[24] it need not be so drastic. Yet by definition the practice is deliberately disruptive, not to say intrusive, and in many cases of state injustice (or wrongdoing more generally) we may well think that no such interference is called for.

2. State Crimes as Violations of Human Rights?

One may be tempted to argue that human rights already play the relevant demarcation role. Here, I am not referring to human rights generically understood as the rights that humans have in virtue of being human—the kind of broad moral understanding to which John Gardner himself seems most attracted.[25] While, all things considered, this conception may be most perspicuous, it is unlikely to be the one that those who analogize state crimes to violations of human rights have in mind. An analogy between violations of human rights so understood and state crimes in particular is not obvious and, insofar as it is, the demarcating potential of the former category is questionable.

There exists an alternate conception, defended by some contemporary political philosophers, which presents a much more direct challenge to the need for a distinct category of state crimes. According to it, the practice of international human rights delineates norms, most often legal, whose violations are so wrongful that they require, or at least permit, external interference with state sovereignty.[26] I will assume its soundness, for the sake of discussion, given the interesting counterpoint it provides.

If, as is traditionally the case, state sovereignty is understood as the normative ability of states to block external actors from interfering with their internal affairs, even when what they are doing is wrong, and human rights define principled limits to this ability, then permissible responses to their violation might conceivably extend to condemnatory punitive interferences. This suggestion is all the more powerful insofar as human rights tend to be conceived as limits on state sovereignty because of their close connection with conditions necessary for decent human lives

[24] See, e.g., John Gardner, 'Introduction' in H.L.A. Hart, *Punishment and Responsibility: Essays in the Philosophy of Law*, 2nd ed (Oxford: Oxford University Press, 2008), pp. xiii–liv, at pp. xiv, xvii–xviii, xxv, xxxi.

[25] See John Gardner, '"Simply in Virtue of Being Human": The Whos and the Whys of Human Rights', *Journal of Ethics and Social Philosophy* 2(2) (2008): pp. 1–22.

[26] See especially Joseph Raz, 'Human Rights without Foundations', in Samantha Besson and John Tasioulas (eds), *The Philosophy of International Law* (Oxford: Oxford University Press, 2010), pp. 321–337; Charles R. Beitz, *The Idea of Human Rights* (Oxford: Oxford University Press, 2009), esp. at ch. 5–7; John Rawls, *The Law of People* (Cambridge, MA: Harvard University Press, 1999), at pp. 78–81.

to be lived. Thus, some, like John Rawls, go so far as to affirm that state violations of human rights are 'to be condemned and in grave cases may be subjected to forceful sanctions and even to intervention'.[27] Obviously, more needs to be said to vindicate the view that violations of human rights, so understood, are equivalent to crimes of states, but one can here begin to see why theorists like Pasternak and Gilbert might be tempted to go down this road.

For many years now, the ideas of individual sovereignty and principled limits to it have been closely associated with efforts to delineate the legitimate scope of state-defined crimes and state-imposed punishments of individuals. Consider Immanuel Kant's understanding of individual domestic crimes as violations of others' sovereignty (individual or collective) through which perpetrators forfeit their right to assert their own sovereignty against state punitive responses.[28] Or think of John Stuart Mill's insistence that '[o]ver himself, over his own body and mind, the individual is sovereign', such that the legitimate scope of 'compulsion and control' that may be exercised over him—including through criminal law and punishment—is limited to behaviour that causes harm to others.[29] No doubt, the analogy between human rights and crimes, as norms the violation of which may legitimize condemnatory and punitive interferences with sovereignty—states' and individuals', respectively—is alluring. Still, one could interject that it is far from perfect.

For one thing, the value of state sovereignty is not the same as the value of individual sovereignty. Whereas the latter arises from the intrinsic importance of respecting individuals' autonomy-related interests and independent status as beings capable of choosing their own ends,[30] such considerations do not apply, or do not apply in the same irreducible way, to institutional organizations such as states. That is, even if, as some argue, states can be persons, in the sense that they can, *qua* organizations, appropriately respond to reason and perform in the space of obligations, they are not persons whose status and interests are irreducibly valuable. States are first and foremost instrumental creations and, in accordance with the commonly accepted principle of value individualism, their worth ought to be assessed 'wholly' based 'on the returns promised for individuals'.[31] Now, endorsement of such value individualism does not entail that state sovereignty is worthless. On the contrary, it is often of tremendous value for individuals. It is valuable given

[27] Rawls, *ibid.*, at p. 81.

[28] Immanuel Kant, *The Metaphysics of Morals* (tr. Mary Gregor) (Cambridge: Cambridge University Press, 1996), at pp. 95–110.

[29] John Stuart Mill, *On Liberty and Other Writings* (ed. Stefan Collini) (Cambridge: Cambridge University Press, 1989), at p. 13.

[30] John Gardner explores and defends important aspects of this idea in the context of his discussion of rape in *Offences and Defences: Selected Essays in the Philosophy of Criminal Law* (Oxford: Oxford University Press, 2007), at pp. 1–32.

[31] Philip Pettit and Christian List, *Group Agency: The Possibility, Design, and Status of Corporate Agents* (Oxford: Oxford University Press, 2011), at pp. 180–183.

the plurality of values in our world, which may legitimately be instantiated in principles and social forms and structures that vary, contingently, from one society or culture to another. Insofar as respect for autonomous and independent state governance facilitates recognition of such diversity, and allows for meaningful responsiveness to local traditions, understandings, and practices, it may then be worthy of great protection against external interferences.[32] So although the analogy between state and individual sovereignty, and permissible grounds of interference with them, must be handled with care due to their different relations to the realm of value, it may still provide a useful point of departure for thinking about the possibility of state crimes.

To be sure, should we really think of violations of human rights as the be-all and end-all of what might otherwise be conceived as 'criminal' grounds for limiting state sovereignty? I have several reasons for doubting it. First, if, as is sometimes the case, human rights are defined as a 'subset of justice'[33]—say, as injustices of a certain degree or kind—then we run into a problem similar to the one I identified above when discussing wrongs like torture and slavery. That is, insistence that all violations of human rights are injustices—including, for example, violations of the rights not to be tortured or enslaved—mischaracterizes what makes many such violations morally problematic. Accordingly, it runs the risk of blurring the parameters of the debate about what kinds of state behaviour properly call for external interference.

Notice, though, that even if the category of human rights is understood more broadly, as including rights grounded in a variety of values, it may still not do an adequate job at delimiting the scope of justified interferences. Indeed, assuming that a state's sufficiently significant wrongdoing is required to justify external interference in its internal affairs, are there not wrongs that meet this threshold, yet cannot be equated with violations of human rights? Genocide, often recognized as a paradigmatic interference-justifying wrong, provides a useful counterpoint. While genocide typically involves multiple violations of individual rights, such as violations of the rights to life and bodily integrity of a group's members, it is unclear that there is any distinctive right against genocide over and beyond these subsidiary rights. Rather, some argue, genocide seems to garner its distinguishing wrongness from the intention with which violations of such other basic rights are perpetrated—namely, the intention to destroy, in whole or in part, a national, ethnic, racial, or religious group, as such—as well as their scale.[34] Joseph

[32] John Rawls first appreciated the importance of this point. See further Samuel Freeman, 'Distributive Justice and the Law of Peoples' in *Justice and the Social Contract: Essays on Rawlsian Political Philosophy* (Oxford: Oxford University Press, 2007), pp. 297–321.

[33] See, e.g., Christopher Heath Wellman, 'Taking Human Rights Seriously', *Journal of Political Philosophy* 20(1) (2012): pp. 119–130, at p. 120, fn 3.

[34] See *Convention on the Prevention and Punishment of the Crime of Genocide*, 9 December 1948, Art. 2, 78 UNTS 277.

Raz expresses such scepticism even more trenchantly. 'To be sure', he writes, 'committing genocide is wrong, but is it the case that I have a right against the genocide of any people' over and above other rights that I have? Indeed, '[d]o I have a right against the annihilation of other groups, for example, of university professors?'[35] Were I to have such rights, one may think, I would be permitted to take steps to prevent members of these groups from voluntarily assimilating into other ones. And surely, that cannot be the case. Insofar as this reasoning is sound, then, not all wrongs, even very significant wrongs, may be equated with, or best understood as, violations of rights. Another good example may be that of state terrorism, against which we do not tend to think that there is any distinctive human right. Still, if any forms of state behaviour warrant condemnatory and punitive interferences, we generally think of genocide and terrorism as two exemplars.

Admittedly, for some who conceive of given communities, perhaps especially political ones, as more fundamental to individuals' meaningful and dignified survival, the genocide example may be less persuasive than the example of state terrorism.[36] In turn, the case of state terrorism may itself be less stark than instances of grave state wrongdoing involving no human victim—think of a state engaging in, or sanctioning, sustained campaigns of mass cruelty against animals. My point is that whatever example one prefers, it seems quite uncontroversial that at least some condemnable and, arguably, punishable state wrongs are not best understood as violations of human rights.

Again, I insist on condemnatory and punitive interferences, since condemnation and punishment are hallmarks of a criminal response—following what is characteristically a process through which alleged wrongdoers are publicly called to account for their legally individuated wrongs and found guilty.[37] This narrow focus is required since, at this stage of the argument, my question remains whether the normative practice of human rights could simply be said to stand in for state crimes. An additional objection could be that while violations of human rights may justify interferences with state sovereignty, there is nothing in the idea of human rights that specifically calls for, or is intrinsically connected to, a punitive response. If sound, as I think it is, this further objection entails that the category of human rights is not only under-inclusive but also over-inclusive, in terms of the wrongs it singles out.

To be sure, theorists who think of human rights as grounds of interference with state sovereignty tend to understand them as exceptionally important and universal

[35] Raz, 'Human Rights without Foundations', note 26, at p. 332.

[36] Cf. Claudia Card, 'Genocide and Social Death', *Hypatia* 18(1) (1993): pp. 63–79.

[37] In *Offences and Defences*, note 30, at p. 80, John Gardner echoes this characterization of criminal law. While he insists that this legal field is 'primarily a vehicle for the public identification of wrongdoing . . . and for responsible agents, whose wrongs have been thus identified, to *answer for* their wrongs by offering justifications and excuses for having committed them', he recognizes that it is also important as 'a vehicle for condemnation, deterrence, and punishment'.

rights, whose violations are morally and legally condemnable. In fact, human rights are often explicitly defended as rights the violation of which states must 'account' for, and can be 'blamed' (condemned, censured) for by 'international tribunals, where jurisdictional conditions are in place', as well as 'responsibly acting people and organisations outside the state'.[38] No doubt, such features of the practice of human rights provide striking parallels with what we otherwise conceive of as the province of criminalization. Since, by and large, violations of human rights are also prohibited legally—think of the plethora of international conventions prohibiting them—the main missing variable to be able to equate them with crimes seems to be punishment.

The kinds of interferences with state sovereignty that violations of human rights may warrant are generally not confined to punitive ones. On the contrary, one may easily conceive of suitable responses that are not intended in any way to set back violator states, but simply seek to prevent the continuation of their wrongful designs, or to alleviate their harmful effects through the provision of benefits or demands for reparations. Rawls foreshadowed this point when, recall, he suggested that while violations of human rights are generally to be condemned, violator states may only permissibly be subjected to forceful sanctions in some grave cases. Here, I take it, the point is not that in less serious cases only non-forceful sanctions are warranted, but that sanctions may sometimes altogether be out of place as a form of responsive interference. Thus, what really seems to be needed here is an account of when state punishment is called for, in contrast to other possible interfering responses which, in domestic parlance, could be better described as 'civil' (e.g. compensatory, restitutive, etc.) or 'preventive' in character. That is, we need an account of what differentiates violations of human rights for which a full-blown *criminal* response may be required, or at least permitted, from those for which it is not.

The key issue here is that the normative function of the practice of human rights—as many political theorists understand it in our current (emerging) world order—is generic. It is to disable, in cases of violations, the 'this is none of your business' response that states could otherwise make to block interferences in their internal affairs. Once this response is disabled, further argument is needed to determine what specific kinds of interferences are either required or permitted, as well as who may interfere. What is missing from the discussion, I suggest, is a core focus on punishment, as the key response that, at least in principle, all criminal wrongs warrant.[39] It is this dimension which, I think, makes the category of state crimes a meaningfully distinct sub-category of state violations of human rights—or, if one

[38] Joseph Raz, 'Human Rights in the Emerging World Order', *Transnational Legal Theory* 1 (2010): pp. 31–47, at p. 42.

[39] John Gardner insists that not every argument for criminal law amounts to an argument for punishment (see, e.g., *Offences and Defences*, note 30, at p. 282). While I regard punishment, *qua* response to criminal wrongdoing, as more central to this legal field than Gardner allows, the 'at least in principle' proviso in the text concedes that, in practice, punishment may not always be a justified response.

accepts my earlier point about the under-inclusiveness of the category of human rights, a meaningfully distinct normative category in its own right. Thus, state crimes do not constitute a redundant idea.

C. State Crimes as Internationally Punishable Wrongs of States

So far, my suggestion has been that a distinct category of state crimes would be useful as a means of singling out those condemnable state wrongdoings that warrant punishment, as well as focusing debate about their proper normative contours. Still, one may question whether there really are any instances of state wrongdoing that warrant a punitive response. Let me focus here on harmful state wrongdoing, which tends to be the kind of state wrongdoing that is deemed most morally urgent. In cases in which such wrongdoing can be adequately compensated *ex post*, one may think that insisting on punishing it would be unjustifiably callous. The argument may go as follows: Even well-tailored punishments of large organizations such as states risk saddling at least some of their individual members with unjustified burdens, losses, or other significant setbacks. Why take this risk? That is, why risk bringing additional unjustified harm into the world when adequate compensation is indeed possible?

One common retort is that punishment may be a deserved response to culpably imposed wrongful harm and, as such, be justified along with its attendant risks as intrinsically good or right. This kind of retributive response has recently been under heavy fire from some theorists of individual wrongdoing, who argue that desert of punishment is either an irremediably obscure idea or insufficiently valuable to justify the ills of the practice.[40] Insofar as this objection is sound in respect of individual desert of punishment, it is a fair question why it should not also be with respect to state desert. To be sure, some may further query whether corporate organizations such as states can, *qua* organizations meaningfully distinct from their individual members, ever intelligibly be said to deserve punishment for wrongdoing. That is, insofar as states are instrumentally valuable entities, why should we think that giving *them* anything that *they* allegedly 'deserve' has any intrinsic value, beyond its consequential value for individuals? Seeking to ascertain the accuracy of either of these provocative suggestions would here be unduly distracting. Thus, I must restrict myself to confessing my inclination to endorse at least the second one of them.[41]

[40] See especially Victor Tadros, *The Ends of Harm: The Moral Foundations of Criminal Law* (Oxford: Oxford University Press, 2011), at p. 321.

[41] I do suggest some marginal ways in which one may be able to make sense of a rather shallow idea of state desert of punishment in Tanguay-Renaud, 'Criminalizing the State', note 4, at p. 274. Constrast David Luban, 'War as Punishment', *Philosophy and Public Affairs* 39(4) (2012): pp. 299–330, who simply

Even if we assume that punishing a state in proportion to some measure of desert can have some marginal intrinsic value, I doubt that it, alone, could justify most instances of state punishment. Rather, if the practice is to be justified, in light of the important resources likely needed to punish states as well as the constant possibility of significant detrimental side-effects on individuals, a wider assessment of its valuable consequences seems called for.[42]

What may other valuable consequences of punishing states be? For one thing, harm occasioned through state wrongdoing may well not be compensable, or only be very partially compensable. In other words, it may not be possible to 'make it up' ex post facto with something as good, or nearly as good. In some cases, even mere attempts to do so only add insult to injury. Consider all the lost lives, or psychological trauma and sense of dehumanization and exploitation, that usually arise from state-led genocides, aggressions, enslavements, or establishment and maintenance by force of colonial dominations. No doubt, such wrongfully imposed harms should ideally be prevented before they arise, or thwarted as they unfold, insofar as this can be done through permissible means, without occasioning even more significant harm. Yet, what if they are not—say, because it was not realistically possible in the circumstances. And what if the most effective way of preventing the recurrence of such abominable wrongs is now to deter the wrongdoing state specifically, as well as other states more generally, by punishing it—say, by expelling it from relevant international organizations, imposing arms embargoes on it, or, more drastically, occupying it, dismantling it, or reconstituting it? In a sense, punishment of the state in question would then serve as a second-best form of remediation for its harmful wrongdoing. It would provide victims (and those related to them by relevant attachments, or perhaps simply by shared humanity) not so much with compensation for the wrongful harm—since, *ex hypothesi*, it is not available—but with very valuable protection against its recurrence. Indeed, one might well think that such protection is so valuable that there is a duty for those relevantly situated to exact it.

Victor Tadros has defended an account of individual crimes along similar lines, which helps give further substance to this proposal in respect of state crimes. Core crimes, Tadros argues, are wrongs whose deleterious consequences are not compensable *ex post*, yet whose perpetrators can permissibly be used, by means of punishment, to deter further similar wrongs.[43] They can be so used because they owe

assumes that states can deserve punishment, and that retributive punishment proportionate to such desert can be intrinsically valuable.

[42] As John Gardner reminds us when laying out the foundations for his pluralistic theory of criminal punishment, even when it comes to punishing individuals, the practice tends to be so costly, both pecuniarily and morally, that it 'patently needs all the justificatory help it can get' (in *Offences and Defences*, note 30, at p. 214). Cf. Scott Hershovitz's contribution to this volume.

[43] See Tadros, *The Ends of Harm*, note 40, chs. 12–14 (especially pp. 278–279).

it to their victims (and those relevantly related to them) to do the next best thing to not having wrongfully harmed them in the first place. That is, when adequate compensation is unavailable, they at least owe it to them to rescue them from further such wrongs. Such secondary duties, Tadros contends, are enforceable, in the sense that wrongdoers may be used as means to ensure the realization of their content. In the cases that concern us, they may be punished as a means of deterring further wrongs.[44]

Now, the objection against intentionally using (and harming) individuals as means to ends which are not their own, to which Tadros seeks to carve an exception for the punishment of wrongdoers, does not apply in the same way to states. One does not need to look for permissible exceptions to treat states as means to further ends, since states' primary value is their very instrumentality to the furtherance of individuals' interests. Still, all states are constituted by individuals, and derive all their matter and energy from them. So one still ought to be careful before vouching for the permissibility of any state punishment that may affect individuals detrimentally, even if it does so only as a side-effect (say, of sanctions targeted at a state's organizational structure or irreducible corporate decisions and plans).

Such care is perhaps especially called for in cases where suitably deterrent state punishments would risk imposing on individuals harms of a considerable magnitude. Still, the level of required care likely varies along with the kind of state wrongdoing and wrongdoer at issue. For example, in the face of wide-scale non-compensable genocides or mass killings, such as those orchestrated by the Nazi state, the Soviet Union in Stalin's time, or Mao's China, one may reasonably think that permissible punitive responses can be significantly less discriminate, as well as much more harmful and intrusive, than for lesser wrongs. In other words, deterring the recurrence of such wrongs may be so valuable, indeed so imperative, as to make it permissible to impose considerable burdens and harms, perhaps including death, on individuals—including individuals who are in no way liable to such treatment. To be sure, individuals' participation in, causal contribution to, or failure to oppose state wrongdoing, individuals' acts of identification or association with a wrongdoing state, or their general benefit from its deeds might make them liable to such ills. Yet, some extreme state wrongs may be such that even

[44] John Gardner disagrees with how Tadros frames his account. In 'Punishment and Compensation: A Comment', in R. Christopher (ed.), *George Fletcher's Essays on Criminal Law* (Oxford: Oxford University Press, 2012), pp. 70–75, at p. 74, Gardner insists:

> [T]here is no way to represent punishment as the fallback performance by the wrongdoer of the duty that he originally failed to perform. Unlike reparation, punishment is not something that the wrongdoer owes. For it is not something that he can give. It is something that is inflicted upon him by others, and the norms regulating it belong, in the final analysis, to their normative position and not to his.

I respond to Gardner on this point, in defence of Tadros, in François Tanguay-Renaud, 'Victor's Justice: The Next Best Moral Theory of Criminal Punishment?', *Law and Philosophy* 32 (2013): pp. 129–157, at pp. 144–145.

deontological constraints such as individual liability are, within reason, overridden by what is at stake.[45] I say 'within reason' to emphasize that of course, to be permissible, state punishment should not occasion bigger problems than it is intended to solve, and must have a reasonable chance of success.

Of course, most state wrongs will not be so extreme as to warrant the abandonment of all deontological constraints, or otherwise make it permissible to harm seriously or kill individual state members. Just war theorists of most stripes go to great lengths to emphasize this point.[46] Even when war is justified in response to wrongdoing, they recognize, it is often the case that not all means of carrying it out will be, due to applicable deontological considerations. Insofar as state wrongs are not significant enough to make it deontologically permissible to kill or harm seriously individuals, state punishments that have few, if any, detrimental effects on individuals are preferable. Yet, given the structure of states as large organized groups of individuals, most conceivable means of punishing them will risk having at least some such significant effects. It will then fall on the punisher to ensure that the individuals impacted are specifically liable to it, or that deviations are kept to a minimum and are offset by the overall value of the punishment. Insofar as this level of precision cannot be ensured, punishers should then strive to make it so that only states in which *all* individuals can permissibly be detrimentally impacted to some relevant extent are punished. Powerful arguments exist about when detrimental effects of state punishment may permissibly be dispersed among all their individual members (including victims), though their reach is typically limited to states that generally respect their citizens' core human rights, and whose authority is otherwise generally legitimate or not widely rejected.[47]

My aim here is not to engage in a detailed exploration of these arguments. Rather, it is to highlight that there may well be instances of state wrongdoing whose punishment would, at least in principle, have great deterrence value, yet for which, all things considered, the perpetrator state cannot permissibly be punished, due to morally unacceptable effects that this would have on individuals. Punishment of such wrongdoing states might then be said to be 'called for', in the subsidiary sense that, were they individual human persons, they could permissibly be (punitively) used as means to deter further wrongdoing. However, given the further problem of

[45] This is one of the lessons of Michael Walzer's discussion of 'supreme emergencies' in, for example, his 'Emergency Ethics', in *Arguing about War* (New Haven: Yale University Press, 2004) pp. 33–50. Constrast Victor Tadros, 'Duty and Liability', *Utilitas* 24(2) (2012): pp. 259–277, at p. 268, who insists on framing some such *in extremis* scenarios in deontological terms.

[46] Compare and contrast Michael Walzer, *Just and Unjust Wars: A Moral Argument with Historical Illustrations* (New York: Basic Books, 1977) and Jeff McMahan, *Killing in War* (Oxford: Oxford University Press, 2009).

[47] Here, I conflate different arguments developed in Avia Pasternak, *Responsible Citizens, Irresponsible States* (Oxford: Oxford University Press, 2021); Anna Stilz, 'Collective Responsibility and the State', *Journal of Political Philosophy* 19(2) (2011): pp. 190–208; Tanguay-Renaud, 'Criminalizing the State', note 4.

dispersion of burdens associated with punishments of wrongdoing states, it may not be possible to punish *them* permissibly.

To clarify, my suggestion here is that states' wrongdoings might still be said, in a derivative sense, to be crimes, insofar as the impermissibility of their punishment is simply due to pragmatic deficiencies on the part of punishers—most notably, unavailable means of enforcing sufficiently discriminate punishments. In such cases, even if the only permissible response to wrongdoing is a 'pure declaration of criminality', it might still properly be designated as such.[48] Indeed, as most theorists of individual criminalization now accept, such a declaration may itself have significant symbolic value, even if its symbolism is ultimately derived from a sense that the wrongdoing in question is one whose punishment, although impermissible, would be of great value. Although secondary, this sense of state crime fits quite seamlessly with the overall account defended here.

Some theorists, though, may be tempted to make more of the kinds of practical limitations I just mentioned and of my proposal. We simply do not have, the claim may be, the kinds of suitably resourced, impartial, reliable, and effective institutions required to adjudicate state wrongdoing justly on a reasonably systematic basis and, when warranted, to impose sufficiently discerning punishment on state wrongdoers. The United Nations Security Council, controlled by its five permanent member states, which tend to be guided primarily by their self-interest, is no such institution. Nor is the International Court of Justice (ICJ), whose jurisdiction is merely optional. Indeed, like the United Nations' Human Rights Committee, the ICJ has always steered clear of even considering the possibility of punitive state sanctions and, in any case, would have no dedicated resources to enforce them discerningly.[49] Of course, one could envisage the possibility of independently structured international institutions with appropriate jurisdiction, procedures, enforcement mechanisms, and resources. However, is it not the case that until such institutions exist, the value of labelling *any* legally recognized state wrongs as crimes is bound to remain symbolic? As I suggested earlier, symbolism matters and, for victims of grave state wrongdoing, symbolic criminal censure may mean a lot. Still, is it really the case that, since we do not have (now or in a foreseeable future) the kinds of international institutions that could ensure, to a reasonable extent, permissible punishment of wrongdoing states, the category of state

[48] This insight might partly explain David Luban's emphasis on the importance that declarations of state criminality could have in the international context. See David Luban, 'State Criminality and the Ambitions of International Criminal Law', in Tracy Isaacs and Richard Vernon (eds), *Accountability for Collective Wrongdoing* (Oxford: Oxford University Press, 2011): pp. 61–91, at p. 90.

[49] The ICJ came close to considering the issue in the *Bosnia v Serbia* case, in which Bosnia accused Serbia of violating its obligations under the Convention against genocide, but it stopped short of doing so. *Case Concerning the Application of the Convention for the Prevention and Punishment of Genocide (Bosnia & Herzegovina v Serbia and Montenegro)*, 2007 I.C.J. General List No. 91 (Judgment of February 26).

crimes must be a symbolic one—or, perhaps at most, an aspirational category inviting the establishment of relevant institutions?

Raz offers an appropriate rejoinder. '[U]ntil such institutions exist', he argues, 'normally one should refrain from attempts to use any coercive measures'.[50] The 'normally' is crucial since, recall, a state's wrongdoing may be so clear and so harmful that its punishment at the hands of other states, groups of individuals, or international organizations can be justified, or perhaps even required, for the sake of deterring its recurrence. That is, a state's wrongdoing may be so clear and so harmful that its punishment may be justified, even required, *despite* its significant and indiscriminate detrimental effects on individuals (and other relevant moral costs). Thus, even in our contemporary world, the possibility of permissible international punishments of states for some of their wrongdoings is very real, although, as Rawls suggests, likely confined to the gravest wrongs. Since prohibitions of such wrongs are generally well entrenched in international legal documents, a category of state crimes reflecting the general permissibility of their punishment is then more than symbolically and aspirationally useful.

D. State Crimes as Domestically Punishable Wrongs of States

What Raz's rejoinder critically omits to consider is the possibility of permissible state punishment at the domestic level. For one thing, states' wrongdoings which are of such magnitude as to warrant, at the international level, relatively unfettered punitive interferences with their sovereignty likely often also undermine the legitimacy of their domestic authority over their individual subjects. Some such individuals may then also be in a position to interfere permissibly with the operation of their state and, sometimes, to do so punitively. Indeed, since the grave wrongs in question are typically conceived as wrongs that humanity as a whole, as opposed to a distinct polity,[51] has the standing to condemn and, within reason, may seek to punish, why should a wrongdoing state's population, often itself victimized by such wrongs, be treated any differently?

Here, the way in which we tend to conceive of tyrannical states' ultimate accountability to their populations is instructive. Such states—which rule through terror, by engaging in unpredictable violence against innocents, including widespread killings and torture, as well as sheer exploitation of certain classes—are commonly cited as examples of states against whose operation individual subjects can permissibly interfere forcefully, even to the point of overthrowing them.[52] In its preamble,

[50] Raz, 'Human Rights in the Emerging World Order', note 38, at p. 43.

[51] See, e.g., note 38.

[52] Even theorists who otherwise deny the permissibility of any forceful resistance against states tend to agree that tyrannies form a special case. See, e.g., Arthur Ripstein, *Force and Freedom: Kant's Legal and Political Philosophy* (Cambridge, MA: Harvard University Press, 2009), at pp. 339–343. While it is true that Ripstein also argues that tyrannical states are so far from the ideal of statehood that they

the *Universal Declaration of Human Rights* clearly sets out that 'if man is not to be compelled to have recourse, as a last resort, to rebellion against tyranny and oppression ... human rights should be protected by the rule of law'.[53] Nowadays, this recourse is explicitly authorized by more than forty state constitutions and, tellingly, is often explicitly recognized as a 'remedy' of last resort.[54] This remedy is clearly not a panacea. It is morally risky, perhaps especially insofar as it involves messy popular uses of force, which may be insufficiently measured and discriminating vis-à-vis valuable aspects of institutions and individuals themselves, as well as unlikely to succeed. Thus, as Tony Honoré insists, the remedy is likely only permissible as an 'ultimate sanction' for state wrongdoing that is 'weighty, crucial, and severe', when other legal remedies are not available.[55] Still, it is unclear what exact types and scale of state wrongdoing may render this remedy of last resort permissible. For example, an argument may be made that since not every wrongdoing that exceeds a state's legitimate domestic authority is a reason for international interference, the threshold of wrongdoing for permissible domestic popular interference, *including* punitive interference, could sometimes be lower.[56] What is more, although some, such as John Locke, argue for the permissibility of forceful popular remediation only against state-led 'unjust and *unlawful* force',[57] and although constitutions typically only authorize it in response to state violations of *legally* entrenched constitutional norms of a fundamental kind, it seems that the permission to resort to it is, at bottom, a moral one—as implied in the *Universal Declaration*. Yet, legal recognition of this remedy for condemnable state legal wrongdoing is significant for my argument. Given the conceivably punitive forms it may take, it conjures up the possibility that some legal wrongs of states may be properly singled out as domestically punishable wrongs—and, thus, in line with my earlier claims, as domestic crimes.

Of course, I am not claiming that all permissible popular acts of rebellion against states for their legal wrongdoing are punitive. Many such acts will be primarily incapacitative in aim, and simply seek to put an end to ongoing harmful wrongdoing. Still, one can imagine scenarios where stopping an instance of state

should not be understood as states properly so called, his framing of the issue is misleading. No conceptual argument can show that what are commonly recognized as states cannot maintain themselves through terror.

53 UN General Assembly, *Universal Declaration of Human Rights*, 10 December 1948, 217 A (III), available at: <https://www.ohchr.org/en/human-rights/universal-declaration/translations/english>.

54 A list of relevant constitutional provisions can be found in an appendix to Tom Ginsburg, Daniel Lansberg-Rodriguez, and Mila Versteeg, 'When to Overthrow Your Government: The Right to Resist in the World's Constitutions', *UCLA Law Review* 60 (2013): pp. 1184–1260.

55 Tony Honoré, 'The Right to Rebel', *Oxford Journal of Legal Studies* 8(1) (1988): pp. 34–54.

56 This question is part of a larger debate about the precise relationship between international sovereignty and domestic legitimacy, which I cannot resolve here.

57 John Locke, *Two Treatises of Government* (Cambridge: Cambridge University Press, 1988), at p. 402 [Emphasis added].

wrongdoing would do little to prevent its recurrence, which might take even worse forms. In some such scenarios, it is at least conceivable that an oppressed population could permissibly seek to set back their wrongdoing state further than is necessary to stop its wrongdoing, so as to deter it, as well as other organizations or individuals inclined to emulate it, from engaging in further misdeeds. Thus, justified domestic popular punishments of state wrongdoers are at least conceivable on grounds of deterrence—whose value may be bolstered by the symbolic and expressive value of explicitly treating the burdens and setbacks deliberately inflicted in response to such wrongdoing as punitive. As I have suggested in previous work, in most societies the description of such deliberately inconveniencing responses as punishment has come to acquire valuable meaning, in that it symbolizes and expresses fitting attitudes towards culpable wrongdoers and their altered moral standing.[58] While, on its own, such symbolism may not be sufficiently valuable to justify detrimental repercussions of state punishment on individuals and other salient moral costs (e.g. the diversion of resources required for such punishment), it may certainly bolster deterrence-based arguments.

Yet, remember that given the moral risks attendant to it, domestic popular remediation of state wrongdoing must remain a last resort. That is, insofar as they are available, better resourced as well as more discerning and measured institutional responses are morally preferable, even when state wrongdoing is of great magnitude. The interesting point to note here is that theorists, as well as constitutional documents, admitting of the possibility of forceful popular responses to state wrongdoing commonly assume that, unlike at the international level, appropriate institutional responses are often domestically available. Before forceful popular remediation can be permissibly carried out, we are reminded, all these other legal remedies must be deemed inadequate. What might these other remedies be? No doubt, those self-imposed by the wrongdoing state itself,[59] or established by those who initially constituted it.

Indeed, in many jurisdictions with which I am familiar, an extensive apparatus for the judicial review and remediation of state constitutional wrongdoing of various kinds and degrees is already operational. I speak of wrongdoing since the constitutions of the states in question typically guarantee a plethora of individual rights and freedoms that bind the state, and whose violations are commonly held to be publicly and legally wrongful.

[58] Tanguay-Renaud, 'Criminalizing the State', note 4, at pp. 279–280.

[59] The possibility of holding oneself to account and punishing oneself is often contemplated for individuals. Thus, in 'Wrongs and Fault' in Andrew Simester (ed.), *Appraising Strict Liability* (Oxford: Oxford University Press, 2005), pp. 51–80, at p. 76, John Gardner writes that 'The remorseful give themselves a hard time for their wrongs, a hard time which they hold themselves to deserve on the model of punishment'. Similarly, I am contemplating here the prospect of states institutionally holding themselves to account, as well as condemning and punishing themselves, for the perpetration of legal wrongs.

Let me focus on the Canadian example, with which I am most familiar. The *Canadian Charter of Rights and Freedoms* prohibits the state from subjecting individuals to cruel and unusual treatment and punishment (s. 12), unreasonable searches and seizures (s. 8), and arbitrary arrest and detention (s. 9). Even more broadly, it prohibits the state from depriving individuals of life, liberty, and security, save in accordance with so-called principles of fundamental justice (s. 7).[60] Should we not think of violations of such prohibitions, irrespective of their scale, as possible domestic crimes of the state, insofar as they can now be institutionally addressed with appropriate discernment and measure? After all, in salient ways, they all seem analogous to forms of individual behaviour otherwise domestically criminalized as *mala in se*.

First off, characterizing violations of such prohibitions as crimes may strike some as awkward because of the structure of the wrongs in question. For example, there is no explicit prohibition of state murder in the *Canadian Charter*, only of state deprivations of life which are not in accordance with principles of fundamental justice. There is no prohibition of state theft, but only of unreasonable searches and seizures. I do not think that the structure of these constitutional wrongs makes them any worse candidates for state crimes. They are what John Gardner calls 'fault-anticipating wrongs', in the sense that they can only be only committed without justification.[61] Yet, and this is part of Gardner's point, many existing individual crimes share this structure. Consider the crime of extortion, which consists in threatening, accusing, menacing, or using violence against another person with the intent of obtaining anything from that person, 'without reasonable justification or excuse'.[62] Or consider property crimes such as mischief or arson that require that one not have a 'legal justification or excuse or colour of right'.[63]

Note, further, that the fact that the *Canadian Charter* allows the state, when judicially called to account for rights infringements, to raise additional defences—most commonly, that infringements were 'reasonable', 'prescribed by law', and 'demonstrably justified in a free and democratic society' (s. 1)—does not make the constitutional norms infringed any worse candidates for state crimes. Indeed, it is uncontroversial that individuals called to account for crimes of murder, assault, theft, and so forth, can themselves invoke justificatory defences as means of exculpation. Admittedly, certain actions which, at the hands of ordinary individuals, would constitute unjustified criminal wrongs may be justified when perpetrated by the state. For example, the state may be able to justify forcefully coercing individuals on a broad scale for the sake of public goods that it is in a position to advance. Ordinary individuals, who are differently situated, may well not be so justified.

[60] *Canadian Charter of Rights and Freedoms*, Part I of the *Constitution Act, 1982* being Schedule B to the *Canada Act 1982* (UK), 1982, c. 11.

[61] Gardner, *Offences and Defences*, note 30, at pp. 150–153; 'Wrongs and Fault', note 59, at pp. 67–70.

[62] *Criminal Code of Canada*, note 15, s. 346.

[63] *Ibid.*, s. 429(2).

That said, the converse is also true. That is, individuals may also be able to justify wrongdoing that the state could not justify—say, because the state's wrongful behaviour was not 'prescribed by law', in dereliction of the prescriptions of the rule of law, which specifically apply to it *qua* organization claiming legitimate authority to govern. Thus, legal definitions of state and individual wrongs (and possible justifications for them) plausibly vary in ways that do not entail that their designation as crimes is unintelligible.

Instead, I would suggest that if constitutional wrongs of states are typically not recognized as crimes, it does not have so much to do with their structure as, once again, with the remedies held to be available for them. Indeed, although constitutional wrongs are routinely condemned, remedies tend to be conceived in primarily incapacitative terms—that is, as means to put an end to ongoing state wrongdoing. Thus, in Canada, state action that violates Charter rights may be 'invalidated' (i.e., deprived of any legal effect); 'nullified' or 'quashed', as in cases of wrongful convictions and sentences; 'stayed', as in cases of wrongful judicial proceedings; or ordered to be reversed, as in cases of injunctions or prerogative writs such as *habeas corpus*, *mandamus*, prohibition, and *certiorari*. Admittedly, in cases of very serious and clear harmful constitutional wrongdoing, courts sometimes also award damages to victims, but, by and large, only of a compensatory kind.

Then again, one may think—with Canada's preeminent authority on constitutional remedies, Kent Roach—that there is a role to play for punitive remedies, such as punitive damages, in the context of Charter adjudication. That role may be 'to respond to cases in which there was no reason why the Charter should not have been respected and to provide incentives to respect it in the future'.[64] Once again, deterrence presents itself as a central reason for responding to state wrongdoing in a punitive way. This time, though, it is discussed in the context of a much more constrained institutional setting. First, the Supreme Court of Canada has made clear that its power to craft and impose 'appropriate and just' remedies for violations of rights under s. 24(1) of the Charter includes the power to monitor closely the implementation and effects of the remedies it imposes.[65] Thus, the prospect of being able to punish the state, through damages or otherwise, in ways that significantly control, if not eradicate, impermissible detrimental impacts on individual members becomes more plausible. This point must be added to the various theoretical arguments, referred to earlier, according to which in a state such as Canada that is reasonably legitimate, rights-abiding, and popularly assented to, some detrimental

[64] Kent Roach, *Constitutional Remedies in Canada* (Aurora: Canada Law Book, 2008), at pp. 11.49–11.50. In *Vancouver (City) v* Ward, [2010] 2 SCR 28, at para. 56, the Supreme Court of Canada also had the following to say about the possibility of imposing punitive damages on the state for violations of the Canadian Charter: 'The reality is that public law damages, in serving the objects of vindication and deterrence, may assume a punitive aspect. Nevertheless, it is worth noting a general reluctance in the international community to award purely punitive damages.'

[65] See especially *Doucet-Boudreau v Nova Scotia (Minister of Education)*, [2003] 3 SCR 3.

costs and burdens of state punishment might permissibly impact the general population as a whole, without the need for individual distinctions. This institutional point should also be added to the possibility that some forms of institutional domestic punitive responses may have no meaningful trickle-down effects on populations. Exclusion of evidence conceived as an inconvenient sanction for the state's constitutionally wrongful acquisition of it may be just such an example, although it is only rarely discussed in such terms in Canada.[66]

If I am right here, a category of domestic state crimes may have a real *raison d'être* that extends much beyond the kinds of grave and wide-scale wrongdoings that warrant punitive popular rebellion or sub-optimally discriminate international punishments. That the category is even more rarely discussed in the context of domestic public law than in the international law context might then have more to do—as John Gardner himself once suggested to me—with the lack of imagination of public judges and lawyers, resulting in the slow and patchy development of their field, than with its unintelligibility or unjustifiability.

E. Of States, Crimes, and Their Deterrence

I want to consider briefly one last objection to state crimes as I have defended them so far. Alice Ristroph, who has explored the question more carefully than any others in terms of the United States constitutional context, suggests that '[d]eterrence theories may simply reflect undue anthropomorphism. Perhaps the state is not much like a person after all, and it cannot be regulated according to the same legal models that we use for private individuals'.[67] I cannot do justice to this objection here, as doing so would require an overly lengthy and complex inquiry into the nature of the state. In this chapter, I have simply accepted John Gardner's wisdom that states can themselves engage in wrongdoing, and may be the object of remediation of various kinds for it. However, let me conclude by sketching some possible avenues of response.

Elsewhere I have argued, following Christian List and Philip Pettit,[68] that suitably constituted states may be corporate moral agents in their own right, which can arrange for criminal wrongdoing in ways that are irreducible to the actions and intentions of their individual members.[69] Some existing crimes already seem sensitive to this possibility—such as the various forms of the international crime of

66 Contrast the position of the Supreme Court of the United States on this question: '[W]e have said time and again that the *sole* purpose of the exclusionary rule is to deter misconduct by law enforcement.' *Davis v United States*, 564 US 229 (2011) at p. 246.

67 Alice Ristroph, 'Covenants for the Sword', *University of Toronto Law Journal* 61 (2011), pp. 657–690, at p. 686.

68 Pettit and List , *Group Agency*, note 31.

69 Tanguay-Renaud, 'Criminalizing the State', note 4.

apartheid that require 'legislative measures' aimed at dominating and systematically oppressing a given racial group.[70] I have also argued that states may meaningfully be held responsible for their crimes *qua* wrongdoing agents (over and above any responsibility that could be ascribed to their individual members). However, as Gardner's work suggests, even when states do not meet the conditions of irreducible agency, there may still be good reasons to hold something we call 'the state'—say, a more loosely defined, territorially bounded collectivity—criminally responsible for the wrongs of relevant individuals (perhaps officials), *as if* the state had perpetrated them.[71] The important point here is that, according to both the first (real agency) and the second (fiction) paradigms of state responsibility, all the matter and energy of states is provided by individuals.

In the case of the real agency paradigm, individuals' participation in the state is modulated through a suitable constitutional framework that sets out aims, divides labour, and ascribes roles and responsibilities. As a result of individuals' adherence to this framework, judgments, attitudes, and plans that cannot be reduced to those of state members arise, and may lead to irreducible state wrongdoing properly so called. Still, it is individuals who provide the state with access to evidence and enable it to gain the understanding required for making evaluative judgments about how it should act. Insofar as these individuals can understand responses to state wrongdoing as punitive, it is then likely that the state will also understand them as such. And insofar as punishment creates disincentives for specific types of action that relevant individual members understand as such, it is also likely that the state will understand it. Of course, the kinds of punitive disincentives that may deter large organizations such as states from engaging in wrongdoing may sometimes differ from those that would deter individuals acting alone. Still, should this realization not be considered more as an invitation to think creatively about ways of deterring state wrongdoing, which may otherwise be irremediable, than as a reason for abdication?

In the case of the fiction paradigm, the link is perhaps even simpler. Insofar as relevant individuals understand the disincentives created by punishment of 'the

[70] International Convention on the Suppression and Punishment of the Crime of Apartheid, G.A. res. 3068 (XXVIII)), 28 U.N. GAOR Supp. (No. 30) at 75, U.N. Doc. A/9030 (1974), 1015 U.N.T.S. 243, entered into force 18 July 1976, Art. III.

[71] In *Law as a Leap of Faith*, note 1, at p. 65, John Gardner argues that 'there is nothing wrong with a legal fiction of concerted agency, if by that phrase we mean simply that the law attributes actions by one agent (an official) to another (an institution) under norms that make the former a representative of, and hence an agent who acts on behalf of, the latter'. In 'Hart and Feinberg on Responsibility', in Matthew H. Kramer, Claire Grant, Ben Colburn, and Antony Hatzistavrou (eds), *The Legacy of H.L.A. Hart: Legal, Political, and Moral Philosophy* (Oxford: Oxford University Press, 2008), pp. 121–140, at p. 138, he goes even further and suggests: 'Aren't there cases in which a fiction of basic responsibility may, with moral propriety, be sustained in the law (or in other institutional settings), so that the advertised precondition of consequential responsibility may be treated as satisfied when it is really not?' On the justified attribution of criminal liability to the state for crimes of its representatives, see also Peter Cane, *Responsibility in Law and Morality* (Oxford: Hart Publishing, 2002), at pp. 266–267.

state', it may take no more for 'the state' to be deterred. So, for example, List and Pettit suggest that it may sometimes be permissible to punish all individual members of a state (to some degree) for the individual wrongdoing of only some, so as to make clear to all members that, unless they develop routines for keeping these individuals in check, they will incur costs.[72] Of course, general punishment of individuals in ways that do not track their personal liability may be objectionable on a variety of grounds. As I suggested, though, this objection may not be valid in all such cases. There may also be cases of collective 'state' punishment where all individuals are indeed liable, if only vicariously and for reasons of fairness. No doubt, state punishments meant to act as a deterrent may fail to do so at an empirical level in both the fictional and real cases, but this problem is not particular to state punishment, and may extend to the punishment of individuals and corporate bodies more generally. In this chapter, I have assumed that criminal punishment of individuals can have significant, if not infallible, deterrent effects, and that the same could be true for organizations like states.

Another reason for thinking that states may not be deterred through punishment is that they may simply legislate themselves out of jeopardy. This is one reason why I have insisted throughout on discussing the possibility of state crimes in terms of legally entrenched norms that, generally, cannot easily be modified by states—namely, international legal norms, such as some key human rights norms, thought to have acquired the status of *jus cogens*, as well as domestic constitutional norms. Of course, in the domestic context, where courts may be suitably independent from the rest of the state to hold it account meaningfully for its constitutional wrongs and punish it as warranted, social and political pressures may still lead them to abdicate their institutional responsibilities. Ristroph harbours this worry to a particularly acute extent, and questions judiciaries' general ability to hold states to account and to deter them through punishment, at least in respect of their deliberately harmful wrongdoing. I tend to be less pessimistic than her about the overall prospects of state accountability—even criminal accountability—through domestic judicial avenues. Given the wide variety of state wrongdoings that courts are called upon to review, both in terms of their seriousness and magnitude, I find it hard to see, considering the judicial history of states such as Canada, Germany, or even India and South Africa, why one would think that they cannot perform their role adequately in relation to a good number of wrongs. Of course, insofar as Ristroph's remarks hold true with respect to the most abusive and violent forms of state legal wrongdoing, domestic judicial accountability may have to give way to popular or international accountability. Yet, as I have sought to argue in this chapter, even at these levels, criminal accountability might have its place.

[72] Pettit and List, *Group Agency*, note 31, at pp. 168–169.

One last note. In this chapter, I have emphasized the possibility of permissibly deterring some state legal wrongdoings through punishment as the primary reason for remaining open to the category of international state crimes. At various points, though, I also suggested that whatever the symbolic value of treating such responses as crimes may be, it should also be factored in. No doubt, those who think that states' desert of punishment for their wrongdoing is an intelligible and at least minimally valuable notion will also argue that it should figure in all-things-considered assessments of state criminality. At the same time, I also suggested that, given the likely high moral costs of treating state wrongdoings as crimes and punishing them, these more marginal values can play no more than a subsidiary role, bolstering the value of deterrence. Now, at the domestic level, when institutions of state accountability are already well established and may impose much more measured and discerning punishment on states, arguments may be made that symbolism (and desert?) ought to be given more play. The variety of state wrongs properly handled as crimes at that level might then turn out to be even broader than I otherwise allowed.

F. Conclusion

I said, initially, that I would investigate the propriety and usefulness of the category of state crimes based on John Gardner's theoretical commitments to the possibility of distinct state agency, the applicability to the state of the general principles of morality that bind us all, and some version of legal moralism as the best way of understanding criminal wrongdoing. I proceeded to argue that, if one takes the way thus paved by Gardner, a good case may be made for upholding the category. Not everyone thinks like Gardner. Among those who do not are more 'politically minded' criminal law theorists, who resist understanding criminal wrongdoing in terms of its relationship with ordinary moral wrongdoing, or understand the state as an entity so radically different, both conceptually and normatively, from ordinary individual moral agents that it is nothing short of unintelligible to analogize it to individual criminals. While I cannot fully answer this more fundamental critique here, I hope to have shown that grounding the analysis in Gardner's key commitments leads to insightful lines of arguments and credible conclusions, with which these sceptics will now have to contend.

11

Rape Trauma and Rape's Wrongness

*Kate Greasley**

A. The 'Pure' Case and the Reasonable Reactions Argument

Rape is paradigmatically harmful. The manifold harms that rapists inflict on their victims can include physical harm, especially when perpetrated with gratuitous violence. Nowadays, though, it is the psychological and emotional damage wrought by rape that tends to take centre stage when people reflect on its harmfulness. Sexual activity need not involve any bodily harm beyond that attendant to the sexual penetration itself to count as rape; it need not even involve the physical violence of overpowering force.[1] This suggests that the badness of rape, for its victims, transcends harm of the brute physical kind. As Alan Wertheimer writes:

> We cannot explain why non-consensual sexual penetration is so traumatic except on the assumption that the invasion of one's sexual organs or the use of one's body for another's sexual pleasure is experienced as a special sort of violation.[2]

The potential mental and emotional harms of rape are abundant and varied.[3] On the one hand, a rape victim might be afflicted by long-term psychological impairments as a result of her assault. These could manifest as post-traumatic stress disorder, liability to being 'triggered', difficulty with developing future intimacy, feelings of shame, reduced self-worth, fear or distrust, to name just a few potential sequelae. Somewhat differently, there is also the intense distress experienced during the rape itself—what Wertheimer called the 'synchronic distress' felt when someone is subjected to sex she experiences as non-consensual throughout its duration. This synchronic distress is a feature of many rapes, but not all: consider, for example, a rape victim who is insensate as a result of heavy intoxication.

* For helpful comments, I am grateful to Michelle Dempsey, James Edwards, Adam Perry, Thomas Adams, Mark Dsouza, Raquel Barradas de Freitas, Andrea Dolcetti, Hasan Dindjer, Kevin Toh, Victor Tadros, Patrick Tomlin; the participants at the Warwick Law and Philosophy Colloquium in January 2019, especially Adam Slavny; and the participants of the Edinburgh Legal Theory Seminar Series in May 2019, especially Maggie O'Brien, Euan MacDonald, and Chloë Kennedy.

[1] Consider, for example, sex undertaken in the context of an egregious, consent-vitiating deception.

[2] A. Wertheimer, *Consent to Sexual Relations* (CUP, 2003) 92.

[3] Cf. Susan Brownmiller, *Against Our Will: Men, Women, and Rape* (1975). See also J. Jordan, *Serial Survivors: Women's Narratives of Surviving Rape* (Federation Press, 2008).

Kate Greasley, *Rape Trauma and Rape's Wrongness* In: *From Morality to Law and Back Again.* Edited by: Michelle Madden Dempsey and François Tanguay-Renaud, Oxford University Press. © Kate Greasley 2023. DOI: 10.1093/oso/9780198860594.003.0011

It is by reference to these various harms, which John Gardner collectively termed the 'trauma of rape',[4] that most people would likely explain the egregious wrongness of committing rape. In a highly influential article co-authored with Stephen Shute, Gardner sought to upend this conventional wisdom.[5] The argument revolves around an imaginary scenario concerning an exceptional rape that is entirely harmless. The key features are that the victim of the rape is drunk or drugged to the point of unconsciousness, the rapist wears a condom, there is no physical harm sustained whatsoever, and the victim continues on with her life exactly as she would have otherwise, forever oblivious to what has happened. For good measure, they even have the rapist run over and killed immediately after committing the crime, so as to preclude any possibility of discovery through confession, and subsequent distress to the victim or anyone else.[6] Here, then, we have an unusual case of an utterly harmless rape; there is no experiential suffering at all, neither synchronic nor after the fact.

Gardner and Shute (hereafter 'G&S') counted on their readers to react to this imaginary case exactly as they did: with horror and disgust. For their point was that, even with every possible harm stripped out of it, it is unarguable that what is imagined in this unusual case *is* a rape and that, as such, it is seriously morally wrong. A harmless rape still qualifies as the same atrocious violation, they argued. Fastening on to this reflection, a core claim of G&S's 'The Wrongness of Rape' is that the wrongness of rape is *not*, in fact, 'a function of the harmfulness of rape'.[7] For all harm has been excluded in their imaginary case and yet, we surely agree, the basic wrong of rape remains.

That basic wrong, as G&S explicate it, is the 'sheer use' of another person for the rapist's own ends, in violation of the Kantian-like maxim that one must never treat another person merely as an instrument.[8] When a rapist uses his victim sexually, indifferent to her consent, he objectifies his victim by treating her as a 'mere repository of use-value'.[9] This specific kind of wrongful objectification, which they also describe as a denial of the victim's personhood, is as present in the imaginary harmless rape as it is in paradigmatic, harmful perpetrations. This is what confirms it as the basic wrong of rape. G&S call the imaginary harmless rape the 'pure' case of rape. Marginal though it is in terms of its typicality, it is precisely here, with all the usual harms stripped away, where the essential wrong of rape can be effectively distilled.[10] Those further harms (the emotional and physical harms which I will

[4] J. Gardner, 'Reasonable Reactions to the Wrongness of Rape' (2017) 29 *Denning Law Journal* 3–16 (henceforth 'Reasonable Reactions') 5.

[5] J. Gardner and S. Shute, 'The Wrongness of Rape', in J Gardner, *Offences and Defences: Selected Essays in the Philosophy of Criminal Law* (OUP, 2007), pp. 1–32 (henceforth 'Wrongness of Rape').

[6] ibid 5.

[7] ibid 3.

[8] ibid 16.

[9] ibid 15.

[10] ibid.

refer to as 'rape trauma') that typically do obtain, but need not, are hence, in G&S's words, only 'epiphenomenal' to that basic wrong, the wrong of sheer use.[11]

B. The Reasonable Reactions Argument

While the argument from the pure case supplies much of the motivating force for G&S's account of the wrongness of rape, it is bolstered by an intriguing supporting argument, more often overlooked. The basic wrong of rape *must* precede its harm rather than follow from it, they argued, if we are to acknowledge the rational agency of rape victims. A crucial premise here is that our emotional reactions to events are answerable to reason. One's feelings may be out of line with good sense for any number of reasons: misplaced values, over-sensitivity, plain bad judgement, and so on. Not all emotional reactions are appropriate responses to what happens. Moreover, treating people as rational agents means appreciating their ability to bring their reactions into line with reason.

If we think our reactions are on the whole evaluable, then this must include reactions to rape. A harm-centric account of rape's wrongness would have it that rape is wrong because it causes trauma to victims, including by causing mental and emotional distress. But we do not think those reactions are irrational or pathological. If that were so, there could be as much reason to recondition victims to be more nonchalant in the face of rape as there is to punish rapists. This is, naturally, a very disquieting prospect. It is not just that people *happen* to react badly to rape, then. We believe it is entirely appropriate for them to react as they do, because of the grave wrong we recognise has been done to them regardless of how they did happen to react.

For G&S, this all entails that the reactions which make up rape trauma '*cannot constitute but rather have to shadow the essential wrongness of rape*', since we must explain 'what it is about the act of rape that gave the victim a reason to react this way' if her reaction is to be regarded as something other than pathology, irrationality, or hysteria.[12] The integral point here is that when a person feels traumatized and violated by a rape, '*this feeling is justified*', as they write.[13] For that to be the case, though, there must be some antecedent wrong to which those victims are justifiably reacting. On G&S's telling, it is the prior wrong of sheer use—the basic wrong of rape—that victims are appropriately responding to with their trauma. The pure case is additionally revealing, then, because it strips out 'the victim's evaluation-dependent reactions to the rape'.[14] By doing so, it pinpoints what the wrong is that

[11] ibid 7.
[12] ibid 6.
[13] ibid 16 (emphasis mine).
[14] ibid 7.

we would take the victim to be legitimately distressed by *had* she been aware of it. For shorthand, I'll refer to this as the *reasonable reactions argument*. Although it tends to attract less attention than its companion argument about the pure case, what follows here will reveal that it is in some respects the more formidable of the two.

The argument in 'The Wrongness of Rape' has garnered ample dissent in the time since it was written. I will not attempt to address all points of objection here, or to offer a full appraisal of G&S's analysis. Rather, after laying out the main pressure points for both the Gardner–Shute thesis and its antithesis, I will zero in on the reasonable reactions argument. As I will elucidate, this argument presents a very special impediment for the alternative view that rape trauma does indeed *ground* the basic wrongness of rape and is not merely 'epiphenomenal' to it.

C. Harming and Wronging in Rape

Gardner and Shute's analysis has some readily apparent pay-offs. Most prominently, anchoring the core wrongness of rape on the sheer sexual use of another person allows us to retain the judgement that the 'pure' case of rape is no less wrong *qua* rape than any other instance.[15] A related pay-off is that the emotional trauma of rape is held out as reason-responsive and non-pathological, which, in turn, asserts the agency and rationality of those whose trauma it is. This just *is* the argumentative force of the reasonable reactions argument.

For all of this, objections have been forthcoming. In the most general terms, dissenters from the G&S thesis allege, in one way or another, that it improperly marginalizes rape trauma in an account of what is so wrong about rape.[16] A more specific and noteworthy objection to G&S's account can be dismissed fairly quickly, though. This is the suggestion, by some scholars, that the wrong of 'sheer use' is too broad to capture the specific wrong of rape, since there are multitudinous possible examples of the sheer use of one person by another which do not amount to rape, or do not even take place in a sexual context.[17] Someone who uses another person merely as a medical dummy or as a human stepladder, totally indifferent to her

[15] Note that a harmless rape may be, nevertheless, less wrong than harmful rapes on other metrics, including all-things-considered wrongness. The same goes for sexual assaults that inflict lesser or greater measures of overall harm.

[16] Cf: bob Watt, 'The Story of Rape: Wrongdoing and Emotional Imagination' (2014) *Denning Law Journal* 46; Victor Tadros, 'The Distinctiveness of Domestic Abuse: A Freedom Based Account' (2005) 65 La. L. Rev.); Daniel Statman, 'Gardner on the Wrongness of Rape' (2012) 1 *Jerusalem Review of Legal Studies* 110, and John Stanton-Ife, 'Horrific Crime' in R.A. Duff et al (eds) *The Boundaries of the Criminal Law* (OUP, 2010).

[17] See, in particular, Statman (2012, above) and Stanton-Ife (2010, above). The examples are drawn from these authors.

interests or her value as a person, engages in the sheer use of that person, but he has not committed a wrong that mirrors rape.

As Gardner adumbrated in later writing,[18] the answer to this objection is already embedded in the explanation of what is so egregious about non-consensual sexual penetration as compared with other physical assaults, including sexual ones. 'Why do violations of *this* kind have such special import for those who suffer them?', G&S ask.[19] Understanding the special badness of rape must 'involve some attention to social meaning', they answer.[20] For better or worse, penetrative sex is socially endowed with a very special symbolism and meaning. The cultural importance of penetrative sex gives, in turn, 'a special social meaning to rape that other sheer uses do not share'.[21] In other words, things can matter because they matter, no less here than anywhere else. Rape is not just any kind of sheer use, then. It is an especially egregious instance of sheer *sexual* use, which 'trades on the social meaning of sexual penetration'.[22] Paying attention to this social meaning, and how rape perverts it, is the key to understanding why rape is a particularly horrendous species of sexual assault, and of instrumentalizing another person.

Uncertainty about G&S's core claim that the harmfulness of rape is merely 'epiphenomenal' to its wrongness may run along different lines, however. To be sure, no one is likely to contest the conclusion that the undiscovered rape of an insensate victim is seriously wrong. Still, we may wonder whether G&S were unduly dazzled, in their theorizing, by the 'pure' case of rape, which is of course still the marginal one. Maybe it is wrong to extrapolate from such an atypical case to the conclusion that harm is not, after all, a grounding feature of rape's wrongness. There are always outliers. But does the conceptual possibility of harmless rape dislodge the place of rape trauma in constituting rape as the distinct wrong that it is? Rare instances of harmless rape do not make harm 'epiphenomenal' to the wrong of rape, argues Victor Tadros, 'just as the fact that there are trunkless elephants does not make trunks merely epiphenomenally related to elephants in the way that dirt is a mere epiphenomenon of elephants'.[23]

We might put this misgiving differently. G&S intentionally go about stripping rape of its characteristic harms so as to focus our attention on the 'basic' wrong that is left over. Yet we might worry that this very stripping away overlooks the importance of rape trauma in making that core wrong the especially iniquitous thing is it for us. The lesson from the pure case cuts against the compelling notion that the

[18] Gardner, 'Reasonable Reactions'.
[19] 'Wrongness of Rape' 21.
[20] ibid 22.
[21] 'Reasonable Reactions' 14.
[22] 'Wrongness of Rape' 24.
[23] Victor Tadros, 'The Distinctiveness of Domestic Abuse: A Freedom Based Account' (2005) 65 La. L. Rev. 1008.

harm typically occasioned by rape has some constitutive role to play in the wrongness of rape, despite exceptional cases.

Support for the idea that rape trauma is more central to the wrongness of rape than G&S's analysis seems to grant could be drawn from considering a counterfactual situation in which harm is *not* a typical consequent of rape. In an imaginary world, let us suppose, victims of rape tend to greet it with about the same degree of dismay as stubbing one's toe—an annoyance, but nothing more alarming than that. Rape in this world is still wrong in G&S's basic or essential sense, we can say: it constitutes the 'sheer use' of the victim for the rapist's own ends and correlative denial of the victim's personhood. What is less clear is that, in this alternative reality, rape retains exactly the same moral valence that it has for us, or constitutes the same wrong. If that is right, it suggests that we cannot abrogate rape's paradigmatic harmfulness from its core wrongness.

Contrariwise, it might be replied that across particular times and cultures, victims *have* borne rape with a fair degree of equanimity. In some contexts, this may owe to social conditioning that dulls victims' own appreciation of the serious violation visited upon them through rape. Social acculturation of this kind may mean that rape victims do not experience what Wertheimer describes as the 'second-order' and 'belief-mediated' distress of rape: the distress predicated on the victim's own sense that her rights have been profoundly violated.[24] Importantly, it does not seem to follow that rape in such cultures and circumstances is any less the basic wrong that it is in contexts in which the 'second-order' distress of rape is ubiquitous.

The upshots of any such thought would also be unsettling. In England and Wales, the marital rape exemption was finally abolished by virtue of a court decision in 1992 (*R v R*).[25] Suppose the defence in that case had argued that, since married women had not, to this point, regarded themselves as having sexual autonomy rights as against their husbands, marital rape per se, as opposed to marital rape attended by further violence, was not particularly harmful, and therefore not wrongful (and thus ought to remain exempt from criminal repercussions). Doubtless, we would recoil at such an argument, and not just because of our scepticism that marital rape was psychologically harmless before 1992. It is unthinkable that the absence of harm attendant to marital rape, even if granted, could in any way militate against its criminalization.

This reflection plays into the hands of G&S's claim that the wrong of rape precedes its harms, not the other way around. If the wrongness of marital rape is not grounded, first and foremost, on its connection to harm, but instead on married women's rights against sheer sexual use, then whether or not marital rape had been the cause of great emotional trauma would be beside the point for its criminal

[24] Wertheimer, *Consent to Sexual Relations* 98–102.

[25] *R v R* [1992] 1 AC 599.

wrongness, as we indeed think it is. Equally as important, their analysis avoids the implication that the utterly harmless rape described in the 'pure' case is *not* seriously wrong, or is not the serious wrong *of* rape, which is what seems to follow, inexorably, if the wrong of rape is grounded in its harmfulness.

Be that as it may, it is difficult to embrace the conclusion that the serious harmfulness of rape is not central to its status as such an abhorrent crime. Indeed, some might prefer to bite the bullet and concede that rape in the very exceptional 'pure' case is not the same distinctive wrong as that of the paradigmatic harmful case, even if it is a serious wrong of a different kind, rather than deny that the basic wrong of rape is at least partly grounded in the trauma inflicted *by* rape. In sum, then, it seems as though we are confronted with a choice between two difficult options: either deny that rape trauma is truly central to the wrongness of rape, or concede that the exceptional, harmless rape is not the same distinctive wrong as the typical, harmful one.

D. Basic and Derivative Wrongs

Above, I tried to set out the points of tension for the Gardner–Shute view that the wrongness of rape 'is not a function of the harmfulness of rape', and for its antithesis. Perhaps, though, G&S's account does not diminish the importance of rape's harmfulness in any way that is difficult to accept. It is not the authors' contention there that rape trauma does not matter. Of course it matters very much. As Gardner clarified in subsequent writing, their claim was not that rape trauma plays a minor or peripheral role in the wrongness of rape.[26] Indeed, the trauma of rape may be the most serious thing of all about any particular rape, and the 'major' or 'dominant' reason why it is wrong to commit rape, he claimed.[27] Their argument, he elaborated, pertained to the logical priority, not the magnitude, of reasons not to rape. The wrong of causing rape trauma is a *derivative* wrong, he argued, being parasitic on the more basic wrong of the sheer sexual use. Because it is legitimate, that trauma points back to some other, primary, reason why the rape is wrong. While being derivative, though, rape trauma is nonetheless the 'most weighty' reason why it is wrong to commit rape, in almost all cases.[28] It is a *derivative* wrong, but not a *lesser* wrong. In much the same way, Gardner suggests, the main reason why it is wrong to break a promise may be because it has been relied upon; however, this reliance, because appropriate, points us back to a more basic reason to keep a promise: the fact that the promise is binding 'and thus fit to be relied upon'.[29] We might then say that the reliance reason is derivative, even though it is the 'most weighty'.

[26] Gardner, 'Reasonable Reactions'.
[27] ibid 4.
[28] ibid.
[29] ibid.

These remarks demonstrate why it would be incorrect to charge the Gardner–Shute thesis with disregarding or diminishing the importance of rape trauma. Rape trauma has a wrong-grounding role to play in most acts of rape, Gardner holds, and, where present, it will always be the wrong-grounding feature with the most clout. The trauma or harm of rape is only epiphenomenal to the basic wrong of which it is derivative; it is of course not epiphenomenal to the wrong it itself constitutes.

Pressing the argument against Gardner beyond this point therefore requires a narrower kind of objection. A true antithesis must contest his assertion that rape trauma is entirely epiphenomenal to the essential or basic wrong of rape. Recall again the imaginary culture in which rape simply is never emotionally distressing. The suspicion arising from this thought-experiment was that the typical trauma of rape in some way informs the moral valence of rape's basic wrongness, and helps to identify it as something which victims are warranted in reacting so strongly *to*. In this vein, Alan Wertheimer has argued that rape's propensity to cause experiential suffering is integral to its character as such a serious violation.[30] If human beings did not typically experience distress when their control over sexual activity is steamrollered, we would simply *not* have such a strong right that other people do not engage in those behaviours, he suggests. While there clearly is such a thing as harmless rape, it is nonetheless true, he argues, that the typical, experiential harm of rape 'precedes and motivates' the right to sexual integrity.[31] Similarly, John Stanton-Ife takes it that although experiential suffering is not 'invariably present' in rape, it is surely 'part and parcel of the horror of rape' and 'indispensable ... to our understanding of the wrongness, badness, and gravity of rape'.[32]

There is one way of understanding Stanton-Ife's remark here that is perfectly in tune with Gardner's analysis. Gardner too, we see, holds that rape trauma is the most horrendous feature of rape, and the gravest thing about it, but that such trauma responds (and responds reasonably) to a more basic wrong of rape, contained in sheer sexual use. A different way of understanding that remark, though, is as calling into question Gardner's sense that the 'basic' wrong of rape sits apart so neatly and independently from the 'derivative' ones. It is hard to shake off the thought that rape's paradigmatic harms are not merely epiphenomenal to, but in some way constitutive of, rape's *basic* wrongness, insofar as they are a crucial part of the story about how rape gets its moral colouring, including in an exceptional, harmless case.

I am not going to fully explore or evaluate this possibility, but I would like to attend to the greatest impediment standing in its way. For how does one square the intuitive notion that the basic wrong of rape would not be what it is were it not

[30] Wertheimer, *Consent to Sexual Relations* 108; 109; 11.
[31] ibid 101.
[32] Stanton-Ife (above, n 16) at 160.

for the intense psychological suffering it tends to cause victims with what I have been calling 'the reasonable reactions argument'? The problem, it appears, is that rape trauma cannot both ground the basic wrong of rape (wholly or partly) *and* constitute a legitimate, reasons-tracking reaction to that same wrong. The tension between these two ideas is a driving force for Gardner's view that the typical harms of rape are parasitic on its basic wrongness and not constitutive of it. To understand the 'strong feelings' about rape as reasonable, Gardner later wrote, requires us to identify an independent 'basic or essential'[33] wrong to which they are reasonably responding.

What is more, the argument from reasonable reactions is an even more powerful defence of the view that the basic wrong of rape 'is not a function of its harmfulness' than is the argument from the pure case. In defence of a harm-centric account of rape's wrongness, there are certain concessions one might make with regard to the 'pure' case that, although challenging, are not obviously and deeply erroneous. Someone may concede, for instance, that G&S's imaginary case is in some respects a marginal case of rape, and that it does not exemplify everything that gives rape its general pernicious moral character. Harmless rape is still very much a wrong, such a person might stress, but a wrong mostly insofar as it shadows the wrong of paradigmatic harmful rape. Furthermore, she may remind us, harm-based reasons for criminalizing acts of harmless rape are surely within easy grasp, as G&S pointed out in their original paper.[34] Since this is the case, we need not worry that a harm-centric view of rape's basic wrongness entails that harmless rapes are outside the proper limits of criminal interference, including if we adopt a harm-principle approach to those limits.[35]

The reasonable reactions argument is not adequately met by these same responses, however. It is incumbent on theorists, it seems, to offer an account of rape's wrongness that explains why rape trauma is rationally appropriate and non-pathological. As Gardner later restated the original idea:

> Rape, we thought, is dehumanising enough already without those who have been raped being condescendingly regarded as having lost their human sensitivity to value, their ability to interpret what has happened . . . The idea that rape survivors can only be passive in the face of their own pain, overwhelmed and trapped by senseless feelings, only adds insult to injury.[36]

[33] Quoation marks are Gardner's own.

[34] See 'Wrongness of Rape' 8; 29–30, where G&S argue that the 'pure' case passes the harm principle test for criminalization 'with flying colours' (29) given that prohibiting harmless rape is in the service of harm prevention.

[35] See, in particular, John Stuart Mill, *On Liberty* (Penguin, 2006 edition).

[36] 'Reasonable Reactions' 5.

This can only be avoided, it is suggested, by positing a prior wrong of rape which is not harm-dependent, and which would remain the thing it is even if rape trauma were rare or non-existent. Whatever judgements one is willing to make about harmless rape, then (whether one accepts it as the 'pure' case, or, contrariwise, regards it as marginal and, although wrong, wrong in a way that is parasitic on the wrongness of typical rape), only the view which holds rape trauma to be epiphenomenal to the essential wrong of rape is capable of affirming the rational agency of rape victims. And the idea that rape victims have good reason to respond as they do to what happens to them—to experience such a sense of horror and violation—is an even harder judgement to relinquish, it appears to me, than the claim that the harmless instance of rape fully exemplifies rape's distinctive wrongness. In what remains here, therefore, let us investigate what scope there is for defusing this problem presented by the argument from reasonable reactions.

E. Reasonable Reactions and the Wrong of Emotional Abuse

The grounding assumption of the reasonable reactions argument is that people traumatized by rape are not merely reacting compulsively, like dogs barking at fireworks. Instead they are, through their distress, exhibiting their capacity to relate properly to the world of reasons. The excellence of the argument is that it sharpens what is at stake in how we construe rape's basic wrongness. In Gardner's framing of things, we must either consign rape trauma to the category of purely compulsive behaviour *or* reject the view that rape's basic wrongness is a function of that trauma. We cannot have it both ways.

Presented this way, my inkling is that the dilemma is somewhat overstated. In this section, I will first consider and dismiss two possible objections to the argument from reasonable reactions before introducing a more challenging objection which arises when studying the wrongness of a different moral crime: emotional abuse.

1. Two Objections to the Reasonable Reactions Argument

First, a note about the response-dependent nature of much of rape's harm. The harm occasioned by an action is response-dependent to the extent that it is conditioned on the harmed party's reactions to what is done. In rape, this includes the emotional and psychological harmed states which rape typically causes. A significant element of rape's response-dependent harm is what, as already noted, Wertheimer terms the 'second-order' and (following Judith Thomson) 'belief-mediated' distress that emanates from the victim's own sense of having been seriously wronged and of having an important right violated.[37] The second-order distress of rape is response-dependent—it depends on the victim's reactions to the rape—and it is also *evaluation*-dependent, since it is a function of the victim's evaluation of what has happened to her and its significance. Evaluation-dependent harms are a species of response-dependent harms, then. In his laudable concern to vindicate the rational agency of rape victims through his account of the wrongness of rape, it is these evaluation-dependent responses which Gardner had foremost in mind, it appears.[38]

This brings me to a first possible objection to the reasonable reactions argument. Patently, not all the harms of rape travel through victims' evaluations about rape. The immediate fear and distress, the terror of the violence, and of further violence (all elements of synchronic distress) and any of rape's physical harms are all independent from the victim's appreciation of how terrible a violation has been perpetrated against her. It might be argued that the reasonable reactions argument thus fails, since all of *these* harms could constitute the basic wrongness of rape and, if so, this would in no way undermine the reason-responsiveness of rape victims. Victims' rational agency is simply not implicated in these wrong-making features at all, as it isn't implicated in the harm I suffer if someone breaks my leg. Perhaps the reasonable reactions argument is only successful, then, if *all* rape's harms are evaluation-dependent.

While not all of rape's harms are evaluation-dependent—indeed, the physical harms of rape are not even *response*-dependent—I doubt that this observation neutralizes the reasonable reactions argument. The nub of that argument is that to the degree that rape trauma *is* a function of second-order, evaluation-dependent distress, these reactions are appropriate, and our account of the wrongness of rape must explain why that is so. Suppose we were to amend the 'pure case' story, and have it that at some future date, after emerging from her stupor, the victim discovers the awful truth about what happened to her. She is shaken to the core, and psychologically damaged, by this realization. Apart from this, though, the rape is as harmless as in the original case (no physical damage, no synchronic distress or terror of violence, and so on). The victim's harmed reaction is a warranted one, we think, in response to discovering the rape alone. Her reaction need not reference any further harm consequent to the rape to register as legitimate or reasons-tracking. If we are to maintain that this second-order trauma would be reasonable and non-pathological we must, it seems, take it to be tracking a prior wrong of rape which isn't harm-dependent. It is beside the point that other potential harms of rape do not implicate the reasonableness of anyone's reactions.

[37] Wertheimer, *Consent to Sexual Relations*, 100–101.

[38] See 'Wrongness of Rape' 6, where G&S describe the emotional and psychological damage of rape in which they are interested as reactions which 'depend on the victim's own evaluation of her ordeal'. They continue, pressing the argument: 'Are we to regard all these evaluation-dependent harms as reflecting the victim's irrationality, her superstition, her over-sensitivity, etc?'

A second objection might proceed as follows. It is wrong knowingly or negligently to inflict response-dependent distress on another person, without good cause, irrespective of the reasonableness of those responses. If I am aware that, owing to your beliefs, it will cause you great distress to eat pork, then I should not manipulate you into eating it, though it may be my view that your response is not in keeping with good reason.[39] Considering this, it might be argued that it does not matter for rape's wrongness whether or not rape trauma is reasons-tracking, in that it responds to a prior wrong. It is enough to know that rape *does* induce such distress to know that it is seriously wrong. Hence, we do not need to identify the wrong of rape with the prior or basic wrong of sheer use to give a suitable account of that wrongness.

Again, I do not think this objection is persuasive against the reasonable reactions argument. It is true that rape could be wrong in virtue of the response-dependent harm it causes whether or not those responses were reasonable and appropriate. Distress is distress, whatever its relationship to reasons. But the reactions and evaluations which ground rape trauma *are* rational and appropriate. We should not be content with an account of rape's wrongness that overlooks this, or presents those reactions as pure, unreasoned facts of nature according to which people should moderate their behaviour. This is far more to the point of the reasonable reactions argument. While the distress occasioned by rape could be wrong-grounding in any event, then, our firm judgement that it is entirely reasonable requires a harm-independent account of the basic wrong of rape, it still seems.

2. The Wrong of Emotional Abuse

The two objections canvassed above do not unravel the argument from reasonable reactions, as I see it. Perhaps, though, there is a more fruitful way of challenging the gist of that argument and the problem that it presents, namely that response-dependent rape trauma must be derivative, not constitutive, of the wrong of rape, if rape trauma is not pathological. It would be quite a significant finding if it turned out that harming someone is never constitutive of wrongdoing wherever that harm is mediated by the victim's emotional or psychological responses. This alone is good reason to reconsider the apparent dichotomy. Rape is not the only wrong which, on the face of it, is wrongful in virtue of its typical harmfulness, and whose harm, or much of it, travels through victims' reactions. What would Gardner's analysis make of other wrongs, the key wrong-grounding features of which are the psychological and emotional damage they predictably cause?

[39] Thank you to Victor Tadros for presenting me with this example.

To bring out this difficulty, consider the wrong of psychological and emotional abuse. It is difficult, ostensibly, to explicate the wrongness of this abuse other than by reference to response-dependent harm. Take, for instance, the now criminal wrong of 'coercive control' defined by section 76 of the Serious Crime Act 2015 as a repeated pattern of behaviour by A towards B (with whom B has an intimate or familial relationship), which has a 'serious effect' on B in that it causes B to fear that violence will be used against them, or it causes B 'serious alarm or distress which has a substantial adverse effect on their day-to-day activities'.[40] Section 76 suggests that the wrong of emotional abuse is partly constituted by the victim's reactions; it requires the victim to respond in particular ways to what the perpetrator is doing, for example with fear, distress, significant self-limiting of day-to-day life, and a sense of helplessness.

Applying the logic of the reasonable reactions argument here, it seems we should say either that a victim's reactions to abusive behaviour are purely pathological, or that they are 'epiphenomenal' to the more basic wrong of emotional abuse—wrong-grounding, certainly, but nevertheless derivative of that prior wrong. Yet neither of these alternatives seems correct here. The harmed states caused by emotional abuse such as coercive control are not symptoms of pathology or irrationality on the part of the victim; they are, in some sense, reasonable reactions to what is being done. At the same time, the basic wrongness of emotional abuse cannot be understood without reference to those reactions. The second we strip away its distinctly insidious harms, whatever is left behind is, arguably, no longer an identifiable example of that wrong. In the case of emotional abuse, therefore, it appears that victims' reactions are legitimate and non-pathological *and* that they ground the essential wrong. This may call into question the gist of the reasonable reactions argument.

It may be replied that the wrongs of rape and of emotional abuse are importantly disanalogous, such that the structure of the wrong of emotional abuse does not undermine the reasonable reactions argument as it pertains to rape. In fact, Gardner drew attention to a potentially salient difference between these two wrongs in response to a different challenge to the wrongness of rape thesis advanced by Victor Tadros, centred on the wrong of domestic abuse.[41] Unlike rape, Gardner pointed out, the definitional ambit of domestic abuse does not appear to include harmless cases.[42] If anything counts as the 'distinctive' wrong

[40] Section 76 of the Serious Crime Act 2015—Controlling or Coercive Behaviour in an Intimate or Family Relationship.

[41] Tadros, 'The Distinctiveness of Domestic Abuse' 1006–1008. Tadros's specific challenge targets G&S's pure case methodology. He questions their extrapolation from the possibility of an exceptional harmless rape to the claim that harm is merely epiphenomenal, rather than central, to the core wrong of rape. It would 'be a mistake', Tadros suggests, analogously to claim that because not all domestic abuse results in psychological trauma, such trauma is 'not central to what is wrong with domestic abuse' (1008).

[42] Gardner, *Offences and Defences* 245–246.

of domestic abuse, he suggests, it is surely the use of terror to exert control over the victim. He continues: 'Now obviously one cannot use terror against a person without terrifying her.'[43] In this respect, domestic abuse is like a 'result crime' in the criminal law, where the bringing about of certain harmful effects partly defines the wrong. With rape, however, things stand differently. Unlike the act of terrorizing someone, which has harm built into its very definition, it *is* possible that an act of rape would not cause any harm whatsoever, as the pure case story shows. Consequently, 'Terrorizing, unlike rape, is a wrong partly constituted by its result, viz. the terror of the person terrorized.'[44]

Gardner's remarks here can be directed at emotional abuse in general and coercive control more particularly (which are both, of course, examples of domestic abuse). As its statutory definition bears out, one cannot coercively control someone without actually *controlling* her. Harm is a definitional (hence constitutive) feature of this wrong. Perhaps the disanalogy can be harnessed, then, to defend the reasonable reactions argument from the counter-example of emotional abuse. We *cannot* separate the distinctive wrong of emotional abuse from its harm. That follows from how the wrong is defined, and it explains why those reactions must part-constitute the wrong even though they are also legitimate reactions to something. But the pure case demonstrates that harm is not, likewise, part of the definition of rape. There is no similar definitional problem, then, in claiming that rape trauma evaluates the prior, core wrong of rape.

I will return briefly, below, to the broader implications of this difference between the wrong of emotional abuse and the wrong of rape. There are one or two things to note here, though, in response to the reliance on this disanalogy to defend the reasonable reactions argument from the apparent counter-example of the wrong of emotional abuse. First, emotional abuse need not mirror rape in the particular respect of having harm built into its very definition in order to put pressure on the basic dilemma offered up by the reasonable reactions argument. In emotional abuse, we have an example of a wrong that is part-constituted by the emotional trauma it inflicts, and where that trauma does not bespeak of any defect of reason or pathology on the part of the victims. Inasmuch as the force of the reasonable reactions argument is that both of these things cannot hold together, the example of emotional abuse undermines the argument in general terms.

Moreover, the fact that the harm of emotional abuse is a definitional requirement of committing the wrong, as Gardner underscores, might only *strengthen* the challenge it poses to the argument from reasonable reactions. Here, there is no question that harm is constitutive of the wrong (if harm is part of its very definition, then it is definitely a wrong-grounding feature), and yet we do not seem to have any problem accounting for the reasonableness of the response-dependent

[43] ibid 245.
[44] ibid 246.

reactions that constitute that harm. They are entirely within the spectrum of appropriate human responses to the perpetrators' behaviour. Despite the disanalogy upon which Gardner alights, then, a closer look at the relationship between wronging and harming in emotional abuse could point the way as to how the rationality of rape victims might be squared with the view that rape trauma is more than 'epiphenomenal' to the basic or essential wrong of rape.

The psychological and emotional traumas inherent to emotional abuse are reasonable reactions, in the sense of being appropriate and non-pathological. (This does not entail that they are the only responses which reason *permits*; a target of emotional abuse who happens to meet abusive behaviour with equanimity and resilience is not acting out of line with reason, but neither are these responses the only ones a rational agent would exhibit.) Those reactions, we saw, part-constitute the wrong of emotional abuse; they are not mere derivative wrongs. Still, in order to be reasonable reactions they must be reactions *to* something.

One way to explain this could be to identify a prior wrong of abusive behaviour. Surely there is some wrong involved in interpersonal abusive actions which, fortuitously, wreak no emotional damage. You cannot gaslight a person without interfering with his perception of reality, but the attempt is still iniquitous. It is this prior bad behaviour to which we might say emotional abuse victims are reasonably responding with their distress.[45] But, as we have seen above, this wrong is not the complete wrong of emotional abuse—for that, we require some actual harm as a consequence. Indeed, I think we should be sooner minded to say that the failed case, the unsuccessful gaslighting attempt, is a different (though related) wrong than to view it as the 'pure' case of emotional abuse.[46] On a closer look, then, it is possible to see how the emotional and psychological trauma experienced by abuse victims is a reasonable reaction and, moreover, part-constitutes the distinctive wrong of emotional abuse.

[45] I should note a certain complication here, which is that the emotional harms of gaslighting or coercive control, though response-dependent, are not similarly second-order as much of the trauma of rape is. The core trauma involved in emotional abuse is not tied to the victim's appreciation of how badly she is being treated. In fact, in the case of some abusive wrongs, such as gaslighting, the completion of the wrong *depends* on the victim's failure to advert to what is really happening and see it for what it is—one cannot not be successfully manipulated or gaslighted if one is able to evaluate what is happening as a form of emotional abuse. In these cases, then, the harmed states which part-constitute the wrong of abuse are response-dependent (and, hence, answerable to reason) but not evaluation-dependent.

[46] Victor Tadros considers this possibility of exceptional, harmless domestic abuse in the context of his challenge to Gardner and Shute's pure case methodology. Unlike Gardner, Tadros seems to regard the harmless example as an unusual or peripheral instance of domestic abuse, rather than as an incident which, because harmless, does not fulfil the conditions required to make out that wrong. (See Tadros, 'The Distinctiveness of Domestic Abuse' at 1007–1008.)

F. Rape Trauma and Rape's Wrongness

A final question here is whether rape could, in any way, emulate the structure of wronging and harming in emotional abuse. This it would do if rape trauma is a rationally appropriate response to something but also, to some degree, grounds the essential wrongness of rape. The first part is easier, and can be explained by carving up the wrongs involved in rape in much the way that Gardner does. Rape trauma is indeed a reasonable reaction to something. Following Gardner, we can understand that something to be the sheer sexual use of the victim, with all the social meaning that carries in a context where penetrative sex is culturally so important. Rape victims do not act pathologically when they respond with great distress to what is done to them, because sheer sexual use really *is* dehumanizing, objectifying, humiliating, and so on. We should agree with Gardner, I think, that there is a harm-independent wrong involved in every act of rape which makes rape trauma rationally intelligible.

How could it be that rape trauma also, then, in some measure, grounds or constitutes the essential wrongness of rape? In emotional abuse, we saw, psychological harm grounds the wrong by being a definitional condition of it. But harm is not likewise a definitional element of rape. Whereas we might accept that the wrong of emotional abuse has not come off, so to speak, unless certain harms eventuate, we are not similarly content to say that the wrong left behind in the pure case, when all harm is stripped away, is a wrong, but not the wrong *of* rape. The identification of a rape, we wish to say, does not require the identification of harm.

There is more than one way, though, in which harm might ground a wrong, and being a definitional element of that wrong is only one way. Another kind of wrong-grounding might stem from the connection between a type of act and the harm that it typically and dependably inflicts. According to this sort of view, the dependability (in the sense of typicality) of rape trauma in response to rape is integral to explaining rape's wrongness and gravity, despite the conceptual possibility of harmless cases. As Wertheimer puts it, it is 'precisely because such acts typically give rise to experiential harm even when they do not do so in a particular case' that serious rights violations exist.[47] This suggestion gets endorsement from the thought, set out earlier, that not everything would remain the same, morally, if rape were not typically so very harmful. No question, the wrong of sheer sexual use would remain intact. Still, it may be that rape's contingent connection to harm in the world as we know it, *and not only the good reason for that connection*, informs its moral character, and the gravity of the right that it violates. Absent this deep connection to experiential suffering of various kinds, rape would not retain exactly the same moral valence, though it would still involve the harm-independent wrong

[47] Wertheimer, *Consent to Sexual Relations* 100.

of sheer sexual use. This, at any rate, is roughly how a harm-based account of rape's core wrongness might proceed.

On this way of thinking, rape trauma inflects the core, essential wrongness of rape, including in the pure case. There, as elsewhere, a proper account of the wrongness of rape cannot omit reference to those dependable adverse reactions, in much the same way that understanding the wrongness of racial slurs must involve attention to the harm they typically cause to targeted individuals and groups, although it is possible to utter a slur which falls only on insouciant ears.

Importantly, to assert that rape part-constitutes the core or basic wrongness of rape in this way does not yield any difficulty in acknowledging the reason-responsiveness of rape victims. For that, we need only to identify something to which they are reasonably reacting, independently of the fact of those reactions. This we have done, in the way of sheer sexual use. Rape trauma entails an appropriate evaluation of that wrong; this, we can say along with Gardner, is the derivative aspect of that harm. But the reasonable reactions argument only prescribes that rape trauma must make essential reference to some other wrong, not that it need make reference to everything which informs the distinctive wrongness of rape. The sheer sexual use of rape is seriously wrong regardless of the reactions it happens to elicit. Still, the damage that rape reliably does do, given how victims have reason to react to it, can be part of what grounds that wrong as especially or additionally egregious, without being a definitional condition of it.

Just as the gravity of sheer sexual use is, on G&S's view, informed by the socially mediated importance of penetrative sex (and note: this social meaning is not a definitional condition of sheer sexual use either), so too, it can be argued, the moral gravity of sheer sexual use is informed by the social fact of its strong connection to serious harm. G&S's insight that some wrong can be particularly odious simply because something happens to matter—as rape matters especially because of the social meaning of penetrative sex—can also underpin the claim that the special wrongness of rape is partly a function of its typical harmfulness, another socially mediated fact. If rape's general connection to harm exacerbates the distinctive wrongfulness of sheer sexual use (what Gardner considers the 'basic' wrong of rape), then rape trauma is not *only* a derivative wrong of rape. It is indeed derivative of a prior wrong, but it also partly grounds the egregiousness of committing that prior wrong.

Whether or not one finds this general account appealing (and far more would need to be said in its defence), one can see that the reasonable reactions argument does not put paid to it. Irrespective of its typical harmfulness, rape trauma is a warranted reaction to the wrong of sheer sexual use. It does not undermine this claim, as far as I can see, if the prevalence of legitimate rape trauma also, in its turn, augments the basic wrongness of rape.

As should be apparent, this is all very much of a piece with—and indeed, guided by—Gardner's main insights about the wrongness of rape. Between his earlier and later work, these included the reflections that (1) there can be more than one wrong-grounding feature in an individual assault which amounts to rape; (2) only some of those wrong-grounding features are definitional necessities of rape; (3) causing distress and harm to victims is the most serious wrong-grounding feature of any rape; (4) one wrong-grounding feature which is inextricable from all rape is the harm-independent wrong of sheer sexual use; and (5) rape victims demonstrate their sensitivity to reason when responding with distress to this wrong.

In a literature in which rape victims tend, perhaps inevitably, to be consigned to roles of passive and hapless sufferers, it is, for me, one of the most appealing and distinctive features of Gardner's work on this topic that the rational agency of victims remained an anchoring thought throughout. As I have hinted at here, perhaps there is nonetheless scope for harmonizing this thought with the intuitive idea that rape trauma is part of what distinguishes rape as such an atrocious moral crime.

12

John Gardner's Continuity Theory of Corrective Justice

Peter Chau[*]

A. Introduction

John Gardner offers an attractive justification of corrective justice, by which he refers to the moral norm that 'wrongdoers are morally required to pay reparative damages in respect of those losses that they wrongfully occasion',[1] which appeals to the idea of continuity of reasons (or what he calls the "'continuity thesis"').[2] My aim in this chapter is to assess the justification for corrective justice offered by Gardner. My conclusion will be that Gardner fails to provide a general justification of reparative damages.

The remaining parts of this chapter will be structured as follows. Section B introduces the continuity theory, by which I refer to a justification of corrective justice based on the continuity thesis. Section C suggests that the continuity theory can come in different versions, and that Gardner can be read either as offering a version that is based on a right to hold on to one's existing life or as offering a version that is based on a right against wrongful loss. Section D criticizes the former version, and Section E criticizes the latter.

* This chapter was presented at a workshop on John Gardner's works in December 2019 at All Souls College, Oxford. I wish to thank all those present, especially Amalia Amaya, Antony Duff, Jeff McMahan, and Ekow Yankah, for their helpful questions. I have also received helpful comments on some ideas in this chapter from Christopher Bennett, Susanne Burri, Cora Chan, Lusina Ho, Nicholas McBride, and James Penner.

I wish to highlight my gratitude to three persons. John Oberdiek and Sandy Steel have provided very helpful written comments. Without their helpful comments, this chapter would have been much worse. My greatest debt is to John Gardner. It is sad that he is no longer able to guide us personally. But I hope he would be pleased to know that his insightful and original contribution to the justification of corrective justice has significantly advanced the debate and has encouraged many—myself included—to think more deeply about related topics.

This work is supported by GRF Grant 17612318 from the Hong Kong Research Grants Council, and I am grateful for the financial support.

[1] John Gardner, *Torts and Other Wrongs* (Oxford University Press 2019) 44 (hereafter Gardner, *Torts and Other Wrongs*).

[2] Ibid, 61.

Peter Chau, *John Gardner's Continuity Theory of Corrective Justice* In: *From Morality to Law and Back Again*. Edited by: Michelle Madden Dempsey and François Tanguay-Renaud, Oxford University Press. © Peter Chau 2023.
DOI: 10.1093/oso/9780198860594.003.0012

B. The Continuity Theory Introduced

Suppose a father had promised his son that he would take him to the beach the previous Sunday, but he failed to do so. Intuitively, when deciding what to do in the future, the father should take this failure into account.[3] But exactly why and how?

Gardner claims that the reasons justifying an obligation are not terminated by a breach of that obligation; those reasons, which have not been conformed with perfectly, continue to exert force post-breach and justify an obligation for 'next-best conformity'.[4] Gardner calls this idea the 'continuity thesis'.[5] The continuity thesis can, according to Gardner, explain why and how the past promise matters in the beach case. Post-breach, there is *nothing* the father can do that can improve his conformity with the breached primary obligation itself—his obligation to take his son to the beach *the previous Sunday*. He cannot dial back the clock; the particular actions required by the primary obligation are simply not available post-breach.[6] But the reason supporting that obligation—say, the reason not to disappoint his son—continues to demand conformity post-breach, and he can still improve his conformity with that reason, which is less particularized than the primary obligation itself. Conforming with that reason may entail, for example, taking his son to the beach on the following Sunday.[7]

Gardner believes that the continuity thesis can similarly explain a wrongdoer's moral duty to repair. Suppose a person removed a victim's arm without justification.[8] The reasons justifying the breached primary obligation towards the victim—his obligation not to remove her arm, in this case—will continue to exert force post-breach, and according to Gardner, compensating the victim would be the course of action that best conforms with those reasons post-breach.[9]

[3] Ibid, 55–56. Gardner borrows this example from Neil MacCormick, 'The Obligation of Reparation' (1977) 78 *Proceedings of the Aristotelian Society* 175 (hereafter MacCormick, 'The Obligation of Reparation').

[4] Gardner, *Torts and Other Wrongs* (n 1) 72.

[5] Ibid, 61.

[6] Ibid, 55, 59. Arthur Ripstein and Ernest Weinrib claim that the primary obligation/right itself, not only the reasons justifying it, continue through the breach. See Arthur Ripstein, *Private Wrongs* (Harvard University Press 2016) 248–251 (hereafter Ripstein, *Private Wrongs*); Ernest Weinrib, *Corrective Justice* (Oxford University Press 2012) 88–91. For the relationship between their accounts and Gardner's, see, e.g., Claudio Michelon, 'Primary Duty = Secondary Duty?' in Harris Psarras and Sandy Steel (eds), *Private Law and Practical Reason: Essays on John Gardner's Private Law Theory* (Oxford University Press forthcoming).

[7] Gardner, *Torts and Other Wrongs* (n 1) 60.

[8] This example is taken from Sandy Steel, 'Compensation and Continuity' (2020) 26 *Legal Theory* 250, 251 (hereafter Steel, 'Compensation and Continuity') (the 'arm' case).

[9] Gardner, *Torts and Other Wrongs* (n 1) 61–62. To my knowledge, Gardner is the first philosopher to defend the continuity theory of corrective justice in detail, although the continuity thesis (and the possibility of justifying corrective justice by appealing to the continuity thesis) has received brief attention in Joseph Raz, 'Personal Practical Conflicts' in Peter Baumann and Monika Betzler (eds), *Practical Conflicts: New Philosophical Essays* (Cambridge University Press 2004).

C. Versions of the Continuity Theory

The continuity theory is a broad theory that is capable of many variations. This is so because all that the continuity theory holds is that the reasons justifying the wrongdoer's primary obligation towards the victim continue through the breach, and those justifying reasons require reparation post-breach. (Instead of the wrongdoer's primary *obligation* towards the victim, I will sometimes write in terms of the victim's primary *right* against the wrongdoer, and I take these expressions to be interchangeable.[10]) The continuity theory, in itself, is *not* committed to any particular answer as to *what those justifying reasons are*. Accordingly, there can be different versions of the continuity theory, depending on what is offered as the justification of the victim's primary right.

Possible justifications of the victim's primary right can be divided into two main camps.[11] First, we can appeal to reasons that are not based on the victim's rights, such as utility, to justify the primary right. Second, we can appeal to a further—*more foundational*—right of the victim to ground the primary right.

Right-based justifications of the victim's primary right—that is, justifications of the primary right that appeal to a more foundational right of hers—can be further divided into two sub-groups, depending on the kind of foundational right being appealed to. The first kind of right, which can be called a 'right against loss',[12] forbids others from causing loss to the right-holder (by 'loss' I refer to a reduction in a person's amount of goods,[13] say, well-being or resources).[14] A right against loss does not have to be 'unqualified', that is, protecting the right-holder from *all kinds* of loss.[15] It can be qualified, that is, protecting the right-holder only from loss caused in a *certain* way (e.g., loss caused by actions that are *wrongful*). I take it that *if* Gardner's account of reparation is based on a right against loss, *then* he would rely on a qualified right against wrongful loss rather than an unqualified right against all kinds of loss, for two reasons. First, the claim that we have an unqualified right against loss, no matter how it is caused, is highly implausible. Second, Gardner is

[10] See also Gardner, *Torts and Other Wrongs* (n 1) 133.

[11] For the idea that the continuity theory is capable of many variations, see also Stephen Smith, 'Duties, Liabilites, and Damages' (2012) 125 *Harvard Law Review* 172, 173. See also the tripartite distinction in Ronald Dworkin, *Taking Rights Seriously* (Duckworth 1977) 169–173.

[12] Charlie Webb, 'Justifying Damages' in Jason Neyers, Richard Bronaugh, and Stephen Pitel (eds), *Exploring Contract Law* (Hart 2009) 142, 158–159 (hereafter Webb, 'Justifying Damages'). For the distinction between rights against loss and loss-independent rights, see, e.g., Arthur Ripstein, 'Beyond the Harm Principle' (2006) 34 *Philosophy and Public Affairs* 21; John Gardner and Stephen Shute, 'The Wrongness of Rape' in John Gardner (ed), *Offences and Defences* (Oxford University Press 2007).

[13] Charlie Webb has drawn (in Webb, 'Justifying Damages' (n 12) 159) a helpful distinction between two senses of loss: (a) 'a worsening of [one's] position' in relation to his amount of goods, and (b) 'specific physical harms or occurrences'. In this chapter, I am referring to loss in sense (a).

[14] For different currencies of distributive justice, see, e.g., G.A. Cohen, 'The Currency of Egalitarian Justice' (1989) 99 *Ethics* 906.

[15] Arthur Ripstein and Ben Zipursky, 'Corrective Justice in the Age of Mass Torts' in Gerald Postema (ed), *Philosophy and the Law of Torts* (Cambridge University Press 2001) 218.

not a utilitarian who believes that all losses count equally; on his view, losses trigger duties of corrective justice only if there is a wrongdoing (though fault—which Gardner distinguishes clearly from wrongdoing—is unnecessary).[16]

The second kind of right, which can be called a 'loss-independent right', forbids certain conducts, regardless of whether they reduce the right-holder's amount of goods. By contrast to right against loss, causing loss to the victim is not necessary for violating her loss-independent right.

Let me illustrate the distinction between the two kinds of right-based justification with the arm case. Consider the following two answers to the question of what justifies the victim's primary right, that is, why does she have a right against the wrongdoer not to have her arm removed? The first answer is that she has *a right not to have her goods (say, welfare) reduced in certain ways (say, wrongful ways)*, and removing her arm would reduce her welfare wrongfully. The second answer is that she has *a right against bodily interference*, regardless of whether such interference reduces her amount of goods, and removing a person's arm amounts to an interference with her body.[17] Both of these answers justify her primary right by appealing to a further right of hers, rather than referring to utility; but the two answers appeal to different rights. The first answer justifies her primary right by appealing to a further right against (wrongful) loss, whereas the second answer appeals to a further loss-independent right.

Based on the tripartite distinction of the possible justifications of the victim's primary right, we can divide possible versions of the continuity theory into three (note that I will assess the version of the continuity theory based on a loss-independent right before I assess the version based on a right against loss in the subsequent sections of this chapter):

(a) Non-Right-Based-Continuity, which holds that the *non-right-based considerations*, say utilitarian concerns, that justify the primary right pre-breach continue through the breach, and post-breach these considerations can ground a reparatory right;

(b) Loss-Independent-Right-Continuity, which holds that the foundational *loss-independent right* that grounds the primary right pre-breach continues through the breach, and post-breach this loss-independent right can ground a reparatory right;[18] and

[16] John Gardner, *From Personal Life to Private Law* (Oxford University Press 2018) 31 (hereafter Gardner, *From Personal Life to Private Law*); Gardner, *Torts and Other Wrongs* (n 1) 70–72; John Gardner, 'Wrongs and Faults' (2005) 59 *The Review of Metaphysics* 95 (hereafter Gardner, 'Wrongs and Faults').

[17] See, e.g., Anton Fagan, 'The Right to Personal Security' in Elspeth Reid and Daniel Visser (eds), *Private Law and Human Rights: Bringing Rights Home in Scotland and South Africa* (Edinburgh University Press 2013) 152.

[18] For duty/right-based versions of the continuity theory, see also Steel, 'Compensation and Continuity' (n 8) 255.

(c) Right-against-Loss-Continuity, which holds that the foundational *right against loss* that grounds the primary right pre-breach continues through the breach, and post-breach this right against loss can ground a reparatory right.

To which version of the continuity theory does Gardner subscribe? I think, for two reasons, that we should not read him as offering Non-Right-Based-Continuity, despite the fact that he is sometimes read that way.[19] First, Non-Right-Based-Continuity is implausible. As Arthur Ripstein argues, there is no reason to believe that the non-right-based considerations, say utility, that justify the primary obligation pre-breach must necessarily be able to justify the reparatory obligation post-breach.[20] Second, textually speaking, Gardner writes that the justification for both the primary obligation and the reparatory obligation, in the context of tort law, is 'rights-based' and the reasons that continue through the breach to justify the reparatory right are themselves 'categorical' and 'mandatory', that is, obligatory reasons.[21]

Suppose I am right that Gardner intends to offer a right-based version of the continuity theory. Does he intend to offer a version of Loss-Independent-Right-Continuity or a version of Right-against-Loss-Continuity? I think there is textual evidence for both in his works.

In some places, he writes that protecting the victim from suffering loss is 'central to the rationale' of both the primary obligations and the reparatory obligations in tort law.[22] This strongly suggests Right-against-Loss-Continuity.

But in his most recent monograph on tort law, *From Personal Life to Private Law*,[23] Gardner claims that the primary obligations and the reparatory obligations in tort law are both concerned with protecting the 'security' of the right-holder,[24] that is, the right-holder's 'ability to hold on'.[25] 'Hold on to *what*?', you may ask. While sometimes Gardner refers to one's security in certain objects—for example, security in one's place of residence[26]—the kind of security on which he focuses more frequently in justifying reparation is a broader kind of security, namely, an

[19] Ripstein, *Private Wrongs* (n 6) 249–251.

[20] Ibid, 250. But see John Oberdiek, 'Wrongs, Remedies, and the Persistence of Reasons: Re-Examining the Continuity Thesis' in Haris Psarras and Sandy Steel (eds), *Private Law and Practical Reason* (Oxford University Press forthcoming), on deriving rights from non-right-based (but nonetheless relational) considerations.

[21] Gardner, *Torts and Other Wrongs* (n 1) 73; Gardner, 'Wrongs and Faults' (n 16) 103, 105. See also his discussion of the 'interpersonal' nature of rights in Gardner, *From Personal Life to Private Law* (n 16) 116–118.

[22] Gardner, *From Personal Life to Private Law* (n 16) 120; Gardner, *Torts and Other Wrongs* (n 1) 10–11, 67–68.

[23] The most recent book by Gardner, *Torts and Other Wrongs* (n 1), is a collection of essays, most of which were published before the publication of *From Personal Life to Private Law* (n 16).

[24] Gardner, *From Personal Life to Private Law* (n 16) 182–186. See also 231.

[25] Ibid, 190.

[26] Ibid.

ability to hold on to *one's existing life*.[27] For our purpose, it is important to notice that holding on to one's existing life (or staying on the 'existing track'[28] of one's life, which I take to be equivalent) is different from avoiding loss, in the sense of not having one's amount of goods reduced.[29] Two lives that contain an equal amount of goods need not be the same: the life of a business executive and the life of a lawyer might contain the same amount of goods—say, resources, happiness, achievement, respect from others, or whatever—but certainly they are very different lives.[30] Accordingly, a person might fail to hold on to her existing life, despite her amount of goods remaining unchanged: imagine, for example, that God suddenly transformed her from a lawyer into a business executive. Conversely, I might stay on the existing track of my life, despite having suffered a loss. Suppose an unimportant tool in my garage is destroyed. My amount of material goods has been reduced, but it is not true that my life has therefore departed from its existing track in any meaningful sense.[31] Accordingly, a right to security, in the sense of a right to hold on to one's existing life, is a loss-*independent* right,[32] and Gardner can be read as offering a version of Loss-Independent-Right-Continuity in claiming that reparation is based on the idea that 'we are to enjoy security against others'.[33]

I will not try to settle the interpretative question of which version is most faithful to Gardner's text. Instead, I will criticize both, starting with the version of the continuity theory based on a right to hold on (Section D) before moving on to the version based on a right against loss (Section E).

[27] Ibid, 181–187, 231. By 'existing life', obviously Gardner refers to the victim's life pre-breach rather than post-breach.

[28] Ibid, 183.

[29] Adam Slavny, 'Negating and Counterbalancing: A Fundamental Distinction in the Concept of a Corrective Duty' (2014) 33 *Law and Philosophy* 143, 151 (hereafter Slavny, 'Negating and Counterbalancing'); Robert Goodin, 'Compensation and Redistribution' in John Chapman (ed), *Compensatory Justice Nomos XXXIII* (New York University Press 1991) 157 (hereafter Goodin, 'Compensation and Redistribution'). See also Gardner's distinction between two senses of 'security interests' in Gardner, *Torts and Other Wrongs* (n 1) 250.

[30] See, e.g., Slavny, 'Negating and Counterbalancing' (n 29) 151; Gardner, *From Personal Life to Private Law* (n 16) 229; Robert Goodin, 'Theories of Compensation' (1989) 9 *Oxford Journal of Legal Studies* 56.

[31] Sandy Steel makes this point in a note on Gardner's Quain Lectures (which form the basis of *From Personal Life to Private Law*), available at: <https://mcbridesguides.com/wp-content/uploads/2014/05/john-gardner-quain-lectures-april-may-2014.pdf> accessed 9 June 2021. See also Steel, 'Compensation and Continuity' (n 8) 272.

[32] Just like a right against loss, a right to hold on to one's existing life can also come in an unqualified version (i.e. a right that you do not push me off the existing track of my life *as such*) or a qualified version (i.e. a right that you do not push me off the existing track of my life *in certain ways*, say through wrongful acts). The qualified version is more plausible, though my critique should apply to both the qualified and unqualified versions.

[33] Gardner, *From Personal Life to Private Law* (n 16) 231.

D. First Interpretation: Loss-Independent-Right-Continuity Based on a Right to Hold On to One's Existing Life

Gardner's account, under the first interpretation, is as follows. The victim has a (loss-independent) right against others, including the wrongdoer, to hold on to her existing life. Pre-breach, this right helps to explain the wrongdoer's primary duty towards her, for example, his duty not to remove her arm: doing so would push her off the existing track of her life. Post-breach, the foundational right will continue to demand conformity. Reparative damages (which can, for example, be used to buy artificial limbs) can help to move the victim back, or closer, to the track of her existing life (i.e. her life pre-breach), and thus are required by the victim's foundational right to hold on to her existing life.[34]

The main problem with this account, as a defence of reparatory duties in general, is that even if we assume that we generally have a right to hold on to our existing lives, such a right does not always require reparation.[35] First, sometimes a wrongdoing would entirely shatter a victim's life. In those cases, it is unclear that reparation can have *any* effect towards restoring the victim to her life pre-breach.[36] Second, in some cases, the victim may have a high amount of goods—far more than what is needed to sustain her existing life. In those cases, reparative damages are not needed to return the victim's life to its original track.[37]

Some may wish to raise the following rule-consequentialist response on behalf of Gardner. It may be argued that while reparation does not always enable a particular victim to hold on to her pre-breach life, there is benefit (say, reduction in administrative costs and false negatives) in having reparation as a general rule rather than judging the effect of reparation on a case-by-case basis.[38] But even setting aside the well-known difficulties of justifying private law by rule-consequentialism,[39] I think we should not ascribe this response to Gardner.[40]

To elaborate, Gardner claims that the 'reconciliatory' account of reparation, which justifies reparation by its ability to ameliorate 'hostility' and 'ill-feeling', cannot be the 'basic story of what ... reparation is about'[41] as reparation is not

[34] Ibid, 184–186.

[35] See also Goodin, 'Compensation and Redistribution' (n 29) 156, 172 fn 35. For the more general point that a right that is not concerned with protecting the victim from suffering loss cannot explain reparation, see, e.g., Stephen Perry, 'The Moral Foundations of Tort Law' (1992) 77 *Iowa Law Review* 449, 483–488.

[36] Scott Hershovitz, 'Tort as a Substitute for Revenge' in John Oberdiek (ed), *Philosophical Foundations of the Law of Torts* (Oxford University Press 2014) 92. Gardner has considered related issues in *From Personal Life to Private Law* (n 16) 187–188, 229. I think his solution at 229 suggests a kind of continuity theory that is loss-based.

[37] See n 31.

[38] For this kind of move, see, e.g., Jules Coleman, *Risks and Wrongs* (Cambridge University Press 1992) 379–380 (hereafter Coleman, *Risks and Wrongs*).

[39] See, e.g., Coleman, *Risks and Wrongs* (n 38) 379–380.

[40] See also Gardner, *Torts and Other Wrongs* (n 1) 131, where he claims that the moral norm of corrective justice is not a 'social norm'.

[41] Gardner, *From Personal Life to Private Law* (n 16) 93.

always necessary for such purpose.[42] Anticipating a rule-consequentialist response on behalf of the reconciliatory account, Gardner argues that while he does not think 'rule-consequentialist gambits are doomed to fail', we should not be 'driven to these gambits so soon'.[43] But if Gardner thinks that it is unsatisfying to defend the reconciliatory account by rule-consequentialism, it is unclear why he would want to resort to such gambits himself in defending the continuity theory.[44]

E. Second Interpretation: Right-against-Loss-Continuity Based on a Right against Wrongful Loss

Under the second interpretation of Gardner's continuity theory, the relevant foundational right is a right against wrongful loss. To illustrate with the arm case, on this account the wrongdoer's obligation not to remove the victim's arm is, at least partly, grounded on a foundational moral right of the victim against wrongful loss—removing her arm is a wrongful action, and this action will reduce her amount of goods such as resources or welfare. Post-breach, while the wrongdoer cannot erase the wrongdoing from history, he can, through reparation, prevent the victim from suffering loss that is caused by his wrongdoing, and thus improve his conformity with his obligation not to cause wrongful loss to her.[45]

This account may appear to avoid the two objections against the account based on a right to hold on to one's existing life, which I discussed in Section D.[46] To recall, the first objection was that some wrongdoings may totally shatter the victim's life such that reparation cannot move her any closer to the track of life she had pre-breach. If the justification of reparation is based on helping the victim to stay at, or stay closer to, the existing track of her life pre-breach, then reparation would be pointless in such cases. But if our goal is merely to *maintain the amount of the victim's goods*, then it seems achievable by reparative damages.[47] The second objection considered also loses some of its bite against Right-against-Loss-Continuity. Reparative damages may be unnecessary to enable the immensely rich victim to

[42] Ibid.

[43] Ibid.

[44] That said, some of Gardner's passages display sympathy towards rule-consequentialism: see, e.g., Gardner, *Torts and Other Wrongs* (n 1) 124–125, 129, 330. For discussion of rule-consequentialist aspects in Gardner's work, see also Sina Akbari, 'Review of From Personal Life to Private Law by John Gardner' (2020) *Modern Law Review* 917.

[45] See, e.g., Gardner, *Torts and Other Wrongs* (n 1) 68; Steel, 'Compensation and Continuity' (n 8) 256–257, 262.

[46] See also, e.g., Steel, 'Compensation and Continuity' (n 8) 255–258, 262; Stephen Smith, 'Remedies for Breach of Contract: One Principle or Two?' in Gregory Klass, George Letsas, and Prince Saprai (eds), *Philosophical Foundations of Contract Law* (Oxford University Press 2014) 352; Webb, 'Justifying Damages' (n 12) 158–159, 162.

[47] Gardner, *From Personal Life to Private Law* (n 16) 229.

hold on to her pre-breach life. But it would still help to prevent her from suffering wrongful loss.

That said, I think that Right-against-Loss-Continuity is vulnerable to another serious challenge. In the real world, many people are unjustly rich. The unjustly rich, of course, still have a valid moral right against bodily injury, including the removal of one's arm.[48] Given the importance to all of us of holding on to one's existing life, as Gardner's illuminating discussion suggests,[49] perhaps we should also accept that even the unjustly rich have a valid (pro tanto) moral right to hold on to their existing lives, or at least a right not to be pushed too far away from the existing tracks of their lives. But, given that they do not have a moral entitlement to their existing amount of goods, it is obscure why they should have any moral protection (that enjoys the status of a right) against loss, including loss that is caused by wrongdoings.[50]

I wish to make one clarification about my challenge. While many have challenged corrective justice by pointing to the unjust distributive status quo, such challenge comes in two different kinds and they are not always clearly distinguished in the literature. The first kind denies the unjustly rich victim's moral right to reparation by arguing that, in light of the unjust distributive status quo, the injurer's act, despite being a violation of the victim's *legal* right, has not in fact violated her *moral* primary right.[51] For example, some may argue that, while legally speaking a poor person is not allowed to break into a rich person's house to get food, morally speaking he has no obligation to refrain; since a moral obligation to repair is premised on a breach of a moral primary obligation, he has no moral obligation to repair. The second kind of distributive justice-based challenge to corrective justice denies the unjustly rich victim's right to repair *without* denying that her primary right has been breached.[52] The challenge that I am raising against Right-against-Loss-Continuity is of the second kind. I do not dispute that torts (such as the removal of another person's arm without good reasons) are often moral wrongs. My

[48] Stephen Perry, 'On the Relationship between Corrective and Distributive Justice' in Jeremy Horder (ed), *Oxford Essays in Jurisprudence: Fourth Series* (Oxford University Press 2000) 247.

[49] Gardner, *From Personal Life to Private Law* (n 16) 168–178.

[50] For similar points, see, e.g., Coleman, *Risks and Wrongs* (n 38) 304–305; Jason Solomon, 'Equal Accountability through Tort Law' (2009) 103 *Northwestern University Law Review* 1765, 1774–1775; William Lucy, 'Rethinking the Common Law' (1994) 14 *Oxford Journal of Legal Studies* 539, 554–557; Diego Papayannis, 'The Morality of Compensation in Tort Law' (draft article presented to the Jurisprudence Discussion Group at the University of Oxford on 22 May 2019), 13–15 (hereafter Papayannis, 'The Morality of Compensation in Tort Law'); James Penner, 'Don't Crash into Mick Jagger When He Is Driving His Rolls Royce', in Paul Miller and John Oberdiek (eds), *Civil Wrongs and Justice in Private Law* (Oxford University Press 2020) 262–263. Cf. Steel, 'Compensation and Continuity' (n 8) 261, 271–272.

[51] But cf., James Nickel, 'Justice in Compensation' (1976) 18 *William and Mary Law Review* 379, 387–388 (hereafter Nickel, 'Justice in Compensation').

[52] For writers who draw a similar distinction and challenge the reparatory obligation without challenging the primary obligation, see, e.g., Papayannis, 'The Morality of Compensation in Tort Law' (n 50) 13; Jenny Steele, '"Far from an Orthodoxy": Assignable Responsibility and Corrective Justice in John Gardner's Account of Tort Law' (2019) 19 *Jerusalem Review of Legal Studies* 50, 64.

claim is rather that some victims—namely, those with an unjustly large amount of goods—do not have a right against wrongful loss.[53] So, if a victim's right to reparation is supposed to be grounded on her right against wrongful loss, as Right-against-Loss-Continuity alleges, then there can be no general right to reparation as there is no general right against wrongful loss.

Gardner discusses—in two places—distributive justice-based challenges to corrective justice. A consideration of those passages will occupy us for the rest of this chapter. I will argue that, while his replies may be effective against some versions of distributive justice-based challenge to corrective justice, they are not effective against mine. This is not meant to be a criticism, as he is not obliged to defend against every possible threat to corrective justice posed by distributive injustice. But it does mean that if the continuity theory is to have a good reply to my version of distributive justice-based challenge, it must look beyond Gardner's writings.[54]

F. 'What Is Tort Law For? Part 2. The Place of Distributive Justice'

The first passage is in 'What Is Tort Law For? Part 2. The Place of Distributive Justice'. Despite remarking at the beginning of that paper that he 'will not be concerned with the desirability of changing the law of torts to cure or alleviate, or otherwise to respond to, distributive injustices that could equally exist quite apart from the law of torts',[55] Gardner nonetheless replies to what he calls the 'perennial student objection to tort law', the objection that 'it cannot be just to restore a distribution that was not itself just'.[56] This is how he lays out the challenge:

> The secondary (corrective) duties of tort law are sometimes imagined to have been, for Calabresi and Melamed, automatic implications of the initial entitlements [i.e. 'the set of primary duties, breach of which constitutes a tort'[57]]. In other words, Calabresi and Melamed are often associated with something like my 'continuity thesis'. Doing corrective justice is responding belatedly to the reasons that one should have responded to in the first place, in not committing the tort. In combination with the Calabresi and Melamed view that these first-place reasons

[53] For a similar distinction between these two rights, see, e.g., Webb, 'Justifying Damages' (n 12) 155–156; Steel, 'Compensation and Continuity' (n 8) 260, 271.

[54] There are of course other attempts in the literature to vindicate corrective justice in circumstances of distributive injustice. See, e.g., Coleman, *Risks and Wrongs* (n 38) 350–354; Helen Eenmaa-Dimitrieva, 'The Problem of Dependency of Corrective Justice' (2019) 32 *Canadian Journal of Law and Jurisprudence* 59; MacCormick, 'The Obligation of Reparation' (n 3) 180; Ripstein, *Private Wrongs* (n 6) 41–43.

[55] Gardner, *Torts and Other Wrongs* (n 1) 81.

[56] Ibid, 91.

[57] Ibid.

> are reasons for the allocation of 'initial entitlements', this lures one into what might be called the 'deflationary view' of corrective justice. Corrective justice is revealed not to be a distinct form of justice, but merely distributive justice re-done following a disruptive intervention (that was not itself licensed by distributive justice). And from here it is a short step to what, in Part 1, I called 'a perennial student objection to tort law', namely that it cannot be just to restore a distribution that was not itself just.[58]

As Gardner believes the 'perennial student objection to tort law' draws its allure from the 'deflationary view of corrective justice' (i.e. the view that the restoration of an antecedently just distribution of initial entitlements forms the point of reparation), he tries to disarm the former by criticizing the latter.

> His critique of the deflationary view begins by drawing a distinction between two versions of the deflationary view. To elaborate, since 'rights' can refer either to (1) rights in 'raw morality', i.e. 'rights that exist independently of the law, and independently of any other kind of use, observance, recognition, or adoption by anyone'[59] or to (2) rights recognized by the law, Gardner distinguishes between two versions of the deflationary view: (1) the raw morality version, according to which justice requires the wrongdoer to repair because it would restore an antecedently just distribution of raw moral primary rights; and (2) the legal version, according to which justice requires the imposition of a legal duty to repair on the wrongdoer because it will restore an antecedently just distribution of legal primary rights.

Gardner then proceeds to reject both versions of the deflationary view.

Against the raw morality version, Gardner claims that we cannot sensibly talk about 'just distribution' of primary rights in raw morality (and accordingly, the restoration of such distribution) because rights and duties in raw morality are *something that we cannot distribute.*

> By their nature, raw moral rights and duties are not allocated by anybody ... It makes no sense to ask what distribution of raw moral rights and duties would be just, even when the interests that they serve conflict, because raw moral rights and duties are incapable of being distributed. They come and go with the reasons for and against their existence, and irrespective ... of their use, observance, recognition, or adoption.[60]

[58] Ibid (his notes omitted).
[59] Ibid, 83.
[60] Ibid, 83–84.

Against the legal version of the deflationary view, Gardner claims that the view is based on the idea that there is some kind of 'automatic [implication]' between legal primary rights and legal reparatory rights.[61] He attacks the legal version of the deflationary view by denying such automatic implication:

In the law, quite apart from the question of which primary duties (= which 'initial entitlements') to recognize, there is the further question of how to deal with the breach of those legally recognized primary duties and, in particular whether to institutionalize a secondary duty of corrective justice . . . the corrective duties are not mere automatic implications of the initial entitlements, whether by the logic of the continuity thesis or otherwise. They are distinct entitlements that also need to be distributed by the law.[62]

In reply to Gardner, while his responses may be effective against the particular versions of distributive justice-based challenge that he considers, they are unhelpful against mine (which, as I will explain below, is in some way more intuitive than the versions that he considers). Let us begin with Gardner's critique of the legal version of the deflationary view. For two reasons, it does not defuse my challenge. First, my challenge is one about raw morality. The crux of my challenge is that unjustly rich victims do not have a right to repair in raw morality. I am not directly making a claim about what rights the law should recognize. Nor do I think that most who raise distributive injustice-based challenges to corrective justice commit to any such claim. Many of them hold that while the unjustly rich victims have no right to repair in raw morality, a rule granting those victims a right to repair in the law may well be justified by consequentialist considerations.[63]

Second, more importantly, Gardner's central move against the legal version of the deflationary view, which involves unbundling the issue of whether one should have a primary right from the issue of whether one should have a reparatory right in case of breach, has no bite against my challenge. To see this, recall my distinction above between the two kinds of distributive justice-based challenge to corrective justice. The first kind of distributive justice-based challenge to corrective justice may presuppose a close connection between the two issues.[64] By contrast, the second kind of distributive justice-based challenge to corrective justice, to which my challenge belongs, presupposes the opposite.

Gardner's critique of the raw morality version of the deflationary view also does not address my challenge. Let us draw a distinction between 'primary rights' and 'goods'. While Gardner has provided a persuasive argument (quoted above) for the claim that the idea of distribution of *primary rights* in raw morality is nonsensical,

[61] Ibid, 91.
[62] Ibid, 92 (emphasis mine).
[63] See e.g., Coleman, *Risks and Wrongs* (n 38) 304–305, 488 fn 21.
[64] See text surrounding nn 48–49.

he has not argued that the idea of distribution of *goods* in raw morality is nonsensical. In fact, plausibly, he writes:

> [The idea that 'there is no such thing as the justice of the ... distribution' of 'raw moral rights and duties'[65]] should not be mistaken for the proposition that there are no raw moral rights and duties of distributive justice. There most certainly are. They bear on the distribution of things other than raw moral rights and duties.[66]

It should now be obvious why Gardner's attack on the raw morality version of the deflationary view has no bearing on my critique and, more generally, on distributive justice-based challenges to corrective justice as commonly understood. When critics of corrective justice, myself included, raise the 'perennial student objection to tort law'—the objection that 'it cannot be just to restore a distribution that was not itself just'—the kind of distributive injustice that most of us have in mind refers to unjust distribution of *goods* rather than unjust distribution of *primary rights*. The question that bugs us is 'why does justice require the poor tortfeasor to transfer some of his goods to the rich victim, if doing so would lead to an even more unjust distribution of goods?' Few would, I suspect, have in mind the different, and rather peculiar, question 'why does justice require the poor tortfeasor to transfer some of his raw moral primary rights to the rich victim, if doing so would lead to an even more unjust distribution of raw moral primary rights?'

G. From Personal Life to Private Law

In *From Personal Life to Private Law*, Gardner considers a well-known quote by Jules Coleman: '[I]f you have no right to your wealth under the relevant principle of distributive justice ... how can you have a right to have it restored?'[67]

Gardner writes that there is 'a possible way of responding to Coleman's troubling question about the conservative aspect of the law of obligations'.[68] He then makes two main points. First, he explains that wealth and security are conceptually distinct. While extra wealth may increase a person's security, we can increase a person's security more specifically by providing a right to repair—as a security right, a right to repair offers security without offering wealth as such.[69] Second, he claims that justice in the distribution of security is distinct from justice in the

65 Gardner, *Torts and Other Wrongs* (n 1) 84.
66 Ibid, 84 fn 18.
67 Coleman, *Risks and Wrongs* (n 38) 304–305. This passage was quoted twice (at 166 and 194) in Gardner, *From Personal Life to Private Law* (n 16). Gardner's response appears after the second quote. For Coleman's own discussion of the challenge, see Coleman, *Risks and Wrongs* (n 38) 350–354.
68 Gardner, *From Personal Life to Private Law* (n 16) 194.
69 Ibid.

distribution of wealth, and tort law, as a system that distributes security rights, must be concerned with the former.[70]

I must confess that I do not have a firm grasp as to how these points are supposed to address Coleman's challenge. One way to understand Gardner's points is this: since justice in the distribution of wealth and justice in the distribution of security are conceptually distinct, even if the unjustly rich have no right to their wealth, they still have a right to security like everyone else. Since reparatory right is a kind of security right, it follows that unjustly rich victims should have the same reparatory right as poor victims.[71]

This possible response to Coleman is unsound, for reasons that I have partly covered. As the right to security is a right to 'hold on' to a certain thing, we can distinguish between three interpretations of the right depending on what the thing being held on to is (the first two interpretations were mentioned in Section C). First, it can refer to a right to hold on to *a particular item* (say, my arm, my house, or my car). Second, it can refer to a right to hold on to *my existing life*. Third, it can refer to a right to hold on to *my amount of goods*—say, my amount of welfare or resources.

It is clear that a right to security in the first sense cannot justify compensation: after my arm has been (irreversibly) removed, I cannot hold on to the relevant particular item, namely *that* arm, regardless of whether I am compensated.[72] The right to security in the second sense also cannot ground a general right to repair, as I explained in Section D.

How about the third sense of security? The problem is that it is very hard to see why one has a right to security in her amount of goods if she does not have a right to that amount in the first place. The fact that we cannot lead meaningful lives without being free (to a certain extent) from disruption may explain why we have a right to hold on (to a certain extent) to whatever lives we are living.[73] But holding on to one's amount of goods is, as I explained in Section C, unnecessary (and also insufficient) for holding on to one's life. What moral consideration—that enjoys the status of a right—is served by ensuring that an unjustly rich person's bank balance maintains the same number of zeroes or her welfare stays at the same obscenely high level post-breach, when doing so has no effect on whether she could stay on the existing track of her life? It is one thing to say, *as a conceptual matter*, the right to *security in* one's amount of wealth is distinct from the right to one's amount of wealth; it is quite another to say that, *as a moral matter*, the lack of the latter does not affect the justification of the former.

[70] Ibid.

[71] See ibid, 167. On a related note, Coleman justifies corrective justice in societies where the distribution of goods is not perfectly just by appealing to the idea of stability: Coleman, *Risks and Wrongs* (n 38) 354.

[72] See, e.g., Gardner, *From Personal Life to Private Law* (n 16) 185–186.

[73] Ibid, 174, 197.

Perhaps I have read Gardner's claims too strongly. Perhaps all that Gardner wants to establish in that passage, through drawing a distinction between security and wealth and noting that justice in distribution of the former is distinct from justice in distribution of the latter, is the more modest claim that tort law is not inherently 'socially conservative'.[74] To elaborate, Gardner plausibly claims that security is something that is valuable to all, regardless of one's amount of wealth, and that while historically tort law often favours the rich (e.g. the rich have much better access to the tort system), in principle, even if the distribution of wealth is unjust, rights in tort law, as a form of security rights, can still be distributed justly—in the sense that one would not have less protection from tort law because one is less wealthy. So, tort law can benefit everyone—rich and poor alike—without discriminating against the poor, and as such, it is not an inherently socially conservative institution.[75]

I agree largely with the modest claim. But the modest claim does not really engage with Coleman's main point. As an analogy, consider a state universal pandemic allowance scheme, where everyone will receive $500 from the government regardless of his or her situation. That this scheme would benefit the rich and poor alike and that access to the scheme is not restricted to the rich—and thus is not inherently socially conservative in the sense above—does not silence the most important objection to the scheme: namely, the rich, in virtue of their wealth, have no claim under justice to extra state benefit in the first place.

H. Conclusion

In this chapter I have argued that the continuity theory can come in many different versions, and that Gardner can be read either as offering a version that is based on a loss-independent right to hold on to one's existing life or a version that is based on a right against wrongful loss. I have argued that the former is unsatisfactory, as a right to hold on to one's existing life cannot ground a general right to reparation post-breach. I have argued against the latter on the basis that, in a distributively unjust society, people do not generally have a right against wrongful loss. I have surveyed two passages in Gardner's work where he responds to distributive justice-based challenges to corrective justice and argued that, while his replies may work against some versions of distributive justice-based challenge to corrective justice, they do not work against mine.

74 Ibid, 193.

75 Ibid, 193–194.

13

Never Let Me Go: Private Law and the Conservative Impulse

Prince Saprai[*]

A. Gardner's Conservatism

In his *From Personal Life to Private Law*, John Gardner revealed himself as a conservative.[1] That will, of course, come as a surprise to most people. If Gardner was anything, he was an unreconstructed, proud, and unapologetic 1960s liberal. That was, of course, one of the things we loved about him. Had Gardner's political views hardened with age? The answer is, of course, no; they most certainly had not.[2] Gardner (quite rightly) had no truck with what he called 'social conservatives'. These are people, he said, who seek to have 'the old social order retained'; never mind that this might be an 'obnoxiously repressive and privilege-entrenching' thing to do.[3]

Rather, Gardner had in mind a different kind of conservatism. He was a conservative in the sense that the vast majority of people are. He believed that there was value in holding onto the lives and things that we already have, even when dispensing with that life and those things might produce better outcomes in the long run. It is a cast of mind deeply at odds with the utilitarian outlook. As G.A. Cohen says: 'To seek to maximize value is to see nothing wrong in the destruction of valuable things, as long as there is no reduction in the total amount of value as a result.'[4]

* Earlier drafts of this chapter were presented at a workshop for this volume at All Souls College, Oxford (2019) and at a Research Seminar at UCL (2020). Thank you to participants on both occasions for extremely helpful feedback. Thank you in particular to Sinead Agnew, Anthony Duff, Nick McBride, Denise Réaume, Irit Samet, Rob Stevens, and Kevin Toh for pressing me on various issues which led me to make a number of revisions. The usual caveat applies.

1 John Gardner, *From Personal Life to Private Law* (Oxford University Press 2018) ch 5 (hereafter Gardner, *Personal Life*).

2 Lest he had created the wrong impression, Gardner makes his card-carrying liberal credentials explicit toward the end of the book. Ibid 198.

3 Ibid 193.

4 G.A. Cohen, 'Rescuing Conservatism: A Defense of Existing Value' in R. Jay Wallace, Rahul Kumar, and Samuel Freeman (eds), *Reasons and Recognition: Essays on the Philosophy of T.M. Scanlon* (Oxford University Press 2011) 203, 211 (hereafter Cohen, 'Conservatism').

Prince Saprai, *Never Let Me Go: Private Law and the Conservative Impulse* In: *From Morality to Law and Back Again*. Edited by: Michelle Madden Dempsey and François Tanguay-Renaud, Oxford University Press. © Prince Saprai 2023.
DOI: 10.1093/oso/9780198860594.003.0013

Gardner thought there was something wrong with such destruction, and he was surely right about this. It's an outlook that is widely shared even among people with otherwise wildly different political views. So, for example, the social conservatives would certainly endorse it, but, as George Orwell pointed out, so too would many a Marxist revolutionary: 'Most revolutionaries are potential Tories, because they imagine that everything can be put right by altering the *shape* of society; once that change is effected, as it sometimes is, they see no need for any other.'[5]

It was a stubborn fact that troubled G.A. Cohen, who, of course, regarded himself as a proud Marxist and certainly no conservative:

> I have a pencil eraser (or in British English, a 'rubber') that I have used ever since I became a lecturer forty-six years ago. When I got it, it was a cube, but now it is a sort of sphere, and although it is small, most of it is still there. It is not because I make very few mistakes that most of my eraser is still there, but because (a) I do not use pencils very much; (b) it takes only a little bit of rubbing to eliminate a mistake; and (c) I do not notice all of my mistakes. I would hate to lose this eraser. I would hate that even if I knew it could be readily replaced, not only, if I so wished, by a pristine cubical one, but even by one of precisely the off-round shape and the same dingy color that mine has now acquired. There is no feature that stands apart from its history that makes me want to keep this eraser. I want *my* eraser, with *its* history. What could be more human than that?[6]

The answer is of course 'nothing', and in that sense Gardner the 1960s liberal and Cohen the Marxist could both agree that they were conservatives in this thin sense.

The difficulty, though, is in unpacking what this conservative value is; in other words, what is good about holding onto the eraser, or the revolution, and so forth? Both Gardner and Cohen had stories to tell about this. My focus is going to be on Gardner's story. It was a story that mattered for Gardner, because he thought that this conservative impulse helped to justify the law of torts and private law more generally. In the next two sections, I am going to express some doubts both about the justification Gardner gives for this conservative impulse and the extent to which it explains very much about private law. In the rest of the chapter, I will suggest that despite these worries, Gardner was right to link private law with conservatism. However, I will claim that, to understand private law, we have to go beyond the thin version of conservatism that Gardner endorsed and towards a thicker conception of the value, while avoiding the error made by social conservatives, that is, believing that there is value in holding onto injustice.[7]

[5] George Orwell, *Essays* (Penguin 2000) 75.
[6] Cohen, 'Conservatism' (n 4) 221.
[7] Ibid, 204.

B. The Story of My Life

Gardner recognizes that the conservative impulse—the desire to hold on to the lives or things that we already have—is a basic feature of human nature. His question was whether it was possible to make rational sense of this disposition. Gardner thought it was. Gardner claims that the conservative impulse reflects a justified desire to keep our lives on the same track. In other words, we have an interest in carrying on with the lives we are already living. It is, of course, not an interest that necessarily prevails against all other interests. Rather, according to Gardner, it is an interest that matters, and carries at least some normative weight in our practical deliberations.[8] I started the PhD and so, other things being equal, I have a reason to carry on with it, because I have an interest, according to Gardner, in keeping my life on the same track that it is already on.

Does Gardner beg the question here? No, he raises a different question: 'Why keep our lives on the same track?' He provides an answer to this new question which sheds light on the value that, he claims, is served by preserving the lives we already have. In other words, he attempts by locating this value to provide a justification for the conservative impulse.

Gardner's answer consists in the claim that it is of fundamental importance for human beings to be able to set, adopt, or pursue personal goals. This is how, according to Gardner, human beings bring value into their own lives. As we are rational and finite creatures, we have to make choices between the great variety of ways in which we might bring value into our lives. We do this by setting certain things as goals or ends to pursue over others.

So, for example, I might set myself the goal this summer of taking as little time off with my family as possible, so that I can write a book. Alternatively, I might set myself the goal this summer of doing very little work, so that I can maximize the time I spend with my family. Both are valuable things to do, but I cannot do both; they are mutually incompatible as ends. Unless I'm willing to compromise, I have to choose which one is most important to me, and I do that by setting one of them as a goal for myself over the other.

Gardner's claim is that our capacity as creatures that bring value into our lives by setting, adopting, or pursuing goals is seriously compromised if we cannot rely on our lives not being seriously knocked off course. So, let's say I set myself the goal of writing a book this summer. That is all very well and good, but in order to achieve that aim I have to be able to rely on my life not being disrupted in unexpected ways that make it impossible or at least very difficult to achieve that goal. In the absence of this kind of security, I can't write the book.

[8] Gardner, *Personal Life* (n 1) 168.

This explains, according to Gardner, why we care about our lives staying on the same track. We can't achieve our goals otherwise. Gardner says:

> Assuming that those who have worthwhile goals have reason to succeed in their goals ... one has reason to fear and to regret failure-inducing disruption of one's life. What one longs for under this heading is not exactly the life that one has lost or is in the course of losing, but the success in it that is to be or has been snatched from one.[9]

On Gardner's view, the explanation for the conservative impulse piggybacks on the value of the capacity to set, adopt, or pursue personal goals. This capacity has importance not only because it enables the rational and finite creatures that we are to engage with value, but also because, by adopting certain goals over others, we define ourselves as the particular people that we are. For Gardner this is what having a life consists in, and it is bound up with the equally important capacity of being able to tell a story about one's life.[10]

For Gardner living valuably, which involves the selective adoption and pursuit of valuable personal goals, is the characteristic end, or *ergon*, of human beings. And it explains why we care about keeping our existing lives on track.[11]

The argument is ingenious. Gardner attempts to connect the justification for a fundamental aspect of human nature—the desire to hold on—with an argument for the role it plays in achieving the organizing end of human beings, that is, living valuably. The trouble though, I think, with Gardner's argument is that the connection he attempts to establish between the two things is not strong enough to sustain the plausibility of his claim.

Here is why. It is all too easy to decouple the link between the preservation of our existing lives and the adoption or pursuit of our personal goals. There is clearly no *necessary* connection between the two things. One may not achieve a goal even when one's existing life is not disrupted in any significant way. So, for example, I might fail to achieve my goal of making a marble cake, because of a lack of skill, or a lack of effort, or just sheer bad luck. This may be true even if my life suffers no disruption when I attempt to make the cake.

Furthermore, there is not even a *sufficient* connection. Take G.A. Cohen's eraser as an example. If Cohen were to lose his eraser, it's very hard to see what possible impact that could have on his goals. As he said, he hardly ever has occasion to use it. Yet, he would still be very upset to lose it. That 'upsetness' is, of course, natural and perfectly intelligible, but *not* according to Gardner's account.

[9] Ibid, 171–172.

[10] On the latter capacity, see: John Gardner, 'The Mark of Responsibility' (2003) 23 Oxford Journal of Legal Studies 157.

[11] Gardner, *Personal Life* (n 1) 175–176.

Now, Gardner might say that he was not making a logical or conceptual claim about the relationship between security and goals. He might argue that he was relying on a looser relationship between disruption to one's life and one's goals or capacity to pursue them. So, for example, perhaps Gardner was arguing that it is *normally* the case that when one's life is disrupted that it inhibits the pursuit of one's goals. Or that typically when we have security, that conduces to the successful pursuit of one's goals. That is a perfectly legitimate response and a reasonable interpretation of Gardner's view. Nevertheless, it means at best that Gardner's account only explains the conservative impulse that we have in *standard* cases, that is, in those cases where the desire to hold on is linked with being able to achieve our personal goals or ends. It does not though explain *all* cases, such as why Cohen would regret the loss of his eraser.

Gardner does accept that we have *impersonal* (not dependent on our own personal goals) reasons to respect already instantiated value, but for Gardner even this has an indirect relation to the pursuit of goals, by creating opportunities for engagement with valuable things and people: 'To have personal goals, to be able to engage selectively with value, is to inhabit a world in which value is instantiated, made concrete, and thereby made available for engagement.'[12] So we might rightly lament the fires that are burning down the Amazon rainforest or the species destruction caused by climate change quite regardless of any role these events might play in the pursuit of our own personal goals. Although Gardner is surely right that we have reasons to preserve impersonal value of this kind, it is important to see that these sorts of reasons cannot explain the unhappiness that Cohen would feel at the loss of his eraser. There the loss would be clearly agent-relative or *personal* in character: that is, I and others would certainly not feel the loss in the same way as Cohen would. Therefore, Gardner's explanation of our reasons to preserve already instantiated value leave at least one important gap. There are cases of the conservative impulse that Gardner's goal-centred account can't capture.

C. Private Law

Gardner might well accept that his account of the conservative impulse has limitations. Nevertheless, he could argue that he has shown one very significant agent-relative reason why human creatures have the conservative leanings that they do. That claim would have a lot going for it.

However, I now want to raise some different doubts which relate to his claim that his explanation of the conservative impulse provides a moral foundation for

[12] Ibid, 179–180. See also 175–176.

tort law and private law more generally, by explaining the structure it takes and the reasons why it operates in the way that it does.

Gardner claims that a central function of the apparatus of private law is the protection of our security interests or our reasons to hold onto the lives that we already have. His focus is mainly on the law of torts, but at various points he brings in discussion of contract and property law too. So, for example, the primary duty not to negligently cause personal injury to others is designed to protect the security interests of people whom we can reasonably foresee that we might harm as a result of our actions. This reflects the conservative impulse that Gardner defends, that is, the desire that people have to hold onto the lives that they already have: 'Our primary duties in the law of tort are mainly duties not to do certain things that set others back (or tend to set others back) in the lives they already have.'[13]

For Gardner tort law characteristically protects people from having their lives unreasonably disrupted, and the reason is tied up with Gardner's explanation of the conservative impulse, that is, that the disruptive effects of wrongdoing make it impossible, or very difficult, for people to be able to plan their lives and successfully pursue their goals. The *primary* duties of tort law give people the security that they need to successfully accomplish their goals. If those duties are breached, *secondary* obligations spring up requiring defendants to comply—albeit imperfectly—with the security-based reasons that they fell short of when they breached the primary duties. They do this by making reparation, usually in the form of monetary compensation, to the victim of the tort.

> So if I do injure your eye with, say, a small retaining screw that flies off my badly-maintained power tool as I used it, your security—the same security that was my reason not to injure your eye in the first place—is now a reason for me to ameliorate what I did, to put you back, so far as it can still be done, in the position you would have been in had I never injured you.[14]

A central purpose of tort law, for Gardner, is to keep people's lives on the tracks that they are already on. If, due to wrongful conduct, people's lives are derailed, tort law imposes reparative duties on wrongdoers to put victims' lives back on the tracks that they were previously on.

In this way, the reasons to hold onto your existing life 'double as reasons for getting that value back'.[15] The same explanation is given for the remedial obligations in contract:

[13] Ibid, 182.
[14] Gardner, *Personal Life* (n 1) 185–186.
[15] Ibid, 188.

> ... the security that is served in the performance of a contract will turn out to be the same one that is served in a fallback way by the reparative damages for breach of contract one obtains when the same security went unserved in the contract's non-performance.[16]

There is no doubt that private law plays the security-protecting role that Gardner puts his finger on. The difficulty, though, is in how much this actually tells us about private law. My worry is that the security-protecting function Gardner describes is not central enough to tell us something sufficiently informative about the practice: that is, it is not a function which infuses the practice and shapes the way that its other functions and aims are pursued.[17] In particular, there are three reasons why Gardner's account of private law falls short.

1. The Omission of Wrongdoing

For Gardner, a central mark of private law is a particular *goal* that it pursues, that is, upholding or protecting security interests, and a particular *mode* or *way in which* it protects those interests, that is, by conferring legal rights on victims or likely victims of wrongs, which they have the legal power to enforce in courts. So, for example, I might obtain an injunction to prevent a nuisance on my land or, if the nuisance has already taken place, monetary compensation for any loss suffered.

The difficulty though is that Gardner's account seems to miss out the notion of *moral* wrongdoing which most people would say plays a foundational role in tort law. Our security interests might be set back in all manner of ways by all manner of people, but private law is only eligible to step in when the cause of the disruption is *wrongful* conduct. So, for example, I might affect my young daughter's security interests by taking away her toys after particularly bad behaviour on her part, or I might affect a coffee shop owner's security interests by opening up a rival coffee shop next door, or my wife might affect my security interests by filing for divorce. These are all significant disruptions, but none of them is legally actionable as a tort because in none of these cases does the person causing the disruption act wrongfully. To the extent that private law is concerned with people's lives not being disrupted, its focus is on *morally wrongful* disruptions to those lives. Yet if we follow Gardner's premises closely it seems that moral wrongdoing or the risk of such wrongdoing would not be a necessary requirement for legitimating a tort.

[16] Ibid, 189.

[17] I rely here on Martha Nussbaum's conception of a focal function: see her 'Aristotle on Human Nature' in J.E.J. Altham and Ross Harrison (eds), *World, Mind, and Ethics: Essays on the Ethical Philosophy of Bernard Williams* (Cambridge University Press 1995) 86, 113–117. See also the distinction Roger Scruton draws between an internal purpose of an institution and its incidental effects: *How to Be a Conservative* (Bloomsbury 2014) 28–29 (hereafter Scruton, *How to Be a Conservative*).

The problem stems from Gardner's capacious view about the legitimacy of legal regulation in general. Gardner would say that in the sorts of cases that I describe (taking away the toys, opening up the rival coffee shop, etc.), the law prima facie at least has a reason to intervene. He says that '[t]he law exists to improve people's conformity with reasons that already apply to them'.[18] So, on Gardner's view, when I take my daughter's toys away, tort law prima facie at least has a reason to intervene to protect her interest in the security of her life. That reason may be more apparent than real (perhaps the law could not due to lack of resources make much difference in this sphere) or outweighed by moral considerations (the justifiability of taking the toys away given her bad behaviour) or legal concerns (e.g. the intrusiveness or disproportionality of legal intervention in such circumstances).[19] *Other things being equal*, though, it seems that the law on Gardner's view would have reason to make the taking away of the toys into a tort or legally actionable wrong—whether or not it constitutes a moral wrong. This is because by doing so the law would make it easier for me to conform to the reason I have not to disrupt my daughter's life by taking away her toys (assuming that the law would be an effective means of achieving this aim and that there is no bad behaviour on my daughter's part to justify my actions, and so forth).

The difficulty is that the notion of moral wrongdoing which most judges, lawyers, and indeed lay people, if asked, would say is at the heart of tort law drops completely out of the picture.[20] Instead, it seems that Gardner's view is that tort law may in principle legitimately intervene in order to prevent or repair disruptions to security interests per se—whether or not they are from a moral point of view wrongfully caused. If that is his view, it clearly misses out on a central feature which makes tort law tort law.

I am not exactly sure how Gardner would reply to this point. He might 'bite the bullet' and say that the common view that links torts to moral wrongs is mistaken. Or he might say that private law as instantiated in past practice is specifically concerned with morally wrongful disruptions to security interests. In chapter 1 of the book, he argues that private law is concerned with duties that we owe to others on account of the special relationships we have with them (he calls these 'strictly relational duties') and duties that we owe to others on account of their special vulnerability to our actions regardless of any pre-existing special relationship (he calls these 'loosely relational duties'). If the latter is how he would respond, my criticism

[18] Gardner, *Personal Life* (n 1) 77.

[19] Ibid, 75–83.

[20] I cannot explore the issue here, but the priority Gardner attaches to reasons over duties may also give rise to a problem with his account of tort law's reparative obligations. This is because arguably wrongdoing on Gardner's view plays a merely causal rather than normative role in justifying secondary duties. Explaining why, see Stephen A. Smith, 'The Significance of a Civil Wrong' in P.B. Miller and J. Oberdick (eds), *Civil Wrongs and Justice in Private Law* (Oxford University Press 2020) 157, 161–163. If Smith's interpretation is correct, Gardner's thesis appears problematic, because the link between wrongdoing and reparation in private law seems to be normative rather than merely causal.

would be that Gardner does not do enough to explain why these particular cases of threats to others' security interests generate moral obligations. I am in a special relationship with my daughter, but I breach no moral duty when I take her toys away. The coffee shop owner is especially vulnerable when I open my rival shop next door, but again I breach no moral duty in doing so. In all these cases security interests are at stake, but Gardner gives little guidance on how to distinguish between those cases that ought to be the concern of private law and those that shouldn't.

Alternatively, Gardner might say that private law plays a constitutive role in determining when we have moral duties not to interfere with the security interests of others.[21] This is no doubt true in some cases, but it seems implausible to suggest that this constitutive role extends to all the duties that private law upholds and enforces. I have a moral duty not to interfere with your security interests by punching you, regardless of what the law has to say on the issue. So, the problem remains: how do we distinguish between those cases where we have moral duties not to upset security interests and those where we don't?

2. Differentiation

This brings me to my second worry. Above I expressed the concern that Gardner's account does not tell us enough about private law. Another related worry is that what Gardner does tell us about private law seems too little to differentiate private law from other areas of law; indeed, I'm not sure that Gardner tells us much about private law that we could not say about most areas of law.

Every area of law seems to be concerned with protecting people's security interests. Isn't this true, for example, of banking law, international law, carriage of goods by sea, family law, corporate insolvency law, competition law, criminal law, constitutional law, human rights law, and so on and so forth? Furthermore, the way that these areas of law protect these security interests is by recognising and upholding legal rights. It is true that tort law grants a victim a right of action against the wrongdoer, whereas for example in criminal law the right to prosecute rests with the state. Nevertheless, even this is a feature that tort possesses with many of the other areas of law in the above list.

Now, it is true that Gardner explicitly rejects that it is any part of his project to provide a timeless definition of private law. Indeed, he claims that the shape that private law takes is a matter of historical contingency and depends on exercises of legal authority in particular jurisdictions at particular times. Nevertheless, he argues that familiar systems of private law from the common law world and beyond share key concerns. One such concern to which Gardner's book attaches great

[21] See Gardner, *Personal Life* (n 1) 13–14, 75–76, 85–86.

weight is the role that private law plays in protecting the security interests of claimants.[22] My point is only that it seems difficult to see why Gardner gives this theme such pride of place, when it is one that we can find in most other areas of law.

3. The Bare Wrong

Related to the difficulty just discussed, that Gardner's account seems to spread itself too thin or is *overinclusive*, is the worry that it is also *underinclusive* when it comes to private law. So far, I have assumed that Gardner was right to claim that private law is concerned with upholding security interests. However, it is important to recognise that the truth of this claim is not obvious or uncontested.

So, for example, there are well-known torts, such as trespass or conversion, that are actionable *per se*, that is, without proof of loss or damage. The existence of these torts suggests that tort law has concerns going beyond the prevention of disruption to people's lives and holdings.[23] Gardner attempts to deal with these cases by saying that the fact that the presence of loss is not an element of the tort in these cases does not show that the avoidance of loss is not part of their underlying rationale.[24]

However, it is much harder to explain away an entire branch of private law, such as contract law, where there is no doubt that private rights are systematically enforced by courts even in the absence of disruption to life plans or any threat to a security interest. So, for example, the law of contract enforces promises in actions for breach of contract, even when a breach of contract would cause no loss or disruption, or even risk of loss or disruption to the life of the promisee. These are cases of 'bare wrongs', and it is unclear how Gardner explains why private law protects claimants from them.[25]

D. Virtue Conservatism

1. A Relational View

The three interconnected worries about Gardner's account are that it: doesn't tell us enough about why we have the private rights that we do; fails to distinguish

[22] Ibid, 12–15.

[23] Indeed, Robert Stevens has argued very influentially that loss is not a requirement for *any* tort and is only relevant to the separate issue of actionability in the case of some of the torts. Robert Stevens, *Torts and Rights* (Oxford University Press 2007).

[24] Ibid, 120.

[25] I borrow the terminology of the 'bare wrong' from David Owens, arguing that they played an important role in David Hume's theory of promising. David Owens, 'The Problem with Promising' in Hanoch Sheinman (ed), *Promises and Agreements: Philosophical Essays* (Oxford University Press, 2011) 58.

sufficiently private law from other areas of law; and, finally, can't explain why private law upholds rights even in the absence or risk of harm. These worries raise doubts in my mind about the plausibility of Gardner's claim that his account of the conservative impulse is a central theme in private law.

Yet, Gardner does show, I think, that the protection of security interests has at least some role in private law. The trouble is this function seems incidental at best, and the problem for Gardner's thesis, I believe, stems from how thin the version of conservatism that he is willing to endorse is.

Recall that Gardner, at the same time as endorsing this thin version of conservatism, was (rightly) keen to disassociate himself from 'social' conservatives, who seek to conserve the existing social order despite the injustices that it perpetuates. However, in his readiness to reject social conservatism, I wonder whether Gardner overlooked the potential relevance to private law of another brand of conservatism, which I will call 'relational' or 'virtue" conservatism.

Whereas Gardner's conservatism focuses on protecting the security interests of rights holders, for the relational conservative what matters is the preservation of a certain kind of relation between the duty bearer and the right holder. The duty bearer has to treat the right holder in a respectful way. The behaviour required depends on the norms in place in particular societies at particular times. What the relational conservative strives to protect are not security interests or existing social orders, but rather instantiations or frameworks of social virtue present in particular societies at particular times.

The relational conservative seeks to uphold forms of social virtue wrapped up or instantiated in our already existing traditions, customs, social and political institutions, laws, and so forth. On this view, the duty of citizens is to support these practices, and cultivate and exhibit the dispositions they require.[26] Ronald Dworkin said that in this sense what I call relational conservatives 'treat the lives of other members of their community as part of their own lives'.[27]

So, for example, in the UK, a conservative of this ilk would defend institutions, such as the free market or the NHS, not only because of their distributive benefits or welfare-maximizing effects, but also because of the social virtues that they exhibit, cultivate, and endorse: for example, in the case of the market encouraging talent and industry, or in the case of the NHS promoting distributive justice or the virtue of charity.[28]

[26] Ronald Dworkin, 'Liberalism' in Stuart Hampshire (ed), *Public and Private Morality* (Cambridge University Press, 1978) 113, 136–137.

[27] Ibid, 137. The most important contemporary proponent of this outlook is Roger Scruton. See his book *How to Be a Conservative* (n 17).

[28] Dworkin, 'Liberalism' (n 26) 137. John Gardner was only too aware of the role that our institutions play in shaping social virtue. See his *Law as a Leap of Faith* (Oxford University Press, 2014) 266, claiming that, as well as justice, the NHS displays 'the public good of spontaneous human compassion'.

The crucial point here is that social virtue depends on our *relations* with other members of the political community to which we belong. Our traditions, institutions, and so forth structure or constitute those relationships, in ways that reflect the values and principles wrapped up in the history and culture of a particular society at a particular time.

2. Tort Law

According to the relational conservative, private law—like other valuable social institutions—attempts to instantiate social virtue and nurture certain qualities or dispositions among citizens. Seana Shiffrin has recently argued that tort law plays this role.

Shiffrin argues that the morality of negligence typically involves an agent's culpable failure to take precautions to avoid harm to others.[29] Culpability turns on the reason that motivated the agent's failure to take reasonable care. Conduct is negligent when the agent unreasonably prioritises the pursuit of her own ends or overestimates her ability to achieve them at the expense of taking steps to avoid harm to others: 'The negligent agent implicitly or explicitly demotes the practical significance of her actions regarding matters that do not occupy her primary focus of concern.'[30]

In cases of negligence there is, Shiffrin argues, 'a procedural defect first and foremost in the deliberations that rise to action.'[31] This failure to show due regard to others is, for Shiffrin, a 'serious moral wrong', because it involves 'a sort of blindness to others.'[32]

I cannot defend Shiffrin's account of negligence fully here. Rather, I put it forward because on Shiffrin's view negligence is a vice and non-negligence 'a significant, but often overlooked, moral virtue'[33] which requires 'sustained and steady moral efforts.'[34] If Shiffrin is right about the morality of negligence, it seems plausible that private law may play a role in enforcing virtue. In contrast to Gardner's view, the focus is not merely on repairing harm, but rather on structuring and upholding respectful relations.

The thin conservativism that Gardner relies on to explain tort law can't do the work to explain the relational underpinning of tort law. The priority Gardner attaches to security interests to explain tort law combined with his more general

[29] Seana Shiffrin, 'The Moral Neglect of Negligence' in David Sobel, Peter Vallentyne, and Steven Wall (eds), *Oxford Studies in Political Philosophy: Volume 3* (Oxford University Press, 2017) 197, 203.
[30] Ibid, 204.
[31] Ibid, 213.
[32] Ibid.
[33] Ibid, 197.
[34] Ibid, 213.

commitment to the legitimacy of law residing in how it facilitates conformity with moral *reasons* that apply outside of law fails to account for tort law's focus on moral *obligations* in particular.

3. Contract Law

The importance of social virtue in private law is a key theme of Charles Fried's *Contract as Promise*.[35] For Fried, trust is the bedrock of promise and contract is founded on promise. He argues that trust exists when we believe that others will behave in a certain manner not for *prudential* reasons, but rather because that conduct is *the right thing to do*.

It is only when people act from that *moral* motive that we can truly rely on them, and engage, for example, in the sorts of valuable cooperative activities that lie at the heart of contract. That is because if we did not have trust and the device of promise, which 'gives trust its sharpest, most palpable form', then we would be left having to depend on prudence. But prudence cannot give us the assurance we need, because the other party's interests might change. On Monday you promise to help me move flat next Saturday. Saturday arrives, but on the way to my flat another friend calls you to say he has a spare ticket for the Cup Final. The scales have shifted. What was in your interests no longer is. If the voluminous literature on efficient breach has taught us anything, it has, at the very least, taught us that what is in the promisor's interests might change.

It is not enough, Fried argued, for us to make *predictions* about how others might behave on the basis of self-interest; rather, we need to *know* that they are committed to perform for moral reasons. Promise which invokes trust provides us with the assurance that we need. Trust is the surest foundation on which institutions such as promise and contract can be built. There are deeply connected instrumental and intrinsic values here that are being served. Let me explain this point further.

The exchange of goods and services using contract involves the making and keeping of reciprocal promises. Making a promise involves invoking trust or morality to achieve what are often, as Fried says, 'humdrum ends: We make appointments, buy and sell, harnessing this loftiest of all forces'.[36] By relying on trust we change the nature of these exchanges. They are no longer merely about getting this or that product or service from the other party, but rather about getting those things in a particular way, which involves morally infused cooperation. That is an end which, as Fried recognised, we pursue 'for its own sake; we prefer doing things cooperatively when we might have relied on fear or interest or worked alone'.[37]

35 *Contract as Promise: A Theory of Contractual Obligation* (Harvard University Press, 1981) 8, 13.
36 Ibid, 8.
37 Ibid, 8.

That is because as well as all the instrumental advantages involving reliance, coordination, and so forth, of invoking trust, when trust is our means we also promote social virtue.

Shiffrin's insight about negligence and Fried's about contract suggest that we should not let the remedial apparatus of private law (which looms so large in the minds of lawyers) obscure the reality that at heart these institutions facilitate the pursuit of our goals against a backdrop of legal constraints aimed at promoting social virtue.

My aim in discussing Shiffrin and Fried here is merely to show how private law might serve virtue. This does not of course by itself make either Shiffrin or Fried into conservatives. Rather, my point is that they offer interpretations of these legal fields which are compatible with a particular strain of conservative thought which I have labelled virtue conservatism, which reflects the desire of a political community to hold onto existing instantiations of social virtue.

I have left much out of the picture. Much more needs to be said, for example, about what respect for others requires in negligence and contract. In my view, the answer depends on local truths about value choices made in particular legal systems at particular times. We have to dig behind past political decisions (constitutions, statutes, case law, and so forth) made in these legal systems to work these out. This was, of course, the truth contained in Dworkin's argument that law is an interpretive practice.[38] This offers a way forward for understanding what constitutes morally wrongful conduct in these legal domains which is, as I have argued, notably absent in Gardner's account of private law.

4. The Given

If private law is connected to cultivating social virtue and law in general is, as Dworkin argued, an interpretive practice, then another important link between private law and the breed of moral and political philosophy we call conservatism comes to light. As well as the cultivation and preservation of social virtue, conservatism has always attached great value to *the given*. Edmund Burke argued that this distinctly conservative value is reflected in the reverence that a political community owes towards the civilisation that they have inherited. For Burke, society was 'a partnership not only between those who are living, but between those who are living, those who are dead, and those who are to be born'.[39] It is an entity that 'is never old, or middle-aged, or young, but in a condition of unchangeable constancy'.[40]

[38] *Law's Empire* (Hart, 1998).

[39] Edmund Burke, *Reflections on the Revolution in France* (Penguin, 1968) 194–195.

[40] Ibid, 120.

It is the 'first duty', Burke argues, of the living to guard the culture they inherit as though a 'treasure'—'not only from invasion, but from decay and corruption'.[41] That culture is made up of laws, constitutions, customs, social practices, and so forth that cradle particular conceptions of social virtue which the living have a duty to respect and preserve for the sake of future generations.[42]

Although looking after this inheritance is something that we have to work hard at (to prevent, as Burke says, its 'decay and corruption'), it is also something that we receive *as a given*. We are subject to its rules, constraints, and expectations, and they shape who we are, how we interact with others, and who we can become, whether we like it or not. In other words, that inheritance is bound up with our identity.[43] The dramatist Arthur Miller put the point best when he said:

> society is inside of man and man is inside society, and you cannot even create a truthfully drawn psychological entity on the stage until you understand his social relations and their power to make him what he is and to prevent him from being what he is not. The fish is in the water and the water is in the fish.[44]

Even in our personal lives, it is this value of the given which explains why we are attached to people and things, sometimes whether we like it or not. Cohen's eraser is bound up with his own personal history, even though he hardly intended this. My sisters are bound up with mine, even though I never chose that. Similarly, being born British, or Irish, or Iranian, or whatever, has—as we all know—huge practical significance for the people we are, even though we had no choice in the matter.

And just as the thin conservatism that Gardner endorses struggles to explain Cohen's attachment to his eraser (recall that if Cohen loses the eraser it would not upset any of his personal goals), it similarly faces an uphill task when it comes to

[41] Ibid, 144–145.

[42] Ibid, 117, 119–120. These duties to protect and promote inherited culture are grounded not only in its inherent value, but also as a way of honouring the sacrifices that past generations have made. On the idea that we may have respect-based reasons to redeem the sacrifices that previous generations have made toward the pursuit of a valuable goal or project more generally, see Thomas Kelly, 'Sunk Costs, Rationality, and Acting for the Sake of the Past' (2004) 38(1) Noûs 60, 76–78. David Portmore has suggested that redeeming such sacrifices may contribute to the welfare of those who suffered them by making their lives more meaningful. See Douglas W. Portmore, 'Welfare and Posthumous Harm' (unpublished) 1, 18 <http://www.public.asu.edu/~dportmor/Welfare_and_Posthumous_Harm.pdf> accessed 19 July 2021. Expressing doubts about Portmore's welfare-based argument, see Nicholas J. McBride, 'Legal Obligations to the Dead' (2020) 1, 10–17 <https://papers.ssrn.com/sol3/papers.cfm?abstract_id=3567197&download=yes> accessed 19 July 2021.

[43] Cf. Harry G. Frankfurt, *The Importance of What We Care About* (Cambridge University Press, 1988) 177–179, 186–190. There is an analogy here with language, which is a set of rules that enable us to express what is on our minds. However, as Fried argues (following Wittgenstein), such constraints also enable us to have thoughts in the first place: 'without types [of language], our minds would be blank.' Charles Fried, 'Contract as Promise: Lessons Learned' (2019) 20 Theoretical Inquiries in Law 367, 377.

[44] *The Collected Essays of Arthur Miller* (Bloomsbury, 2015) 151. See also Joseph Raz, *The Morality of Freedom* (Clarendon Press, 1988) 391: 'For those who live in an autonomy-supporting environment there is no choice but to be autonomous: there is no other way to prosper in such a society' (hereafter Raz, *Morality of Freedom*).

explaining the sense of loyalty and affection that many people feel towards the political communities to which they belong. These are sentiments that exist quite independently of any goals we have; indeed, they *precede* our goals, because they constitute *who we are.*

E. A ½ Myth

In the previous section, I defended a thicker version of conservatism—virtue conservatism—and the role it might play in justifying private law. It tells us more about private law than the thin version that Gardner endorses, and indeed it helps to overcome some important gaps in Gardner's account, such as the omission of the central role that moral wrongdoing plays in tort, or at least the lack of guidance Gardner provides on what constitutes moral wrongdoing for tort law, or why disruption to personal goals is not a requirement for certain torts or breach of contract claims.

Nevertheless, there is no getting around the fact that conservatism is a hard sell (especially in academic circles!). I suspect one of the main problems is that people too quickly associate conservatism of whatever stripe with the brand that Gardner called social conservatism, according to which there is value even in preserving injustice.[45] That is, as Gardner (rightly!) said, an obnoxious view to hold. Luckily, few conservatives actually hold it. Nevertheless, the myth sticks.

Why? The reason, I suspect, is that at least in the case of virtue conservatism, there is a half-truth buried in the myth that all conservatives are at heart social conservatives. This is because different political communities will protect and promote distinct virtues, which may be incompatible with the pursuit of others. As Joseph Raz argued, this is a feature of moral pluralism, which 'is the view that there are various forms and styles of life which exemplify different virtues and which are incompatible.'[46] Just as a single person cannot both be a nun and a mother,[47] a single society cannot be both liberty-supporting and radically egalitarian.[48] The result is that when a culture attaches priority to the pursuit of certain virtues or forms of life, it inevitably sacrifices other perfectly legitimate but incompatible ways of living.

These political choices infuse the social forms that exist in a society, which makes it harder or even impossible for individuals to pursue virtues that are not

[45] Making the point, see Cohen, 'Conservatism' (n 4) 225.

[46] Raz, *Morality of Freedom* (n 44) 395.

[47] Ibid.

[48] This is because, as Robert Nozick showed, 'liberty upsets patterns': *Anarchy, State, and Utopia* (Basil Blackwell 1974) 160–164. See also Isaiah Berlin, *The Proper Study of Mankind: An Anthology of Essays* (Vintage Classics, 2013) 197: 'To avoid glaring inequality or widespread misery I am ready to sacrifice some, or all, of my freedom: I may do so willingly and freely; but it is freedom that I am giving up for the sake of justice or equality or the love of my fellow men.' And see Charles Fried, *Modern Liberty* (WW Norton & Co, 2007) ch 2.

already embedded in existing social practices. So, for example, as Raz argued, if a society embraces an autonomy-supporting culture, this will 'affect the nature of the opportunities it provides'.[49] For instance, it will likely have a very different conception of work compared to one where children take up a trade carried on by their parents. In an autonomy-supporting culture, a premium will be attached to the freedom of the individual to move her labour freely. Attempts to unduly interfere with this freedom will be frowned upon.[50] This commitment to autonomy will affect 'Attitudes to work, expectations from it, and conceptions of its role in one's life generally'; in other words, it plays a constitutive role in determining the nature and purpose of work. This changes the options that are available to citizens in such a society.[51]

The result is that there will always be people in any society who feel estranged or constrained by prevailing social forms. They want to pursue potentially incompatible forms of life. They might feel that existing social attitudes and practices are unjust or oppressive and ripe for radical reform. That can lead to resentment, even when society embraces virtue rather than social conservativism. Such societies are not necessarily unjust, but they do preserve and promote certain social forms and virtues at the expense of others. That is, as I have argued, bound to be the case given the existence of moral pluralism. However, the regret which should be the natural response to this aspect of the human predicament all too often spills over into (unjustified) resentment about the social order. This is why there may be a grain of truth in the tendency to conflate virtue and social conservatism.

However, there may be a more problematic way in which virtue conservatism and social conservatism are related. It has been claimed that, in some cases, injustice is *required* for the pursuit of virtue. So, for example, Aristotle thought that a good education depended on citizens having leisure time, which in turn relied on labour being carried out by slaves.[52] It could be argued that while social conservatives in their commitment to uphold existing social orders are comfortable with preserving injustice *per se*, virtue conservatives are in the same ballpark, because they are willing to endorse injustice where it contributes to the pursuit of virtue.

Some virtue conservatives might hold such views. However, I doubt that injustice can ever legitimately be used for the pursuit of virtue. I cannot defend this view fully here, but there are two reasons why I reject this strand of virtue conservatism.

49 Raz, *Morality of Freedom* (n 44) 392.

50 Reflected, for example, in the common law's restraint of trade doctrine. See Prince Saprai, *Contract Law Without Foundations: Toward a Republican Theory of Contract Law* (Oxford University Press, 2019) ch 7.

51 Raz, *Morality of Freedom* (n 44) 393.

52 See C.D.C. Reeve, 'The Well-Educated Person' (2019) (*Aeon*, 23 September 2009) <https://aeon.co/essays/for-aristotle-education-is-what-equips-us-for-a-better-life> accessed 16 July 2021.

First, John Rawls was surely right that justice 'is the first virtue of social institutions'.[53] This explains why our intuitions rebel at the thought that slavery might be pursued even for the sake of virtue. It seems morally abhorrent. It is hard to see why any intelligent conservative would seriously entertain such a political outlook.

Secondly, even if there might be cases where injustice is justified for the sake of the pursuit of virtue, there is a deeper problem. It is the assumption that it is even *possible* to pursue virtue when it is built on injustice. In his recent book *The Humanity of Private Law*, Nicholas McBride raises a doubt about this assumption by relying on a short story, *The Ones Who Walk Away from Omelas*, by the science fiction writer Ursula K. Le Guin.[54] The story describes a community full of 'boundless and generous contentment', but where this happiness depends on one child living a life of squalor in a locked, windowless cellar. The child must suffer for the community to be happy. But McBride argues—quite rightly—that, despite appearances, the community cannot possibly be truly happy, given the misery that is being inflicted on the child. Omelas, McBride says, is 'located on accursed ground—a kind of Hell which dooms anyone who chooses to live there to endure a non-flourishing existence'.[55] The injustice taints the flourishing of the community, and this is why some people in the story choose to walk away.

For these two reasons, I doubt that a conception of virtue conservatism according to which the pursuit by a political community of at least some virtues depends on the commission of injustice is at all a defensible view to hold. However, I do accept that the pursuit of virtue may come at the expense of other virtues that might have been pursued—for example, liberty may come at the expense of achieving equality—and that this may be a legitimate source of regret for some in such a society. It is in this latter sense that there is a half-truth in the claim that virtue conservatism is linked to social conservatism.

F. Conclusion

In conclusion, Gardner made a major contribution to understanding the sense in which private law is a conservative institution. His claim that private law exists to protect the security interests in the lives we already have reveals something important about private law. My criticism has been though that it does not tell us enough. By prioritizing reasons for action, the crucial significance of moral wrongdoing to tort law seems to drop out of Gardner's account or at least he tells us too little about what constitutes moral wrongdoing for the purposes of tort. Nor is it

[53] *A Theory of Justice* (Rev. edn, Oxford University Press, 2019) 3.

[54] In Ursula K. Le Guin, *The Unreal & The Real: Selected Stories Volume 2 Outer Space, Inner Lands* (Orion, 2015) 1.

[55] Nicholas J. McBride, *The Humanity of Private Law: Part 1: Explanation* (Hart, 2018) 102.

clear how the thin conservatism that Gardner endorses differentiates private law from other areas of law, nor how it is meant to explain that private law upholds rights even in the absence of harm.

The remedy for these defects in Gardner's account lies in embracing a deeper form of conservatism, virtue conservatism, which not only places emphasis on the importance of protecting people's security but also has a relational dimension, which is focused on the value of preserving existing forms of civility, or ways of living together, that are embedded in the conventions, customs, laws, and so forth that constitute society. I have tried to illustrate, by relying on the work of Shiffrin and Fried, how the law of tort and contract might plausibly cultivate and promote social virtue in a political community. It is these valuable social forms, which we are given on trust from previous generations, that private law refuses to let go.

We get a better and more accurate picture of private law if we allow ourselves to twin Gardner's thin conservatism with the more relational conservatism that I have defended here. There may though have been a number of reasons why Gardner did not follow me along this path. Perhaps his positivism obscured his view of the particular way that valuable conceptions of social virtue are bound up with our legal practices? Or perhaps his liberalism meant that he could not accept a more deeply conservative outlook—which might take or leave the importance of personal freedom? Or perhaps he, like many others, conflated, for understandable reasons, social conservatism with virtue conservatism?

With regard to that last possibility, I have tried to show why it is important to prise these different versions of conservatism apart. As for the others, those are debates for another day.

14
Virtuously Discriminating: John Gardner's Contributions to Discrimination Theory

Sophia Moreau

A. Introduction

John Gardner always maintained that philosophers' analyses of discrimination should reflect the fact that people use the term 'discriminatory' approvingly as well as disapprovingly. Although we treat many instances of discrimination as wrongful, there are times when we regard it as a virtue for a person or their writing to be discriminating. Gardner's work on discrimination displays this virtue in abundance. Over the course of twenty years, he circled back to discrimination over and over again, from 'Liberals and Unlawful Discrimination', written in 1989,[1] to the Diversa Lectures he gave in San Paulo in 2016 on 'Discrimination, Disadvantage, Diversity',[2] and finally to his graduate seminar on discrimination, which he finished teaching just weeks before he died. His writings on discrimination eagerly challenge established intellectual orthodoxies, demonstrating both ingenuity in moral theorizing and a deep understanding of discrimination as a social problem. John Gardner came as close as anyone I know to being the kind of person that Henry James told us that we all ought to be—that is, 'someone on whom nothing is lost'.[3] And his writings on discrimination reflect this. They are packed full of surprising details and claims that are worth pondering and coming back to as sources of illumination, even outside of the context of the particular arguments in which they are made. So it is a great sadness to those of us who work in this field that John Gardner was not able to complete his planned book on discrimination before he died. However, even without that book he has left us a rich legacy in discrimination theory, one that opens up many possibilities both for future philosophical work on discrimination and for potential reforms of anti-discrimination laws.

One of the aims of this chapter is to lay out what I believe to be the most important of the many original contributions that John Gardner has made to

[1] John Gardner, 'Liberals and Unlawful Discrimination', Oxford Journal of Legal Studies 9 (1989), 1.

[2] Lecture 2 was subsequently published as 'Discrimination: The Good, the Bad, and the Wrongful', Proceedings of the Aristotelian Society 118 (2018), 55; the other lectures were not published.

[3] Henry James, 'The Art of Fiction', Longman's Magazine 4 (September 1884).

Sophia Moreau, *Virtuously Discriminating: John Gardner's Contributions to Discrimination Theory* In: *From Morality to Law and Back Again.* Edited by: Michelle Madden Dempsey and François Tanguay-Renaud, Oxford University Press.
 DOI: 10.1093/oso/9780198860594.003.0014

discrimination theory. In Section B I shall outline and explain the significance of the view of discrimination that he defended, particularly in his most recent work. It is a view that departs quite radically from a number of commonly held views about discrimination. For instance, it presents indirect discrimination as just another form of direct discrimination. Moreover, Gardner argues that discrimination is ultimately a *malum prohibitum*, something that is wrong because our governing bodies have decided to prohibit it, rather than a *malum in se*, wrong in itself. But he urges that the elimination of certain forms of discrimination is no less urgent or important just because such acts are wrong by virtue of having been prohibited. On the contrary, by seeing why certain forms of discrimination are not wrongful until legislatures prohibit them, we will develop a better understanding of how discrimination in certain social contexts begets cycles of permissible discrimination, leaving certain social groups severely disadvantaged across a number of different areas of social life. I shall explain why, in my view, Gardner's account displays considerable insight into how such cycles of discrimination perpetuate themselves. I shall also suggest that we need to follow his lead in thinking that the distinction between direct and indirect discrimination is not that significant from a moral standpoint.

I shall then turn in Section C to some criticisms of his account. Of course, no person and no theory can really be 'one on whom nothing is lost'. All have their blind spots. The question is which blind spots we are willing to live with and which seem to be too high a price to pay. I shall argue that even on Gardner's rich account, there are some important facts about discrimination that recede from view in ways that we have reason to regret. In particular, when we treat indirect discrimination as just another form of direct discrimination on the basis of a different trait—such as height, or strength—it becomes more difficult to see the ways in which these forms of discrimination contribute to discrimination on the basis of conventionally prohibited traits, such as sex. And this is a problem on Gardner's own terms, because it may prevent us from seeing the ways in which different forms of discrimination work together to disadvantage particular groups and sub-groups within society. So we should not, I argue, reduce indirect discrimination to direct discrimination. But we can decline Gardner's invitation to do this while still agreeing with him that direct and indirect discrimination are often morally problematic for the same sorts of reasons. I shall argue, further, that discrimination is ultimately problematic not just because it disadvantages people, but because it treats them as inferior to others. Many of the things we do disadvantage others, often in very significant ways. This is an inevitable result of living in a society with scarce resources and among other people with different aims and values. What seems to make the kinds of disadvantages that result from discriminatory acts especially problematic is the fact that they turn some people into the inferiors of others. This, I shall argue, is enough to make discriminatory policies and practices wrongful, regardless of whether any governing body has actually prohibited them. But we can only see this if we focus, not just on disadvantage, but also on subordination.

B. Gardner's Innovations

Gardner's work on discrimination aims quite deliberately to resurrect and modernize a view of discrimination that is no longer fashionable. Legal prohibitions on discrimination between private parties—for instance, between employers and employees, or shop-owners and clients, or clubs and their members—were originally treated as a form of quasi-criminal regulation, regulation of behaviour that was believed to be problematic primarily because of its agents' intentions or motives.[4] Discrimination was understood as morally troubling because of the *reasoning* of the discriminator. However, as discrimination laws have evolved in many countries, the reasons for which discriminators have acted have been treated as less important—relevant when assessing the extent of the insult to the discriminatee and the dignitary damages owed to her, but not determinative of whether the discriminatee has been wrongfully discriminated against in the first place. This is partly because most jurisdictions now recognize a form of discrimination called 'indirect discrimination'. In cases of indirect discrimination, a rule or practice constitutes a greater impediment to a certain group of people than it does to others because they possess a certain protected trait, but this group is not explicitly singled out as such by the rule or practice.[5] This form of discrimination is often taken to be wrongful simply because of its disadvantageous effects on the discriminated group, and not because of the discriminator's reasons for acting. But even in cases of direct discrimination, countries such as the UK no longer require proof of discriminatory intent. It can seem, therefore, as though the reasoning of the discriminator should be irrelevant in our assessment of their actions.

The starting point of Gardner's account of discrimination, however, is that even if we applaud recent developments in discrimination law, and even if we agree that an intent to discriminate or an intent to harm others is not necessary for wrongful discrimination, we need not assume that the discriminator's reasons for acting are morally irrelevant. On the contrary, the most natural account of what discrimination involves—the one that best accords with our ordinary use of the term 'discriminate'—appeals to the discriminator's reasons. According to what Gardner called the 'Discriminator's Reasons Analysis' ('DRA' for short):

[4] For more detailed discussion of the legal movement away from thinking of the discriminator's reasons and intentions as relevant to wrongful discrimination, see Denise Reaume, 'Harm and Fault in Discrimination Law: The Transition from Intentional to Adverse Effect Discrimination', Theoretical Inquiries in Law 2.1 (2002) 349; and Moreau, 'Equality and Discrimination', Chapter 9 of *The Cambridge Companion to the Philosophy of Law*, ed. John Tasioulas (Cambridge University Press, 2020) 171.

[5] See e.g. UK Equality Act 2010, s.19.

> To discriminate is to treat someone or something that (supposedly) has property *p* differently, doing so for the (supposed) reason that he or she or it (supposedly) has property *p*.[6]

Note that, on this definition, it is possible to discriminate either well or badly—so this understanding of discrimination has the advantage of preserving the neutral valence of the term 'discrimination', as it is ordinarily used. It also allows for what Gardner called 'Robinson Crusoe discrimination'. This is discrimination in which there is no actual comparator group that the agent treats better than he treats the victim of discrimination, but where it is nevertheless true that victim is treated worse than he would have been treated had he been a member of a different group (as would have happened had Robinson Crusoe maltreated Man Friday on that deserted island because of his race). But the real ingenuity of the account that Gardner builds using the DRA lies, in my view, in three places: first, the way in which he argues that indirect discrimination, too, can be captured by the DRA, and so is not a form of discrimination that is unconcerned with the discriminator's reasons; second, his explanation of what makes both direct and indirect discrimination *bad*; and third, his explanation of what makes them *wrongful*. Let us look at each of these in turn.

First, consider Gardner's contention that indirect discrimination is fully captured by the DRA. Gardner asserts that in cases of indirect discrimination, it is still true that the discriminator looks for a certain property and treats some people differently if and when he does not find that property in them. So, for instance, when a luxury car company requires employees to meet a certain height requirement, it treats some people differently from others on the basis of their height. If far fewer women meet this requirement than men, then this, Gardner says, is just height discrimination that indirectly affects women. Likewise, when a department store requires all employees to work evening shifts once a week and this is more difficult for women because they provide most of the childcare for their families in the evenings, we have a straightforward case of discrimination on the basis of 'not being available in the evening'. In both cases, what we think of as indirect sex discrimination is just 'ordinary ('direct') discrimination against people with some *other* property (people of less height, or with less availability for evening work)'.[7] So although we might not have realized it, anti-discrimination laws regulate 'in a derivative and circumscribed way, height discrimination, strength discrimination, and so on'.[8] I am going to postpone for the moment my criticisms of this view, because I want in this section of the chapter to dwell on the progress made by Gardner's analyses.

[6] Gardner, 'Discrimination: The Good, the Bad and the Wrongful', note 2 at 56.
[7] Gardner, 'The Good, the Bad and the Wrongful', note 2 at 60.
[8] *Ibid*, 60.

This is an ingenious way of trying to capture, in one coherent account, both direct and indirect discrimination. Moreover, Gardner's analysis has the important implication that we waste our time when we try to figure out whether a discriminatory act is best characterized as direct or indirect discrimination. Instead of worrying about which box to fit it into, we should be thinking about the reasons on the basis of which the discriminator acted, whether they are *good* reasons or not, and whether acting in this way contributes to patterns of disadvantage in society at large. Of course, the reason why litigators worry about how to characterize a given case of discrimination is that, in certain jurisdictions, all cases of direct discrimination that occur on the basis of protected traits are treated as unjustifiable, whereas cases of indirect discrimination can sometimes be justified—for instance, based on factors like the legitimacy of their purpose and how closely tailored they are to achieving that purpose. If Gardner is right, however, the idea that direct and indirect discrimination differ in terms of their justifiability is mistaken. In order to know whether a given act of discrimination is justifiable, we need to look in all cases at the *reasons* on the basis of which the discriminator acted. These will, on Gardner's view (for reasons that I will explain shortly), tell us whether the discrimination is rudimentarily bad or not. And we need to look to other considerations, such as the social disadvantage caused by such acts of discrimination, to determine whether even perfectly justifiable acts of discrimination ought nevertheless to be legally prohibited. So, both in cases of direct discrimination and in cases of indirect discrimination, what matter from a moral and a political standpoint are the reasons for which the discriminator has acted and the social disadvantages that he or she has exacerbated, not whether the discrimination is direct or indirect.

What about Gardner's account of the badness of discrimination? Before we examine this account, it is worth pausing to note how original it is of Gardner to start by asking about the badness of discrimination, rather than leaping straight into an analysis of its wrongfulness. Many scholars working today on discrimination theory start from the question of what makes discrimination wrongful, not from the question of what makes it morally bad. For example, Deborah Hellman has argued that discrimination is morally wrongful either because it demeans or because it compounds historical injustices.[9] In my own account of discrimination, I too have focused on the properties of discriminatory practices that make them wrongful.[10] Like Hellman, I have avoided the use of the term 'morally bad'—partly because I am not sure what it adds to the claim that a particular act is morally wrong, and partly because I worry that we will confuse judgements about the moral badness of actions with judgements about whether an act is *bad for* someone, in the sense of lowering their well-being. Wrongfully discriminatory acts are often

[9] Deborah Hellman, *When Is Discrimination Wrong?* (Harvard University Press, 2010).
[10] Moreau, *Faces of Inequality* (Oxford University Press, 2020).

bad for their victims, but not always so. Sometimes these acts benefit their victims, even though they are morally wrong.

But Gardner's account starts with the bad, rather than with the wrongful. He uses the DRA to give a distinctive meaning to moral badness in the context of discrimination. Discrimination is 'rudimentarily bad', he notes, if the property, *p*, that the discriminator takes as a reason for treating a person or group differently from others 'is actually no reason at all'.[11] This would be true, for instance, of an employer who declines to hire a young woman simply because she is a woman, assuming that all such women are likely to quit work in order to have children and that it is therefore not worth investing time and training in them.

As I understand Gardner's account, the badness of this sort of discrimination is morally primary, relative to the wrongness of discrimination, in at least two senses. First, it is the only thing that is *intrinsically morally problematic* about discrimination. As we will go on to see, discrimination is wrongful on Gardner's account only if a legislature deems it so, as a way of addressing the pressing social problem that arises when too many of us start discriminating against others on the basis of properties such as race, sex, and so on. But discriminatory acts can be bad simply because the agent acts on what is not a valid reason. Second, the badness of discrimination is morally primary for Gardner in the sense that it is *the beginning of the broad and enduring cycles of discrimination* that we see in our societies today, according to which discrimination begets more discrimination. Gardner—both in his later paper and in earlier pieces—offers deeply insightful analyses of how, once enough people engage in discrimination on a ground such as sex, other people end up with quite valid reasons for excluding members of this group on this ground, and the cycle is perpetuated until the legislature intervenes by prohibiting this form of discrimination, thereby finally giving people reasons to stop this sort of discrimination.[12] For instance, if enough employers in a particular profession engage in rudimentarily bad discrimination (say, by denying young women a fair chance at a first job on the grounds that they will likely quit their job to have children), it will then become true that young women will, as a group, have less experience and less training in this profession than their male counterparts. This lack of training and experience will then furnish a *valid* reason for employers not to hire young women in the first place. So cases of rudimentarily bad discrimination beget cases of valid discrimination. One of Gardner's most lasting contributions, in my view, will be

[11] Gardner, 'Discrimination: The Good, the Bad and the Wrongful', note 2 at 64.

[12] The argument is only made explicit in Gardner, 'Discrimination: The Good, the Bad and the Wrongful', note 2 at 70–71, but the building blocks for it are present in the discussions of disadvantage and systemic discrimination in the following earlier pieces: Gardner, 'On the Ground of Her Sex(uality)', Oxford Journal of Legal Studies, 18.1 (1998) 167–187; Gardner, 'Private Activities and Personal Autonomy: At the Margins of Anti-Discrimination Law', in B. Hepple and E. Szyszczak (eds), *Discrimination: The Limits of Law?* (London: Mansell 1992); 'Liberals and Unlawful Discrimination', Oxford Journal of Legal Studies 9 (1989), 1; 'Discrimination as Injustice', Oxford Journal of Legal Studies 16 (1996), 353.

this nuanced analysis of cycles of discrimination, which carry us from a state of affairs in which we have no reasons for acting in these ways to a society in which many people have many valid reasons for discriminating—reasons that depend in deeply unsettling ways on other people's discriminatory behaviour.

It is these cycles of discrimination—or of what Gardner calls 'discrimination-led disadvantage'—that, in his view, give rise to the need to regulate discrimination, prohibiting certain forms of it by law and attaching sanctions to them.[13] For anti-discrimination laws, Gardner argues, aim to give us the reasons we would otherwise have lacked for not discriminating against people on the basis of certain properties. This is why discrimination is, on Gardner's view, a *malum prohibitum* rather than a *malum in se*.[14] When it is wrong, it is wrong only because certain law-givers have decided to prohibit it. This does not, of course, mean that legislatures' decisions about which forms of discrimination to prohibit are arbitrary. On the contrary, they are motivated by the need to break these cycles of discrimination-led disadvantage. So anti-discrimination laws are, on Gardner's view, a response to a real social and moral problem. But most scholars have misunderstood what this problem is. The problem is not that many people are acting wrongly and we need laws in order to prevent their wrongful behaviour. The problem is that many people are acting in ways that, when compounded, severely *disadvantage* certain social groups relative to others, leaving them without access to opportunities that other social groups have. When a legislature or a constitution prohibits discrimination of a certain sort, it is a response to this cycle of disadvantage. But discriminatory acts themselves are not wrongful until and unless they are so prohibited.

I think a helpful analogy can be drawn here between Gardner's view of the function of anti-discrimination law, on the one hand, and the view of tort law defended by certain law and economics scholars such as Richard Posner, on the other hand. Posner maintains that tort law operates under a kind of necessary illusion.[15] It is structured to give the impression that it aims to compensate the plaintiff for a wrong done to her by the defendant. But this, he says, is merely the 'necessary inducement' for the plaintiff to play his regulatory role of identifying inefficient behaviour or pressing for changes in the law that will bring about more efficient behaviour. Tort law does not in fact track any wrong that is actually done to the plaintiff: it is just a regulatory system designed to incentivize efficient social behaviour. But it works best to accomplish this goal if it is structured in such a way as to give the impression that the plaintiff has been wronged. Similarly, on Gardner's view, anti-discrimination laws do not track a wrong that is done to victims of discrimination. Like tort law on Posner's view, anti-discrimination laws are a form of social regulation. They aim to eliminate the patterns of disadvantage that result from

[13] Gardner, 'Discrimination: The Good, the Bad and the Wrongful', note 2 at 75.
[14] *Ibid*, 74–75.
[15] Richard Posner, 'A Theory of Negligence' (1972) 1 Journal of Legal Studies 29 at 29–34.

these self-perpetuating cycles of 'discrimination-led disadvantage'. But these laws work most effectively if the population *believes* that a wrong has been done and that discrimination is a *malum in se*: they will then be motivated to bring their complaints before human rights tribunals and work to change their own and others' behaviour.

C. Potential Problems for this Account

Gardner's account of discrimination departs from both our intuitive understanding of discrimination and from scholarly trends in a number of ways, and so therefore raises many questions. I shall focus mainly on the two sets of issues that I think are most important. But before I turn to these, I want briefly to raise some of the other questions that are worth exploring –in particular, questions about how, on this account, we are to understand the duties of legislators and the principles that ought to guide them.

1. Duties of Legislators

Gardner notes that in some cases, Parliament may have 'a duty to assign these [anti-discrimination] duties exactly as they were in fact assigned' and that when this is true, it brings the wrong of discrimination 'very close to being *mala in se*'.[16] This can sound rather as though the account is trying to have its cake and eat it too. One might object that, if legislatures are under a duty of justice to enact anti-discrimination laws, then perhaps it is true that the wrong here is close to a *malum in se*—but that will only be because the reason why the legislature stands under such a duty of justice is that these forms of discrimination fail to treat people as equals and are *wrong* for this very reason. So it looks as though, on this reading, discrimination is not, in fact, a *malum prohibitum*. On the other hand, perhaps the suggestion is rather that legislatures sometimes have not a moral duty, but a duty given by positive law (perhaps constitutional law), to protect a certain group from discrimination. One example of such a duty was at issue in the Canadian case of *Vriend*.[17] Here, the Canadian Supreme Court held that, once a particular provincial government had chosen to protect certain social groups under its anti-discrimination laws, it could not then deny protection to people on the basis of their sexual orientation without violating Canada's constitutional equality rights. In this case, the duty of the legislature to protect certain groups from discrimination was not treated as a moral duty or a duty of justice—it was treated as a duty

[16] Gardner, 'Discrimination: The Good, the Bad and the Wrongful', note 2 at 75.
[17] *Vriend v Alberta* [1998] 1 S.C.R. 493.

generated by the Constitution, which was engaged only because the government chose to become involved in protecting groups from discrimination law in the first place. It is clear that the legislature might, in such a case, stand under a duty to enact certain anti-discrimination laws. But on this scenario it is unclear how the mere fact that the legislature stands under a duty would affect the nature of the wrong done by discrimination, turning it into a *malum in se*. As a wrong, it is surely still a *malum prohibitum*—because it is only wrong once the legislature chooses to become involved in prohibiting discrimination and once there is a Constitution requiring it to do this equally for all such groups.

It is also true that Gardner's account sits uncomfortably with many legislators' understanding of their task. Many understand themselves not as trying to decide which forms of discrimination should be *turned into* wrongs, but as trying to figure out which forms of discrimination *really are* wrong and ought to be eliminated. Of course, Gardner would say that such legislators are under the same kind of necessary illusion as the populus is, so this objection is hardly decisive. But I wonder what he would say to legislators who demand: 'You have told us that none of these acts are wrong, prior to our deciding that they are. So how, exactly, should we decide which forms of discrimination to prohibit? How should we decide which disadvantaging properties are to be given protection by anti-discrimination laws? Should we protect people from cycles of disadvantage based on gender? Or from cycles of disadvantage based on prior criminal conviction? What about the cycles of disadvantage that white supremacists believe they are facing? Do they have an equal claim to be protected from these?'

Gardner notes that questions about which particular groups legislators ought to protect through anti-discrimination laws are 'questions of policy' whose answer is 'whatever works best'. But this sounds rather like Lord Denning when he admits that he has no principled way of deciding a particular legal question.[18] And in response, our legislators would likely ask: 'Whatever works best *at doing what*?' Many social practices give rise to cycles of disadvantage. Gardner's account has nothing to say about which are the relevant cycles for the purposes of anti-discrimination laws. Are they only the most severe or the most pervasive? Looking at actual discrimination laws, one would have to say no. Very few jurisdictions have prohibited discrimination on the grounds of poverty, even though the social groups that are further disadvantaged on the basis of their poverty are undoubtedly among the worst off across many social contexts. Is the answer, perhaps, any cycle of disadvantage? Again, I think not. White supremacists, we feel, have no claim to protection from anti-discrimination laws for those disadvantages that accrue to them because of their racist beliefs. When asked why this is, most of us would reply: because they have not been *wronged* by being disadvantaged on the basis of their racist beliefs.

[18] See, e.g., *Lamb v London Borough of Camden* [1981] QB 625 (CA).

But this is not a line of argument that Gardner can accept, because on his account the wrongfulness of a particular kind of discrimination is a function of its having been prohibited, not a factor that legislators can consult in assessing whether it should be prohibited.

2. Not Disadvantage, but Status

I think that this problem brings us to a more significant problem with Gardner's account. This is that, although understanding how cycles of disadvantage are perpetuated is a tremendously important step in grappling with how wrongful discrimination is sustained, the bare concept of disadvantage simply cannot do all of the work for us. It cannot do the explanatory work of making sense of our actual anti-discrimination laws—for these laws do not in fact protect against all, or even all of the most severe, cycles of disadvantage that result from excluding people on the basis of certain personal traits. And the concept of disadvantage also cannot do the normative work that needs to be done here, helping legislatures to pick out which forms of discrimination should be prohibited.[19] In order to answer our hypothetical legislators' questions, we need to hone in on a particular *kind* of disadvantage. And in my view, once we do, we will see that whatever criterion we use to determine the relevant kind of disadvantage, this criterion will on its own be sufficient to render discrimination a *malum in se.* So we do not need an account of discrimination that derives its wrongfulness, in a roundabout way, from the fact that it has been prohibited.

What kind of disadvantage is it that we need to focus on here? Anti-discrimination laws are, in my view, fundamentally concerned with eliminating disadvantages that leave some people with a *lower social status* than others. Some discriminatory acts and rules treat certain social groups as thought they were the social inferiors of others. This is what outrages us about the treatment of Blacks by non-Blacks in many societies; and it is, similarly, what underlies the calls of women for equal standing in public life and in employment, and what moves marginalized, subordinated groups such as the LGBTQ community and persons with disabilities to call for an end to the discrimination that they face. In order to understand why these groups need protection from anti-discrimination laws, we need the concept

[19] Gardner seems at one point to acknowledge this. He notes in passing that his account is not 'wedded to any sectarian account of what counts as a relevant disadvantage' and he suggests that this is a 'boon', presumably because it means that his account is compatible with many different views of discrimination ('Discrimination: The Good, the Bad and the Wrongful', note 2 at 79). But I worry that, once we pair Gardner's account with a separate account of the relevant disadvantages, then (i) most of the normative work in the account will be done by this separate account, so it matters very much what this other account states, and (ii) a natural way to spell out what the relevant disadvantages are is to look to what makes discrimination wrongful, and of course if we proceed in this way then our account will not imply that discrimination is, as Gardner claims, a *malum prohibitum.*

of someone being not just disadvantaged, but treated as though they were inferior to another person or group of people. I have argued elsewhere that we can flesh out this idea of being treated as someone else's inferior in a number of different ways.[20] One way in which a policy can treat someone as inferior to others is by denying them and other members of their social group the power, authority, or deference that is given to other social groups (defined by other traits), or by rendering people like them invisible in certain areas of society, through structural accommodations to the needs of groups with a superior social standing. Another way that a policy can treat some as inferior to others is by denying them deliberative freedoms that others commonly have, and to which they have a right—thereby implying that obstacles to these people's attempts to exercise their autonomy matter less than do obstacles faced by others. And sometimes, discriminatory practices deny people goods that they need to have if they are to function in their society as equals, such as access to the institution of marriage.

For the purposes of our discussion here, it does not matter whether you agree with my understanding of what it is to treat someone as the inferior of another person or whether you would substitute a different conception. The important point is that we need *some* such conception, some idea of what it is to treat people as inferior to others, if are to make sense of when and why discrimination is wrong. And once we have such a conception, we will have a ready answer to the legislator who asks the question I posed above: 'How should I decide which forms of discrimination to prohibit?' The answer is not 'Those that disadvantage people' but rather 'Those that treat some people as the inferiors of others'.

Note that this answer is quite consistent with the recognition that what constitutes wrongful discrimination in a given time and place can change over time. Gardner always insisted that we need an account of discrimination that recognizes that 'changes in social form alter the structure of the possibilities for, and obstacles in the way of our thriving'.[21] But an account of discrimination as a *malum in se* need not overlook this truth. It need not assume that the history of anti-discrimination laws is a history of our coming to realize certain eternal truths. On the contrary, which types of discrimination treat people as the inferiors of others in a given society depends very much on the institutions in that society, on common forms of behaviour, and on shared understandings and misunderstandings, all of which change over time. So there is ample room, on such an account, for recognition that what constitutes wrongful discrimination and what constitutes a properly attentive body of anti-discrimination laws will change over time.

[20] Moreau, *Faces of Inequality*, note 10.

[21] John Gardner, 'On the Ground of her Sex(uality)', note 11 at 177.

3. Conceptualizing Indirect Discrimination

I want now to turn to a separate objection to Gardner's account of discrimination, concerning his treatment of indirect discrimination. I suggested earlier that one of Gardner's insights into discrimination is that we need not assume that direct and indirect discrimination are so very different, from a moral standpoint. Perhaps, when they are wrong, they are wrong for the same kind of reason. I think this is exactly right—and I think that an account of discrimination that appeals to the idea that wrongful discrimination turns some people into the inferiors of others can accommodate this intuition nicely, because both direct and indirect discrimination can, and often do, leave some people as the social inferiors of others. But I think there is a problem with Gardner's own explanation of why direct and indirect discrimination are not importantly different. And it is a problem on his theory's own terms, because his way of conceptualizing indirect discrimination seems to make it *more* difficult to recognize the kinds of cycles of discrimination that he thinks it is discrimination law's job to identify and halt.

Recall that on Gardner's view, indirect discrimination is just direct discrimination on the basis of another property. I mentioned two examples earlier. First, the luxury car dealer that requires employees to meet a certain height requirement, and so treats some people differently from others on the basis of their height. If far fewer women meet this requirement than men, this is, according to Gardner's DRA, an instance of direct discrimination on the basis of height. Likewise, if a department store requires all employees to work evening shifts once a week and this is more difficult for women because they provide most of the childcare for their families in the evenings, Gardner would say that this is a straightforward case of discrimination on the basis of 'not being available in the evening'.

One difficulty with this re-interpretation of indirect discrimination is that it is not clear that it can capture all cases of indirect discrimination. Some practices that are indirectly discriminatory don't explicitly employ any criteria at all in order to distinguish between different groups. They simply lavish resources on particular causes that happen to satisfy the needs of some groups, while leaving another group invisible, without its needs being met. For example, when a federal government fails to fund water purification on Indigenous reserves, while watching the local governments of cities and towns fund excellent water treatment systems for the predominantly non-Indigenous inhabitants of these areas, the federal government is not itself drawing any distinction between any groups, on the basis of any properties at all. We cannot redescribe this as direct discrimination on the basis of some other ground: it is simply an omission. But this omission has the effect of leaving Indigenous communities without a good that they need if they are to function in society as equals, in circumstances where all other social groups have access to that good. Many of us would see this as a form of indirect discrimination. However, it cannot helpfully be re-described as just another kind of direct discrimination, on the basis of some property other than 'being Indigenous'. One worry, then, is that if we assume that all forms of indirect discrimination can be re-described as direct discrimination under the DRA, we may be left unable to see certain genuinely troubling cases of discrimination for what they really are.

Another difficulty with this way of conceptualizing indirect discrimination is that even in the case of those indirectly discriminatory practices that *can* be re-described as acts of drawing a distinction on the basis of some other property, it is unclear that we will be able to pick out the particular social group that is in fact problematically disadvantaged, or to explain *why* there is a troubling disadvantage, if we see the discrimination as connected only to the property on the basis of which people are directly discriminated against. It is, of course, not generally problematic to distinguish between people based on their height or their availability for evening work. What makes it morally problematic to do this in the case of female employees is precisely that it perpetuates *women's* inferior status in the workplace and piles disadvantages upon women, who are already disadvantaged both at work and at home. In the case of the luxury car dealer, we might add that women are already underrepresented in this sort of employment: they are deemed less suitable for employment as car salespeople for reasons that have nothing to do with their abilities and everything to do with stereotyped views about women (for instance, that they are less good at taking risks, less strong, and less authoritative, and consequently both less good at selling cars and less good at personifying the cars they are trying to sell, which are supposed to be powerful and liberating). In the case of women who have too many childcare obligations to be able to work in the evenings, we need to note that women are disproportionately saddled with childcare obligations relative to their male counterparts, for many different reasons, and that when they choose not to work in the evenings this is a choice that is constrained by social and familial pressures that many men simply do not face. In both examples, these truths will be obscured if we treat the discrimination simply as discrimination 'on the basis of height' or discrimination 'on the basis of lack of evening availability'. We need to see the impact that such policies have on women because of their sex, and because of the pre-existing disadvantages that they face because of their sex, in order to understand how they contribute to the kinds of cycles of discrimination and disadvantage that Gardner has in mind. So even on Gardner's own terms, cases of indirect discrimination will need a kind of special treatment, beyond the treatment that we give to ordinary cases of direct discrimination. In ordinary cases of direct discrimination, the ground (or the intersecting grounds) on which the discrimination is directly based can tell us most of what we need to know concerning whom discrimination of this type harms, and why. But in cases of indirect discrimination that have been re-described as direct discrimination, on Gardner's view, we will have to appeal to other grounds—the ones that are commonly listed as prohibited grounds of discrimination—in order to understand why these policies cause disadvantage, and to whom. And this seems to me to amount, in effect, to an admission that indirect discrimination is *not* just direct discrimination on the basis of another property. It works in a different way to disadvantage and subordinate those who possess, or are believed to possess, particular traits.

The concern I have been expressing here about Gardner's re-conceptualization of indirect discrimination is not purely an academic one. That is, the people who risk failing to see genuine cases of discrimination for what they really are, when they adopt this view, are not only scholars. A naïve version of this view has been, and is still, endorsed by certain judges, and it is almost always used to deny remedies to claimants on the grounds that a particular case of indirect discrimination actually involves no discrimination at all on the basis of a prohibited ground and is instead really just discrimination on the basis of some innocuous ground. The recent Canadian case of *Fraser v Canada* illustrates this.[22] The three claimants in this case were female police officers, all of whom had opted to work part-time as part of the RCMP's job-sharing programme because they had significant caregiving duties that took up much of their time. The RCMP permitted full-time officers who took unpaid leave to 'buy back' pension credits. But it did not permit part-time officers in the job-sharing programme to buy back these pension credits. The claimants challenged this policy as discrimination under s. 15 of Canada's *Charter of Rights and Freedoms*. The Majority of the Court ruled that the policy amounted to unjustifiable indirect sex discrimination, since the overwhelming majority of officers in the job-sharing programme were women who had chosen to enter the programme because they were already overburdened with childcare responsibilities, and the refusal to let them buy back their pension credits heaped an additional disadvantage on a group that was already significantly disadvantaged because of their sex. But Justice Coté held, in dissent, that this rule did not amount to indirect sex discrimination at all. In her view, it was simply an innocuous form of direct discrimination on the basis of another property: 'having caregiving responsibilities'. 'The distinction exists', she wrote, 'not because one is a *woman*, but because one has *caregiving* responsibilities'.[23] She noted that there is no prohibition in the Constitution on discriminating on the basis of caregiving responsibilities, and she would have dismissed the appeal.

Although Gardner himself did not intend judges to reason in this way about indirect discrimination, this is precisely the kind of reasoning that his account inadvertently invites on the part of the judiciary. If courts treat indirect discrimination as direct discrimination on the basis of a different ground, they may become overly focused on that other ground and may think that the discrimination does not, in fact, amount to discrimination on the basis of a prohibited ground and is therefore perfectly permissible. So the account risks blinding courts to the often hidden connections between any given case of indirect discrimination and the properties that

22 *Fraser v Canada*, 2020 SCC 28.
23 *Fraser v Canada*, note 22 at para 234.

are recognized as prohibited grounds of discrimination, such as sex. And in the process, it risks blinding courts to the complex processes that work to subordinate various social groups.

For these reasons, I think it is most helpful to retain the distinction between direct and indirect discrimination and to treat indirect discrimination as an indirect way of disadvantaging people on the basis of the same prohibited grounds that we recognize in cases of direct discrimination. But we can do this while recognizing, as Gardner emphasizes, that direct and indirect discrimination contribute to the same social problem, and that when they are wrong, they are wrong for the same reasons.

D. Conclusion

I have argued that we can learn from Gardner about how cycles of discrimination perpetuate themselves and that we ought to follow his lead in thinking that the distinction between direct and indirect discrimination is not that significant from a moral standpoint. I have also suggested, however, that it is a mistake to think that discrimination is a *malum prohibitum*, and that in order to see why it is genuinely a *malum in se* we need to move beyond the concept of mere disadvantage and focus on the particular way of disadvantaging people that makes discrimination wrongful. In my view, this involves treating some people as the inferiors of others.

I said at the beginning of this chapter that John Gardner was close to being 'someone on whom nothing is lost'. Henry James gave a more detailed description of the gifts possessed by such a person, and I want to close by mentioning these gifts. For now that I have given you a taste of Gardner's writings on discrimination, I think you will be in an even better position to appreciate the extent to which his writings on discrimination display these gifts. They involve, James said, 'the power to guess the unseen from the seen, to trace the implication of things, to judge the whole piece by the pattern'.[24] We are fortunate to have his work to inspire us as we continue—both in our roles as scholars and in our roles as citizens of countries with unfortunate legacies of discrimination—to work our way through the difficult and urgent problems that discrimination poses.

[24] James, note 3.

15
Indigenous Rights and Decolonized Legal Positivism

Dwight Newman KC[*]

A. Introduction

While some do not see issues of legal philosophy as matters in the headlines, a set of contemporary developments on Indigenous rights have involved significant confrontations on issues of legal philosophy. Indigenous rights theorists have shown a tendency to attack theories of legal positivism, suggesting that these theories have constrained Indigenous rights. The key aims of this chapter are twofold. First, the chapter raises issues with some of the Indigenous attacks on legal positivism. These attacks are understandable in light of the colonial history and legal positivism of a past era, and the chapter thus recognizes some of the colonizing history of legal philosophy. However, these attacks are misplaced in the context of more contemporary theories of legal positivism, which have adapted and/or are further adaptable in ways that remove some of the sting of historical versions of legal positivism. Moreover, suggesting that it is necessary to abandon theories of legal positivism in order to find a place for Indigenous rights risks making Indigenous rights less attainable than need be. Second, the chapter tries to search for a more constructive interaction of Indigenous rights and legal positivism, in which legal positivism can be adjusted so as to have a place for Indigenous rights and in which discussion of Indigenous rights may help to enrich legal positivism itself. In light of the clarity that he brings to legal positivism, and the ways in which he has so effectively cleared away myths that can be attached to it, those latter phases of the chapter draw significantly on the work of John Gardner.

[*] Due to schedule conflicts, it was not possible to present this chapter at the workshop at which most chapters in this collection were presented. I presented a version of it at a Juris North meeting at Liverpool University and am grateful to Jorge Emilio Núñez for his organization of that; I appreciated comments and queries from participants including Patrick Butchard, Michelle Farrell, Michael Gordon, Padraig McAuliffe, and Veronica Rodriguez-Blanco. I also presented a later version at the 2021 Law and Society Association Annual Meeting and I thank Paul Schiff Berman for organizing the panel and offering his comments and Kirsty Gover for acting as discussant and offering her extensive oral and written comments. I appreciate the work of Michelle Dempsey and François Tanguay-Renaud on this volume. They also arranged for Michael Giudice to offer comments on the penultimate version of the chapter, and I am grateful to him for those comments. I have endeavoured to learn from all of these comments but of course remain responsible for remaining shortcomings.

Dwight Newman KC, *Indigenous Rights and Decolonized Legal Positivism* In: *From Morality to Law and Back Again*.
Edited by: Michelle Madden Dempsey and François Tanguay-Renaud, Oxford University Press.
DOI: 10.1093/oso/9780198860594.003.0015

By way of background, there has been to at least some degree a worldwide embrace of Indigenous rights norms in recent decades. Most notably, the adoption by the United Nations General Assembly of the United Nations Declaration on the Rights of Indigenous Peoples (UNDRIP) in 2007 marked a sort of turning point.[1] If still an instrument of complex and limited legal weight in formal terms,[2] the UNDRIP's adoption nonetheless marked a recognition of the normative significance of Indigenous rights. The UNDRIP emerged from a multi-decade process involving Indigenous peoples themselves alongside state negotiators, with the fact that those affected by the instrument were involved in its development endowing it with significant legitimacy. Live, ongoing discussions on 'implementation' of the UNDRIP show attention to the instrument that goes beyond a formalistic approach to its legal status and instead recognize this legitimacy dimension of the instrument. Those discussions also manifest, though, the reality that the meaningful recognition of Indigenous rights will not be solely in one universal instrument, but perhaps more in the context of domestic legal systems yielding to a recognition of Indigenous peoples within the state.

While some who have not thought as much about Indigenous claims might first think of Indigenous rights in terms of rights to carry on certain ceremonies or to carry on traditional harvesting practices, a full recognition of Indigenous rights obviously goes beyond simple liberties. Some Indigenous rights involve at least substantial claim rights, such as in the context of rights to the Indigenous ownership of certain lands and to non-interference by others with those Indigenous lands. But Indigenous rights go farther yet. Indeed, a contemporary approach to understanding Indigenous rights would be inclined to think of them less as simple rights claimed against the state than as grounded in underlying power or jurisdiction shaped by Indigenous legal systems.[3] This conception is closely connected to a view that Indigenous rights are inherent in Indigenous peoples themselves, as opposed to being granted by the contemporary state or flowing from state law. This chapter is thus concerned not simply with Indigenous rights but with the space for Indigenous legal norms within states that have implemented systems of state law that have historically not appeared to leave room for legal norms emanating from the prior-existing political societies of Indigenous peoples.

This chapter builds upon a conceptualization of Indigenous legal norms having status within states through incipient forms of legal pluralism. It conceives of those as 'incipient' for three distinct reasons. First, the actual recognition of Indigenous

[1] Declaration on the Rights of Indigenous Peoples UN Doc A/RES/61/295 (2007). For discussion of the instrument, see Mauro Barelli, *Seeking Justice in International Law: The Significance and Implications of the UN Declaration on the Rights of Indigenous Peoples* (London: Routledge 2016).

[2] See the various discussions in Stephen Allen & Alexandra Xanthaki (eds), *Reflections on the UN Declaration on the Rights of Indigenous Peoples* (Oxford: Hart Publishing 2011).

[3] See e.g. Maggie Blackhawk, 'Federal Indian Law as Paradigm within Public Law' (2019) 132 Harvard L Rev 1787. See also the group of papers on self-determination in Dwight Newman (ed), *Research Handbook on Indigenous Rights in International Law* (London: Edward Elgar 2022).

legal norms within states in which there have been claims about legal pluralism has sometimes been more limited than claimed.[4] In Canada, for example, while some have attempted to make more of them, the historic cases recognizing Indigenous legal norms tended to be within limited areas of case law and to involve a continuity of vested rights from prior-existing legal orders as opposed to any full recognition of those legal orders.[5] Second, for reasons detailed elsewhere, there are complex discussions to be had about how to understand the forms of legal pluralism at issue as between traditional categories within the legal pluralism literature of 'weak' and 'strong' legal pluralism.[6] Third, the future shape of these forms of legal pluralism in such jurisdictions simply remains to be seen.

In the course of challenges to various sorts of prior colonial assumptions that the shape of Indigenous rights was permissibly determined in state law, Indigenous rights theorists have ended up launching broad attacks on legal positivism, some of which are set out in section B of the chapter. The challenges concern whether legal positivism has room for Indigenous legal conceptions and thus for Indigenous rights as properly understood as connected to those underlying legal conceptions. In response, it is important to consider the significant theoretical clarifications in recent decades in the dominant understanding of legal positivism and, notably, the clarifications of positivism offered by John Gardner's work. Turning to challenges, though, section C of the chapter wrestles with what it might mean to say that Indigenous rights within a legal system are entitlements arising prior to the legal system that are both legal and from outside the system, thus adding complexities to the concept of a legal system conventionally employed within positivist analyses. The chapter will argue that positivist values call for further modifications to positivism itself in order to engage in sufficiently rich description of the phenomenon of law. The chapter will not, then, argue against positivism, but rather for an improved positivism. The concluding section D will wrestle with what could seem to be a resulting conclusion that there may then be positivist-oriented exceptions to standard positivist theses, with room for accounts of several different kinds of 'law' becoming a means of reconciling positivism with more complex phenomena of law.

[4] Attention to a larger group of states might well change this claim. In many states where colonizing groups remained relatively small as compared to the population as a whole, there was no possibility of prior-existing norms not continuing in a fuller pluralism. For an important recent discussion, see Brian Z Tamanaha, *Legal Pluralism Explained: History, Theory, Consequences* (Oxford: Oxford University Press, 2021).

[5] See Dwight Newman, 'Indigenous Rights and Instrastate Multijuridicalism', in Paul Schiff Berman (ed) *The Oxford Handbook of Global Legal Pluralism* (Oxford: Oxford University Press, 2020) 833, 837.

[6] See ibid.

B. Unhelpful Attacks on 'Positivism' by Indigenous Rights Theorists

Indigenous rights theorists have prominently attributed problems in the Western colonial interaction with Indigenous peoples to legal positivism. Their attacks on positivism have taken several different forms, with some making more specific links between claimed aspects of legal positivism and particular legal outcomes and others suggesting less precise links, but with the term 'positivism' almost coming to function as an epithet. This form of engagement with 'positivism' may not differ from that of other human rights advocates, but it is unfortunately unhelpful in the context of the distinctive claims of Indigenous peoples to the recognition of Indigenous legal systems.

In terms of an example of a more specific link with attention to specific legal positivists, some prominent Indigenous scholars, such as John Borrows, have objected specifically to the lack of room in Austinian accounts of positivism for Indigenous law. Borrows notes that 'for legal positivists like Austin, centralized authority and explicit command are necessary for a legal system'[7] and Borrows objects to these characteristics for their potential to exclude Indigenous law, including systems of Indigenous customary law.[8]

Aside from the general significance of whether Indigenous legal systems are recognized and treated as part of potentially applicable law within the contemporary state, their recognition or non-recognition in particular circumstances as 'legal systems' has actually become part of the legal test for certain more specific Indigenous claims. Notably, under the Australian system on Native title, one element of proving Native title is establishing the existence of a continuous normative system from prior to the assertion of British sovereignty in Australia.[9] In other words, part of the legal test for establishing land rights in Australia may depend on whether an Indigenous legal system has existed continuously since a particular point in time, making the legal theory question of the nature of a legal system now a matter with intensely practical implications. Some legal analysts have considered whether subsequent Australian case law has been more attached to an Austinian vision of legal positivism or has made use of Indigenous perspectives on the nature of

[7] John Borrows, 'Indigenous Legal Traditions in Canada' (2005) 19 Washington U J L & Pol'y 164, 176.

[8] In some of his work, Borrows has emphasized that not all Indigenous law is properly called 'customary' law, but this focus tracks the article under discussion here. A more extended, recent account that critiques the ability of a 'liberal positivist' model to make room for Indigenous rights, but with other elements mixed with positivism, appears in Gordon Christie, *Canadian Law and Indigenous Self-Determination: A Naturalist Analysis* (Toronto: University of Toronto Press, 2019) 258–301.

[9] This was a significant interpretive development in *Members of the Yorta Yorta Aboriginal Community v Victoria* (2002) 214 CLR 422. On the evidentiary obstacle it poses, see e.g. Simon Young, *The Trouble with Tradition: Native Title and Cultural Change* (Alexandria NSW: Federation Press 2008).

a legal system, with some variation seemingly evident from case to case and some criticism directed at those cases too closely fixated on Austinian approaches.[10]

However, the terminology of 'positivism' has not always been as focused on any specific account of positivism in legal theory. Some Indigenous critics have ended up using the word 'positivist' to describe versions of international law in which only states have standing.[11] James Anaya writes that positivist versions of international law effectively removed the possibility of international law standing above states and committed international law to being described solely in terms of voluntarist agreement by states.[12] Other international law scholars arguing on behalf of Indigenous rights, such as Benedict Kingsbury, have claimed the term 'positivist' for particular purposes in this context, such as approaches attached to formalistic legal definitions that he argues against.[13]

That there would be some lack of clarity on implications of 'positivism' in the international law context is not surprising. The terminology of 'positivism' has been used in highly distorted ways in international law scholarship more generally, entirely apart from Indigenous contexts of any sort, and these uses have often focused on very unsophisticated versions of positivism far from contemporary philosophical conceptions.[14] However, many of those discussing"positivism' in other international law contexts are not engaged in advocating for the recognition of additional legal systems, as is commonly an important focus of Indigenous scholars or those advocating for Indigenous rights.

Some Indigenous scholars, such as Sákéj Henderson, have made more general statements linking 'positivism' to visions of Europeanist supremacy without precise explanation of the connection.[15] If one were seeking to link this usage with the discussion thus far, one would consider such possibilities as seeing this along the lines of the Borrows concern with Austinian accounts of positivism failing to have room for Indigenous legal systems or along the lines of the discussions about 'positivism' in international law. But, in some ways, there has come to be simply a more general concern about 'positivism', and a wide variety of Indigenous rights theorists use the term in broad ways where it almost starts to function less as a clear conceptual distinction and more as an epithet.[16] That usage similarly does

[10] See Marcelle Burns, 'Challenging the Assumptions of Positivism: An Analysis of the Concept of Society in *Sampi on Behalf of The Bardi and Jawa People v Western Australia* [2010] and *Bodney v Bennell* [2008]' (2011) 4 Land, Rights, Laws: Issues of Native Title 1.

[11] Odette Mazel, 'The Evolution of Rights: Indigenous Peoples and International Law' (2009) 13(1) Australian Indigenous L Rev 140, 140.

[12] S. James Anaya, *Indigenous Peoples in International Law* (Oxford: OUP, 1996) 26.

[13] Benedict Kingsbury, '"Indigenous Peoples" in International Law: A Constructivist Approach to the Asian Controversy' (1998) 92 Am J Int'l L 414, 414.

[14] Joerg Kammerhofer, 'International Legal Positivism', in Anne Orford & Florian Hoffmann (eds), *The Oxford Handbook of the Theory of International Law* (Oxford: OUP, 2016).

[15] James (Sákéj) Youngblood Henderson, 'Postcolonial Indigenous Legal Consciousness' (2002) 1 Indigenous LJ 1, 9, 12, 13, 20.

[16] For broad-ranging critical references to 'positivism' by Indigenous rights theorists, another important example would be the discussion in Robert A. Williams Jr, 'Encounters on the Frontiers of

not necessarily differ from that of others in fields like international human rights law.[17] But it nonetheless departs from precision in this context—almost inserting an additional thesis into positivism that would see it as committed to recognizing only state law[18]—and it does so in a way that inadvertently does harm to the cause of Indigenous advocates themselves.

There may be a role for legal epithets in marking out resistance to colonial legal systems that have brought injustices in the context of colonialism. However, to use "positivism" in such ways is unhelpful insofar as it involves distancing Indigenous rights and Indigenous law from the dominant legal philosophical framework concerning the nature of law and the scope of a legal system. If the adoption of legal protections for Indigenous rights and the recognition of Indigenous law is seen as entailing abandonment of a key paradigm of legal philosophy, it is rendered more difficult than need be the case. There are, in effect, strategic reasons for those who support Indigenous rights not to launch unnecessary assaults on legal positivism writ large. Making Indigenous rights sound unnecessarily exotic may needlessly undermine openness to Indigenous rights causes.

Moreover, the key positivist concept of legal validity also serves key moral purposes of law insofar as it is precisely because law is source-based that it is possible to effect morally valuable ends through the law, or, as Maris Köpcke's important study puts it, 'The techniques of legal validity can confer on us the power to craft justice'.[19] Obviously, those techniques can and have been used to impose injustice as well, but it is within an ability to alter the content of the sources of the law that it is also possible to change the law and to thereby achieve greater justice.

To challenge the attacks on positivism in the context at issue is not to question some of the impacts of historical versions of legal positivism. Indeed, the history of theories of legal positivism is more intertwined with colonial history than has often been realized. An important recent legal history paper by Coel Kirkby shows that Anglo-American legal theorists of the mid-nineteenth to mid-twentieth centuries were more focused on colonial issues than has previously drawn attention, even while this interest was simply part of a longer historical pattern of legal theory being shaped by—but also shaping—colonial approaches.[20] The period on which Kirkby focuses, that between Austin and Hart, is not one normally regarded as

International Human Rights Law: Redefining the Terms of Indigenous Peoples' Survival in the World' [1990] Duke Law J 660.

[17] I thank Kirsty Gover for emphasizing this point to me.

[18] See Michael Giudice & Eric Scarffe, 'Transnational Law and Legal Positivism', in Peer Zumbansen, *The Oxford Handbook of Transnational Law* (Oxford: OUP, 2021) 971, 981.

[19] Maris Köpcke, *Legal Validity: The Fabric of Justice* (Oxford: Hart Publishing, 2019) 158. For a different take on positivism's moral dimensions, arguing its value in some different ways, see David Dyzenhaus, 'The Inevitable Social Contract' (2021) 27 Res Publica 187.

[20] Coel Kirkby, 'Law Evolves: The Uses of Primitive Law in Anglo-American Concepts of Modern Law, 1861–1961' (2018) 58 Am J Legal History 535.

containing much jurisprudential vitality,[21] and Kirkby's contribution is partly to show that it was more active than commonly thought.

There was also an important transition under way that bears on matters of Indigenous rights. Austin's mid-nineteenth-century account, even if we strive to overcome the cartoonish readings of him to which he arguably made himself subject, has a character clearly tending to reinforce a colonial order. From the first words of *The Province of Jurisprudence Determined*, there rings out the pronouncement that '[l]aws proper, or properly so called, are commands'.[22] And, while Austin's account of positive law is interlaced more with morality than sometimes acknowledged in so far as his first several chapters actually concern divine law, there are nonetheless continuous strands focused on ideas of 'law set by political superiors to political inferiors' and, generally, demands that law be set in precise forms by determinate bodies.[23]

By the mid-twentieth century, Hart's account of the concept of law, while still not being particularly welcoming of international law and customary law,[24] nonetheless had shifted methodology so as to be taking in the results of legal anthropology rather than simply to be imposing an account of law that shuts out *a priori* many world legal systems, as had Austin's.[25] Hart's concept of law still remained mired in older terminology of 'primitive' law and in not seeing those systems as having all of the features of a full legal system.[26] However, Gardner's reading of Hart may help to contextualize these dimensions and suggest the potential for a legal positivist approach to find room for systems that Hart had not yet fully understood to be included in the concept of law. Gardner writes of Hart as having written of 'primitive law' in a 'legal fable' ' that served certain pedagogic purposes within his book but that did not yet embrace a full understanding of the already-present legal dimensions of differing legal systems.[27] The history of legal positivism, then, illustrates a movement forward in an expanded ability to incorporate more divergent legal systems within understandings.

Indeed, the contemporary account of legal positivism from Gardner himself—even if Gardner is usually seen as not overly engaged with or obviously receptive

[21] For a useful history, see Neil Duxbury, 'English Jurisprudence Between Austin and Hart' (2005) 91 Virginia L Rev 1.

[22] John Austin, *The Province of Jurisprudence Determined* (1832), ed. Wilfred E. Rumble (Cambridge: Cambridge University Press, 1995) 10.

[23] Ibid 18, 123ff.

[24] H.L.A. Hart, *The Concept of Law* 3rd edn (Oxford: Clarendon Press, 2012) 213ff.

[25] On Hart and legal anthropology, see Kirkby (n 20).

[26] Hart, *Concept of Law* (n 24) 3, 4. That said, there may be more constructive potential in Hart in relation to legal pluralism, as argued suggestively in Jeremy Waldron, 'Legal Pluralism and the Contrast Between Hart's Jurisprudence and Fuller's', in Peter Cane (ed), *The Hart–Fuller Debate in the Twenty-First Century* (Oxford: Hart Publishing, 2010) 135.

[27] John Gardner, 'Why Law Might Emerge: Hart's Problematic Fable', in Luís Duarte D'Almeida, James Edwards, & Andrea Dolcetti (eds) *Reading HLA Hart's The Concept of Law* (Oxford: Hart Publishing, 2013) 81.

to customary legal systems—does much to make room for customary legal systems simply by clearing unnecessary baggage away from the central claims of legal positivism. Gardner focuses on the straightforward legal positivist claim that '[i]n any legal system, whether a given norm is legally valid, and hence whether it forms part of the law of that system, depends on its sources, not its merits'.[28] One of his important contributions in his '5 ½ Myths' article was to show that nothing follows from this essential claim that directly requires formalistic theories of adjudication, specific roles of judges, or specific approaches to interpretation.[29] Nor is what legal positivism recognizes as law necessarily the preferable state of the law but, rather, the legal positivist account provides certain minimal requirements applicable equally to what natural law theorists call central cases and peripheral cases,[30] simply recognizing what a legal system is and contains.

Beyond this, however, Gardner's later work on legal positivism also more explicitly envisions specific room for customary law within a legal positivist theory, indeed highlighting that Hart's whole account depends on there being at least one (but not necessarily just one) norm of customary law in the rule of recognition, with the rule of recognition necessarily depending on customary law 'identifying a legislator (as it were) from below, not from above'.[31] The Austinian theory of commands and political superiors comes precisely to be reversed in contemporary accounts of legal positivism focused away from particular colonial forms towards its more essential features.

Later sections of this chapter will turn to yet further contemporary developments in legal positivism that emerge from loosening other implicit assumptions. Of particular note are Nicole Roughan's account of potentially pluralistic authorities and the account of Keith Culver and Michael Giudice that loosens assumptions about complete control by the state within particular borders.[32] There is a significant trend in legal positivist scholarship towards a more general account of law.

While some of the earlier Indigenous theorists attacking positivism might not have been positioned to anticipate all of these developments, the fact that attacks on legal positivism as inherently oppressive are ongoing in the Indigenous rights literature illustrates an unfortunate disciplinary divide, albeit involving the perhaps usual time lags in diffusion of new scholarly ideas. For the most part, Indigenous

[28] John Gardner, 'Legal Positivism: 5 ½ Myths' (2001) 46 Am J Jurisprudence 199, 199.

[29] Ibid 211–222.

[30] Ibid 225–227.

[31] John Gardner, *Law as a Leap of Faith* (Oxford: Oxford University Press, 2012) 69. Cf generally David J Bederman, *Custom as a Source of Law* (Cambridge: Cambridge University Press, 2010).

[32] Nicole Roughan, *Authorities: Conflicts, Cooperation, and Transnational Legal Theory* (Oxford: Oxford University Press 2013); Keith Culver & Michael Giudice, *The Unsteady State: General Jurisprudence for Dynamic Social Phenomena* (Cambridge: Cambridge University Press, 2017). Also notable, but arguably departing in some more challenging ways, is Brian Tamanaha, *A Realistic Theory of Law* (Cambridge: Cambridge University Press, 2017).

rights scholarship and legal philosophy do not occur in prominent ways at the same institutions, so there are few immediate connections between these disciplines, although there are certainly new generations of scholars who will have been schooled in now-contemporary forms of both. The present chapter is, in part, an attempt to urge an ongoing bridging of gaps.

The historical adaptation of legal positivism that has already occurred may be just the beginning of important developments in legal philosophical understandings that make more room for Indigenous rights and Indigenous law, and there would be important strategic advantages for those working within these fields in avoiding unnecessary conflict with this key movement in legal philosophy.

At the same time, developments in fields such as Indigenous rights and Indigenous law may continue to inform better development of legal positivism and legal philosophy more generally. This point speaks not to an onus on Indigenous legal theorists—to whom this chapter is a comment in principally strategic terms—but to an onus on positivists to find fuller accounts of the law within a jurisdiction that has space for Indigenous rights and Indigenous law recognized within a state legal system.

C. Indigenous Rights Prior, Legal, and Outside the System

My claim here is that state legal systems increasingly recognize Indigenous rights while treating them as arising from sources that are prior, legal, and outside the system. To the extent that state legal systems do this, a positivist account of law must take account of this complexity in the texture of law within the jurisdiction. That might seem to require one of the sort of further-reaching approaches adopted in some of the new scholarship mentioned a moment ago, but I will argue that those further innovations may not be necessary and that Gardner's account of positivism can itself make space for the necessary sort of recognition of Indigenous rights placed within a sort of set of exceptions to standard positivist requirements nonetheless grounded in positivist principle.

Gardner engaged directly with the concept of legal pluralism on at least two occasions, these being in presentations at McGill's Faculty of Law in 2012 and at Osgoode Hall's Nathanson Centre on Transnational Human Rights in 2013. True to form, one of his key hopes was to attempt to clarify what was meant by 'legal pluralism' and whether it was a 'theme' or a 'thesis'. Gardner rightly suggested in his remarks on both occasions that if there are theses that fit under the term 'legal pluralism', they must be analysed and tested. His approaches are not necessarily closed to legal pluralism, but what matters is the truth of particular propositions about legal pluralism.

Approaches that would effect larger changes in the concepts of positivist analysis in order to accommodate Indigenous rights raise some profound questions.

For example, when Nicole Roughan develops an account of pluralistic authorities that all operate simultaneously,[33] one needs to ask serious questions about whether the approach proposed is consistent with the very concept of authority in the first instance. When Culver and Giudice propose a loosening of assumptions about the degree of a state's authority within its boundaries,[34] they propose what could be seen as a particular idea within Roughan's larger claims about the potential to have competing pluralistic authorities within a legal order, so their account is subject to similar types of questions.

Both accounts represent important, creative work. But it may not be necessary to adopt such accounts in order to have space within positivism for Indigenous rights and even recognition of Indigenous law within a state's legal system.

An important starting point here is that legal systems routinely recognize rights arising from prior sources outside of the legal system, and any positivist account of law would properly identify legal systems as having rules by which they do so. For example, when a foreigner arrives into a state, that individual's property rights in personal property acquired in a foreign legal system are recognized and respected, even where the rules related to that acquisition are different in that other legal system. A prior source outside the host legal system is thus recognized within the host legal system as altering legal rights within that host system. In the example, it will also often or even typically be the case that the rules concerning the acquisition were legal rules but simply the legal rules of a different legal system.

The ways in which a legal system respects and recognizes Indigenous rights arising from a historically prior political society are in some ways analogous to this example. Vested rights of various sorts continue into the legal system that subsequently asserted sovereignty. A prior source outside that new legal system is recognized within that legal system as having resulted in various vested rights. These may take on complex forms and consist in, for example, a right to carry on a certain traditional activity, though with the possibility of doing so in a modernized form. But there is in any event a recognition of legal rights arising from a prior source from outside the legal system.

If the current state legal system recognizes ongoing alterations of certain legal rights and obligations based on the operations of an Indigenous legal system subsequent to the assertion of state sovereignty, that too can be accommodated within this account. In this instance, as with the individual arriving from a foreign state, there are ongoing determinations of legal rights to be recognized within the state's legal system that operate outside the legal system itself and, in that sense, prior to the state legal system. Without any larger change in the concept of authority, it is possible to give a positivist account of legal systems recognizing rights coming from systems prior to and outside the state legal system.

[33] Roughan (n 32).
[34] Culver & Giudice (n 32).

Where matters may get more delicate is in describing whether a right such as those under consideration was a legal right prior to its recognition as a legal right by the state legal system in question. Here, Gardner's account of positivism is both potentially accommodating and potentially unaccommodating. First, Gardner suggests that it would be entirely possible to recognize law in some very different systems. He writes that 'Hart did not go, clipboard in hand, to Nunavut or Badakhshan or to the Ogaden, to see whether there were practices or attitudes or institutions there meeting the specifications set out in his book' but accepts the possibility that there could have been law to be identified in some of these examples.[35] Second, though, Gardner would also suggest that law might not exist in every society visited.[36] Indeed, he rejects any functionalist account that would say that it is necessary to identify something in each society as law based on it serving the same social functions as law.[37] Gardner writes that 'Law is not "whatever resolves disputes" but a special *way* of resolving disputes',[38] something potentially not actually utilized in every society. Gardner would be potentially accommodating of the notion of describing the right recognized by the state legal system that comes from a system prior to and outside the state legal system as always having been a 'legal right', but only if it fits within the 'way' of dealing with rights within the positivist account of law. But if he were to insist on labelling it as not having always been from a system of 'law', he would not thereby be denying that the other system in question serves many of the same functions as a legal system. He would simply be saying that there are different types of classifications.

However, in this latter example, there would be some kind of claim that became a legal right the instant it came into contact with the state legal system in question. To the extent that positivism has value in the fact that it classifies, it has that value because classification describes something about the world. So, even if Gardner suggests that Hart's lack of a clipboard means that Hart was engaged in developing classifications rather than engaging in description,[39] there is nonetheless an underlying descriptive impulse to positivism. Do I, though, suggest positivism has a descriptive attitude, or do I suggest a thesis here about positivism that it has an inherent connection to description? I do suggest the latter, precisely because its classifications would have no point if they did not enable description. Positivism is inherently linked to an aspiration of accurate description, and it is only that aspiration that leads it to its classifications or, indeed, that makes positivism valuable in offering descriptions of the law that enable discussion of changes to the law.

Given that positivism is committed to accurate description, there needs to be room for it to recognize something that becomes a legal right within a legal system

[35] Gardner, *Law as a Leap of Faith* (n 31) 277.
[36] Ibid.
[37] Ibid 292.
[38] Ibid.
[39] Ibid 274–279.

as potentially to have come from something linked to law in the first instance. Of course, that claim may seem overgeneralized. Obviously, the objection might run, there are non-legal dimensions to what becomes a legal right within a system, with for instance the legal system itself determining that certain acts attempting to form a contract do or do not amount to acts that generate a legal right but with those acts in themselves not being 'legal' acts. But their immediate effects in the legal system also make them 'legal' acts. Especially when those acting had intentions related to the legal system, there must be room for recognizing them as something other than mere physical gyrations that randomly result in legal rights and obligations. There must be room for a bit of play around the edges of what the positivist legal system is ready to describe as law for purposes of its relationship to law in the strictest sense. And I thus suggest that whether or not Hart's account would treat a particular Indigenous right as arising from 'law', whether or not the system from which it derived deals with things in the legal 'way' that Gardner would seek, the underlying values of positivism call for acceptance of the right and its underlying system as having a legal character. While the motivation is accurate description, this approach has the result of manifesting respect for different systems of political organization.

There are, of course, arguments for going farther than this to give full respect for different sorts of political systems. Even Gardner himself hints at one point at the possibility of describing the existence of European law within a European member state not simply in terms of the member state's inclusion of EU law within its rule of recognition—as would be both most analogous to what I have said here and most parsimonious in approach—but in terms of recognizing the coexistence of different legal systems within one geographic territory. He writes: 'There is no paradox in holding that two legal systems with conflicting constitutions, and hence with potentially conflicting subordinate laws, are in force simultaneously in the same territory. Propositions of law are true or false only relative to legal systems, not relative to territories.'[40] Explaining the underlying assumptions, he writes that '[t]erritoriality, never mind exclusive territoriality, is no part of the nature of law'.[41]

Such an account marks, perhaps, a great openness to a fuller legal pluralism than one might have anticipated in the context of other discussions. And I do not exclude the possibility of positivism going in such a direction or in directions like those proposed by Roughan or by Culver and Giudice. All I claim here is that it is not necessary to do so for the moment insofar as it is possible for present purposes to incorporate a principled exception to any narrower requirements of positivism in light of positivism's deeper values. In doing so, while describing the state legal system, it is possible to recognize Indigenous rights (and Indigenous laws) as arising from prior legal sources outside the state legal system.

[40] John Gardner, 'Fifteen Themes from *Law as a Leap of Faith*' (2015) 6 Jurisprudence 601, 606.
[41] Ibid.

To say as much makes no assumption on whether Indigenous norms will be recognized as operating in the legal 'way' inherent within Gardner's theory. Remaining agnostic on that point for the present moment—and leaving room for different, nuanced interactions—manifests more respect for the challenging work ahead. It is very possible for different normative systems to do law-like things while not operating in the legal 'way' present in the category of law within legal positivism. Saying as much does not say that legal positivism is committed to a state-centric vision—the very point I have tried to challenge—but it says that the scope of a category should not be immediately expanded to encompass every adjacent activity, or one distorts both the category and perhaps the activities to which attention has been newly focused. There is, quite simply, very careful work to be done, and trying to move everything quickly into particular categories based on an unnecessary idea that being in those particular categories is necessary to equal recognition of cultures and societies carries two problematic risks. First, it risks distortion of the categories. Second it risks encouraging distortion of understandings of the cultures and societies at issue.[42] These both arise from an attempt to fit them into a slightly adjusted category at the expense of considering the possibility of further categories that could bring additional understanding.

Considering this point another way, one could note the important observations of Dale Turner, who notes that 'many Aboriginal peoples do not understand their rights in terms that are amenable to the state's legal and political discourses. This is because many Aboriginal peoples do not perceive the political relationship as one of subservience.'[43] On the one hand, the consequence flowing from this important point might appear to be that it is important to move quickly beyond any conception of Indigenous normative orders being analysed through their entry into Canadian law, as Culver and Giudice have sensibly suggested in relation to this very quote,[44] and thus focusing on fitting Indigenous normative orders into the category of law and/or making the category of law encompass Indigenous normative orders. However, the further implications of Turner's statement about Indigenous peoples not seeing their rights in ways 'amenable to the state's legal and political discourses' may speak to a more radical otherness. While I argued earlier that Indigenous advocates should be careful not to make their normative orders appear too exotic for positivism, there should also not be an erasure of difference, which could risk a different sort of disrespect for Indigenous systems.

[42] I have work-in-progress that I will soon publish on ways in which the broad scholarly community in relation to a very prominent article has sometimes inadvertently drawn upon problematic work on Indigenous history, seemingly out of a wish that the research were correct so that its consequences would follow. The risks I mention here have some analogy to phenomena in that discussion.

[43] Dale Turner, *This is Not a Peace Pipe: Towards a Critical Indigenous Philosophy* (Toronto: University of Toronto Press, 2006) 4.

[44] See discussion in Keith Culver & Michael Giudice, 'Entanglement of State and Indigenous Legal Orders in Canada', in Nico Krisch (ed.), *Entangled Legalities beyond the State* (Cambridge: Cambridge University Press, 2022).

There must be very careful work done in analysing the nexus of the concepts here, and the direction I have suggested is sufficient as a starting point. I have shown that positivism can make room for Indigenous normative orders, even while I am also frankly saying that there is significant work ahead in developing the soundest descriptions and analyses. This work represents an important scholarly agenda that requires close attention simultaneously to details of legal philosophy and details of Indigenous orders.

D. Conclusion: Towards a Decolonized Positivism

The matters under discussion here may raise more questions than I have offered answers for. But I have made and defended two important claims that I hope can contribute to further discussions. First, I argued that positivism itself has changed already from certain historical movements of 'positivism' such that it may not be necessary, and is probably a strategic mistake, for Indigenous theorists and Indigenous advocates to imply that their claims are necessarily incompatible with positivism. Gardner's simplified account of positivism makes clear that 'positivism' need not imply everything ever said within positivist traditions, some of whose historical manifestations have indeed been interlinked with the colonial project and have thus properly evoked criticism even while continuing with that criticism could today endanger the prospects of the Indigenous rights project if the criticism makes that project appear incompatible with the dominant account of law. Second, I have argued that it is possible to adjust positivism so as to ensure it has space for Indigenous rights and Indigenous law. I have noted that there are arguments in existence for larger adjustments to fundamental concepts of positivism, and a significant scholarly agenda arising, even while arguing that these larger adjustments are not necessary to face the immediate issue. Drawing on Gardner's later writings on what law claims and on the character of law in general, I have argued that his account of positivism has some potential to be both accommodating and unaccommodating of the matters at issue. However, I have argued that any plausible positivist account already describes phenomena with analogies to Indigenous rights and Indigenous law, and I have extrapolated from an example of that claim that a positivist account can see a legal system recognizing Indigenous rights (and Indigenous law) that are prior to and outside that legal system and, in light of a deep commitment to descriptive accuracy, it would also properly see those Indigenous rights as having always had a legal character, even if coming from a very differently organized political society.

Separating contemporary positivism from its historical manifestations, some of which did have intersections with colonial policy, thus offers a 'decolonized' positivism, though much of this process is simply removing positivism from the power of overly narrow descriptions of itself. Gardner's account of the essence of positivism makes clear that positivism need not have colonial commitments. And Gardner's further discussions of positivism open various possibilities. There may be further discussions to be had, but the present discussion has already illustrated the power of working carefully with the concept of positivism and its concept of law so as to see it already transcending unnecessary limitations upon it. 'Decolonizing' positivism may consist in the first instance simply in clarifying positivism.

16

Big-E Equity, Small-C Conservatism

Irit Samet[*]

A. Introduction

Theoretical engagement with the law of Equity has become trendy.[1] Even in the USA, where Equity has been declared dead, or at least irreversibly 'fused' with the common law, a renewed interest in Equity as a distinct body of law is clearly apparent.[2] Hot debate surrounds basic questions such as what Equity can do for us, and whether its benefits justify its costs—in terms of the split between Equity and Law, and the way it compromises clarity and predictability by relying heavily on legal standards rather than rules. John Gardner did not venture into these arguments. As you would expect of writers on theory of law, Gardner pays tribute to the great contribution of Aristotle's concept of equity to the science of law.[3] But the relationship between small-e equity—as in Aristotle's discussions—and big-E equity—as in the body of law developed by the courts of Chancery in England—is hardly straightforward.[4] And on big-E equity Gardner had very little to say. In his, sadly, final book-length account of the law of obligations, he had only this to say:

> There are also equitable wrongs, such as breach of trust and breach of confidence, that have something in common with torts but also some of their own doctrinal apparatus. You will not be surprised to find me saying nothing specific about them.[5]

[*] I am grateful to Prince Saprai for very helpful comments.

[1] Some examples of the new crop of volumes devoted to the subject are D. Klimchuk, I. Samet, and H.E. Smith, *Philosophical Foundations of the Law of Equity* (OUP 2020); Peter G. Turner, 'Fusion and Theories of Equity in Common Law Systems' in John C.P. Goldberg, Henry E. Smith, and P.G. Turner (eds), *Equity and Law: Fusion and Fission* (CUP 2019); Irit Samet, *Equity: Conscience Goes to Market* (1st edn, Oxford University Press 2018).

[2] See for instance H.E. Smith, 'Fusion of Law and Confusion of Equity' in D. Klimchuk, I. Samet, and H.E. Smith (eds), *Philosophical Foundations of the Law of Equity* (OUP 2019); Kellen Funk, 'Equity Without Chancery: The Fusion of Law and Equity in the Field Code of Civil Procedure, New York 1846–76' 36 J Leg Hist (2015) 152.

[3] See for example John Gardner, *Law as a Leap of Faith: Essays on Law in General* (Oxford University Press 2012), pp.254–256.

[4] See discussion (and terminology) in D. Klimchuk, 'Aristotle at the Foundations of the Law of Equity' in D. Klimchuk, I. Samet, and H.E. Smith (eds), *Philosophical Foundations of the Law of Equity* (OUP 2020).

[5] John Gardner, *From Personal Life to Private Law* (OUP 2018), p.14. He also makes some remarks on Aristotelian Equity without referring back to our law of Equity (Gardner, *Law as a Leap of Faith*,

Irit Samet, *Big-E Equity, Small-C Conservatism* In: *From Morality to Law and Back Again.* Edited by: Michelle Madden Dempsey and François Tanguay-Renaud, Oxford University Press.
DOI: 10.1093/oso/9780198860594.003.0016

In this chapter, I attempt to dig a little deeper into the relationship between the general theory advanced by Gardner and big-E Equity. What I wish to propose is indeed 'nothing specific', but rather an overview of the applicability of his account of the underlying justifying principle of the law of obligation to Equity. The question, I believe, is interesting for scholars and students of Equity, even if Gardner himself did not pay much attention to it.

First, if the account he offers of the values that animate the law of obligations can successfully explain large swathes of the law of obligations—including tort, contract, property (which he views as a branch of tort law), and unjust enrichment—it would be telling us something important about Equity if this body of law did not fall in line. If Equity is the odd one out, this could, for example, lend support to a new conceptualization of Equity according to which it is a species of public, rather than private, law. In a string of thoughtful papers by eminent public lawyers, an attempt is made to reconceptualize Equity as a public or hybrid public/private law concept.[6] If this novel way of categorizing Equity is successful, namely, if it can explain the values Equity promotes and the machinations it employs to do so by using the matrix of public law, we would indeed expect to find that accounts such as Gardner's that focus solely on private law would falter when applied to Equity. If Equity can indeed be better understood as a public/private law hybrid, that would be a radical departure from the way it is widely understood by scholars and jurists in the field.

But perhaps a mismatch between the theory of law of obligations and Equity does not tell us something interesting about the latter, but rather reflects negatively on the theory itself. The extent of a theory's inability to explain one aspect of the law which one purports to rationalize is an indication that the whole project is on the wrong track, if indeed that particular aspect is central to the explanandum. In the USA, many scholars of private law would not see Equity as a cardinal building block of contract, property or succession law (which are the areas of the law of obligations in which Equity is mostly active). Given the merger ('fusion') between law and Equity in most areas, many lawyers would not even be able to point out those parts of the law of obligations that originate in Equity.[7] But in other common law jurisdictions which did not go through a similar fusion process, equitable doctrines play a central role in those areas of the law of obligations in which the common law is largely

pp.254–255). On the relationship between Aristotle's Equity and the law of Equity see Klimchuk, and sources cited there. In his *Torts and Other Wrongs*, Gardner criticizes Goldberg and Zipursky for the way their 'civil recourse' theory fails to account for equitable wrongs (p.5). He explains his arguments with reference to some equitable remedies (pp.7–15), but he does not offer an account of the field as a whole or how it fits in with his grand theory (John Gardner, *Torts and Other Wrongs* (OUP 2019)).

[6] See Evan Fox-Decent, 'The Constitution of Equity' in Dennis Klimchuk, Irit Samet, and Henry Smith (eds), *Philosophical Foundations of the Law of Equity* (OUP 2020), and sources cited there.

[7] See review in S. Bray, 'Equity: Notes on the American Reception' in J. Goldberg, H. Smith, and P. Turner (eds), *Equity and Law: Fusion and Fission* (Cambridge University Press 2019).

dominated by formal sets of rules such as property and contract. In areas where it is active, Equity intervenes in the common law rights of the parties by offering defences, claims, and remedies whose effect goes deep and wide into the terrain shaped by the common law (and, sometimes, statute). Moreover, being the source of trust law, equitable doctrines dominate large portions of the law that applies to wealth and savings, from pension schemes to individual investment portfolios. Failure to explain the law of Equity therefore does not reflect well on an account of the law of obligations.

Thus, in spite of openly avoiding the question, I believe that Gardner would have found it interesting to ask whether the central ideas he explored in *From Personal Life to Private Law* apply to the law of Equity. In this chapter I suggest that the answer to this question, which he did not ask, is 'yes, albeit in a unique way that reflects the unusual nature of this area of law'. I start by looking briefly at Gardner's explanation of why the law of obligations operates in the way that it does (mainly in his chapter 5), and then explain why, at first glance, it does not seem to account for Equity. However, so I argue next, if we correctly identify the unique role of Equity within the legal system, it can help us reveal the way in which the themes Gardner suggests reverberate under its surface. The law of Equity is a large and complicated area of law, and it is not possible in this short space to address all the manners in which it departs from or expresses Gardner's theory. I will focus on three aspects of the law of Equity which, to my mind, exemplify the complex and unusual way in which it corresponds with Gardner's ideas: the vocation of Equity, its effect on common law rights, and the nature of equitable rights.

B. The Way Equity Undermines Security

In chapter 5 of *From Personal Life to Private Law*, Gardner sets out to answer a question that gets right to the foundations of the law of obligations: '[If] you have no right to your wealth under the relevant principle of distributive justice ... how can you have a right to have it restored . . ? [W]hat sort of justice is it that permits ... injustice?'[8] Following a successful claim—so we learn in the first weeks of every law of obligations course—defendants are offered remedies whose aim is to place them where they would have been if the facts on which their claim is based did not materialize; the consequences of the breach, the tortious act, or the unjust enrichment are to be wiped out, as far as is possible, so as to reinstate the status quo ante. But the claim that people are entitled to get the state's help in getting back what they had, or what was promised to them, is not even intuitive. Surely, we first need to ask whether the initial state of affairs was just, before we employ

[8] Jules L. Coleman, *Risks and Wrongs* (Cambridge University Press 1992), pp.304–305.

the justice system to restore it? If we cannot provide a satisfactory answer to this question, the whole edifice of the law of obligations as we know it would collapse. Gardner weaves his nuanced and profound treatment of this complex issue around an interest of security—in our chosen lifestyle, property, or ability to make life-determining plans—that we can legitimately expect the state to protect: '[t]he law of obligations … could be thought of as a scheme for allocating security, indeed for allocating security rights in a certain distinctive pre-packaged form.'[9] In a bold attempt to break through the deadlock between those who believe that private law (just like public law) is animated by considerations of distributive justice and those who argue that private law can only do corrective justice, Gardner argues that the role of this body of law is to bring about justice in the *distribution* of corrective justice. The corrective justice which the law of obligations sees as its mission to carry out is 'a specialized juridical scheme for allowing some people, often at the expense of others, to hold on more tightly … to what they already have, or recently had, in their lives'.[10] Since the rights distributed by the law of obligations are a type of security right, the question we should ask is not whether the pre-wrong distribution of wealth as between defendant and claimant was just (and therefore ought to be restored), but rather whether the claimant was entitled to hold securely to her position in the pre-wrong state of affairs.

Gardner explains the right to hold on to our way of life by appeal to what Jerry Cohen dubbed 'small c conservatism'.[11] Small-c conservatives, unlike the social conservative, would not hesitate to dispense with traditional social values where these lead to injustice. But they do stand for the belief that one is entitled to prefer a present state of affairs to an alternative one even if the latter is a little better; it is, in other words, a rejection of the utilitarian calculus as a universal measure for the correct order of preferences. Many would agree with Cohen that attachment to possessions one has had for a long time, or the way the neighbourhood looked and felt for years, or the habit of playing music at a regular time in the evening, and so on are a mark of humanity; but not all of them will see such preferences as rational. Unless you can show that the status quo is of a higher value to the alternatives (and the calculation can be highly complex and account for myriad factors), they can argue, you cannot *rationally* prefer it to the reformed state of affairs. Posing such condition on the rationality of a choice, Gardner wants to show, is a mistake: preferences can be rational without being supported by a calculation of utilities. Our ability to commit and be truly invested in something external to us (a life goal, friendship, home) is dependent on our ability to see it as possessing special value over and above the alternatives: 'when certain goals are ours, we

[9] Gardner, *From Personal Life to Private Law*, p.218.

[10] Ibid, p.219.

[11] J.A. Cohen, 'Rescuing Conservatism: A Defense of Existing Value' in *Finding Oneself in the Other* (Princeton University Press 2012), p.1.

cannot regard them as just possible goals among others ... [for while in] the grand scheme of things, as we might admit in a reflective moment, they are nothing special ... adopting them as ours means coming to stand in a special relationship of commitment to them'.[12] Even if we could, or do at times, recognise that in fact we could have chosen otherwise and be just as (or even slightly more) happy, we must stick to the illusion that what we have is worth holding on to; without it, our life would be empty and sad.[13] I do not have room here to discuss the merits of this theory, for which I have much sympathy.[14] Instead, the space here will be devoted to the question with which we started, namely: can Gardner's account of the law of obligations in terms of the distribution of security interests explain how and why Equity intervenes in the common law rights of the parties? Central features of the way in which Equity operates as a 'gloss' on the common law seem to suggest that people's entitlement to hold on to their property is not an important concern of this body of law.[15] In the following three sub-sections I focus on three such features to demonstrate this point: the vocation of Equity; the effect its intervention has on *common law* rights; and the way *equitable* rights are protected.

1. The Vocation of Equity

The question 'what is Equity for' is fraught with controversy. Some say that Equity is not even a category of which you can ask the question 'what is its purpose', as it is no more than a collection of doctrines that were historically administered by the Courts of Chancery.[16] This is not the place to refute such nominalist views of Equity. Instead, I will assume here that Equity has an essence, that is, that it is a body of law that comprises principles, rules, and doctrines with, at least, a 'family resemblance', about which we can meaningfully ask what common purpose they serve. Of the different answers to the questions 'of what the family resemblance between the doctrines of Equity is' and 'what we can learn from it about the vocation of Equity', I will focus on one dominant strand: the doctrines of Equity are a response to a concern about the way the clear and formal rules of common law can be exploited in an unconscionable way to 'game' the system.[17] Take an example from contract: the common law rule that contracts to transfer or create a right in land are

[12] Gardner, *From Personal Life to Private Law*, pp.195–196.

[13] Ibid, p.198.

[14] See further Irit Samet, 'On Tradition and the Conservation of Equity' (2020) 65 American Journal of Jurisprudence 109.

[15] As Maitland famously referred to Equity: (Frederic William Maitland, *Equity, also, the Forms of Action at Common Law: Two Courses of Lectures* (CUP 1909), p.18).

[16] See for instance Frederic William Maitland, *Equity: A Course of Lectures* (2nd edn, CUP 1936); Lionel Smith, 'Equity Is Not a Thing' in D. Klimchuk, I. Samet, and H.E. Smith (eds), *Philosophical Foundations of the Law of Equity* (OUP 2019).

[17] See for instance *Earl of Oxford's case* (1615) 21 ER 485; Samet, *Equity: Conscience Goes to Market*, chapter 1; Henry Smith, 'Equity as Meta-Law' 130 Yale Law Journal.

binding only once formalized in writing can be used by crafty negotiators to skew the fair and efficient balance between the parties. In common law, the seller can make a representation that encourages the other party to make a pre-contractual investment in anticipation of a duly formalized contract, and subsequently renege on the representation with no repercussions. The result would be a 'hold up' problem as the seller can threaten to withdraw from the negotiation unless the price is raised thus enabling her to scoop the profit up to the value of the buyer's sunk investment.[18]

If such practices are allowed to take root, buyers would be discouraged from investing in the pre-contractual stage even where it is efficient to do so, trust among contracting parties would erode, and the reputation of the legal system that allows such a rift between the moral and legal obligations would be badly damaged.[19] Equity steps in to 'estop' the seller, that is, to force her to take responsibility for the effect that her representation has had on the buyer and make good the expenses he incurred in relying on her representation.[20] A similar pattern of interventions which stem manipulative use of the legal rules to avoid clear moral obligation can be identified in many, if not all, of the doctrines of Equity.[21] The concern that animates Equity, according to this account, sets it apart from other private law areas, as it is focused on the proper, decent, and efficient performance of the legal system as a whole. The language of unconscionability does not grant the courts *carte blanche* to interfere whenever the result in (common) law strikes the courts as unfair. Rather, the law of Equity is there to correct those pockets of law where fixation on clear bright-line rules creates an opportunity for the canny to serve their interests at the expense of others. Indeed, in areas where open-ended principles cannot easily be used in such manipulative ways, such as tort law, Equity maintain a low profile.[22] If so, then, at least from the perspective of the overall purpose that Equity serves, it does not seem to be subsumed under Gardner's account of private law as protecting the interest of security. Equity's interventions target pockets of law in which the Chancery Court identifies a very specific problem of uncurbed enthusiasm for formalism, and their aim is to add a layer that would protect not only litigants, but the wellbeing of the legal system as a whole, from the damage it can cause.[23]

[18] Arye Bebchuk and Omri Ben-Shahar, 'Precontractual Reliance' 30 The Journal of Legal Studies (2001) 423.

[19] Samet, *Equity: Conscience Goes to Market*, chapter 2.

[20] *Gillett v Holt & Anor [2000] EWCA Civ* 66 CA.

[21] See examples in Smith, 'Equity as Meta-Law'.

[22] Benjamin C. Zipursky, 'The Inner Morality of Private Law' 58 The American Journal of Jurisprudence (2013) 27; Irit Samet, 'On Trusts, Angels, Morality and Fusion: Reply to My Critics' 21 Jerusalem Review of Legal Studies (2020) 50.

[23] Thus, equity never introduced an 'easy rescue' duty, or even an 'abuse of rights' doctrine—two issues where, you may think, the common law is cut adrift from ethics. These and other chestnuts which equity avoided show that it does not operate as a general patch for areas where the common law seems to fall short of what interpersonal morality would require.

2. The Interaction with Common Law Rights

But while this account of '*what* Equity is for' seems problematic for Gardner as it avoids the value of security, the answer to the more practical question of '*how* Equity achieves its aims' indicates that equity positively undermines the interest of security in one's possessions. For whatever one's views on the vocation of Equity, there is no controversy about the way it operates to achieve them, namely, by means of open-ended principles that leave the courts discretion to assess the defendant's actions in retrospect. The extent to which this assessment involves moral judgement (via the element of unconscionability), or just how wide the discretion is and whether we should aspire to narrow it down as precedent builds up, are all hotly debated.[24] But if Equity is to bear any resemblance to its early incarnation, it must retain the standard-based, *ad hoc*, morality-freighted character of its norms. It is argued by many that, be the merit of such norms as it may, they score pretty badly on 'serving people's security interests'.[25] For example, owners of land who know that, unless they signed a document to transfer it, they are entitled to keep their land—as the common law has it—would feel much more secure in their current status than owners who know that their actions (or even omissions) can give rise to claims against their property—as is stipulated by Equity.[26] When it comes to rights to one's home, the chances are that the sense of security that is tied up with homeownership would go straight to the core of Gardner's justification of the duty to reinstate owners to their previous position regardless of the justice of the initial allocation of wealth which it reflected. For one's home can play a crucial role in her life goals, as the locus of various activities from gardening to decoration, as well as her connection to local communities and personal and family history. The highly formal set of rules on the transfer and creation of property rights in land that we find in the common law does a great service to the security interest of homeowners; the doctrines of equity that suspend these rules do the opposite.

The same pattern reoccurs with regards to the security of contracting parties as to the deal they will be held committed to, the remedies they can expect in case of a breach, or the level of protection they can expect in case their autonomy is compromised during the negotiations: where the common law reassures you with bright-line ex-ante rules, Equity introduces nuanced, morally judgemental ex-post caveats.[27] Parties' ability to rescind a voluntary disposition on grounds of

[24] For very different views on these issues, see e.g. Peter Birks, 'Equity in the Modern Law: An Exercise in Taxonomy' 25 U Western Australia L Rev (1996) 1; Sarah Worthington, *Equity* (2nd edn, Oxford University Press 2006), chapter 1; and sources in Irit Samet, 'What Conscience Can Do for Equity' 3 Jurisprudence (2012) 13.

[25] As do all legal standards: Joseph Raz, 'Legal Principles and the Limits of Law' 81 The Yale Law Journal (1972) 823.

[26] As would be the case if they made a representation about their right on which another relied to his detriment: *Crabb v Arun District Council [1976] Ch. 179* CA.

[27] You can find examples in Phillip Sales, 'The Interface between Contract and Equity', Lehane Memorial Lecture 2019.

mistake is a good example. In a recent decision, the UKSC ruled that rescission would be allowed where the donor worked under a causative mistake of sufficient gravity which made it unconscionable to leave the mistake uncorrected. The question whether it would be unconscionable to leave a mistaken transaction uncorrected, Lord Walker explained, cannot be decided 'by an elaborate set of rules' but must be decided by an exercise of judicial discretion following review of all the circumstances 'in the round'.[28] Thus, in contrast with common law, Equity awards a proprietary remedy when a successful claim for rescission is made, with the result that property rights of the parties are decided on the basis of open-ended, morally freighted criteria, and a particularistic standard of unconscionability. It is therefore tempting to conclude that in this and other instances where it interposes, Equity diminishes the sense of security that accompanies the knowledge of the precise boundaries of our rights.

3. Equitable Rights

If we turn our attention to the structure of the rights that Equity creates, we find further evidence for the proposition that for Equity, security interests are nowhere near the top of the normativity agenda. If in the last paragraph we looked at the way in which Equity may be seen as reducing the level of security that people can enjoy with regards to their *common law* rights, here we focus on the rights that are *created* by Equity and the relatively low level of security they come with. The most conspicuous example is the right beneficiaries to the trust property. Commonly seen as the most original and influential invention of Equity, the trust is a highly popular instrument for the creation of flexible property rights. From the way in which Equity structures the beneficiary's right to the property that is the subject matter of the trust, one can easily conclude that the security interest of the right's owner is not a priority—for the beneficiary's rights vis-à-vis the property are much more prone to expire in a competition with third parties than are common law property rights. In some conspicuous cases of competition between the beneficiary's security in the property and other values such as the dynamics of markets or the integrity of the legal system, the law of Equity prefers the latter where its common law counterpart places security at the top.[29] The comparison is particularly stark in English law, where common law property rights are almost completely resistant to involuntary transfers, whereas the right of the beneficiary to the trust property expires whenever the property is transferred by the trustee to a bona fide purchaser.[30]

[28] *Pitt v Holt* [2013] UKSC 26 SC [128].

[29] See cases discussed in A. Nair and I. Samet, 'What Can "Equity's Darling" Tell Us about Equity?' in D. Klimchuk, I. Samet, and H.E. Smith (eds), *Philosophical Foundtions of the Law of Equity* (OUP 2019)

[30] Compare, for example, *Akers & Ors v Samba Financial Group* [2017] UKSC 6 UKSC [51] to Sale of Goods (Amendment) Act 1994. Registered land is an exception: see section 58 of Land Registration Act (2002).

Being based on private arrangement between the trustee and the settlor, trusts are often hidden from the public, and the chances that a purchaser of trust property will indeed satisfy Equity's innocence requirement are therefore high.

The preference given to an innocent third party in circumstances of trust (the 'Equity's darling' rule) is not a mere technicality. As an essential part of the law which governs the trust relationship, it supports an amalgam of other values. For example, the ability to structure rights to property in the form of a beneficial interest is a boost to people's autonomy, as the flexibility it affords breaks through the mould of the closed list ('numerus clausus') of property rights.[31] The trustee's duty to hold the property for the beneficiary is an expression of the duty to follow one's conscience even if legal formalities would have allowed her to deny them.[32] But the value of security seems to lag way behind these (and maybe other) values that are instantiated by the trust in particular, and Equity in general. For Equity, it seems, the value of securing people's right to hold on to their property rights is, at best, just one of a number of values that animate the trust; the relative ease with which the security interest is waived in the context of trust indicates that it does not play a particularly important role. If so, Gardner's account of the law of obligations does not encompass Equity, and hence fails to address an important branch of what it purports to explain. In section C I attempt to show why this conclusion is unwarranted.

C. Protecting Security Equity's Way

In this section I argue that a deeper look reveals that Equity does show great concern for the interest of security—but it does so in a unique manner which complements the more conventional ways in which the common law of obligations protects this interest. To see that, we need to revisit the three aspects of Equity we discussed in section A. We will find that (a) Equity in fact *strengthens* the overall protection of security interests by enabling the common law to remain a staunch defender of the interest of security without endangering its legitimacy, and (b) various other aspects of the equitable right demonstrate a commitment to the value of security that goes over and above that of the common law, or so I will argue.

[31] Hanoch Dagan and Irit Samet, 'The Trust as the Missing Piece in the Property Jigsaw' in Simone Degeling, Jessica Hadson, and Irit Samet (eds), *Philosophical Foundations of Express Trusts* (OUP 2023).

[32] *Westdeutsche Landesbank Girozentrale Respondent v Islington London Borough Council [1996] 2 W.L.R. 802* HL, 705.

1. Allowing the Common Law to Be Itself

In his account of the way the law of obligation promotes the interest of security, Gardner takes as his model the law of tort. Property is conceived as 'mainly a long footnote to the law of torts'.[33] Even without going into the deep difficulties such conceptualization of property encounters, it is clear that in order to understand how Equity works to protect security interests we must pay close attention to the profound differences between tort law on the one hand, and property and contract (common) law on the other: beyond the obvious difference in the content of the law, there is a profound *structural* dissimilarity between norms we find in these areas of law. The core norm of tort—negligence—is formulated as an open-ended standard which leaves the court ample discretion to fit the norm to novel situations, in a retroactive and ad hoc manner where necessary. This flexibility may detract from the protection that the norm offers to the interest of security, as right owners do not have a comprehensive picture of what the court may order with regards to it. On the other hand, when the interest of security is threatened in ways that come before the courts for the first time, the court has the tools to tackle the threat on the spot without having to wait for parliament to amend the rules—a lengthy process that will not help the litigants who suffered harm before the game changed. The common law of property and contract operates differently. By formulating the norms in these areas of law as sets of closed, neat, clear-edge rules, the common law was able to offer elevated protection to the security interests of rightholders. For this reason, we saw, Equity may be viewed as disrupting the security-protection project of the law of obligations.

I want to suggest, however, that without Equity's intervention in the common law rights of the parties when results 'shock the conscience of the court', the common law would not have been able to protect the interest of security as fiercely as it does now.[34] The first way in which Equity works as a champion of security has already been hinted at. The hyper-formalistic approach of the common law in contract and property fields can lead to a dangerous schism between legal rules and moral conventions. Profound and/or multiple cases of such disharmony undermine the legitimacy of the system and place a big question mark on the ability of the law to serve morality.[35] One way to tackle the problem would be to change the nature of rules by introducing open-ended exceptions, or 'super principles', like the negligence standard in tort or the good-faith requirement in civil laws of contract.

[33] Gardner, *From Personal Life to Private Law*, p.14.

[34] An expression used by courts to describe the condition for Equity interventions, e.g. by Lord Walker in *Yeoman's Row Management Limited and another v Cobbe* [2008] UKHL 55, at 92.

[35] Examples of the rich empirical research into the connection between the legitimacy of the legal system in the eyes of the community and the extent to which it reflects their moral beliefs can be found in Janice Nadler, 'Flouting the Law' 83 Texas Law Review 1399; Paul H. Robinson and John M. Darley, *Justice, Liability, and Blame: Community Views and the Criminal Law* (Westview Press 1995) (especially around p.457).

With its openly particularistic stance, Equity can fix the problem in a more subtle way, as it surgically tackles instances of unconscionable insistence on rights while allowing most interactions around contract and property to be governed by the common law's clear set of rules.[36] In that way, owners of property and contractual rights can enjoy—most of the time—the excellent protection for their security interests which is offered by the bright-line rules of common law, without thereby incurring the risk that widespread frustration with the system would undermine its very foundations.[37]

Thus, the interventions of Equity, which may strike you at first as detracting from the protection of security interests in the areas in which it operates, are in fact a second-line defence to right holders' security interests as they facilitate the superior shield which the common law offers to property and contract right holders. Equity, if you wish, aligns the law of contract and property with the law of tort by introducing into these fields a healthy balance between rules and standards which the common law failed to promote. For Gardner, who takes tort law as his archetype of the law of obligations, this should be a welcome intervention. In earlier writing, he warned against viewing the rule-of-law requirement that norms should be clear, predictable, ex ante and general as the 'the be-all-and-end-all of sound government, the one and only valid political ideal'.[38] Gardner was very much aware of the socially conservative political agenda behind a fixation with the rule of law, even if it often presents itself as a politically neutral pursuit.[39] He would, I expect, have greatly approved of the fix that Equity offers to the flaw of myopic adherence to formalism, and deem the sacrifice in terms of the defendants' security interests as worthwhile; in the conflict between security interests and the legitimacy of the system as a whole, the former has got to give ground sometimes.

But the relationship between equity's role in the legal system and the level of security it affords is not exhausted by reference to the better balance it introduces between conscionability and rule-of-law values. In what I have said up to now, I accepted the assumption that as we move from a set of norms that are formulated as rules to a web of open-ended standards, the level of protection which the law affords to the interest of security declines.[40] The intuition behind this is that with legal standards, people cannot draw with certainty the boundaries of their rights

[36] Samet, *Equity: Conscience Goes to Market*, chapter 1, section 2.

[37] On the link between conventional morality and the legitimacy of law in the context of contract law see Prince Saprai, *Contract Law Without Foundations: Toward a Republican Theory of Contract Law* (1st edn, OUP 2019), chapter 4.

[38] John Gardner, 'The Supposed Formality of the Rule of Law' in *Law as a Leap of Faith: Essays on Law in General* (OUP 2012), p.196. For such an approach see for instance Friedrich A. von Hayek, *The Constitution of Liberty* (The University of Chicago Press 1978), chapter 15.

[39] See also Duncan Kennedy, 'Form and Substance in Private Law Adjudication' 89 Harv L Rev (1976) 1685, at 1685.

[40] See for example, Raz, p.841; Louis Kaplow, 'General Characteristics of Rules' in Gerrit de Geest and Francesco Parisi (eds), *Production of Legal Rules* (Edward Elgar 2011) 512–513; and Cass R. Sunstein, 'Problems with Rules' 83 Cal L Rev (1995) 1121–1122.

beyond which they are safe from state and third-party intervention. This is not a merely epistemological problem; the boundaries of rights that are created by standards *are* underdetermined at any given moment, as the court has a strong discretion to decide whether right owners lose them in novel situations. But in fact, a host of empirical and theoretical research rejects the automatic association of standards with reduced certainty for right holders. Researchers found that in areas where the complexity of the human interaction they regulate requires a 'thicket' of rules, the addressees of the norm are in a better position to assess the boundary of their right if the governing norms are formulated as standards rather than rules.[41] The law of obligations, or parts of it, seems to exhibit the complexity that leads to the reversal of roles whereby standards promote security better than rules. If so, the doctrines of Equity which are formulated as standards—most notably, the conscionability standard—offer better protection for the citizens' security interest than their common law counterparts. The protection of the unmarried woman's share in the family house is one prominent example. According to common law rules, ownership is determined (nearly) exclusively by registration in HM Land Registry. This highly formalistic rule, while upholding the security of property rightholders and buyers who are in no doubt as to the boundaries of the rights, can lead to an intolerable injustice and total disregard for the security of an *unregistered* partner. Thus, one partner, usually the woman, who is not registered as an owner may find herself with no rights to her home regardless of the contributions she made—financial and otherwise—to the purchase or upkeep of the family home along the years.

If lawmakers had tried to address the problem by drafting detailed exceptions to the rule, they would end up with a highly intricate set of exceptions that purports to offer a solution to the complicated question of the criteria for awarding an unregistered partner a share in the property, the size of the share, and ways to mitigate its effect on innocent third parties. The countless permutations of the tripartite relationships would inevitably lead to a thicket of rules which would require unceasing 'patching' until the law loses its coherence and ability to guide courts and parties as to the basic question, namely: 'what security is afforded by registered ownership?' Equity offers a different course. The tool which courts use to approach the intricate problem of unregistered partners' rights to their home is the constructive trust.[42] Having laid general standards for the acquisition of rights by unregistered partners, the courts can look into each situation in particular and apply these flexible standards in a way that balances the security rights of home ownership with the rights of third parties. Forms of contributions that people would normally expect to grant them a right to the home they build for their family are taken into account, and banks and other lenders know what to look for when granting a mortgage

[41] John Braithwaite, 'Rules and Principles: A Theory of Legal Certainty' 27 Austl J Leg Phil (2002) 47, p.53.

[42] *Stack v Dowden* [2007] UKHL 17.

over a family home. The flexible standard of constructive trust is thus a better answer to the problem of security, of both unregistered partners and third parties. By forgoing the formality requirements of property law, Equity prevents registered owners from exploiting the rules of registered land to deprive their partners of one of the most basic security rights one may possess—the security of one's home.

It is also important to remember that Equity is the source of (most) remedies that are designed to augment the ability of the claimant to hold on to *exactly* what she had before the wrong was committed. Two examples that come to mind are injunctions and specific performance. In both of these remedies, Equity deems the monetary compensation for damages that is offered by the common law as insufficient to address the plight of the claimant. Instead, Equity offers the claimant a mechanism for protecting her right to hold on by nipping in the bud an attempt to destabilize it, or by restoring the situation to be exactly (or very close to) the way it was before the wrong. Note that Equity is not merely the historical origin of these remedies: its principles also inform the day-to-day application and management of many remedies whose origins we can trace to Chancery. The case of injunctions in the USA is particularly enlightening: in the face of a widespread fusion of Equity with common law, civil remedies stuck by the law/Equity divide, and continue to be viewed as distinctively equitable.[43] The ad hoc, particularistic, and hands-on approach of Equity to justice enables the court to closely manage the situation on the ground so as to make sure that the claimant's right (to a good name, a quiet dwelling, enjoyment of sunlight, etc.) remains intact, as far as possible.[44] For Gardner, who was very well aware of the drawbacks of monetary compensation, this should be a most welcome intervention, as the court of Equity excels in what Larry David in Gardner's example fails to do: manage the preservation of the claimant's right in a professional, measured manner.[45] We can see then that in its response to failures of the common law, Equity makes a vital contribution to the way in which the law of obligations protects our security interests. For the interventions of Equity allow the common law to pursue a rigorous agenda of protecting people's right to hold on to what they have by mitigating its most lopsided results, by introducing flexible standards where a thicket of rules would undermine clarity and predictability, and by advancing remedies that go far beyond the standard monetary remedy offered by the common law.

[43] See review in Gergen, Golden and Smith, 'The Supreme Court's Accidental Revolution? The Test for Permanent Injunctions' 112 Columbia Law Review (2012) 204.

[44] Samuel L. Bray, 'The System of Equitable Remedies' 63 UCLA L Rev (2016).

[45] See Gardner, *From Personal Life to Private Law*, chapter 3.

2. How Equitable Rights Protect Security

The best way to learn about the extent to which concern with security of rights informs the choices made by Equity is by studying equitable rights. For unlike claims in Equity in which it merely responds to a fault in the common law—as in estoppel—in formulating standalone equitable rights the courts of Equity had more of a free hand to imbue them with the values they believe in. What is the place of security in this set of values? We already saw that in one critical respect the courts of Equity chose to downgrade the importance of security, as they left owners of equitable rights defenceless in the face of innocent purchasers. Especially when compared to the fierce protection awarded by the English common law to the original owner's right—which can defeat almost any third party who happens to possess the property—Equity is much more open to the possibility that the original owner must lose her right when the new owner acted with clean conscience. But that does not mean that Equity disregards or even downplays the interest of security. There are, as we shall presently see, important aspects of security that Equity promotes in a *far more* rigorous way than the common law. The picture as a whole, I believe, is one that sits comfortably with Gardner's theory about the fundamental purpose of private law. But Equity, as is often the case, does things its own way.

Let us go back to the innocent purchaser of trust property. It would be hard to say that by preferring this purchaser over the beneficiary, Equity protects *his* security rights (in the trust property he purchased)—at least not in the sense Gardner has in mind. Recall that according to Gardner, our right to hold on to what we have is rooted in the human need to adopt life goals in order to lead a meaningful life and the rationality of preferring the life goals we adopted over alternative ones, since it is a necessary condition for commitment to these goals. Attachment to property and other conditions that facilitate the pursuit of our goals naturally lends itself to be rationalized on that basis. But in the case of a purchaser of trust property, it is unlikely that their life goals have been embedded in the property before it turns out to belong to a trust. The beneficiary, on the other hand, may well have formed some life goal with regard to, or reliance on, the trust property. Inasmuch as the purchaser's interest can be couched in terms of 'security', it would be 'security of receipt' or 'dynamic security' which has instrumental value for the swiftness of commerce; it has very little to do with security as 'the right to hold on' in Gardner's sense.[46] Thus, when Equity prefers the innocent purchaser, that purchaser's security interest, in the sense that we are exploring here, takes a back seat. The decisive consideration here is one that goes back to the basic principles that underlie this body of law: the courts of Equity only intervene in the parties' common law rights when unconscionability is at play. Where no unconscionability is involved,

[46] See e.g. The Law Commission Consultation Paper No 227: 'Updating the Land Registration Act 2002: A Consultation Paper', sec. 13.21.

Equity lets the chips fall where they may, and since in common law the beneficiary has no right to the property, the purchaser from the trustee gets clean title.[47] Given the fundamental nature of Equity's reluctance to act against a bona fide defendant, I think there is very little we can learn from the 'Equity's darling' rule about the place of security interests in the value system that informs Equity.

But if we turn to look at situations where unconscionability *is* present, we will see that Equity is even more keen than the common law to protect the right of the beneficiary to 'hold on'. When a transferee of trust property knew or should have known that the trustee breached the trust in transferring the property to him, or if he did not pay for it, the beneficiary has a *proprietary* claim against him; thus, if the transferee still has the property, or traceable proceeds, she will have to hand them *in specie* to the beneficiary.[48] In stark contrast to the common law, Equity deems the restorative monetary damages as only a second-line remedy, which is ordered only where there is a good reason why the property itself cannot be restored. The order to hand back the property itself would include in it any profits that arise from the property, such as dividends or rent, so as to get the beneficiary as close as possible to the position she would have been in had the breach of trust never taken place.[49] Moreover, in an attempt to secure the beneficiary's right to hold on to her position as a beneficiary of a trust, Equity provides her with recourse not only against an unconscionable recipient of the property, but also against whoever dishonestly assisted the trustee to transfer the property in breach of trust.[50] The remedy against the assistant cannot be *in specie*, of course, but the claim she has against him provides the beneficiary with an extra safety net in case neither the trustee nor the recipient of the trust property can be made to restore her to the pre-wrong position. Deep reverence towards people's right not to be deprived of what they have by actions of private people is the most plausible explanation of Equity's willingness to offer proprietary remedies for beneficiaries in these circumstances.

However, from the perspective of Gardner's theory, the really interesting action happens in the relationship between the beneficiary and the trustee in breach. For here, Equity adopts an unusual perspective on the remedial process—a perspective that fits particularly well with Gardner's thought on the limits of the remedial response of the common law. In short, as against the trustee in breach of trust, Equity enforces the beneficiary's *primary rights* and not some secondary right that arises as a result of the breach. Here is how it works: the primary duty of trustees is 'properly to preserve the trust fund, to pay the income and the corpus to those who are entitled to them respectively, and to give all [the beneficiaries] information

[47] As explained, for example, by Lloyd LJ in Independent Trustee Services Ltd v GP Noble Trustees Ltd [2012] EWCA Civ 195.

[48] *Royal Brunei Airlines v Tan* [1995] UKPC 4.

[49] See discussion in Charles Mitchell and Stephen Watterson, 'Remedies for Knowing Receipt' in Charles Mitchell (ed), *Constructive and Resulting Trusts* (Hart Publishing 2010).

[50] *BCCI v Akindele* [2000] EWCA 502.

with respect to the mode in which the trust fund has been dealt with, and where it is'.[51] The beneficiary can then object to any entry in the account which strikes her as unauthorized according to the terms of the trust, and it is then up to the trustee to prove that the entry was justified. The beneficiary can go to court and ask for an order commending the trustee to abide by this duty. But to obtain such an order, the beneficiary need not show that the trustee has done wrong (in breaching the trust terms), since all she is asking for is that the *primary duty* is complied with. If the trustee cannot comply with his duty *in specie*, say because he sold the trust property, the beneficiary can ask for 'substitutive performance'. This remedy can be given in the form of money, but unlike damages for a breach of contract or of one's duty of care, Equity insists that it is still forcing the trustee to comply with his *primary* rights, albeit in a substitutive manner. This is not mere theoretical hair-splitting; the manner in which the remedy unfolds is expressive of this unusual view of what the defendant is being asked to do, as 'it looks not so much to the loss suffered as to what is required to restore the trust fund'.[52]

Accordingly, a beneficiary need not base her claim that the trustee account for the trust property on an alleged loss which the trustee's action or omission caused. Traditional principles of Equity therefore dictate that the concepts of remoteness or contributory negligence do not apply as they would in a claim for damages in tort or contract.[53] If the trustee cannot justify an entry on the account, it is 'falsified', and the expense is treated *as if it never happened*: '[t]here is no need to conduct a causal analysis as to whether the assets which were in fact disbursed would have been lost to the trust fund in some other way, as they ought still to be in the trust fund.'[54] Instead, the courts of Equity insist that what looks like an unauthorized withdrawal of trust money, for example to make an investment that is not allowed according to the trust terms, was in fact an unauthorized loan taken by the trustee. The trustee will therefore have to pay it back (i.e., reinstate the trust fund) and the investment will be his.[55] If, however, the unauthorized investment was successful, the beneficiary can authorize it retroactively, and keep the investment and its fruit.[56] This fiction according to which the trustee has in fact acted as he should, and that he can therefore be ordered to comply with his primary duty, informs a set of complicated rules of equitable tracing that give the beneficiary advantages

[51] *Low v Bouverie* [1891] 3 ch.82 at [99].

[52] *New Corp v General Cologne* (2004) 7 I.T.E.L.R. 295 at [55].

[53] In England, the courts moved away from these traditional principles of Equity towards a more 'fused' approach according to which the remedy for breach of trust should conform to common law principles of causality: see *Target Holdings Ltd v Redferns* [1996] AC 421; *AIB Group (UK) plc v Mark Redler & Co Solicitors* [2015] AC 1503. This development has been heavily criticized by scholars of Equity, as in Matthew Conaglen, 'Equitable Compensation for Breach of Trust. Off Target' 40 Melbourne University Law Review (2016) 126.

[54] Ibid p.136; *Ultraframe (UK) Ltd v Fielding* [2005] EWHC 1638 (Ch), at [1513].

[55] See e.g. *Jackson v Dickenson* [1903] 1CH 947.

[56] On this right to cherry-pick the investments see *Re Oatway* [1903] Ch 356.

way beyond the common law rules of tracing that protect the rights of ordinary owners.[57]

The nature and measure of the trustee's responsibility to ensure that trust assets are managed and held exactly as the trust terms dictate, and the remedies that are on offer when this does not happen, are a highly complicated subject. I hope to have given you a taste of the uniquely rigorous way in which Equity protects the beneficiary's right to hold on to her interest in the trust.[58] The unusual character of trust as a private arrangement of a proprietary nature requires a cautious approach to interventions by third parties, lest innocent strangers to the trust suffer. This caution may come at the expense of the beneficiary since she is the one who enjoys the fruit of the private arrangement with the trustee to split the ownership in the property (to 'legal' and 'equitable'). In that respect her security interest is indeed fragile. But another characteristic of the trust relationship, namely the imbalance of power and knowledge between the trustee and the beneficiary whose interests the trustee ought to promote, motivates Equity to offer a particularly rigorous protection of the beneficiary's sense that she can hold securely to her interest in the trust. Moreover, Equity's eagerness to pursue unconscionable recipients of trust property provides the beneficiary with extraordinary remedies as against third parties who are not innocent. The picture as a whole reveals, in my view, that the protection of security interests features high up on Equity's list of priorities, even if it has to give ground to other values when circumstances call for it.

D. Conclusion

In this chapter I wanted to show that the law of Equity can lend support to Gardner's view about security interests as the animating force behind the law of obligations. Despite getting very little attention in his work, Equity plays a major role in the law of obligations, and had it been the case that protecting the interest of security is not an important mission for Equity, that would have been a blow to Gardner's theory. In some respects, we saw, Equity indeed gives up quite quickly on security interests; this can be true for the way equitable rights themselves operate, and also for some of Equity's interventions in the parties' common law rights on grounds of unconscionability. But a wider look at the role of Equity in the legal system reveals that its measured interpositions are necessary in order to allow the common law to pursue an agenda that fiercely protects our 'right to hold on'. Moreover, in

[57] *Foskett v McKeown* [2000] UKHL 29.

[58] The rule according to which beneficiaries need not prove a loss to make a claim for account could be seen as a problem for Gardner (see Prince Saprai's chapter in this volume about torts actionable per se). But in the present context there are good practical as well as conceptual reasons for not placing the beneficiary (or any other principal) under a duty to provide evidence that the trustee (or fiduciary) caused her loss.

particularly complicated areas of private law, the open-ended discretionary norms of Equity do not undermine the sense of security enjoyed by right holders, but rather increase the clarity they have with regards to the boundaries of their rights. When we turned to equitable rights, we saw that while the right of the beneficiary is far less secure than an ordinary common law right when it comes to competition with innocent buyers, this does not express a lack of concern towards the interest of security. A brief review of the remedies to which a beneficiary can resort against a trustee in breach and third parties who did not act innocently reveals Equity's deep respect for people's right to keep what they have. Having developed in a separate system of courts, with its unique set of concerns, it is no wonder that Equity acts to protect the interest of security in ways that are very different to the common law. But as the source of many of the *in specie* remedies that we now have in our law of obligations, Equity is no less devoted to the just distribution of the right to preserve the pre-wrong state of affairs that the claimant enjoyed. In that, Equity fits well with the ambitious explanation that Gardner offers for the justifying principle behind the law of obligations.

Index

For the benefit of digital users, indexed terms that span two pages (e.g., 52–53) may, on occasion, appear on only one of those pages.